Effective and Efficient Organisations?

Contributions to Economics

www.springer.com/series/1262

Further volumes of this series can be found at our homepage.

Pablo Coto-Millán
Utility and Production, 2nd Edition
2003. ISBN 3-7908-1423-7

Emilio Colombo/John Driffill (Eds.)
The Role of Financial Markets in the Transition Process
2003. ISBN 3-7908-0004-X

Guido S. Merzoni
Strategic Delegation in Firms and in the Trade Union
2003. ISBN 3-7908-1432-6

Jan B. Kuné
On Global Aging
2003. ISBN 3-7908-0030-9

Sugata Marjit, Rajat Acharyya
International Trade, Wage Inequality and the Developing Economy
2003. ISBN 3-7908-0031-7

Francesco C. Billari/Alexia Prskawetz (Eds.)
Agent-Based Computational Demography
2003. ISBN 3-7908-1550-0

Georg Bol/Gholamreza Nakhaeizadeh/
Svetlozar T. Rachev/Thomas Ridder/
Karl-Heinz Vollmer (Eds.)
Credit Risk
2003. ISBN 3-7908-0054-6

Christian Müller
Money Demand in Europe
2003. ISBN 3-7908-0064-3

Cristina Nardi Spiller
The Dynamics of the Price Structure and the Business Cycle
2003. ISBN 3-7908-0063-5

Michael Bräuninger
Public Debt and Endogenous Growth
2003. ISBN 3-7908-0056-1

Brigitte Preissl/Laura Solimene
The Dynamics of Clusters and Innovation
2003. ISBN 3-7908-0077-5

Markus Gangl
Unemployment Dynamics in the United States and West Germany
2003. ISBN 3-7908-1533-0

Pablo Coto-Millán (Ed.)
Essays on Microeconomics and Industrial Organisation, 2nd Edition
2004. ISBN 3-7908-0104-6

Wendelin Schnedler
The Value of Signals in Hidden Action Models
2004. ISBN 3-7908-0173-9

Carsten Schröder
Variable Income Equivalence Scales
2004. ISBN 3-7908-0183-6

Wilhelm J. Meester
Locational Preferences of Entrepreneurs
2004. ISBN 3-7908-0178-X

Russel Cooper/Gary Madden (Eds.)
Frontiers of Broadband, Electronic and Mobile Commerce
2004. ISBN 3-7908-0087-2

Sardar M.N. Islam
Empirical Finance
2004. ISBN 3-7908-1551-9

Jan-Egbert Sturm/Timo Wollmershäuser (Eds.)
Ifo Survey Data in Business Cycle and Monetary Policy Analysis
2005. ISBN 3-7908-0174-7

Bernard Michael Gilroy/Thomas Gries/
Willem A. Naudé (Eds.)
Multinational Enterprises, Foreign Direct Investment and Growth in Africa
2005. ISBN 3-7908-0276-X

Günter S. Heiduk/Kar-yiu Wong (Eds.)
WTO and World Trade
2005. ISBN 3-7908-1579-9

Emilio Colombo/Luca Stanca
Financial Market Imperfections and Corporate Decisions
2006. ISBN 3-7908-1581-0

Birgit Mattil
Pension Systems
2006. ISBN 3-7908-1675-2

Francesco C. Billari et al. (Eds.)
Agent-Based Computational Modelling
2006. ISBN 3-7908-1640-X

Kerstin Press
A Life Cycle for Clusters?
2006. ISBN 3-7908-1710-4

Russel Cooper et al. (Eds.)
The Economics of Online Markets and ICT Networks
2006. ISBN 3-7908-1706-6

Renato Giannetti/Michelangelo Vasta (Eds.)
Evolution of Italian Enterprises in the 20th Century
2006. ISBN 3-7908-1711-2

Ralph Setzer
The Politics of Exchange Rates in Developing Countries
2006. ISBN 3-7908-1715-5

Dora Borbély
Trade Specialization in the Enlarged European Union
2006. ISBN 3-7908-1704-X

Iris A. Hauswirth

Effective and Efficient Organisations?

Government Export Promotion in Germany and the UK from an Organisational Economics Perspective

With 15 Figures and 18 Tables

Physica-Verlag
A Springer Company

Series Editors
Werner A. Müller
Martina Bihn

Author
Dr. Iris A. Hauswirth
iris.hauswirth@gmail.com

ISSN 1431-1933
ISBN-10 3-7908-1730-9 Physica-Verlag Heidelberg New York
ISBN-13 978-3-7908-1730-0 Physica-Verlag Heidelberg New York

Physica-Verlag is a part of Springer Science+Business Media

springer.com

Printed in Germany

Typesetting: Camera ready by the author
Cover: Erich Kirchner, Heidelberg
Production: LE-TEX, Jelonek, Schmidt & Vöckler GbR, Leipzig

SPIN 11756361 Printed on acid-free paper – 88/3100 – 5 4 3 2 1 0

Acknowledgements

There are many people who made the preparation of this book possible, providing help in both content and other matters. My first thanks go to Professor Andres Rodriguez Posé for unimposing supervision, collegiality, patience and encouragement. I also owe thanks to Professor Ian Gordon for comments, and to Professor R.J. Bennett, with whom the work started.

Several friends and colleagues read draft chapters and were willing to engage in discussions. I am grateful to Catarina Cardoso, Yonn Dierwechter, Jacob Jordan, Charles Maddison, Andy Pratt, Karen West, Matthias Wissman, and to Ruth O'Rourke for her editing work.

Many others helped by keeping me in good spirits. Among my colleagues I would like to thank in particular Yiannis Chorianopoulos, Liljana Grubovic, Holger Münt, Miguel Jimenez, Cesar Nava-Escudero, Juan Osorio, Hulya Özdil, Asato Saito, Javier Sanchez, Murat Yalcintan. Outside LSE I was fortunate to have the encouragement and friendship of Isa Brelowski, Tassilo Herrschel, Carol Kidwell, Don MacMenamin, Cornelia Messing, Olga Milosavljevic, Uli Pfeiffer, Govind Venuprasad, Regine Wagner, and my family. Without them the book would never have been completed.

It would also have been impossible without the many people who readily shared their time and knowledge in interviews. I am very grateful to all individuals listed in the Annex and hope that they may somehow benefit from university research. Equally, I am grateful for financial support from the Friedrich Flick Foundation and the London School of Economics and Political Science.

The book is dedicated to my grandparents and grandaunts, who taught me that a new beginning is a matter of personal choice.

April 2006 Iris A. Hauswirth

Table of contents

List of abbreviations

AHKs	Außenhandelskammern – overseas chambers of commerce
AHS	Außenhandelsstelle – a body set up jointly by the chambers of industry and commerce and the association of trade corporations in Northrhine-Westphalia to execute the trade fair programme and the consultancy programme of the Northrhine-Westphalian ministery of economics
AUMA	German umbrella organisation for the trade fair industry and main player in the German trade fair support
BAW	Bundesamt fuer Wirtschaft – an agency of the BMWi
BCC	British Chambers of Commerce
BDI	Top umbrella associations of German industry
BEDG	British European Design Group
BESA	British Educational Suppliers Association
BFAI	Bundesagentur für Außenwirtschaft – German Office for Foreign Trade
BMWi	Bundesministerium für Wirtschaft und Arbeit – German Ministry of Economics and Technology
BOTB	British Overseas Trade Board
BPF	British Plastics Federation
BPI	British Phonographic Industry Association
BTI	British Trade International
CBI	Confederation of British Industry
CEBIT	the world's largest annual trade show for information and telecommunications technology
CEMA	Circuit Equipment and Materials Association
COI	Central Office of Information
CSSA	Computing Services and Software Association
D-A, D-B, …, D-X	Interviewees in Germany
DFG	Durchführungsgesellschaft – Trade fair company
DIHK	Deutscher Industrie- und Handelskammertag – umbrella organisation of the German Chambers of Industry and Commerce
DIHT	former acronym for DIHK
DIP	Dokumentations- und Informationssystem für Parlamentarische Vorgänge - parliamentary documentation system
DMA	Direct Marketing Association

DTI	Department of Trade and Industry
ECGD	Export Credit Guarantee Department
EIC	Energy Industries Council
FCO	Foreign and Commonwealth Office
FEI	Federation of the Electronics Industry
FMCEC	Federation of Manufacturers of Construction Equipment and Cranes
FT	Financial Times
GDP	Gross Domestic Product
IBS	International Business Schemes
ICT	Information and Communication Technology
IHK	Chamber of Industry and Commerce
IMF	International Monetary Fund
ISG	Institut für Sozialforschung und Gesellschaftspolitk – Institute for social research and policy
JEPD	Joint export promotion directorate
KFW	Kreditanstalt fuer Wiederaufbau
LGA	Landesgewerbeamt – executive agency for the Ministry of Economics and Technology
MPA	Music Publishers' Association
NAFTA	North Atlantic Free Trade Agreement
NAO	National Audit Office, UK
NIE	New Institutional Economics
NPM	New Public Management
OE	Organisational Economics
OECD	Organisation for Economic Co-operation and Development
PLASA	Professional Lighting and Sound Association
PPMA	Processing and Packaging Machinery Association
PR	Property rights
QMS	Quality Management Surveys
REMM	Resourceful, Evaluative, Maximising Man
SBAC	Society of British Aerospace Companies
SESA	Support for Exhibitions and Seminars Abroad
SME	Small and medium size enterprises
SMM	Sector Market Matrix
SMMT	Society of Motor Manufacturers and Traders
TIA	Telecoms Industry Association
TPUK	Trade Partners UK
UK-A, UK-B,…, UK-X	Interviewees in the UK
UKOP	United Kingdom Official Publications
VDMA	Verband der Investitionsgüterindustrie – Federation of German engineering industries
VFM	Value for money

Chapter 1: Introduction

1.1 Overview

'...as never before, governments are involved in supporting the export activities of companies. Sizeable budgets and numerous programmes have been put in place so as to help draw companies into exporting for the first time, and enable existing exporters to expand or consolidate their foreign market operations' (Seringhaus and Rosson 1990:3).

This importance of export support to governments was not just a passing phenomenon in 1990, but is equally prevalent today. All western industrialised countries and many other countries are involved in export promotion, and provide strikingly similar types of services to encourage their domestic firms' international sales activities. But despite the similarity in the content of their export promotion programmes, the delivery of the support services is organised differently from one country to another (Seringhaus and Rosson 1990:34ff, 1991; Camino 1991; Schultz et al. 1991; Jaramillo 1992; NAO 1996; Habuda et al.1998a). Various governments have restructured their services' organisation fundamentally to 'improve' them. Yet little is known about the relative performance of different export support organisations, and indeed of different public sector organisations in general.

This thesis is concerned with the relationship between *organisation* of export support services and their *effectiveness and efficiency*. The objective is to explore two assumptions, which underlie decisions about services' reorganisation: the belief that *organisation matters*; and the belief that *restructuring organisations can increase their effectiveness and efficiency.*

In this brief introductory chapter, the background for the topic is set, and an outline of the thesis is provided: after an overview of the reasons for government export promotion, and a more detailed presentation of the research question, the research approach is summarised. The last section gives a synopsis of the following chapters.

1.2 Export promotion

An OECD compilation of member states' industrial policies in the 1990s shows that the primary goal pursued by *all* countries is to raise the *international competitiveness* of domestic firms (OECD 1998:1). Together, the French and Swedish reports to the OECD (1998) summarise the concerns that lie behind this strategy: *'There is now a consensus that to reactivate growth, enterprises must have the means to make the most of the opportunities opened up to them by the globalisation of trade and to capitalise on their assets in the global market-place'* (OECD 1998:41). *'The ability of companies to compete and expand sales in international markets is essential for industrial growth and welfare'* (OECD 1998:137). According to 'The Economist' foreign policy and development aid have also been used increasingly to promote domestic firms abroad (The Economist, 1997a; 1997b; 1997c; 2000).

The benefits which firms are expected to derive from selling abroad are various: Increased demand enables companies to expand, to spend more on research, and to benefit from economies of scale. For small and medium sized enterprises (SMEs), which often produce a narrow range of specialised goods, and serve a limited or shrinking domestic market, exporting can be the easiest option to increase their customer numbers. By supplying foreign markets, companies are also better safeguarded against cyclical and seasonal variations in demand. Moreover, the profit margins might be higher elsewhere and in many cases product life cycles can be extended. Furthermore, firms' competitiveness is strengthened because the exposure to and feedback from international markets tends to raise businesses' level of technological development and marketing competence. The macroeconomic results can ultimately be: a reduction in unemployment, increased stability, and economic growth (e.g. Nothdurft 1992; Conway and Nothdurft 1996; Czinkota 1996; MacBean 2000).

While this line of reasoning is not new, it has attracted more attention in view of the global changes over the last decades. The results of the GATT Uruguay Round, the creation of NAFTA and the European Single Market, the opening-up of Eastern Europe and the former Soviet Union and the rapid growth of newly industrialising countries, particularly in Asia, have led to a rapid expansion of international markets. New and faster means of transport and communication, and the liberalisation of financial markets have lowered the costs of doing business abroad (Engelhard 1992; Deutscher Bundestag 1995b; Weidig and Ruprecht 1996). This has been reflected in the growth of international trade, which has averaged 6% per year over the past 20 years, twice as much as the growth of world output (IMF 2001). On the one hand these developments have opened up new opportunities for a country's competitive enterprises, but on the other hand they have also exposed weaker firms to competition from abroad (OECD 1997a). Asia, for example, expanded its share in world merchandise exports from 16% in 1980 to 23% in 1990 and 29% in 2000, while Western Europe's share dropped from 48% in 1990 to 38% in 2000 (WTO 2001). Alarmed by the trade figures, and also by the recession in most European countries in the early 1990s, governments have put emphasis on supporting their industries' internationalisation, especially their export activities.

While all of a country's policies which affect the economy – e.g. infrastructure development, education, labour market regulation, or tax policies – affect the international competitiveness of resident firms, governments have exerted a direct influence on external trade by shaping international trade agreements, by reducing trade barriers, and by their currency policy. Undoubtedly the latter have had the strongest impact on changes in export volumes (Bank of England 1998).

But the term 'government export promotion' is usually used in a narrower sense. It describes those public sector activities that are designed explicitly and specifically to encourage and support companies in the process of winning market shares abroad. They can range from activities to create awareness of exporting as a growth and market expansion option to the creation of incentives and various forms of export assistance (Camino 1991; Engelhard 1992:22f).

The programmes generally target SMEs because of their importance for the economies, and because SMEs are perceived to be disadvantaged in international trade. It is also believed that SMEs' export volume can be raised more easily than that of large firms since SME's growth rates are higher and their exports, so far, disproportionately low (e.g. Conway and Nothdurft 1996; OECD 1998:43): in OECD countries SMEs contribute between 30 and 70% to GDP and between 40 and 80% to employment. As employers, they have been more resilient to recession than large firms, and most new jobs in recent years have been created in small and micro firms. In the US, the UK, Germany, and Spain for example, employment growth was almost exclusively confined to firms with fewer than 20 employees. The fastest-growing SMEs are those in niche markets and new industries, which particularly benefit from global strategies. Besides their role for employment, SMEs are also perceived to contribute significantly to competition, to an entrepreneurial culture, and to a country's innovation capacity (Bannock and Peacock 1989; Hemmersbach 1993; OECD 1997a). But in contrast to SMEs' important role in the domestic markets, their contribution to national exports is limited. On OECD average, excluding Italy and Taiwan, it is only about 25% (OECD 1997a:77).

Researchers argue that there are two major reasons: SMEs find it more difficult to bridge the time gap between relatively high fixed costs of investing in market expansion abroad, and the returns from these markets once they succeed, e.g. costs in terms of management time for information search, or of expenditures for sales promotions abroad. They also find it harder to cope with the risk attached to this investment, which is likely to be relatively higher for them than for a larger firm (Bank of England 1998; Bannock and Peacock 1989; Czinkota 1996; Hauswirth and Borger 1997).

Governments have responded to these problems in a similar fashion. More or less universally, developed countries (and many developing countries) provide information services, market research, and contact-facilitating programmes for SMEs to reduce the high entry costs into exporting. Trade fair support, i.e. subsidising SMEs directly or indirectly in exhibiting their products at trade fairs abroad, is particularly wide-spread, receives generally the very largest share of the export promotion budgets (Nothdurft 1992), and is considered to be a very effective policy (Nugent et al. 1999:264). Governments also offer export credit guarantees and credit insurance to improve firms' access to finance for their export ventures and to reduce the direct risk of overseas activities (Seringhaus and Rosson 1990:34ff, 1991; Camino 1991; Schultz et al. 1991; NAO 1996; OECD 1997a; The Economist 1997b; Habuda et al.1998a). But in stark contrast to the similarity in programmes, the significant differences as to the programmes' organisation stand out, especially concerning the mix of public and private actors who are involved in the service delivery (Seringhaus and Rosson 1990; Schultz et al. 1991; NAO 1996; BDI 1998; Habuda et al. 1998a; Onida 2002). Regarding trade fair support for example, the organisational arrangements have varied from having civil servants design even the advertising boards for firms' overseas exhibition stands, to giving them only a limited role in the decision-making process how the trade fair budget should be spent. Roles attributed to chambers of commerce, business associations, private firms, and local and regional governments, and development agencies have also varied significantly.

Seringhaus and Rosson (1990:43,64), two of the very few academics who work in the field, argued that evaluations of the relative performance of the different organisational arrangements were not possible. They made the point that there was a certain 'path consistency' in the development of countries' administrative systems and that due to different business cultures different systems might be required. But their major reason for refraining from a judgmental comparison of different export promotion organisations was that: *'evaluation...of export promotion activity is in its infancy, so that uniform or broadly comprehensive comparisons of different export promotion systems are not currently feasible...Whether or not one system is better than another remains open to question...'*

1.3 The research question

The question raised by Seringhaus and Rosson, whether one organisation is better than another, is the challenge that this thesis intends to tackle. It is relevant, because governments have behaved as if the question was answered, while academics have continued to ignore it.

In the last decade many governments have reviewed the organisation of their export support services (Austrade 1994, 2000; Conway and Nothdurft 1996; Weidig and Ruprecht 1996; DTI and FCO 1997, 1999; Lorot 1998; Auditor General of Canada 1999; Soederman 2002). They have commissioned reports to find out how competitor countries deliver export support services (Schultz et al. 1991; Bannock c.{1995}[1]; Habuda et al. 1998a; House of Representatives 2001), and the United States, the United Kingdom, Australia, Canada, France, and Austria all restructured their export promotion organisations fundamentally under the banner of efficiency and effectiveness considerations (Habuda et al. 1998; Auditor General of Canada 1999; Austrade 2000). Other countries like Germany or Japan discussed and introduced some changes for the same reasons (Habuda et al. 1998).

That organisation plays a role in performance is a reasonable expectation, considering that simple reorganisations of production in private firms have frequently

[1] This report, commissioned by the British Department of Trade and Industry and the British Institute of Export was never published. The various parties involved could not agree on how the results should be presented (UK-T).

yielded substantial efficiency increases (De Alessi 1983). Regarding public sector services, for instance in the context of development aid, academics have argued that the failure of many approaches could not solely be explained with inadequate policies, but lay to a major extent in the inappropriate design of the donor organisations (Koerner 1989). Egeberg (1994:88) claimed that organisation studies from a wide range of countries revealed a clear correlation between formal structures and actual behaviour regarding information exchange and other co-ordination processes.

Yet organisational aspects of government export support services have been little researched. At the time Seringhaus and Rosson published their two books on government export promotion (1990, 1991) they were *'hard-pressed to come up with a single piece of public organisation export research aside from those of national governments and quasi-government bodies'* (Rosson and Seringhaus 1991:322f). A decade later, the 'glaring gap' (321) they identified still exists. McAleese and O'Donnell (2000:28) complain about the 'dearth of literature' on organisational aspects of government export promotion.

Information that does exist are a few reports commissioned by governments and business associations, and some brochures or websites of export promotion agencies. But where their authors compare countries' export services, positive or negative assessments of different organisational structures appear to be made on the basis of superficial information, or to be influenced by the political agenda of the publishing body.[2]

On the academic side, only a few books and articles have been published that deal with export promotion services of developed countries in a descriptive or evaluative way (Nothdurft 1992; Engelhard 1992; Kotabe and Czinkota 1992; Hemmersbach 1993; Cavusgil and Yeoh 1994; Wilkinson and Brouthers 2000). Others have discussed export promotion, but with a very different focus [e.g. trade distortion by export insurance (Abraham and Dewit 2000), the efforts of supranational organisations to influence national export-promotion (Walzenbach 1998), finding evidence for market failure (Richards and Patterson 1998)]. A further group of authors has tried to evaluate the impact of very specific export promotion strategies, often for US agricultural products [e.g. apples (Richards et al. 1997), almonds (Halliburton and Henneberry 1995; Kinnucan and Christian 1997); the

---

2 For example when German researchers assessed British export services (BDI, 1998; Habuda et al. 1998b; Schultz et al., 1991) they did not do enough research to value the actual relevance of certain organisational features. It seems that the information was largely based on the British Department of Trade and Industry's promotional material to the public. This led to misjudgements, for example regarding the role of the British 'Whitehall Export Promotion Committee' (WEBCO). While the German authors of a comparative report singled out WEBCO as a model for an efficient co-ordination mechanism (BDI 1998:12), comments in British reports (DTI & FCO, 1997; DTI & FCO, 1999), and comments of British export promotion experts in interviews (UK-N; UK-O; UK-R) suggested that WEBCO has been ineffective. One of the purposes of the BDI report was to point out that the German export promotion efforts should be co-ordinated better. But the report also supports the point that publicly available information about how exactly service delivery is organised in different countries is very limited.

promotion of exporter networks (Welch et al. 1998)]. It seems that no academic research has taken place that has focused on the impact of organisation on the efficiency and effectiveness of export support services' delivery.

Moreover, the scanning of research on other government business support services did not lead any further. Most of those studies have also been either descriptive or have tried to evaluate the rationale for specific services. They have rarely been concerned with the organisational structure of the service delivery, not to speak of delivering an evaluation of organisation with regard to its efficiency and effectiveness impact.[3]

Given this mismatch between what is practically attempted by governments on the one hand, and what is known about its consequences on the other, research into the relevance of export promotion organisation for service delivery appears relevant. Since governments' re-organisation efforts seem to be based on two implicit assumptions, the focus of the research is on the validity of these assumptions:

1. The fact that these re-organisations have taken place in the context of efficiency and effectiveness debates suggests that governments believe *organisation matters for efficiency and effectiveness.*
2. Re-organisation on the premises of efficiency and effectiveness considerations suggests a belief that the 'new' organisations are more efficient and effective than the old ones, i.e. it takes for granted what Seringhaus and Rosson (1990) questioned: that *one organisation is more efficient and effective than another.*

Since organisation can only matter if there is a causal link between 'organisation' and 'efficiency and effectiveness', the primary goal or 'research question' is to identify which causal link may exist between the two. This link can then be scrutinised with regard to the second notion, that one organisation is better or worse than another. In addition to the first assumption, this implies that the link between organisation and efficiency and effectiveness is either mono-causal, or that it is multi-causal but without trade-offs in organisation's impacts on the different causes for efficiency and effectiveness.

It is acknowledged that by focusing on the efficiency and effectiveness with which export support services are delivered, other concerns of public sector management like equity, democratic decision making, or accountability are neglected. However, the focus on efficiency and effectiveness is justified in this context, because they have been the key concepts in the debate about public sector reform

[3] Both BIDs, the extensive database of journal articles, and the catalogue of BLPES, the biggest social science library in Europe were searched, and abstracts and keywords regarding the books and articles were evaluated. The few exceptions to the statement that there is no published research on organisational aspects of service delivery dealt with business services in England (e.g. Otzel and Martin 1998; Priest 1999; Robson and Bennett 1999). But none of these authors attempt to analyse the impact of organisation on efficiency in a systematic manner.

from the late 1970s and export promotion re-organisations (Metcalfe and Richards 1990; Naschold and Proehl 1994; Dowding 1995; Pollitt and Summa 1999).

It is also acknowledged that by focusing on the organisational structures for the delivery of export promotion services, questions about the value of these services and their opportunity costs are neglected. Camino (1991:119f) for example stated that the costs of export promotion programmes, as well as the benefits generated by them, are still being questioned. Zwonieck (1988:46) argued that countries with an aggressive export credit and insurance policy have not been shown to be able to improve their relative share of the world market compared to those countries that do not have such policies. And the OECD (1997a:54) found in a survey that SMEs do not widely acknowledge government assistance programmes to be a significant success factor. But here, in order to focus on the question of the *organisation* of the service delivery, the task in form of the specific export promotion policy is taken as externally determined. The research is therefore not concerned with the question whether an export support service should be provided, but with its efficient and effective realisation, once the government has made the decision that it should be provided.

This requires finding whether and how organisation impacts on effectiveness and efficiency, since only if there is a causal link, can export support organisation 'matter', and can alternative organisational structures lead to more efficient and effective services.

1.4 A synopsis of the chapters

After this brief outline of government export promotion activities and the research focus here, the second chapter sets the context for the questions raised. It deals with the concepts 'organisation' and 'efficiency and effectiveness', and defines their meaning for the research. Then the state of knowledge about causal links between organisation and outputs is explored. Of the wide field of research on public sector management and organisation theories, organisational economics is identified as the most promising theoretical basis for the purpose of this thesis.

Chapter 3 is concerned with finding the determinants for efficient and effective organisations. It introduces the reader to three different theories within organisational economics – property rights theory, agency theory and transaction cost theory – and explores which fundamental cause–effect mechanisms they hold responsible for the success and failure of different organisations. The chapter also presents the empirical evidence for each of the theories and the criticisms they have been confronted with. On this basis a 'model' is developed, which synthesises the findings. It puts forward three key variables and their inter-relationships, through which organisational structures are thought to affect outputs: the incentives of the actors, their knowledge, and the organisation's adaptability.

In Chapter 4 the challenge is to turn the 'model' into an operational framework to analyse export support organisations. It examines the three variables in more detail and identifies the criteria that can be used to assess existing organisations' effect on them. While the discussed theories have provided a framework for judging the impact of organisation on incentives, they have made little contribution to the question of how the knowledge of the actors and the adaptability of the structures can be assessed. Research from other fields is used to explore these issues further. The chapter ends with a summary of criteria in the form of a list of questions, which are going to be used as a guideline for the comparative empirical research in the second part of the thesis.

Chapter 5 sets the scene for the empirical research. A case study approach appeared to be the research method best suited for acquiring the necessary detail of information about sparsely documented export support organisations, and for capturing their complexity. Trade fair support, as the most important export support service for small and medium sized enterprises, and Britain and Germany, as two contrasting examples of public sector services organisation, are chosen. Thus, some background information about the export promotion systems in Germany and the United Kingdom is provided before the chapter proceeds to outline the rationale and significance of trade fair support in both countries. Then the research framework is developed further. A pattern-matching technique is used for analysing the cases, where the real organisations are compared with hypothetical ones. For this end the features of a hypothetical 'ideal' trade fair support organisation are defined, based on what the two governments pronounce to be the goals of their trade fair support services.

Chapter 6 and 7 look at the German and the British governments' trade fair support organisations respectively. Using the analytical framework that was developed in the previous chapters, they present information about the two organisations in a way that allows predictions about service delivery outputs. These predictions are then compared with empirical evidence about the actual outputs. The material for the comparative case studies is based on a wide range of sources, since each offer only limited information. Detailed knowledge about the structures relies on a series of semi-structured interviews, conducted with leading members of the public, private, and voluntary bodies that are involved in the production and provision of the services. Websites, annual reports, government commissioned research, parliamentary papers, government press releases, and newspapers provide additional information, particularly about the outputs of the respective services. The two chapters' conclusions present a summary judgement of each organisation's effectiveness in view to the goals of governments' trade fair support services.

Chapter 8 draws together the British and the German cases. It re-visits the relationships that were identified in the previous two chapters, and tries to validate the conclusions that were drawn about the organisations' impacts through direct comparisons. It looks at the comparative efficiency of the organisations, the question of which organisation is 'better' than the other, and at the impact of the variable 'institutions'. In the concluding part, the contribution of the research to understanding in the fields covered is underlined, but the work is also critically assessed, and directions for future research, necessary to validate and deepen our knowledge, are given.

Chapter 2: The context

2.1 Overview

The purpose of this chapter is to provide the reader with information on the concepts with which the thesis deals – 'organisation' and 'efficiency and effectiveness' – and the theoretical settings that relate to the topic. Accordingly, the first section specifies the research question by defining how the terms 'organisation', 'efficiency', and 'effectiveness' are used, and which difficulties underlie research into the latter two. In the second section the focus is on theories that may help to explain how organisation is related to the efficiency and effectiveness of public sector services delivery. First, the field of 'New Public Management' (NPM) is scrutinized for explanations. Attention is then turned to the wider field of organisation theory, to conclude that organisational economics promises to offer the most fruitful contributions to the research question.

2.2 Concepts

2.2.1 Organisations

Before the research interest – whether and how organisation matters for efficiency and effectiveness – can be pursued, it is necessary to define what is meant by 'organisation' and by 'efficiency and effectiveness'.

A look at different English language dictionaries shows that the word 'organisation' is used with several meanings, of which the three most common are: 1. a group such as a club or business that has formed for a particular purpose; 2. the act of planning and arranging things effectively; 3. the way in which the different parts of a system are arranged and work together.

In everyday language and in academic publications people mostly use 'organisation' in the first sense, referring to 'units' or 'bodies', which usually have an independent legal identity. In these 'units', e.g. companies, universities, or churches, two or more people work together to attain specific goals. A government export promotion agency is an organisation in this sense of the word. But as Pollitt and Mul, who use this meaning of 'organisation', write, *'nowadays it is a commonplace that many public policies and programmes are delivered not through single organisations, but through networks or partnerships of various organisations, both public and, in some cases, private or mixed. Thus it is the broad co-ordination and guidance of a whole squadron of organisations that will determine the ultimate effectiveness of the programme, rather than the individual productivity or efficiency of a single process or even a single component body.'* (Pollitt and Mul 1999:90).

Complying with this concern, 'organisation' is used here in the sense of the third definition – the way in which the different actors, who together produce and deliver a service, work together. Goodman and Pennings (1977:3) talk of *'a rational set of arrangements oriented towards achieving certain goals'*. In this spirit 'organisation' is used interchangeably with the term 'organisational structure', not only of one legal unit, the export promotion agency, but of the service delivery from the beginning to the end. Only the *formal 'ways in which the different parts of a system are arranged and work together'* are scrutinised. Informal co-ordination mechanisms, based for example on friendship between different individuals, are ignored. This is not because they are considered irrelevant, but because they are not within the design remit of the politicians or civil servants, who have to decide about organisational structures, not knowing which individuals will fill the posts. In contrast to the first definition of 'organisation', the interpretation of the word used here means that a production and delivery process for trade fair services or other export promotion services has an organisation, which is a tool to reach an end.

To have an organisation, or structure, order, or system of rules, for the entire service production and delivery process is a necessity. But which features it takes is a deliberate choice, and possibly a means to achieve the combination of all input factors in the most efficient and effective way (Etzioni 1964; Woehe 1986:153). Different countries have made different choices, and different organisations may have different implications. This is what the research tries to assess.

The government body that is in charge of export promotion has to ensure that a whole series of composite tasks – e.g. advising firms, doing research for adaptations of the service, dealing with financing – are carried out in a co-ordinated manner. For each of these tasks, the government has at least three alternatives: 1. to do it inside one public sector agency; 2. to buy it in individual market transactions; 3. to develop a co-operative agreement with one or more public, private or voluntary sector body (Mariti and Smiley 1983). The 'organisation' of trade fair services can therefore involve a whole range of different actors, only a few, or only the government export promotion unit itself. But in all cases the latter can be perceived as the *core unit* of the structure. It allocates roles to different actors and co-ordinates their contributions, so that the goal of the service will be attained.

To avoid ambiguity it is also necessary to define how the term 'institution' is used in contrast to the term 'organisation'. Institutions are generally agreed to be the mechanisms that structure economic and social actions. They are a mixture of interlinked systems of formal laws, norms, customs, conventions and paradigms, and their respective enforcement mechanisms, which differ from society to society (North 1990:33f). They are similar to organisational structures, since both constrain and inform action. The difference in the use of the terms here is that 'institutions' refer to rules and regularities in a society that are fairly stable and have developed over long periods of time. They are impersonal and non-arbitrary in that they apply to all members of a certain group or society and preclude individual choices (Schotter 1981; Ostrom 1986; Williamson 1993; Neale 1994). With regard to organisational analysis, institutions can therefore be depicted as the fairly stable framework within which organisations operate. Organisations, or more precisely the individuals within them, cannot change this framework purposefully in the short or even medium term.[1] Instead, organisational structures are adjusted to the prevailing institutions. For a comparative organisational analysis it is therefore necessary to take into account how the organisations are affected by their specific institutional framework. Organisations themselves then form a set of 'secondary institutions', i.e. a more specific framework for the action of the individuals and/or the different legal units that are involved in the respective production and delivery processes. The formal structures are designed deliberately and purpose-orientedly within the framework allowed for by the 'primary institutions' and can be changed in the short and medium term.

Thus, 'organisations' are defined here as deliberate structures set up by a core unit to co-ordinate the activities of different actors towards a goal. Institutions can enable some structures while precluding others.[2]

2.2.2 Efficiency, effectiveness and their measurement

In discussions about the performance of public sector organisations, the concepts of efficiency and effectiveness (or 'efficiency' as a more general term, which encompasses both) stand in the foreground. In broad terms they are measures of how well the public sector uses its resources to accomplish its goals (NAO c.{1994}). More specifically, 'efficiency' is taken to describe the relationship between inputs and outputs, whereas 'effectiveness' is used to describe the relationship between outputs and the intended results of the organisation (Brudney and Morgan 1988; Dalton and Dalton 1988; Metcalfe and Richards 1990; Glynn et al. 1991; Rosen 1993; Naschold 1994; Dowding 1995). Here, effectiveness is used as a term that refers to goal attainment, while efficiency is used as a term referring to the cost incurred in this effort (Hannan and Freeman 1977:110). These definitions seem to be straightforward, if somewhat broad. But when starting to look at 'efficiency' more closely, it becomes clear that the terms are not unambiguous, and that both efficiency and effectiveness are difficult to measure:

'Efficiency' is held to be *the relationship between output in terms of goods, services and other results, and the resources used to produce them* (NAO

---

[1] From this definition of institutions as a 'framework' it follows that what is defined as an institution depends on the viewpoint. For example, from the perspective of firms, tax legislation is an institution (which might only be changed through persistent lobbying) whereas from the point of view of the ministry of finance, it is a work output on which they have direct influence.

[2] The 'technology', which is available to co-ordinate different actors also impacts on choices. But since the technological options do not differ in two developed countries at a specific point in time, 'technology' is not considered as a differentiating factor. However, it would need to be considered as a 'framework' factor if organisational structures were compared over time.

c.{1994}:3). To increase efficiency means to increase the outputs of an activity with a given input, or to reduce the input for a given output. The reference scale is the cost of inputs vs. the value of outputs.

At first sight this conceptualisation of efficiency is very appealing, because it implies that precise and comparable statements about the efficiency of different organisations are possible. But the problem with such an approach is that one needs to be able to measure inputs and outputs:

To quantify the *inputs* for a service one would have to ensure that all the resources that are used in the production and delivery process, and their cost, are identified. This covers not only human and financial resources, but also the use of equipment, offices etc. But even countries' national audit offices can find it difficult to assemble this information, although they have legal access to all documents and accounts of the public agencies they investigate. Apart from the challenge to keep track of *all* inputs, there are problems with representing overheads adequately, and there are problems with changes in the measurement of inputs (NAO c.{1994}:10). When for example the British National Audit Office (NAO) reviewed the 'Overseas Trade Services' in 1995, they found that full cost information was not readily available on individual programmes (NAO 1996:3). For an 'outsider', who has no right to access 'sensitive' financial information, the task of obtaining meaningful cost information is incomparably more difficult. And for countries like Germany, which still rely on a cameralistic budgeting system for the public sector, it is impossible to trace the exact total input cost for specific programmes and activities.

Furthermore, there are problems with comparing countries' input expenditures, because they are estimated and calculated in different ways. This is highlighted by Conway and Nothdurft's (1996:19f) paragraph on comparative export support expenditures:

> *'In a 1992 study the U.S. General Accounting Office found that the U.S. federal government spent only 59 cents on promotion for every $1000 of non-agricultural exports, compared to $1.62 for the United Kingdom, $1.71 for Italy and $1.99 for France. The German government spent less – 22 cents – but that is only because German export promotion is handled through massive investments by its chamber of commerce system. – But note that the chambers receive a government subsidy, which was presumably not considered in the calculation (I.H.) – The spending includes estimates provided by government officials, except for the U.S.. Outlays do not include state and local government export promotion spending and are only for 'traditional' export promotion activities such as awareness promotion, counselling, information, and trade event programs. For France it includes spending on agricultural promotion, because officials were unable to separate the agricultural spending from the total.'*

In short, in the attempt to compare inputs, due to different accounting systems and to varying information availability, apples might be compared with pears. The 'input' figures become deceptive, because they are based on the same unit of measurement without being truly comparable.

But while one could devise accounting systems that reduce the problem of measuring inputs, to measure public sector *outputs* is incomparably more difficult. All the goods produced or the services provided have a quality as well as a quantity dimension. Many outputs are intangible, for example information. Often they are dissimilar, so that it is difficult to form a summary picture of an agency's performance (Brudney and Morgan 1988; Ganley and Cubbin 1992:8; Kelly 1988:8ff).

The output measurement problems have led to the development of proxy or substitute measures. But even if good proxy measures can be found, they still need to be 'weighed', as soon as an organisation produces more than one output. The weighing poses a problem because utilities are totally subjective. For example, how should 'supplying client firms with contact addresses abroad' be 'objectively' weighed in comparison with 'supplying client firms with information about customs laws', so that a value can be attributed to the export advice organisation's overall output? And how does one take into account that the firm A derives twice or half as much benefit from the same information as firm B? Whichever weighing of outputs is chosen is therefore questionable (Cordato 1994; Dowding 1995:35; Kasper and Streit 1998:57; Kelly 1988:6f).

Short of a 'value' for the outputs, audit offices apply weights which attempt to reflect either the relative complexity of the work needed to produce specific outputs, or the different amounts of resources they require (NAO c.{1994}). But at least the latter seems to defeat the purpose of measuring the 'efficiency' in transforming inputs into outputs.

The whole problem of measuring outputs becomes even more complicated as one attempts comparisons. *'...One hospital or school or church is more efficient than another only if it produces the same product at a lower cost, and this 'sameness' is a very difficult thing to establish'* (Etzioni 1964:9).

And this is the point where the difference between comparing the 'efficiency' and the *'effectiveness'*, i.e. the 'goal attainment' aspect, of two organisations becomes blurred. The efficiency concept implicitly presupposes that all outputs are exactly defined in content, quantity and quality. But usually, only the broad output categories are pre-defined. The chief decision makers in a public agency are able to decide about some programme features, e.g. in trade fair support programmes they may decide which type of trade fairs can be attended, how the beneficiaries are selected etc. On the one hand this can be perceived as an 'output quality' issue, and is thus conceptually a part of the efficiency measurement question. On the other hand the 'output design' may affect the goal attainment of the organisation, and is thus part of the effectiveness question.

But this consequently means that the concept of 'effectiveness' itself can have different meanings. It is useful to distinguish between two types of 'effectiveness' 'policy effectiveness', and 'operational effectiveness': The first refers to the extent to which a certain SME support programme meets the goals for which it was introduced. The second refers to the extent to which a 'given' policy, i.e. a broadly pre-defined output, is shaped in a way that produces results conducive to reaching the policy goals, not comparing it with alternative policies but with alternative output designs. For example, if the goal of trade fair support is to increase SME's exports, trade fair support's 'policy effectiveness' in reaching this goal may be high or low in comparison with alternative policies. But the specific shape which trade fair support takes may also influence to what extent the goal is reached.

Figure 2.1. shows these relationships. As stated above, the question of 'policy effectiveness', i.e. whether export support policies as such are effective in promoting exports, is not part of the thesis.

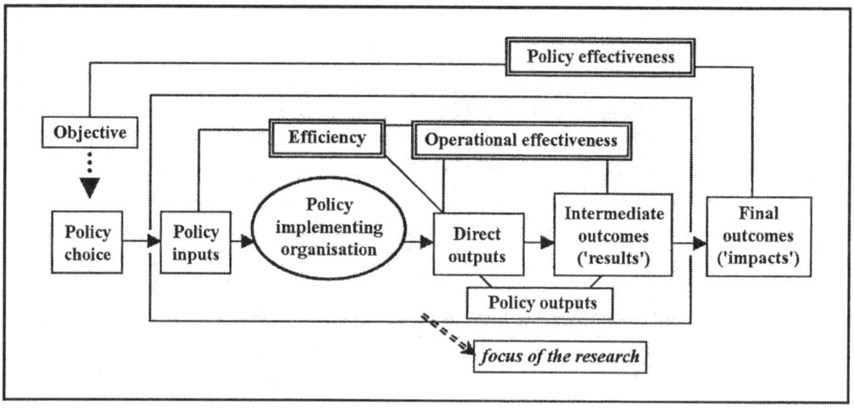

Fig. 2.1. Efficiency, operational effectiveness, and policy effectiveness
Source: adapted from Pollitt and Summa (1999:10)

As a result of the discussed measurement problems, the range of cases where input–output assessments have actually been attempted to assess efficiency have been limited (Brinckmann 1994; NAO c.{1994}:17). *'We have seen an overwhelming focus upon the evaluation of well-structured tasks where output is definable and measurable with relative ease...'* (Tomkins 1987:48). For most public sector organisations the tasks are not like that, and where measurement is attempted nevertheless, there is the danger that *'the effort to measure services is reduced to gauging those characteristics that are tangible or quantifiable without regard to their importance'* (Brudney and Morgan 1988:163). More problems lie in the fact that a measured input–output ratio is pointless, unless a 'benchmark' as to what represents 'efficiency' has been set (Etzioni 1964), and unless it is certain that input and output fall into the same period of measurement (Pfaff 1994).

Regarding effectiveness, the measurement problem presents an even bigger challenge. Glynn et al. (1991) found that practitioners and academics were reluctant to develop a definitional framework. They also found that since outcomes, i.e. the direct consequences of the produced outputs, are even more difficult to define than the outputs themselves, effectiveness measurement has tended to focus on outputs as proxies, 'often inadequately and potentially misleading'. Metcalfe and Richards (1990:33f) as well as Hannan and Freeman (1977) questioned the feasibility of effectiveness assessments, given the notorious difficulty with defining the objectives of public services. And Pfaff (1994) made the point that comprehensive effectiveness studies would have to take negative external effects into consideration as well as their impact on goals.

Thus, in most cases the efficiency and effectiveness of public sector service delivery cannot be determined unambiguously, because inputs, outputs, and outcomes cannot be measured objectively. Confronted with this problem, audit offices have resorted to judging efficiency and effectiveness by examining observable features of the organisation. This is reflected in the British National Audit Office's internal guide (NAO c.{1994}:19): *'The measurement of efficiency is followed by an assessment of the management of the activity or programme. This is also an approach that can be adopted in circumstances where the measurement of efficiency is not a feasible proposition because complete, reliable, quantified information on inputs, outputs or performance standards is not available.'*

To do this assessment, the NAO's 'value for money' (VFM) unit devised a catalogue of questions, which guides their staff through a review. These include for example: *'are operations satisfactorily planned? Are the progress and status of operations monitored? Is information reported frequently enough? Have efficiency factors been given due consideration in strategic plans?'* (NAO c.{1994}:20ff). But although all of these questions seem reasonable, and have presumably proven valid in the experience of the staff involved in VFM audits, it is not evident that these are the most important questions, nor how one would assess a situation where one question is answered satisfactorily while another is not. It is also likely that different people would come to different conclusions about what, for example, 'satisfactorily planned' means. No justification is given as to why these questions rather than others are asked, and the relative weight of the different questions, their detailed assessment, and possible omissions remain in the dark. However, other countries' audit offices judge 'effectiveness' and 'efficiency' in a similar manner, as Pollitt and Mul (1999:86) found in their research: *'...a good part of their performance audit work has taken place on the basis of judgements not so much about effectiveness or efficiency, strictly defined, but about the presence or absence of good management practices'*, i.e. the presence or absence of certain features that are taken to affect efficiency and effectiveness.

It is evident that the value of such an approach relies entirely on the validity of the underlying cause–effect assumptions. The question is therefore, what is known about these cause–effect links in public sector organisations?

2.3 What makes organisations efficient and effective?

2.3.1 New Public Management

The past two decades were characterised by discussions about public sector organisation and by administrative reforms in most countries. Given that the primary aim was to increase efficiency and effectiveness in the public sector (Ferlie 2000; Naschold 1994; Pollitt and Bouckaert 2000), one could expect that there was a clear understanding of how to judge whether an organisation delivers services efficiently and effectively or not. However, as the information about auditing practises already indicated, and a review of the public management literature confirms, a commonly recognised framework for assessing organisational performance does not exist.

The public sector reform movement, which has been labelled 'New Public Management' (NPM), has been described as *'a set of beliefs or ideology from which actions followed in anticipation of particular consequences'* (Dawson and Dargie 1999:1) and for which no single definitive 'master manual' (Dunleavy and Hood 1994:10) exists. The reforms were carried out by politicians and civil servants in different countries in response to various pressures, and were only subsequently analysed and commented by 'public administration' academics (Dunsire 1999).

The core driving forces for the reforms and their shape were public sector budget difficulties and the belief that service provision through traditional bureaucracies was inefficient and often ineffective. To improve, the public sector would have to learn from the private sector and leave activities to the private sector, wherever possible. Consequently, while there have been variants of the NPM movement, the two major avenues of reform were to simulate market processes within the public sector and to make greater use of the private sector through privatisation and contracting-out (Brinckmann 1994; Ferlie 2000; Dawson and Dargie 1999; Naschold 1994; Newman 1999; OECD 1991).

However, so far no convincing empirical evidence is available for the assumption that public sector organisational structures lead to less efficiency *per se* (Brinckmann 1994; Tomkins 1987:16ff). Studies of the effect of privatisation on efficiency have been inconclusive and suggest that privatisation on its own does not lead to higher efficiency of service production and delivery (Vickers and Yarrow 1987; Barnekov and Raffel 1990; Galal et al. 1994). 'Contracting-out' has received more positive assessments, but it could also be observed that in some public administrations service production that had been contracted out was placed back into the public sector (Naschold 1994). Hirsch (1995), comparing in-house and contracted-out urban government services found mixed evidence. Dunsire and Hood (1989) gave to consider that increased production efficiency might not be sufficient to compensate for the costs of finding and controlling the contractor.

As to the 'marketisation' of the public sector itself, Hood (1991) composed a list of seven overlapping precepts, which have characterised 'internal' public sector organisation under NPM in different countries. More efficient and effective public sector activities were expected from reforms that ensure: 1. an active, visible and discretionary control of organisations by named persons at the top; 2. an explicit definition of goals and performance targets; 3. resource and reward allocation according to performance; 4. the creation of decentralised 'single purpose' units, which deal on an 'arms-length' basis with each other; 5. the introduction of term contracts and competitive tendering; 6. flexibility in hiring and rewards; and 7. a focus on cost-cutting. As suggested by such a list of 'recipes', and the fact that when applied, not all reforms have been equally present, the reform ideas have not been derived from one coherent and comprehensive concept of what causes public sector efficiency and effectiveness.

Aucoin (1990) observed that the different NPM prescriptions are not fully consistent. He traced the contradictions back to two major sources of inspiration for reform ideas: one school of thought, – labelled 'managerialist' because the ideas stem from 'business guru' prescriptions for the private sector[3] – identified the freedom of line managers to decide about their activities as the key feature affecting efficiency. According to this view hierarchical control and tight rules and regulations within public administrations hinder the line manager from deciding what action is best in the given situation to achieve the desired results and 'de-bureaucratisation' is necessary. To find out about the needs of the clients, consultation and external communication are essential. The other school of thought– the 'public choice' approach – perceived the possibility for bureaucrats to act in their own self-interest as the major problem. Efficient organisational structures must therefore enable politicians and the taxpayer to determine and control the activities of the public sector employees. The 'capture' of bureaucrats by interest groups must be prevented.

Due to the different perception of what the key problem with public organisations has been, the organisational design solutions that have followed these paradigms have taken different directions. To curb self-interested behaviour centralisation and control have been favoured whereas to provide the freedom to respond to specific situations decentralisation, deregulation and delegation have been asked for. Aucoin (1990) argued that principles from both paradigms have been simultaneously applied for administrative reforms, in most cases creating uncertainty as to what is the best management structure, and leading to perpetual changes. Some governments have, for example, tried to emulate the Swedish model of delegated authority at the same time as the Swedish government attempted to secure better control over its system of administration (Aucoin 1990:133). The NPM checklist for 'good' public sector organisation, the features of which were mainly gained on a trial and error basis, has not illuminated the issues and the conflicts have remained unresolved. Dunleavy and Hood (1994:15), judging NPM reform 'doctrines' as a basis for organisational design, go as far as suggesting that they are nothing more than '*simple mantras of the 'four legs good, two legs bad' variety...*'.

Controversy exists as to the assessment of the experiences from public sector re-organisation experiments. There is not enough evidence to judge the reform impacts on the quantity and quality of service provision and there are different perceptions of cause–effect links. This has been demonstrated by Dunsire and Hood (1989) who looked at the effects of cost-cutting strategies. They offered three competing interpretations of the medium- and long-term effects, which are based on different perceptions of how the public sector works. According to the 'lean and fit credo' cost-cutting leads to higher efficiency because it puts public sector employees under pressure to perform better and reduces the managers' scope to waste money. According to the 'anorexia credo' cost-cutting reduces mo-

[3] The bestselling book 'In Search of Excellence' by Thomas Peters and Robert Waterman was singled out as the most influential example. The book proposed a list of eight key attributes, possessed by successful companies (Aucoin 1990; Tomkins 1989:86).

tivation and may reduce efficiency.[4] The 'gattopardismo credo' suggests that there is no firm relationship between the amount of resources used and public sector efficiency and that therefore the effects of cutbacks are indeterminate. Regarding the efficiency effects of short term contracts, Hood (1995:171) remarks that *'...it cannot even be taken for granted that the new orthodoxy...even contributes to effective cost restraint. Focusing on narrow quantifiable savings through short-term contracting may be convenient, like the old joke of the drunk who chooses to search for his lost key under a lamp-post because the light is better there.'*

These examples should be sufficient to demonstrate that the NPM 'recipes' cannot be adopted as a guideline to the key organisational features that affect efficiency.

'The need therefore is for conceptual frameworks with which to determine what factors in organisational design and management deserve analysis.' (Aucoin 1990:135).

2.3.2 Organisation theories – a bazaar of approaches

If it is argued that NPM does not provide a useful framework for the research question, because it is not based on a coherent and empirically confirmed model of what causes efficiency and effectiveness, and how this relates to organisational structures, the obvious place to look for alternatives is in the field of 'organisation theory'.

Doing that, one finds a field of academic research in which a wide variety of disciplines are active. Apart from sociology, psychology, economics, political science, engineering to name just a few, each of them with their specific subject perspective, interdisciplinary as well as non-academic literature are strongly present as well. Yet the diversity does not end here. The paradigms which are used by different organisational researchers cover the whole field of different social science approaches and, to make things even more varied, in different regions of the world different strands of theory have been developed (Chanlat 1994; Donaldson 1995; Uesdiken and Pasadenos 1995; Pfeffer 1997). It is therefore not surprising that 'organisation theory' and 'organisational analysis' are spoken of as a *'theoretical and methodological bazaar'* (Chanlat 1994:52).

But without claiming to do justice to each approach, one can narrow down the field in view of the research interest here. Burrell and Morgan (1985(1979)) have categorised organisation theories into two major groups according to their underlying paradigms – the functionalist and the interpretative. The former implies that concrete, real structures that can be researched exist, that human actions are shaped by their environment, and that there are causal relationships between different aspects of organisations. The interpretative paradigm on the other hand sees the world as a social process, which is created by the individuals concerned. There

---

[4] An example would be the decision by the Thames Valley NHS management board to keep their first aid helicopter on the ground on Tuesdays and Wednesdays in order to cut back the cost of the service (BBC1 9pm News, 16.6.00)

is no objective standpoint of evaluation, and there are no systematic causal connections between events.

As was made clear by the discussion of 'organisation' above, 'organisation' is defined here in a functionalist way – 'as a social tool…' (Cooper and Burrell 1988) for a productive purpose. Theories based on the interpretative paradigm cannot contribute to the research question, because they reject the functionalist approach as such.[5] 'Postmodern' approaches to organisation, for example, belong to this group, focussing on subjective perceptions and on the *'production of organisation, rather than the organisation of production'* (Cooper and Burrell 1988:106; Parker 1992; Payne 1993).

Although functionalist, 'radical organisation theories' (Burrell and Morgan 1985 (1979):365ff), do not promise to illuminate organisation's effects on efficiency and effectiveness either. Here the focus is on organisations as reflections of society's power structures, as tools to promote the interests of dominant groups (Kieser 1987; Reed 1992).

Of the remaining group of 'mainstream' organisational theories (Scott 1981; Astley and Van de Ven 1983; Burrell and Morgan 1985 (1979); Morgan 1990; Pfeffer 1993; Donaldson 1994), 'natural systems approaches' can be excluded, following Scott's (1987) classification. They pay little attention to formal organisational structures and concentrate instead on those features that characterise organisations as 'social groups', especially on informal patterns of human interrelations. They have brought insights about facets of organisations that develop beyond formal organisational structures and they have drawn attention to the fact that issues like human interrelations also influence outputs. However, 'natural systems' theories do not help to illuminate relationships between formal organisation and efficiency and effectiveness.

This leaves the group of theories classified as 'rational systems' approaches (Scott 1987). They focus on organisations as instruments, designed to best attain specified goals. Implicit in some approaches is the argument that formal structures per se contribute to efficiency. Organisation as such matters, because it specifies roles and positions of the actors and the rules that govern the relationship among them. Thus, each participant can have 'stable expectations' regarding the behaviour of the others. Roles and positions appear 'objective' and externally determined, which means that status battles are reduced and that activities can be carried out in collaboration with others, independent of the personal feelings between the participants. Appropriately trained actors can replace each other, even the leaders whose power and influence is determined by the definition of their offices and not necessarily by their personal qualities (Scott 1987:33ff).

Beyond contributing to an understanding why formal structures as such are functional, rational systems theories have also been concerned with aspects of the nature of those structures. Of interest here is whether the theories identify factors that are responsible for efficiency and effectiveness, and how they are affected by formal organisation.

[5] Should the proponents of the interpretative paradigm be right, there is no relationship between organisation and outputs, and a functionalist approach will not lead to any results.

Scott (1987) divided the 'rational systems approaches' into two groups depending on whether the theories approached organisations as 'closed' or as 'open' systems. The 'closed' rational systems approaches, all of which were developed in the first decades of the last century, are only concerned with the structures of one legal entity, the 'core organisation'. They do not look at structures that regulate inputs from suppliers, or connect the entity with its customers or wider environment, nor are they concerned with the question how the separation of tasks between the core unit and other actors may affect efficiency.

The three most prominent *'closed rational system approaches'* used different perspectives to theorise about the core unit's 'efficient' structure:

Max Weber's 'theory of bureaucracy' can be seen as the first work producing any organisational categories (Pugh et al. 1964). He argued that large organisations managed by traditional or charismatic authority had over centuries gradually given way to bureaucracies because the latter had proved more efficient. The superiority of bureaucracies stemmed from the rational–legal basis, which legitimised bureaucracies' administrative structures. This structure led to a calculability of bureaucracies' results, and meant that posts could be filled on the basis of technical knowledge and experience. The rational–legal structures also led to an increase in bureaucracies' scope, since post-holders could be given some discretion to make decisions as long as they complied with the rules defining their role (Weber 1997 (1924):12ff).

Weber's descriptive portrait of the characteristics of bureaucratic structures has been highly influential. However, it is precisely these described features of 'bureaucratic' structures, e.g. the formalisation of rules, strict hierarchies, payment according to seniority, need for paperwork, etc. that have been criticised in the last decades as leading to inefficiency in the public sector. While in Weber's context the point of reference were earlier forms of organisation, led by hereditary or charismatic rulers, if one 'bureaucracy' is to be compared with another, those features would not serve as a guideline to assess which bureaucratic organisation is more efficient. However, it should be noted that Weber was explicit as to what he saw as the fundamental cause of bureaucracies' higher efficiency: *'Bureaucratic administration means fundamentally the exercise of control on the basis of knowledge'* (Weber 1997 (1924):14). According to Weber higher efficiency thus results from a structure, which better ensures that those who make decisions have sufficient knowledge to make them, or respectively, that those who have the required knowledge have the discretion to make decisions.

Frederick W. Taylor and others engaged in 'Scientific Management' had a more practical outlook. They were concerned with the question of how to increase efficiency in a given production company. They segmented the work process into its smallest components and then analysed the individual manual tasks from the perspective of engineering, industrial psychology, ergonomics, and physiology. The aim was to discover 'scientifically' the most efficient way of doing each task, meaning finding ways of production that eliminated workers' waste time and waste motion. Once this was discovered, workers would be trained in handling their jobs accordingly and benchmarks for work output would be set. The work processes as such would be redesigned, also paying attention to eliminate waste between the different steps of work (Taylor 1997 (1912)).

Scientific management had a large impact on production efficiency since it provided a conceptual and practical framework for increasing specialisation and for standardising manufacturing processes. Thereby it also contributed significantly to the development of mass production. As a technique, it calls for an empirical analysis of every single task component *'through hundreds of experiments'* (Taylor 1997 (1912)), for task regrouping, and for task output control. But apart from establishing the importance of 'know-how' for efficient task fulfilment it offers no guidelines as to how 'waste' in and between tasks can be identified when it comes to activities which are not entirely repetitive, and to work processes that contain few manual activities so that motion studies are not possible.

The third 'classic' closed rational system approach is 'administrative theory', which developed concurrently with scientific management and has Henri Fayol as its most famous proponent. Fayol, based on his own experience as an industrialist, tried to generate broad administrative or 'management' principles that would initiate the discussion about a 'management code' – a guideline of what managers have to do and how. He devised a list of 14 principles, such as 'division of work', 'authority and responsibility', 'discipline', 'unity of command', 'fair remuneration' etc. Other administrative theorists, who pursued the same objective, came up with different numbers of principles (Scott 1987:38). Fayol himself wrote that *'the list has no precise limits'* (1997 (1916):273), and that *'seldom do we have to apply the same principle twice in identical conditions; allowance must be made for different changing circumstances...'* (253).

Critics stated that many of the principles were mere truisms or common sense pronouncements and offered little guidance for practical use, since they failed to specify the limits of the applicability to particular situations, or to types of organisations (Scott 1987:39f). While they were an advance in identifying the fundamental features of formal organisational structure, they did not constitute a model of what causes efficiency and effectiveness. In their disconnectedness, incoherency and lack of a conceptual framework they appear a bit like the NPM 'recipes'.

Several decades after these three famous 'closed rational systems approaches' were first publicised, structural thinkers started to argue for the need to analyse the 'working environment' of the organisation, to view them as *'open systems'*.

For the theorists, who put forward 'situational approaches' to organisation, the search was no longer for *'the'* one best way to organise (Lawrence and Lorsch 1997 (1967):129), but for structures coping effectively with different states of the environment. A whole set of theories emerged, which identified different 'contingency' factors like technology, sources of inputs, customers etc., and their respective 'optimal' structures (Scott 1981). Some were based on large quantitative studies in which statistical links between 'dependent' variables for structure and 'independent' variables for context were tested. Pugh and colleagues for example devised measures for the degree of specialisation, formalisation, standardisation, centralisation and configuration of organisations, and correlated them with seven context variables such as size, technology, ownership. They found that *context* is *'a'* or *'the' determining factor which designs, shapes and modifies the structure of any organisation. But within these contextual limits top management has plenty of leeway left to make its influence felt* – about 50% of the structural features were not 'explained' or determined by the context (Pugh 1997 (1973):28) The result was presented as a major step forward, as a 'proof' that there is a link between structure and context. But the research stopped at the descriptive stage and lacked a comprehensive theoretical framework that explained the pattern and the 50% leeway.

Another strand of 'situational theorists' worked qualitatively to explore how differences in internal states and processes were related to differences in organisations' external environment (Lawrence and Lorsch 1997 (1967)). They also concluded that design decisions are contingent on environmental conditions, particularly on environmental diversity. The higher it was, the more differentiated the organisation would have to be; and from a large degree of differentiation an elaborate design of integration devices would have to follow. Based on the results from an analysis of three high performing organisations Lawrence and Lorsch (1997 (1967):129) concluded that organisation should be such that each sub-unit should be suited to the specific environment in which it operates. *'The locus of influence to resolve conflict is at a level where the required knowledge about the environment is available. The more unpredictable and uncertain the parts of the environment the lower in the organisational hierarchy this tends to be.'* In other words, like Max Weber and Frederick W. Taylor they saw the performance of organisations as being determined by the knowledge of the decision-makers. The difference is that the former appear to have perceived 'knowledge' as only a kind of static expertise, whereas the 'contingency' theorists put emphasis on the need for processing information about the environment.

However, despite their attention to context and environment, the situational theorists did not pay any attention to questions regarding the division of tasks between the core organisation and other actors, e.g. how different ways of segmenting the work process into separate tasks would affect efficiency, or whether different choices of co-ordinating the actors would affect the overall output. According to Pfeffer (1996) structural contingency theory, popular in the 1960s and 70s, 'has virtually faded from the scene'. One reason was that it was too complicated and too disconnected from variables about which managers could decide, the other that it was beset with theoretical and empirical problems, like a lack of clarity about cause–effect relationships or the failure to differentiate between linear and non-linear relationships.

Another 'open system rational approach' presented in Scott's (1987) discussion of major organisation theories is Oliver Williamson's transaction cost approach. This is one of the 'organisational economics' (OE) theories, which in contrast to the theories above approach the problem of organisation deductively. They have focused on the different actors' contributions to the overall output of an organisation by conceptualising them as contributions the actors make in exchange for something else. Efficiency is created by finding forms of organisation, which keep the cost of all the exchanges as low as possible.

A 1990 edition of the 'Academy of Management Review', one of the most prestigious academic management journals, was dedicated to reviewing what OE had to offer to 'management theory'. Hesterley, Liebeskind, and Zenger (1990) produced an account of the advantages OE has as an analytical paradigm for organisational analysis:

1. Organisation is perceived as a governance mechanism that resolves differences in individual interests via exchanges, so that joint effort towards a goal becomes possible. This means that for the analysis of organisational arrangements the same tools of analysis can be used for looking at governance mechanisms within the firm as at governance mechanisms with external actors, e.g. suppliers or joint venture partners. It is also irrelevant whether one looks at public, non-profit, co-operative or hybrid organisations.
2. The authors argue that compared with those other organisation theories that also look at issues like the boundaries of the core unit or at employment contracts, OE provides many more insights, highlights more variables that are important regarding organisation structures, and also looks at the relationships between these variables.
3. Empirical tests of the OE ideas have for the most part been confirmatory. Interest in this field expanded in the 1970s, and has grown exponentially in the last decade. With increasing success in the attempts of trying to explain a wide range of organisational issues, organisational economics has become an established field of research.
4. Since OE is based on deductive reasoning, it is logically coherent (Hesterley et al. 1990). This is in contrast to most organisation theories, which have usually been empirically motivated and are therefore 'quite broad and lack rigor' (Winship and Rosen 1988:S5). This deductive, rather than inductive approach, built on assumptions about human nature in general, means that OE ideas can also be generalised across countries.

These advantages make OE look attractive for the research topic in question. For the comparative analysis of export support services delivery organisations, which are made up of a variety of actors and internal–external relationships, the fact that whole organisations instead of just core organisations can be analysed from a unified perspective is an important advantage compared with other approaches. Moe (1984), a sympathetic critic of organisational economics, remarked on the value of organisational economics that: *'...the theories have 'value in clarifying what the relevant aspects of hierarchical relationships are. (They) cut through the inherent complexity of organisational relationships by identifying distinct aspects of individuals and their environments that are most worthy of investigation and integrate these elements into a logically coherent whole' (Moe 1984:757).*

2.4 Summary

International competitiveness in general, and SME exports in particular, have increasingly concerned governments over the past decades. This has led to reviews, comparisons, and to the restructuring of national export promotion systems, with the aim to increase their efficiency and effectiveness. Yet the relationship between organisation and these performance measures has been far from clear. One major impediment is that the efficiency and effectiveness of service delivery usually cannot be measured in a comparable way. It is therefore difficult to judge directly whether 'organisation matters', or whether one organisation is 'better' than another one. The measurement problem makes inductive explanations about cause–effect links between organisation and performance difficult, and also hinders the testing of any theories, once they are developed.

This may be a reason why the academic literature on 'new public management' has so far rather focused on exploring the political reasons for changes in service delivery, and on criticising the convictions that guided the shape of changes. 'Organisation theory' on the other hand does not offer a coherent, integrated body of knowledge on the issue either. Of the variety of those 'rational systems approaches', which have dealt with organisations as functional, production-oriented, formal structures, organisational economics appears to be most useful for developing the wanted *'conceptual framework with which to determine which factors deserve analysis'* (Aucoin 1990, see above). From the other presented theories the tentative argument emerged that organisation efficiency and effectiveness is related to the expertise and environmental knowledge of the actors. But none of the approaches appeared sufficiently broad and versatile to offer a base for comparative analyses, nor did they offer an in-depth explanation of efficiency or effectiveness. The focus in the following chapter will therefore be only on organisational economics, to examine in detail which cause–effect explanations for organisations' efficiency and effectiveness it offers.

Chapter 3: Efficient and effective organisations – Approaches in organisational economics

3.1 Overview

The purpose of this chapter is to engage with different theories in organisational economics, to explore and synthesise their contributions to the question of which factors in organisational design are linked to 'efficiency and effectiveness'.

'Organisational economics' is a name that was given to approaches within New Institutional Economics (NIE) by non-economists (Moe 1984; Barney and Ouchi 1986; Perrow 1986; Donaldson 1990; Donaldson and Barney 1990). Its definition depends as much on the author as the definition of NIE itself, a label that has been applied to a large number of economic approaches, which analyse institutions and organisations from the perspective of methodological individualism (Langlois 1989; Mayhew 1989; Hodgson 1989, 1993; Reuter 1994; Rutherford 1989, 1994; Cheung 1992). Here, in line with some authors (e.g. Picot et al. 1997; Furobotn 1997), 'organisational economics' is used as a term that subsumes property rights theory, agency theory, and transaction cost theory.

To provide a backdrop for the three theories' arguments, the first section of the chapter gives a brief introduction to the main themes in the field, followed by a discussion of the basic assumptions on which the deductive theories are based.

Attention is then focused on the main theoretical arguments of property rights theory, agency theory and transaction cost theory. Each is presented on its own, with an outline of the reasoning, a summary of the applications and empirical evidence, and a look at the criticisms, followed by a summary of major insights into the causal links between organisation and 'efficiency and effectiveness'.

In the last part of the chapter the findings are synthesised.

3.2 The foundations of organisational economics

3.2.1 Organisation as a facilitator of exchanges

Economics is concerned with the question of how scarce resources are allocated efficiently.[1] This perspective, as a normative concept, has for a long time been

[1] 'Efficiency', as used by economists, goes beyond the definition of the previous chapter. It broadly encompasses both 'effectiveness' – that the 'right' outputs are to be produced

used to discuss how 'the economy' should be organised. The two co-ordination mechanisms around which the discussion has revolved (e.g. in the famous Mises/Hayek vs. Lange/Lerner debate) have been the allocation of scarce resources through the price-mechanism, as opposed to allocation by a central decision maker. Economists' mainstream consensus has been that price allocation is superior to the central direction alternative, since it involves far lower information costs, and since it triggers an automatic adaptation to changed scarcity patterns. Prices enable very many agents to make simultaneous 'small computations' with only low information requirements, whereas centralised allocation needs vast information inputs and matching computation capacities (Hayek 1945). A further factor in favour of price allocation is the reduced incentive for individuals to distort the allocation by giving wrong signals to the central decision maker, e.g. for rent-seeking purposes (Samuelson 1954, Marschak 1987). The price mechanism has thus been seen as the structure which co-ordinates the use of scarce resources in a way that is beneficial to society as a whole, although each individual is following his or her self-interest.

But some scholars looked more closely at the implicit assumptions of the argument. Ronald Coase (1937) made the point that if prices and the associated markets were always the best allocative mechanism, firms would not exist. As they did exist, the economy in fact worked with a mixture of price and administrative allocation processes. It was necessary to find an explanation when and why co-ordination occurred through 'planning' as opposed to 'markets'.

Coase argued that economic activity was based on exchanges or 'transactions', which all involved search, negotiation, monitoring and enforcement efforts, i.e. they were not costless. The efficiency of alternative modes of co-ordinating exchanges was determined by their comparative cost, and the way economic activity was organised influenced these costs. In some cases 'hierarchies' were more efficient than markets.

More than twenty years later Coase (1960) made a second important contribution to organisational economics. He pointed out that there were constraints to exchanges, as the prerequisite to market exchange was a clear delimitation of rights. Any exchange required a prior specification of what individuals were allowed to exchange. Moreover, since 'ownership' was often not complete or not specified, the choices of one individual could have 'external effects' on others. Organisation, i.e. a specific allocation of property rights, mattered, since in a world with transaction costs, it delineated actors' choices.

Other scholars have developed the arguments further, as will be presented below. However, Coase's ideas that 'exchange' as such had to be investigated, and that 'transaction costs' and 'property rights' specifications were important for the way in which exchanges took place, have shaped the whole school of thought. In combination with fundamental assumptions about the nature of human beings and the methodological individualist approach, they have formed the basis of organisational economics' reasoning about what makes organisations efficient.

---

from scarce resources, and 'efficiency' – that they are produced at the lowest possible cost.

The three approaches within 'organisational economics' have taken different perspectives on analysing organisation. *Property rights theory* has concentrated on the implications of organisations and institutions for individuals' behaviour. *Agency theory* has focused on the implications of alternative ways of delegating decision rights to other actors. *Transaction cost theory* has been concerned with the efficient boundaries of 'hierarchies' vs. 'markets'.

Before the three approaches are presented in detail, the conceptual foundations of organisation economics – methodological individualism and specific assumptions about human nature – will be discussed. This is necessary because the theories are deductive, and their credibility thus relies on the credibility of the assumptions on which they are built.

3.2.2 Methodological individualism

The basis of organisational economics' deductive reasoning is methodological individualism – the idea that social phenomena should be analysed as the outcome of individuals' actions. It is one of the major areas of attack by OE critics (e.g. Perrow 1986; Schreyoegg 1988; Donaldson 1990, 1994, 1995), and distinguishes organisational economics fundamentally from most other approaches to organisation (Donaldson and Barney 1990).

The term was coined by Schumpeter to make the distinction between political and methodological individualism explicit. While political individualism is a normative concept that favours the rights of the individual, methodological individualism per se 'asserts nothing and has no particular premises' (Machlup 1978:472). It simply means that the description of economic processes centres on individual ends. In Max Weber's words, *'truly empirical sociological investigation begins only with the question, what did and still does motivate the individual...Any formal functional analysis which uses the 'whole' as its point of departure can accomplish only preliminary preparations for further investigation'* (cited in Agassi 1975:145).

The brief explanation of the term makes it clear that much of the criticism of the approach is misconceived. Critics and some scholars of organisational economics, who see methodological individualism as implying a political programme such as 'laissez faire' (Tietzel 1981; Kirsch 1993), fail to distinguish between political and methodological individualism (Hodgson 1994). Those who reject the notion that the structure and change of social phenomena are explicable only in terms of exogenously given individuals, who are not influenced by their social environment, criticise a reductionist version of methodological individualism (Hodgson 1989; Donaldson and Barney 1990; Rutherford 1994), which Agassi (1960; 1975) calls 'psychologistic individualism'.

But the 'institutional individualism' version of 'methodological individualism' (Agassi 1960; 1975), which underlies most OE analysis, accepts the existence of distinct social entities (called institutions, customs, traditions, societies, etc.). They constitute a part of the individuals' circumstances that might affect their preferences and that together with their aims determine their behaviour (Frey 1990;

Khalil 1995a). What is not accepted is that these entities should have distinct aims and interests. *'An institution may have aims and interests only when people give it an aim or act in accord with what they consider should be its interest'* (Agassi 1960:247). Institutions are therefore exogenous and endogenous at the same time, which means that it depends on the research question what is left exogenous and what made endogenous (Basu et al. according to Rutherford 1994:49). Institutional individualism also permits that an organisation, a firm, a household etc. may be taken as an 'entity', but it is understood that organisational goals in the end always derive from individuals' goals, and are not some independent feature.

3.2.3 The model of the individual

For any theory based on methodological individualism, it is obviously of fundamental importance which assumptions are made about human behaviour.

Organisational economics, especially transaction cost economics, uses a wider model of the human decision-maker than the much criticised 'Homo Economicus' model, who is only interested in maximising his profits or consumption, and who makes fully rational decisions about every possible alternative for action. Meckling (1976) described this wider model as 'REMM' - *R*esourceful, *E*valuative, *M*aximising *M*an:

Resourceful: 'Man is Resourceful, he 'reasons' about the consequences of changes in his environment and in his own behaviour' (Meckling 1976:545).
This assumption is a necessity for seeing individuals as a major force behind social and cultural evolution. Without it, conscious adaptation, search, innovation and experimentation would not exist and man would be a passive element.

Evaluating: Being evaluative is a necessity for making choices. Choices have to be made as soon as individuals have preferences, and resources are scarce. As far as preferences are concerned, REMM, in comparison to Homo Economicus, may care about many different things from money, prestige, power, beauty, leisure to knowledge, altruism etc. His valuation of specific goods is relative, which means that depending on how much he already has of one in comparison to others, he values an additional unit more or less. (Meckling 1976:554f)

Maximising: REMM uses her resourcefulness and evaluation ability to pick the option that promises the highest returns in the specific circumstances.
But whereas Homo Economicus makes entirely rational choices because she has all relevant information and the capability to process it, REMM is only *boundedly rational*. She intends to be rational but is unable to foresee all the consequences of choosing alternatives. She also has finite abilities of receiving, storing, processing, and retrieving information. This costs time and effort, and to maximise her utility REMM has to take those costs into account. Therefore, REMM will in many instances not optimise, but 'satisfice'. REMM will set up more or less conscious routines and rules of thumb for some types of decisions and adjust them in a trial

and error process (Simon 1959; Zald 1987).[2] In organisations, the main consequence of bounded rationality, aside from the establishment of routines, are that all complex contracts are unavoidably incomplete and ways have to be found to deal with this incompleteness (Williamson 1993).

REMM, as a maximiser of utility, is as self-interested as Homo Economicus even if 'utility' for her might mean making presents to other people. Self-interest is seen to be a genetic characteristic (Brunner 1987). But whereas the standard self-interested utility maximiser is honest in her dealings with other individuals, in transaction cost theory and agency theory she might pursue her self-interest at the cost of others at any given chance. She is *opportunistic.* She might not tell the truth or might not act as she agreed to. Not everybody lies and cheats, and fewer do it all the time, but in many circumstances it is very costly or impossible to assess this. For a self-interested, boundedly-rational individual it is therefore wise to assume that who he is dealing with might act opportunistically (Williamson 1985).

Although this new model of man seems far closer to reality than 'Homo Economicus', there are still many problems with it. The major ones have to be noted here since the results of the research will be based on this model.

The first major criticism concerns the extension of maximising behaviour towards 'utility' instead of profit or consumption. Applied to a specific case, it is necessary to assume a specific utility function, which reflects the preferences of the decision-maker. An explanation constructing such a utility function ad hoc would degenerate into a tautology. Any empirical observation could be 'explained' by a 'specific' utility function (Tietzel 1981:219ff).

The hazard can be avoided by applying assumptions about preference functions universally, but the trade-off is that the REMM model becomes less open. People are judged as if they all reacted the same. This is a problem for an assessment of the actual efficiency of a given organisation with specific individuals. But in the context of the research question it has to be considered that governments do not usually set up organisational structures for export support services delivery with specific individuals' in mind. They have to design structures that produce results independently of who exactly fills a certain post.

A second major problem has been highlighted by empirical research, which suggests that utility functions for ranking choices are not complete. They are also inconsistent due to varying mental procedures for decision making or even due to biological and chemical processes within the brain (Roth 1996). Moreover, there are reasons to assume that human behaviour might not be rational at all: Selten (1990) developed a decision-emergence theory, according to which the conscious mind evaluates alternatives, but functions only 'like an advisor to the king'. The king may or may not listen to the advice; i.e. rationality has limited control over behaviour. Rationality is, in addition, reduced by emotions 'like anger or hunger (which) focus the attention on a narrow set of activities related to temporary goals

[2] To what extent this behaviour is interpreted as being explained by the concept of 'bounded rationality' and to what extent it is taken into account by different authors varies. Schlicht (1990), for example, does not consider the use of routines to be explained by bounded rationality.

and fears and thereby control the direction of thinking and imagination' (Selten 1990:652).

However, a realistic behavioural theory (if it existed) may be far too complicated to the point of intractability and, therefore, not theoretically useful. Although predictions might be made for specific individuals, it is impossible so far to generalise, due to insufficient evidence (Schlicht 1990). As has been claimed by many economists, the motivations, which underlie economic behaviour, may be diverse, but theorising with the assumption that people behave as if consciously maximising utility has so far delivered useful approximations (Roth 1996). Therefore, given that organisational structures have to co-ordinate the behaviour of 'anonymous' individuals, and that a better model does not exist so far, the REMM generalisation seems to be an adequate option, compared with the choice not to generalise at all. The critics, who suggest that the results of organisational economics are redundant, because they are based on inappropriate assumptions, have been proven wrong by the empirical evidence in favour of OE.

3.3 Property rights theory

3.3.1 Incentive structures as a cause of allocative choices

According to property rights theory, the effective and efficient use of resources depends on individuals' incentives to choose 'right' actions. 'Right' actions result in a larger net benefit for the individual, than they cost him and others, or cost the individual less than they benefit him and others. Efficiency and effectiveness also depend on the cost of assigning, monitoring, enforcing, and changing property rights.

Organisation is of crucial importance for efficiency and effectiveness because it represents a purpose-designed system of property rights. Alternative organisational arrangements confront individual decision-makers with different choices and different incentives, at different costs.

The theory developed on the basis of three notions. 1. PR theorists have argued that ownership means holding 'a bundle of rights' and that not all rights to resources are fully allocated, or privately held. 2. PR theorists take REMM as their basic units of analysis and distinguish between the effects a decision has on the decision maker, and on others. 3. PR theorists recognise that the allocation and the exchange of ownership rights are not costless:

1) 'Bundles of rights'

While in neoclassical economics, as well as in contemporary English, it is generally understood that 'owning' a resource means that the resource 'belongs to this person and nobody else', PR theorists point out that ownership relationships are in fact varied and complex, and that an asset rarely 'belongs' to one individual alone:

With the example of the meaning of 'owning land', Alchian and Demsetz (1973:17) demonstrated that it is not the resource itself that is owned, but a bundle of legally and socially recognised rights to use the resource: *'To own land usually means to have the right to till (or not to till) the soil, to mine the soil, to offer those rights for sale etc. but not to have the right to throw soil at a passer-by, to use it to change the course of a stream, or to force someone to buy it.'* When exchanges take place, e.g. a good is bought or sold, it involves a transfer of 'property rights'.

For any good, a range of different property rights exist and the rights are often held by many different parties *(complexity of rights).* In many cases the rights to choose what to do with an asset are restricted *(restriction of rights)*, or might even be withdrawn, e.g. by the state *(non-security of rights).* Moreover, one specific property right is not always exclusive to one individual *(non-exclusivity of rights)*, and not all rights over assets are completely defined *(non-specification of rights).*

These common forms of 'incomplete' ownership may cause problems, as property rights have two interwoven attributes that are relevant for the allocation of resources: They formally or informally assign to particular individuals *'the 'authority' to select, for specific goods, any use from an unprohibited class of uses'* (Alchian 1965:130), i.e. they define who has which decision rights about a good. Property rights also *'specify how a person may be benefited or harmed'* by their own decisions, or decisions of others who hold some decision rights over the good (Demsetz 1967:347). Combined with the notion of REMMs, this can lead to individual choices that are ineffective or inefficient from a group's, or society's perspective:

2) REMMs and 'external effects'

Resourceful, Evaluating, Maximising individuals will use their decision rights to choose those actions, from which they expect a net benefit for themselves. For PR theorists this assumption, together with an analysis of the distribution of property rights, makes the behaviour of different actors, and resulting efficiency and effectiveness problems predictable:

In the case of complete ownership of an asset, income streams are exclusive to the owner, who can decide freely and exclusively over the use of the asset, its alteration, or sale. In other words, the incentive to take account of both positive and negative effects of a decision is structured in a way that the wealth maximising outcomes for the individual and for society are identical.

But whenever ownership is not complete, i.e. property rights over a good are distributed among different parties, or are not fully specified, it is likely that not only the decision-maker is affected by her decision, but other individuals as well – *external effects* occur. External effects are a problem, because the costs and the benefits of an allocative choice are not fully weighed against each other. If an individual chooses an action from which he benefits less than someone else suffers, the action is inefficient from society's point of view. Nevertheless, for the individual the choice is perfectly rational, as long as his own net benefit is positive.

3) Transaction costs

If the lack of complete or fully specified private property rights creates incentives that make individual decisions inefficient from society's point of view, why do these situations exist? PR theorists have argued that it is mainly due to transaction costs (Coase 1960). It can be 'efficient to be inefficient' if the costs caused by externalities are lower than the costs of putting in place property rights structures that would prevent these externalities. This can frequently be the case, because it is expensive to define rights, and to monitor and enforce them. In addition, it is expensive to exchange rights, since this not only involves defining them, but also searching for exchange partners, examining what is to be exchanged, and negotiating (Demsetz 1967; Furubotn and Pejkovich 1972; Alchian and Demsety 1972).

Since both transaction costs, and the costs of external effects can change over time, be it due to new technologies, changed scarcity conditions, scientific or philosophical discoveries, or socio–psychological attitude changes (North 1990), what are efficient and effective property rights structures at present may not be so in future (Furubotn and Pejkovich 1972: 1145).

3.3.2 Applications and empirical tests of the property rights approach

To give an overview of the use of property rights reasoning in past and present research is difficult. It has been used in hundreds of analyses and explanations of different ownership patterns and their effects, ranging from: the productivity of socialist versus capitalist systems; the effects of and reasons for certain laws; alternative business structures; diverging historical developments of countries or businesses; to slavery regimes, and environmental problems (e.g. De Alessi 1980, 1990; Alston et. al. 1996; Barzel 1997). It seems that the last comprehensive literature review was carried out by De Alessi (1980), who concluded that *'the effects of alternative systems of property rights on behaviour and welfare are substantial and pervasive.'* (40).

The largest field of application has probably been the study of ownership rights to natural resources, and the consequences for their use. By outlining the application of property rights theory in this context, it can be demonstrated how the three building blocks described above have been brought together:

Compared with privately-owned assets, commonly-owned pasturelands or fisheries, hunting grounds, forests, etc. are typically used more intensely, and receive less maintenance or upgrading investment.[3] With a property rights approach, focusing on each individual actor's decision rights and incentives, the explanation is straightforward: In cases of 'communal' ownership (Demsetz 1967) the income shares of the group members are not fixed to some input measure, and each individual in the group can make private decisions that affect the communal resource. If an individual does not have the exclusive right to the income from an asset, it means that any benefits from investments have to be shared with 'free riders', who did not contribute to the investment costs. Therefore, rational decision-makers do not invest. The same dynamic applies to voluntary self-restraint in the use of the resource. The damage done by one individual, overusing or depleting the com-

[3] Hardin (1968) produced a classic piece of work in the field. De Alessi (1980:6ff) and Milgrom and Roberts (1994:288ff) review various studies. Demsetz (1967) discusses anthropological research on land use patterns; Besley (1995) presents research on farming in Ghana. Database searches show that hundreds of studies have been carried out in this field (e.g. IBSS, keyword 'property rights')

monly-owned asset has to be borne by all owners, not only by the person receiving the immediate benefits. Furthermore, in cases where the ownership to the income stream is assigned on a 'first come, first serve' basis, each individual has the incentive to serve himself before others do. He also has an incentive to invest in private improved 'harvesting' techniques (e.g. more powerful fishing boats in the case of communal fishing rights), as the benefit from such an investment only flows to the investor.

Additional institutional features of common ownership regimes could be explained as mechanisms that were set up to mitigate the consequences of common ownership. There are institutions to prevent overuse e.g. hunting and fishing seasons, limits on catches, specification of admissible harvesting techniques, or rules for maintaining physical assets. Another 'solution' has been to establish common rights not only for the use, but also for the income stream from the asset, e.g. in some tribes hunting catches have to be shared (Demsetz 1967; Ostrom 1990).

Property rights theory has also been able to explain observed changes in the property rights pattern of natural resources. Demsetz (1967), for example, traced changes in Canadian Indian hunting rights to the development of a fur market (i.e. the benefits of an internalisation of external effects increased), and Anderson and Hill traced the development of private land in Western America to the innovation of barbed wire (i.e. the transaction costs of enforcing rights fell) (De Alessi 1980:6).

Existing property rights structures could therefore be seen as efficient 'market outcomes'. However, as other researchers have argued, existing property rights structures might prevent new, more efficient ones to develop, or might even support the development of inefficient ones (Olson 1982; Eggertson 1990:271ff; North 1990; Bates 1995). Rational individuals, who hold property rights that are likely to lose value if new ones emerge, will resist changes. Also, structures may exist that make it profitable for specific groups to engage in rent-seeking activities, pressing for property rights patterns that benefit them (e.g., tariff barriers on certain products; subsidies) but have negative effects overall. Because of that, the adaptability of property rights structures to certain changes depends largely on how they are structured at present

Libecap (1988) found evidence for these points in four case studies of natural resources property rights change in the US. The property rights that were developed and maintained despite alternatives that appeared to be more rational, depended on the preferences of the individual bargaining parties, and on the details of the bargaining process. Various factors appeared to be relevant for the outcomes. Firstly, the greater the size of the anticipated benefits, the more likely it was that new property rights were sought and adopted. Secondly, whether institutional change was delayed or blocked depended on the number and on the heterogeneity of the contracting parties involved. A further issue was information asymmetry, which if known to exist among the competing parties intensified the distributional conflicts. Also, the greater the concentration of wealth under the proposed property rights allocation, the greater the likelihood of political opposition and the less likely was an unmodified adoption of the proposals by politicians.

More specific examples for problems with the adaptability of property rights are institutions that restrict or deny the right of sale (e.g. water rights in California cannot be transferred from farmers to others who value them more – Milgrom and Roberts 1992: 298ff), or the rights of changing organisational structures. Granick (1988) made the case that socialist firms were handicapped because they did not have these rights. The centrally-determined protection of employees against dismissal, their right to mobility, and their right to equal earnings for equal work, regardless of the enterprise at which they worked, undermined organisational adaptability, and limited the boundaries for still profitable transactions. Someren (1992) reflected on the effects on adaptability of such restrictions by discussing the interaction between technical and organisational changes. He demonstrated that technical changes cannot be implemented without any change in organisational structures.

Further successful applications of the theory have been, for example, to Yugoslav enterprises, where under-investment could be explained (Pejovich 1995:231), or to the institution of 'owner-managed' firms, which was explained as representing a low cost solution to the problem of monitoring in teams (Alchian and Demsetz 1972), or to state-owned enterprises whose lower output was explained via the incentive patterns of their managers and their monitors (e.g. Gravelle 1981; Borcherding et al.1982; Bonus 1987; Laffont and Tirole 1991; Dunn 1994).

3.3.3 Criticisms of the property rights approach

Most of the criticisms of the property rights approach concern its assumptions about human behaviour, not the rationale of the argument itself. As the objections to methodological individualism and REMM were already examined, few controversial issues remain to be considered. The following points are based on Tietzel's (1981) critical review:

First, property rights theory's focus on allocative efficiency rather than on distribution is disapproved of. This can be ignored here, because distributional implications of organisational structures are as such not part of the research question. However, linked to this issue is the recognition that different systems of rights have different side effects. As Coase (1960) implicitly noted, the person who supports one way of allocating property rights over another often has to make value judgements concerning the trade-offs.

Second, it is problematic to introduce non-quantifiable transaction costs or informal institutions as attenuating or enforcing property rights, and thereby 'explain' existing structures as efficient. If transaction costs cannot be quantified, there have to be credible arguments for any assumptions regarding their level. But this is also not an argument against the logic of the property rights approach, more a note of caution against functionalist 'explanations', and regarding the value of efficiency statements in an empirical context. Here, the interest lies not in using property rights theory to explain organisations as being efficient, but in the identified relationships between organisation and outputs.

Third, Tietzel did not find a study that tried to falsify property rights theory, and therefore concluded that there was uncertainty regarding its factual substance. The above-mentioned database research has also not identified any reviews that had the explicit objective to test the theory. This leaves Tietzel's doubts open. But the wide application of the property rights concept for over two decades demonstrates that many researchers have found it fruitful. Given that, despite this popularity, no substantive arguments against the theory – beyond the general criticisms against an 'economic' approach to social science themes – seem to have developed, it appears reasonable to accept the logic of the property rights argument.

However, this does not imply that property rights are necessarily the only explanatory factor for allocative choices. Moxnes (1998) presented the result of an experiment, where 83 subjects were asked individually to manage simulated fish stock, having been granted exclusive property rights. Despite perfect property rights they consistently 'overfished'. The author explained this outcome with 'misperceptions of feedback'. Godoy et al. (2000) relate the efforts of Honduran Indians to increase farming productivity, not only to security of land tenure, but also to education. One could argue that these 'knowledge factors' are encapsulated in the 'bounded rationality' assumptions of organisational economics. But property rights approaches do not make them part of the analysis.

3.3.4 A summary of property rights theory's insights into the cause–effect relationships between 'organisation' and 'efficiency and effectiveness'

The basic argument of property rights theory, backed by empirical evidence, supports the assumption that 'organisation matters'. The cause–effect link between 'organisation' and 'effectiveness and efficiency' is incentives. Organisational structures shape actors' cost–benefit expectations regarding alternative actions. Organisations represent a system of rights, which defines not only who can decide about what, but also who gets to enjoy the positive or suffer the negative consequences of those decisions. Inefficiency and ineffectiveness arise when actors benefit individually while imposing negative external effects on others. As Alchian and Demsetz (1972) argued, this means that the efficiency and effectiveness of 'team production' depend on the organisation's ability to align changes in actors' individual rewards with their contribution to the overall goal, i.e. on internalising external effects.

Property rights theory points out as well that 'organisation' as such involves costs. In an efficient organisation, the costs of designing and enforcing the structures that provide the right incentives are lower than the costs of the external effects they prevent. As both costs can change over time, organisations can only be efficient and effective in the long run if the property rights structures can be adapted accordingly.

Some case studies have suggested that 'incentives' do not explain all decisions about the use of resources, and can therefore not be taken as the sole cause of variations in decision making. There are indications that the knowledge of the actors plays a role in choices as well. This will be kept in mind when looking at agency theory and transaction cost theory, theories that have helped to identify in what circumstances the costs of defining and enforcing property rights are high, and what organisational structures help to reduce the cost.

3.4 Agency theory

3.4.1 Information asymmetry as a source of delegation problems

Agency theory pictures organisations as contractual arrangements in which one party (the principal) has delegated decision rights to other parties (the agents), whose decisions will then affect both of them. In efficient and effective organisations the principal has ensured contractually that the agents have an incentive to choose those actions that produce outcomes desired by the principal, at a minimum cost for the principal.

While property rights theory has made the point that costs arise when property rights over one good are distributed among several individuals, agency theory focuses on the question of how these costs can be kept low when such a situation is inevitable.

In a society characterised by division of labour, there are ubiquitous situations in which one party delegates tasks and the corresponding decision rights to another party in exchange for monetary or other types of compensation. Agency relationships exist, for example, between employer and employee, a firm and its suppliers and distributors, politicians and bureaucrats, or, in the terminology used here, between the core organisation and the other actors that are part of the organisation. More elaborate settings are also omnipresent. There are chains of principal–agent relations in which each party assumes alternating roles of both principal and agent, e.g. shareholders – boards of directors – managers – employees, and there are situations in which one principal has many agents, or in which multiple principals compete for agents.

Based on the assumptions that agents are self-interested and opportunistic (they might cheat to pursue their self-interest), that the environment is uncertain, and that information is imperfect, agency theory shows that delegation is almost always fraught with problems for the principal:[4]

Standard economic theory pictures exchanges between two parties as situations in which one party pays the other party for having performed a particular task, e.g. a household pays a baker in exchange for a loaf of bread. If the 'agent' has performed the task, he receives the compensation, if not, he does not. But, according to agency theory, this type of straightforward exchange is the exception, not the rule (Stiglitz 1989). The problem is that the principal is interested in, and willing to pay for the results produced by the agent, while the agent wants an adequate

[4] The agents might also have problems with their self-interested and opportunistic principals, but the theory focuses on the problem from the principal's perspective.

compensation for his efforts. If the results were a direct function of the agents' efforts, and either of the two could be measured, both effort- and results-based compensation would work for both parties. However, in most cases results depend on the agent's actions *and* on a whole range of other 'chance factors' (see Figure 3.1.). It is difficult to predict the occurrence of these 'chance factors', their impact on the output is not precisely known, and the principal cannot always observe them. Moreover, in most cases efforts or results cannot be measured easily.

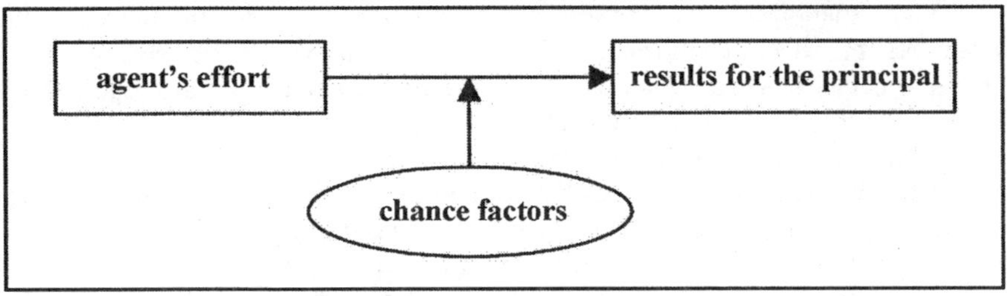

Fig. 3.1. The agent's effort and results

Based on these notions, agency theory frames the question of organisation as a problem for the principal to choose between a results oriented contract or an effort- oriented contract with the agent (e.g. Ross 1973, Jensen and Meckling 1976, Grossman and Hart 1983; Sappington 1991).

While, from an incentive perspective, the *results-oriented contract* (which corresponds with the simple exchange described above) appears to be ideal, agency theory points out that it might not always be the most efficient: The agent has the incentive to produce the output required by the principal, because his compensation depends on it. Yet, given that there are 'chance factors', e.g. the weather in the case of farming, the agent also demands a risk premium from the principal. If the principal's risk tolerance is higher than the agent's, it could be cheaper for the principal to take on part, or all of the risk, and to pay the agent for 'effort'. (In principle–agent models, it is usually assumed that the agent is more risk averse, e.g. because an individual employee cannot pool risks in the way that the firm he works in can (Sappington 1991)). Neither may output-based contracts be efficient when it is very costly or unfeasible to measure the outputs, or when agents are supposed to do many different tasks, of which only some can be measured. If compensation is then based on the measurable outputs, the agents focus their effort on those, rather than on the whole range of their tasks (Holmstrom and Milgrom 1991). Thus, in many exchange situations it might be necessary, or better for the principal to make an effort-oriented contract with the agent.

But *effort-oriented contracts* are problematic as well. The principal needs to know which actions the agent has undertaken, and whether these are the actions the agent should undertake, was he acting in the principal's interest? Since one of the major reasons for delegating a task is to take advantage of an agent's specialised knowledge (e.g. in the patient–doctor relationship) these conditions are not always easily fulfilled. If the principal then pays the agent according to some proxy measure for effort like the agent's time, the self-interested agent has the opportunity to engage in actions that are not in the interest of the principal (e.g. leisure on the job), without the principal noticing it. In fact, the principal cannot even be certain whether the chosen agent is capable of doing the task.

To prevent these problems, the principal has to use mechanisms that reduce the 'information asymmetry' between him and the agent. He has to avoid 'adverse selection' (Akerlof 1970), i.e. the choice of an exchange partner, who misrepresents his qualities to receive more favourable exchange terms. He also has to avoid an exchange situation that exposes him to 'moral hazard', i.e. the possibility that the agent uses his superior information and knowledge to make decisions that are not in the principal's interest, including 'shirking', i.e. the agent putting in less effort than implicitly promised in the contract.

For agency theorists the overall challenge of organising the efficient and effective completion of a task thus consists of designing an optimal incentive system, considering the risk attitude of the agents, and considering the information acquisition possibilities, and costs for the principal. 'Agency costs' – the costs of setting-up controlling and incentive devices, as well as the unavoidable losses that arise because it is too costly to control all actions should be kept as low as possible (Jensen and Meckling 1976).

3.4.2 Applications and empirical tests of agency theory

There have been a vast number of studies that have used or explored agency theory, as well as some reviews of that work, on which the following is based.

Jensen (1983) has distinguished the applications of agency theory into two strands: the more formal 'principal–agent theory', and the more empirically oriented 'positive agency theory'.

Principal–agent theory focuses on determining optimal contracts for different situations, using formal models that provide mathematically testable implications (Jensen 1983). As follows from the presentation above, they are based on variables, which define the information asymmetry between the principal and the agent, and on assumptions about the agent's risk aversion combined with assumptions about the uncertainty of the environment.

The following are examples of some of the mechanisms that have been identified as reducing the principal's information deficit: The *programmability of tasks*, i.e. the degree to which the appropriate behaviour can be specified in advance, reduces agents' freedom for 'hidden action' (Eisenhardt 1989:62); the use of *competitive tenders* allows the principal to gain information about the task, and identify the best agent, while it simultaneously reduces the agent's incentive to demand excessive compensation (McAfee and McMillan 1987); the use of *several agents*, who perform the same task, allows output comparisons; it also allows a *'tournament'* as an output-based incentive mechanism, (for example, the promotion of the best agent) while not imposing the risk of 'chance factors' on the agents (Lazear and Rosen 1981). Tasks for which there is a *repeated interaction* between the principal and the agent allow the principal to reduce the risk for the agent by basing the compensation on average performance (Sappington 1991:54ff).

'Principal–agent' researchers have carried out some empirical research to confirm their models (see Eisenhardt 1989; Prendergast 1999), but the bulk has been carried out by the 'positive agency theory' group:

Positive agency theorists have tried to answer the question, 'why do certain observable contractual relationships arise?' (Jensen 1983:326), concentrating mainly on the relationships between owners and managers of large corporations (This is because it is the only field where US contract data is readily available). The focus is on observed governance mechanisms that limit the self-serving behaviour of the managers. In doing so, positive agency theorists found additional variables to be relevant for contract design. These concerned the contracting environment (e.g. capital intensity, information cost, capital markets, labour markets), the available monitoring technology, and the design of institutions that allocate and enforce decision and ownership rights (Jensen 1983). Nevertheless, the findings of positive agency theory about the relevance of incentives and information systems are in accordance with those of principal agent theory: In situations where the principals' (shareholders) and the agents' (managers) interests strongly diverge, opportunism tends to be curbed by outcome-related contract components (e.g. equity ownership, partnerships, possibility of dismissal) and/or by information systems (Eisenhardt 1989). Regarding information systems, the literature has identified many different mechanisms like stock prices, boards of directors, budgeting and accounting systems, competition etc. More generally, Akerlof (1970) emphasised mechanisms like guarantees, brand names, certifications, and interpersonal ties to avoid adverse selection. These mechanisms have later been labelled 'signalling' and 'screening' mechanisms, and more have been found in contracting practise. They are used by the agent to convince the principal of his ability (e.g. degrees), or are used by the principal to find out more about the agent before the contract is made (e.g. assessment centres) (see Milgrom and Roberts 1992:154ff).

Overall, research from an agency theory perspective has been able to explain many observed contract features in terms of their incentive impact (Moe 1984:757; Arrow 1985). Eisenhardt (1989:58) concluded from her review that the ideas on risk, outcome uncertainty, incentives, and information systems are novel contributions to organisation theory, and that the empirical evidence has been supportive. Sappington (1991:64) found that even the simple models are helpful 'in identifying some possible sources of friction within organisations and in exploring efficient ways to mitigate these frictions.' In the more recent literature though, emphasis on the importance of information (both on outputs and on effort) has even increased, while the factor 'risk-attitude' has lost significance (Gibbons 1998). Prendergast (1999), in her very extensive 'agency literature' review, even found that there is no conclusive evidence on a trade-off between risks and incentives. While the literature has been limitedly successful in finding empirical evidence for 'optimal' contracts such as predicted by the theory, there is strong evidence that 'firms get what they pay for'. Agents do respond to incentives and are evidently self-interested.

3.4.3 Criticisms of agency theory

Agency theory has been criticised from various sides. Not surprisingly, taking aside the general criticism against neoclassical assumptions, the focus on the principal's perspective, and some NIE theorists' assumption that observed institutions are necessarily efficient (e.g. Perrow 1986), the bulk of attacks is directed against the inevitable shortcomings of principal agency theory's formal analytical approach. Stiglitz (1987; 1991:21f) acknowledges that the existing contractual structures look little like those predicted, and that they do not change in response to variations in the kind of variables that are considered most important in the models. In practice, most employment contracts are relatively simple.

Pratt and Zeckhauser (1985), Arrow (1985), Sappington (1991), Gibbons (1998), and Prendergast (1999) all give explanations for this divergence between theory and practise: real life is more complex than models. On the contract side, there are practical limitations to how detailed and tailor cut they can be, especially in the usual multi-task settings with outputs that are difficult to measure. Specifying and enforcing contracts that depend on many variables is costly, while the incentive benefits of the complication might be marginal. Also, contracts that provide strong incentives, but choose the wrong output proxy variables, can be much more dysfunctional than contracts with weaker, more balanced incentives. And there are institutional restrictions to the contract design, for example civil service grades, or agreements with trade unions. On the 'agent' side, the analytic models are too simplistic to take into account all the incentive and control mechanisms that the real world provides (Stiglitz 1991). Rewards or penalties do not only have a monetary aspect but also social ones, and they have different time frames. Opportunistic behaviour has much to do with structures of personal relations (MOE 1984). Besides, as Simon (1991) has emphasised, issues like identification with the organisation (or the principal's goals), or professional pride are at work as well. These are issues that also pose problems to positive agency theorists, as they are nearly as difficult to assess empirically as formally.

But while these points are highly relevant when it comes to attempts for blueprint designs of 'optimal contracts', they do not undermine the general agency theory notion that 'organisation matters' because of its impact on the agents' incentives. But the criticisms suggest that 'incentives' are determined by a wider range of variables than formalistic approaches have looked at, and, as argued by the positive agency theorists, that the institutional context of a specific contractual arrangement is relevant.

Williamson (1985, 1990b) makes the further point that agency theory completely neglects the fact that contracts have to be adaptable. Although principals are supposed to lack information, and are in that sense only boundedly rational, they are taken to be fully aware of all incentive problems at the time the contract is set up. As this is unrealistic, contracts are unavoidably incomplete, and not as elaborate as agency theory suggests.

Lastly, while agency theory acknowledges the importance of the agent's expertise in its 'adverse selection' considerations, and there have been agency authors recently looking at incentives for skills acquisition (Gibbons 1998), output in the general model is related only to agents' efforts. Similarly, the 'optimal information' considerations of agency theorists focus exclusively on 'control' information. However, it is reasonable to expect that an agent's total contribution depends not only on his effort, but also on his task-related knowledge. Prendergast (1999:17), for example, found in her review that studies that allowed the effects of incentives to be separated from worker selection issues, suggest that perhaps one-third of the increase in performance arises from attracting better workers. Also, one of the major reasons why a principal would want to delegate decision rights is that she expects the agent to take actions based on knowledge that the agent, but not she, has. The bigger the 'task-related' knowledge asymmetry between the principal and the agent, the bigger the 'control-related' information asymmetry will be. This suggests a potential trade-off in contract design between the feasibility and cost of avoiding agents' self-serving behaviour, and the benefits from specialisation, which has not been addressed by the theory.

3.4.4 A digression on the similarities and differences between agency theory and the economic theory of bureaucracy

The economic theory of bureaucracy developed independently from agency theory, but has many similar features, and deals specifically with the public sector. Therefore, it is necessary to briefly outline its major arguments (which will partly be picked up in the next chapter), and justify why here, it is neglected in favour of agency theory.

The economic theory of bureaucracy is one strand of 'public choice theory' – the application of neoclassical tools to the analysis of political processes (Tullock 1987). Niskanen (1971) argued that bureaucrats were as self-interested as anyone else. Instead of focusing on the goals of their bureaux, they would attempt to maximise their own utility. This utility was made up of variables like salary, perquisites of the office, public reputation, power, patronage, output of the bureau, security, ease of making changes and ease of managing the bureau. All but the last two were a positive function of the bureau's total budget during the bureaucrat's tenure (Niskanen 1971:23). Information asymmetry between the bureaucrat and the elected representatives gave the bureaucrat the opportunity to pursue his self-interest. As he was a monopolist, he was able to make a 'take it or leave it' offer to the legislators, who could either accept it, or get nothing. The legislators were confronted with both 'adverse selection' and 'moral hazard' problems (this terminology was not used by Niskanen). While they could observe whether the bureau actually produced the output they agreed on, they did not have the information to evaluate whether this amount served their interest best, and hence the bureaucrat had the opportunity to produce in excess of demand. Also, if the bureaucrat could produce the output at lower cost than she pretended was necessary, she had the opportunity to spend the legislators' (principal's) resources on non-optimal input combinations. In any case, resources were allocated inefficiently.

Although these arguments employ a similar logic as the agency theory literature, they are more restricted in their application. While in agency theory chains of relationships could be analysed, in the highly abstract 'bureaucracy approach' only two players – the bureaucrat and the legislators – are involved. Furthermore, in Niskanen's view the legislators are largely passive. Their funding choice depends on the information provided by the bureaucrat; they themselves do not have any influence on the outcomes. They cannot issue orders, adopt incentive systems, control the bureaucratic agenda, or otherwise structure the principal–agent relationship (Moe 1984:770). The bureaucrats, as the agents, are also very restricted in their behaviour. Whereas in agency theory they can either be productive or unproductive, depending on how the incentives are set, according to Niskanen they are always unproductive. Lastly, agency theory allows for a reduction in information asymmetry, for example in the case of various government bureaux providing certain services, and for the possibility that legislators have a choice between a variety of proposed expenditures, and that bureaux therefore might have to compete for the resources.

Although when it was first published, Niskanen's model was 'a major advance over the prevailing assumption of a benevolent government, which could costlessly remedy all sorts of market failures' (Frant 1991:119), it seems that now agency theory can offer a wider approach to analysing bureaucratic organisation.

3.4.5 A summary of agency theory's insights into the cause-effect relationships between 'organisation' and 'efficiency and effectiveness'

Agency theory asserts that organisations (contracts and other secondary institutions) can be designed so that agents working in their own self-interests will also work in the interest of the principal (the core organisation). Organisation matters for efficiency and effectiveness because it impacts on agents' incentives.

Like property rights theory, agency theory holds the agent's behaviour to be influenced by the degree to which he can/must appropriate the results of his actions, although in agency theory this becomes even more important as individuals are not only self-interested but also opportunistic. In addition to property rights theory, both strands of agency theory emphasise that in principal–agent settings information asymmetry makes self-interested opportunism possible, and that to 'internalise external effects' the interests of principal and agent have to be aligned. Empirical evidence is supportive of these issues, although not to the extent that practical contracts could be devised solely by theoretical deduction. There is recognition that the institutional context plays a role for contract design, and that more factors influence incentives than those that have found entry into formal models.

What is, however, only indirectly addressed, as part of the agent selection problem, is task-related information. But to contribute to organisational goals, even an agent whose interests are perfectly aligned with the principal's must know-how to fulfil his tasks. Since with an increasing information asymmetry between principal and agent agency-costs increase, it appears that in terms of effectiveness and efficiency there may be a trade-off between incentives and knowledge of actors, which has not been addressed by the theory.

Another criticised gap of agency theory – the neglect of a need for contract adaptability – has been dealt with by transaction cost theorists.

3.5 Transaction cost theory

3.5.1 Dependency as a problem for adaptation

Transaction cost theory pictures organisations as 'governance structures', i.e. formal and informal arrangements that allow mutually satisfactory exchanges between transaction partners. Efficient and effective firms have governance structures that allow adaptation in the execution stage of contracts at low cost, because the exchange partners do not have the incentive to behave opportunistically.

Transaction cost theory, like agency theory, adopts a contractual approach to analysing organisations, but problems of hierarchical control lose their predominance in favour of a focus on firms' boundaries. The question is, what activities would be carried out within a firm and what would be contracted out on the market, given that the environment and the commitment of exchange partners, may change in the execution stage of contracts. The approach is closely associated with the work of Oliver Williamson[5], who has built on Coase's (1937) insights into the cost of market exchanges:

Interpreting economic activity as a series of transactions, as 'trading at a microanalytic level' (1985:6), Williamson's central assumption is that effective and efficient organisations would be those, which *ceteris paribus* minimise the cost of carrying out transactions.

Transactions occur 'when a good or service is transferred across a technologically separable interface. One stage of activity terminates and another begins' (1985:1).

Transaction costs have not been rigorously specified by Williamson, and different authors have defined them in various ways (e.g. Boessmann 1982:664f; Hodgson 1988:199ff; Allen 1991). But Williamson emphasises that they comprise not only the 'cost of using the price mechanism' (Coase 1937:390) – e.g. price negotiations, but also the cost of internal organisation – e.g. control costs, *and* potential 'ex post costs' of contracting – e.g. costs of maladaptation or costs for setting up and running governance structures to deal with disputes. These potential *ex post costs* of contracting are so important for Williamson's argument that he focuses almost exclusively on them (Alchian and Woodward 1988).

[5] The following outline is mainly based on his book 'The Economic Institutions of Capitalism' (1985) in which Williamson refined his ideas on transaction costs, which he had presented in 'Markets and Hierarchies' (1975) a decade earlier. Since then, certain aspects have been highlighted in various papers, and summaries have been provided, but the central logic of the argument, as outlined here, has remained the same (e.g. Williamson 1998, 1993; 1991; 1990a,b, 1989a,b).

By identifying the crucial factors that cause (ex post) transaction problems, Williamson has demonstrated that organisation impacts on transaction costs. The transaction attribute of utmost importance is *asset specificity*, i.e. the extent to which the value of an investment depends on a specific exchange partner. The impact of asset specificity is influenced by *frequency, uncertainty* and *complexity*, where the frequency of a certain transaction determines how lucrative it is to invest in specific contractual structures for it. Combining the assumptions about human behaviour – *bounded rationality* and *opportunism* – with the characteristics of a transaction situation, Williamson has demonstrated how these variables can lead to problems with market exchanges:

As a result of *bounded rationality*, all contracts for complex transactions and those reaching into the future are incomplete. This would cause no concern if the exchanging actors were honest, since all gaps in contracts could be filled when required. But if the actors are *opportunistic*, incomplete contracts can be hazardous for both parties. Each side has to take into account that the other might use the opportunity to increase their own share of the benefits. This 'behavioural uncertainty' (Williamson 1985:58) means that both parties have to take precautions, unless their partner's trustworthiness is transparent from the outset, or unless exchanges are only of a 'thick market' type (Williamson 1985:30ff, 58ff, 64ff, 69).

'Thick markets' (Williamson 1991:271) represent the neoclassical idea of markets. They imply that there are no dependency relationships between the parties, and information is not a problem. Exchanges are easily arranged and monitored, there are many potential transaction partners, and each transaction is immediate. Under these circumstances every contract can be made according to the specific circumstances of the day, and exchange partners can be easily switched. Knowing that, everyone's scope for opportunistic behaviour is very limited. Adaptation to changes in the environment is brought about by prices, which provide sufficient statistics, and set incentives. The incentives are 'high powered' with positive effects on production costs, since the consequences of decisions are tightly linked to the decision makers who receive the net benefits (Williamson 1991).

However, this scenario applies only to some transactions, if an economy is to benefit from specialisation. For an investor, durable special purpose investments in machines, employees, specific locations etc. are often necessary, or would lower production costs in view of planned transactions with a certain exchange partner (Williamson 1985:54ff). Yet such investment is risky, since it loses significantly in value if it has to be used for a different purpose. The investor thus becomes dependent on exchanging with a specific partner, who could exploit this dependency opportunistically by trying to re-negotiate the contract conditions up to the point where she only receives the benefits she would get from a 'second best' use of the asset. The exchange partner on the other hand risks that after the specific investment has been made, the investor is the only supplier who matches his requirements, and can behave opportunistically on her part.

This transaction situation, characterised by its *'asset specificity'* becomes the more problematic the more *uncertain* the environment and the more *complex* the exchange. The two factors lead to increasingly incomplete contracts, and therefore to an increasing scope for opportunistic re-negotiation attempts. Furthermore, a lack of quick mutual consent about how to adjust to new situations leads to maladaptation and bargaining costs until the conflict is settled. Walker (1988) pointed out that the problem is made worse if the transaction is strategically important for one or both parties.

Attempts to protect oneself against dependency's hazards create costs. According to transaction cost economics, these costs are lower if the asset specific transaction is carried out within a 'hierarchy', because here the various actors' interests are more aligned than among actors in the market. Transaction costs are also reduced because hierarchies' co-ordination mechanism 'fiat' allows for a sequential adaptation to changes without the need to consult, or to revise inter-firm agreements. In the case of disputes, hierarchy is its own court of ultimate appeal, with the advantage that decisions are based on more information than could ever be communicated to courts. As a result, hierarchies can adapt more cheaply to disturbances, where co-ordinated adaptation is required, and contracts can be more incomplete (Williamson 1991).

But there are also major drawbacks of transacting in hierarchies. They are characterised by bureaucratic problems, e.g. a failure to manage complexity, and they only offer 'low-powered' incentives to the actors within, since consequences of their decisions are 'collectivised' (Williamson 1985: Chapter 6). Hierarchies are therefore only an 'organisation form of last resort' for cases where transactions have especially high degrees of asset specificity and added uncertainty strongly requires co-operative adaptation (Williamson 1998).

For medium degrees of asset specificity, according to transaction cost economists, hybrid governance structures have developed. They aim to balance the advantages and disadvantages of both market and hierarchies in a way, which is suitable for the particular transactions. The result is a large variety of different forms. But a general feature is that by offering signs of 'credible commitment', e.g. warranties, or equity in the exchange partner's firm, legally independent parties signal trustworthiness (Williamson 1985:163ff).

Williamson sees the force of asset specificity to push transactions into hierarchies as universal, but he is also aware that contextual differences for the choice of organisation have to be taken into account. The institutional environment affects for example contract law or the security of property rights. The 'atmosphere' for the transaction, involving issues like friendship, trust, loyalty, etc. has an impact on perception and reality of hazards stemming from opportunism (Williamson 1975:20;38f; 1985:405f). But Williamson himself concedes that 'understanding of informal organisation is still primitive and the economics of atmosphere is similarly underdeveloped' (1998:52).

3.5.2 Applications and empirical tests of the transaction cost approach

The theoretical propositions of transaction cost economics have been used to explain a variety of contractual structures, and have been applied in over 400 empirical studies (Williamson 1998) examining organisational structures like franchising, joint ventures, and especially vertical integration. In the studies, the organisational forms are treated as a dependent variable of independent transaction characteristics. Reviewers (Sydow 1992; Shelanski and Klein 1995; Lyons 1996; Coerderoy and Quelin 1997) conclude that the empirical results on the whole support Williamson's approach.

The evidence, that asset specificity combined with product complexity and uncertainty has significant effects on vertical integration, was judged as 'striking' (Shelanski and Klein 1995:344). Lyons (1996), looking at 'buy' decisions, noted that long term contracts in the presence of specific investments seemed to be used when vertical integration had been prevented by government regulation. The same seems to be the case for some informal agreements between firms (Shelanski and Klein 1995:348). Many 'nonstandard' contracting practices – likē, for example, closed shop arrangements – could be explained as offering safeguards for specific investments, as do hybrid forms like contracts with reciprocity agreements, or exclusive dealing contracts (Lyons 1996). Hierarchies appeared to lose their comparative advantages when dealing with transactions of low complexity and a large number of exchange partners, but also in cases where hybrid forms could combine some of the advantages of markets and hierarchies (Sydow 1992:133).

But the empirical evidence appears insufficient so far to judge fully when certain hybrid forms are preferred to either market or hierarchy, and Coeurderoy and Quelin (1997) criticise the 'flavour of ex post rationalisation' of some studies. Little evidence is available on the performance effects of firm's internal structure, and findings are mixed (Shelanski and Klein 1995). Perhaps this state of research is not surprising, considering the problem of access to information on contracts. And even in those few cases where written contracts are available, their interpretation is extremely difficult since many aspects often remain unwritten and the institutional context is important.[6] Comparing organisational structures across firms, industries, or countries is therefore a complex exercise, which explains why case studies dominate the empirical literature. However, although based on the evidence no detailed predictions can be made which organisation leads to highest effectiveness and efficiency, the general propositions, that those firms survive, which safeguard themselves best against opportunism and remain adaptive to the environment, seem to be supported.

3.5.3 Criticisms of the transaction cost approach

Although the usefulness of the transaction cost idea has not been denied by most of its critics, some find that the theory is unsuitable to explain existing institutions, others consider it too limited to give satisfactory answers. Disregarding the al-

[6] Lyons (1996) cites for example Lane and Bachmann (1996), who demonstrate that different legal systems have an important influence, both in setting out implied terms and in providing differing degrees of certainty of legal redress. In Germany, with its detailed, systematic Civil Code of commercial law, firms apparently have more confidence in the law and so rely more on contractual detail than British firms do.

ready discussed general condemnations of the behavioural assumptions, and a further group of criticisms, which do not take into account Williamson's acknowledgement of institutions and 'atmosphere' as influencing factors,[7] major remaining objections concern the theory's 'vague concepts', its allegedly 'static' approach, and its neglect of 'knowledge' as an important variable.

Vague concepts

All cited surveys of empirical literature stress the problem of clarifying, and making precise the variables of the transaction cost approach. This does not only apply to the use of a vague concept like 'atmosphere' in a case study, by which any form of organisation could be justified as efficient in a transaction cost minimising sense, while on the other hand a disregard of 'atmosphere' might distort results as well. It also applies to asset specificity, uncertainty, strategic importance or complexity, which seem to be only definable in relation to a certain context. That the fundamental problem, of how to measure transaction costs, has not been solved means that cost variances of alternative forms of governance cannot really be specified (Coerderoy and Quelin 1997). Often, it cannot even be defined where a transaction begins and ends.[8]

Williamson (1998:43) suggests a 'remediableness criterion' according to which an existing mode of organisation is presumed to be efficient, if no superior feasible alternative can be described and implemented. If there is such an alternative, the cost of overcoming pre-existing conditions would need to be taken into account. This, however, does not really solve the problem of a lack in the analytical preciseness of the concepts, as a consequence impeding a stringent test and application of the theory. Nonetheless, it is a pragmatic approach to the problem. Even

---

[7] e.g. Granovetter (1985), Martin (1993) or Moe (1984) suggest that Williamson is not aware of the importance of the institutional context (traditions, customs, politics, norms and values, 'externalities' across individuals, or the structures of personal relations, or does not acknowledge their impact. Williamson is (see above), but excuses himself for not integrating these issues more formally, by pointing to the lack of operational academic knowledge in this area. Perrow (1987), Zald (1987), Martin (1993) accuse Williamson of ignoring that power shapes contracts and behaviour both inside and outside the organisation. Williamson defends his approach, discussing 'power' in the context of various examples (1985:124ff, 231ff). According to his interpretation, power is a secondary issue, which only has an impact on the form of organisation if the transaction cost savings that could be achieved by a change are not large. This is supported by Spiller's studies. He tested market power theory in comparison with the transaction cost approach as an alternative explanation for vertical integration with the result that the explanatory power of asset specificity proved to be superior (Shelanski and Klein 1995).

[8] Williamson (1975:256) states 'I submit however that technological separability is merely a necessary and not a sufficient condition for transactions to be regarded independently. Attitudinal separability must also be established'. This could affect, for example, new exchanges with a party, with whom other transactions have been carried out before, affecting, for example, perceptions on the risk of opportunism. Therefore it is possible that there are spill-over effects in pricing and metering of these transactions. Several other authors (e.g. Milgrom and Roberts 1992, Foss 1993, Madhok 1996) point out that it is often difficult to distinguish between transaction and production costs.

if the effectiveness and efficiency of an organisation cannot be specified as such, it can be judged how it compares with an alternative organisation set up for the same purpose.

A static approach
Several authors (e.g. Martin 1993, Demsetz 1992, Casson 1997) argue that contrary to Williamson's emphasis on *adaptability* as the ultimate criterion for effective and efficient organisation (1985, 1991, 1998), his claim, that a vertical integration of highly asset specific exchanges was efficient, would only hold in a static environment. In conditions of high uncertainty, market exchanges would leave firms more flexibility, and therefore be preferable. But Schreiter (1994) resolves this dilemma with reference to the importance of both production and transaction cost as outlined in Williamson's heuristic model (1985:90ff). He assumes that with increasing asset specificity the comparative advantage of market exchange is reduced, because asset specificity reduces the possibility of exploiting economies of scale. However, if there is not only one way of producing a good, the degree of asset specificity can be chosen. While high-asset specificity might normally be desirable because of the specialisation advantage, there is a risk of sunk cost in conditions of very high uncertainty. This risk is reduced by engaging in transactions with lower-asset specificity, which is why such exchanges are chosen and markets are preferred.

Neglect of 'knowledge' as a factor influencing efficiency
Linked to the criticism of a static approach to organisational efficiency is the more fundamental charge that Williamson neglects the importance of knowledge (Demsety 1992, Dietrich 1992; Nooteboom 1992; Foss 1993; Connor and Prahalad 1996, Madhok 1996). The critics see firms as *'bundles of resources and capabilities linked together through various idiosyncratic routines'* (Madhok 1996:583), rather than as contractual entities. Therefore they argue that when determining the boundaries of firms, the focus must be on firms' unique competencies rather than on the costs of preventing potential opportunism.

Given that bounded rationality not only implies an inability to monitor and control behaviour effectively, but also a constraint on an organisation's capability of absorbing and combining knowledge, organisations necessarily specialise, particularly if the environment changes rapidly. Path-dependent, specific firm competencies develop. These are difficult to communicate or copy, and therefore production functions differ across firms. A firm with specific competencies might decide to vertically integrate transactions, even if they are not asset specific, if it can do so at lower cost than any potential supplier, and it cannot transfer that knowledge to the market (Foss 1993). On the other hand, a firm requiring a component that involves an asset-specific transaction, the production knowledge of which is not related to its own major production activity, will find it difficult to produce at a cost which is comparable to that of a potential supplier who has the specialised production knowledge. Since 'knowledge' is not static, a major component of this are productivity advantages that arise because knowledge can be adapted much faster if the competence to select and process information in the particular field is already available. Even if, for example, 'experts' could be bought, a buyer without knowledge could not judge their value. If the value of the experts' knowledge depended partly on their surrounding support structure, the experts would also be worth more to their current employer than the prospective one (Madhok 1996).

The authors with a 'resource-based' view of the firm conclude that opportunism is not a necessary assumption to explain the boundaries of firms. However, to the question of why the buyer could not just buy the entire supplier or distributor organisation, and thereby acquire the whole 'competence bundle', only Williamson (1985:Chapter 6) offers a solution. Even if the new firm was run as an entirely separate unit, i.e. it could uphold and develop its specific competencies, efficiency losses would occur because all parties would try to protect themselves against opportunism.[9]

But this still does not explain why market transactions can be observed even in the case of asset specificity, as Nooteboom (1992) suggests. Williamson (1985:131) offers production costs, i.e. economies of scale and scope, as another reason why a firm would eschew integration. But then he dismisses the economies of scale argument by pointing to the fact that if economies of scale are realised by the outside supplier, the same economies could be preserved by continuing to sell the product in the market, while producing it internally. His point is that only asset-specific transactions should be vertically integrated and those exclude economies of scale by definition. The economies of scope argument is not discussed further, except in a passage in a previous chapter regarding a case of forward integration (1985:112ff). However, the unique competence of an organisation is a result of its activities in the past and present, and their imprint on the interaction of its different parts. Economies of scope, as far as they relate to superior production or marketing knowledge,[10] are therefore an essential part of the argument. But the 'knowledge' or competence argument goes further, because superior competencies can also affect the firm's transaction costs, for example regarding the knowledge of suppliers. In order to vertically integrate transactions with actors who benefit from lower costs based on competence, all parts which contribute to the knowledge would have to be integrated, not just the particular unit which produces the good or service in question. Nevertheless, in order to answer why this is usually

[9] The argument is that the owners of the firm that is going to be acquired have to discount very heavily any promise that they would continue to gain the profits from their firm once they have come under someone else's ownership since they would be exposed to potentially opportunistic accounting practices by the new owners. The second reason is that the former owners turned employees would not utilise their assets with due care any more since they could externalise the costs to the new owners. They might, for example, not care to keep their knowledge up to date. Monitoring would be required which implies costs. As here a wide discrepancy of knowledge between buyer and seller is assumed, these costs would be particularly high (Foss 1996a, Chi 1994). The only other option are low powered incentives (e.g. a fixed salary for the former owner) which have negative effects on performance compared with the high-powered incentives of the market. These costs of vertical integration would of course come in addition to the very high transaction costs of determining a fair price for the firm.

[10] Economies of scope can for example arise if several products share the same retail outlets.

not efficient, one has to resort again to the effects of opportunism on governance costs.

Therefore, the points raised do not contradict Williamson. Both approaches are ultimately based on the belief that resource interdependence characterises organisations. The empirical finding, that vertical integration is most important in cases of human asset specificity, for example, clearly supports both approaches. But the 'resource-based view of the firm' is a useful contribution, because it puts emphasis on the importance of aspects Williamson has not developed further. If knowledge has a major effect on production cost (and some transaction costs), and if the transfer of knowledge is very expensive because of those transaction costs that are related to information asymmetry, the relevance of the transaction costs that are related to dependency could be less predominant than Williamson's approach might lead to suggest. However, Williamson himself is only too aware of these issues, and one of his 1985 books' conclusions concern the underdeveloped state of knowledge regarding tradeoffs between production cost economies and transaction costs, as well as between different types of transaction costs (1985:390). An implication of possible tradeoffs is however that different combinations of transaction and production costs can have the same level of efficiency and effectiveness. Therefore, there may be different ways to organise co-operation equally effectively and efficiently.

3.5.4 A summary of transaction cost theory's insights into the cause–effect relationships between 'organisation' and 'efficiency and effectiveness'

Going beyond the adverse selection and moral hazard concerns of agency theory that agency theorists found to be rooted in information asymmetry between contracting parties at the time contracts are made, Williamson has introduced a new cause of co-ordination cost – dependency of one party on another after contracts have been signed. This situation develops whenever the transactions between the parties involve specific investments.

The focus on this aspect of the co-ordination problem, rather than on measurement difficulties per se, comes from a conviction that adaptability is the most important quality that organisational structures need to ensure in a world of complexity and uncertainty, inhabited by boundedly rational decision-makers. Organisation matters, because it affects the cost of adaptability.

But in terms of the argument on what are the links between organisation and transaction costs, transaction cost theory argues ultimately in the same way as property rights theory and agency theory: Its major variable, asset specificity, affects adaptability through the way in which it influences the incentive structure for the actors. Like 'measurability' 'asset specificity' is an important transaction characteristic because it has an effect on the degree to which opportunism is possible, and hence on the cost that opportunism and protection against it incur. Opportunism arises when actors assume that they can obtain benefits without having to carry the costs. Credible commitments, for example, as a suggested contractual remedy, are a means to reassure the other party that the costs of decisions will not be externalised.

Williamson' suggested organisational solutions, with the assertion that in the case of asset specific transactions hierarchies achieve the aim of adaptability at a lower cost than markets, is essentially based on property rights considerations as well. The co-ordination mechanism 'fiat' implies extended decision rights, most importantly the rights to change existing structures, for the party whose goals are at stake. Improved auditing means that inside hierarchies, the 'core' party's control rights go further than in market exchanges. The assumption that the interests of actors within firms are more aligned than those of market exchange partners ultimately stem from the idea that the firm's fate is more directly related to that of the individuals within it, i.e. if their activities affect their own firm, they will perceive the consequences less as an 'external effect' than outsiders would. Equally, Williamson's arguments about low-powered incentives within hierarchies versus high-powered incentives in markets rest on the effects which the rights to appropriate residual benefits and the costs of being liable for wrong decisions have on decision makers.

Thus the transaction cost approach essentially puts forward that incentives and adaptability are the relevant features for effectiveness and efficiency, both of them shaped by the allocation of property rights to the different parties, and the cost of adaptability being influenced by actors' incentives. The property rights are expressed through the organisational structures chosen, while the choice is limited and influenced by primary institutions, including issues of 'atmosphere'. What the efficient choice is within the range of possibilities depends on the characteristics of the transaction as long as production costs are assumed to be constant.

But critics have pointed out that since specialisation can alter production costs, the effectiveness and efficiency are also affected by organisation through its impact on productive (or task-related) knowledge.

3.6 The links between organisation and effectiveness and efficiency

The purpose of this chapter was to investigate organisational economics' insights into causal relationships between organisational structures and outputs. That causal relationships exist is the underlying precondition for the validity of the two assumptions that shape public sector services' re-organisation: 1. that organisation matters for effectiveness and efficiency, and 2. that one (new) organisation is more effective and efficient than another (old) organisation.

Since property rights theory, agency theory, and transaction cost theory are based on broadly the same assumptions, their arguments are compatible. But as their foci of analysis differ, all three theories, and the criticisms against them, have offered their own contributions.

All three are fundamentally about the influence of organisation on actors' incentives. These **incentives** influence how actors decide about the use of available resources. As discussed especially in property rights theory, but also in the context of contracts in agency theory and transaction cost theory, decision making in pursuit of self-interest takes place within a framework of assigned rights that define the options an actor has. The rights also define the costs or benefits to be expected from taking particular decisions. Organisational structures provide such a framework within the context of given institutions, and thus affect incentives.

In effective organisations, all actors have the incentive to carry out their particular task in a manner that contributes best to the goals of the organisation. If efficiency is taken into account as well, the marginal cost of implementing such an incentive structure has to be set in relation to the marginal benefits that arise from better aligning the actors' incentives. As agency and transaction cost theory point out, it is up to the core organisation (the principal/the hierarchy), who defined the goal, to design contracts that contain appropriate decision rights and benefits distributions.

Property rights and transaction cost theorists also argue that the **adaptability** to respond to changed scarcity patterns is a necessary feature of effective and efficient organisations. It concerns the distribution of rights between actors. Apart from the question to what extent the institutional framework allows organisations to change their structure, the issue is whether rights within an organisation are distributed in a way that allows for redistribution and flexible decision-making. This depends on the one hand on the decision rights of those actors who set the goal – as transaction cost theory points out, continuous small adaptations are for example easier within a hierarchy because of fiat – on the other hand it depends on the incentives that individual actors have to support, or hinder, a restructuring of rights that might benefit or cost them.

In context of the criticism of transaction cost theory, the considerations regarding agency theory's exclusive emphasis on 'control information', and the findings that the explanatory powers of property rights theory are strong but not all-encompassing, a third variable has emerged as being relevant – the **knowledge** actors have about doing their tasks. Agency theory has addressed the issue to some extent, by putting the knowledge that is necessary for the task of controlling agents into the centre of their analysis, and by pointing out how the requirements for this knowledge change with contract structures. Bounded rationality as an important factor in transaction cost theory also hints to the importance of knowledge, and adaptability presupposes that changes in the environment are known. But none of the NIE theories directly took into account that productivity is generally increased by specialisation, i.e. that task-related knowledge impacts on effectiveness and efficiency. Nevertheless, 'knowledge' seems to be a variable that is influenced by organisation, be it only through the choice of actors or also through the incentives actors have, to learn more about fulfilling their tasks.

On the basis of these points, the following 'model' is suggested for explaining the cause–effect relationships between 'organisation' and 'efficiency and effectiveness' (see Figure 3.2.):

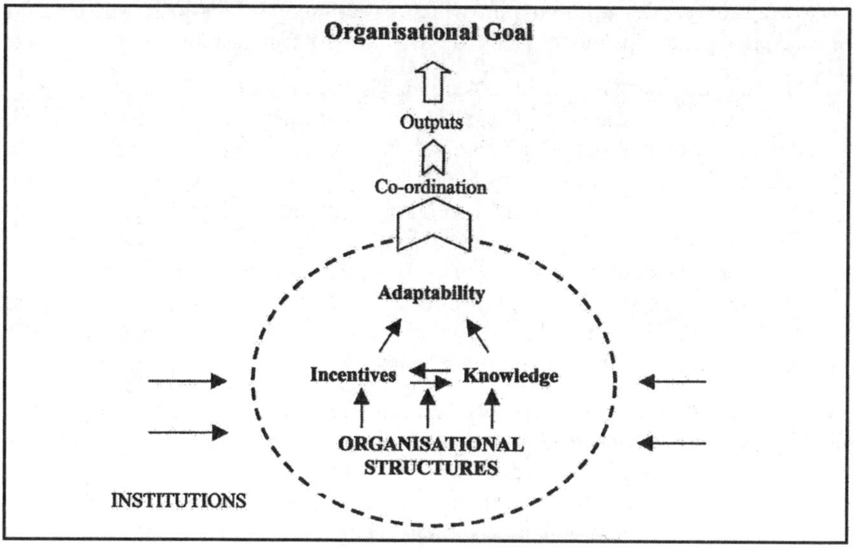

Fig. 3.2. The relationship between 'organisation' and 'effectiveness and efficiency'

Organisations are set up deliberately to co-ordinate the activities of self-interested actors towards a goal. Some of the actors are part of a hierarchy designed for the pursuit of the goal, others stand outside this core unit, and their contributions are co-ordinated via hybrid or market contracts. Effective and efficient organisations produce the outputs that are thought to advance the goal, at present and in the future, in a way and at a cost that cannot be improved compared with other feasible organisations that could operate within the given institutional framework (see Chapter 2, and Williamson's 'remediableness criterion' above).

Organisation influences what knowledge the actors can apply to perform their task in the interest of the core organisation, and which incentives they have to contribute to the organisational goal (or not). Organisation also influences to which extent the structures can be adapted to new environmental conditions, within the given institutional framework.

The three variables – knowledge, incentives and adaptability – are not completely independent of each other. Control-related knowledge impacts on actors' incentives, whereas incentives can impact on actors' motivation to acquire new knowledge. Adaptability is on a different level, concerning the dynamic aspect of organisational structures. It is affected by incentives and knowledge, as control- and task-related knowledge are necessary for knowing when it is time to change structures, and as within the given framework of rights, actors have incentives to pursue or oppose the changes that would contribute to the organisational goal.

Viewing the two assumptions on which export support services' restructuring are based in light of this model leads to the following conclusions:

1. Organisation does matter for effectiveness and efficiency.
2. There may be trade-offs between the variables, and one organisation might therefore not be 'better' or 'worse' than another. For example, incentive structures that motivate actors to fulfil their tasks most effectively at a given point in time, might create incentives that make them oppose any re-allocation of rights; high degrees of specialisation, e.g. in the extreme form of a very specialised machine, may be more efficient than a multi-purpose machine, but make adaptation more difficult. As it was already pointed out in the concluding section of agency theory, highly-knowledgeable actors might be more difficult to monitor, which can affect their incentives.

And as all three theories have stressed, it is necessary to consider the cost of improving organisational structures, since higher effectiveness, e.g. by setting better incentives for actors, may be pursued at the cost of efficiency.

This would mean that the effectiveness and efficiency effects of organisations are researchable via the three major variables, but also that the conclusions are debatable. However, as DiLorenzo (1988:327) states, *'there is nothing particularly 'unscientific' about investigating the economic consequences of alternative property rights structures and then, based on that research, trying to persuade others of what one believes to be a more 'ideal' structure of rights. This would involve value judgements, but would make them explicit. This approach would emphasise making greater efforts to understand the tradeoffs involved in political economy.'*

The aim in the following chapters is to apply the model to the export support services. The objective is to establish how the existing forms of organising support affect the three factors, and whether there are indications for the variables' expected effects on the organisation outputs. Then it can be tried to 'persuade' the reader about the benefits and deficits of the organisations. First, however, it is necessary to specify how the three variables can be operationalised.

Chapter 4: Incentives, knowledge and adaptability

4.1 Overview

The previous chapter argued in favour of a framework, which holds that actors' incentives and knowledge, as well as organisational adaptability, are the causal link between 'organisation' and 'effectiveness and efficiency'. Organisational structures have to be examined in terms of their impact on these key variables.

The purpose of this chapter is to discuss these three variables in more detail, to develop a framework for using them in an empirical context.

4.2 Incentives

4.2.1 Benefiting in exchange relationships

The incentive effects of institutions and organisational structures on individuals and firms are the central theme of Organisational Economics, and the arguments of the three major approaches with their different foci have been presented in the previous chapter. The question here is how to assess the incentives of actors in real organisations and their impact on the organisation's goal.

To this end, an organisational structure is conceptualised as defining an exchange relationship between a principal dealing with agents. The management of the core organisation, endowed with a range of property rights over assets, has a goal.[1] It has defined chains of activities, necessary to produce the outputs related to the goal. It has exchanged rights with other actors, who are supposed to produce these outputs, either because the others are specialised in doing so, or because teamwork is required.

---

[1] In the case of export promotion it would be the top civil servants, who are in charge. They are obviously 'agents' of their ministers, parliament and ultimately the public, but the constraints these 'principals' impose are interpreted as 'institutional constraints'. For the time being it is assumed that the core management aims to achieve the task goal for which the organisation has been set up and therefore acts like an 'owner' would. But the incentives framework presented here could be equally applied to analyse core management's incentives to contribute to the organisational goal.

The exchanges can be of various natures: In the case of a purchase on a spot market, management exchanges their property rights over a fixed amount of money for the complete property rights over the good. In the case where they require customised goods and services from a specialised actor in the market, or from an employee in their core organisation, management exchanges some *decision rights* over some of their assets and rights over *financial and/or other resources*. The 'agents' might additionally experience *external benefits* stemming from their engagement in this exchange, i.e. benefits that are not paid for by the principal. In return they offer some or all property rights over the *good or service* they provide. To produce the goods and services they use the delegated decision rights in combination with the assets they hold independently, most importantly their expertise.

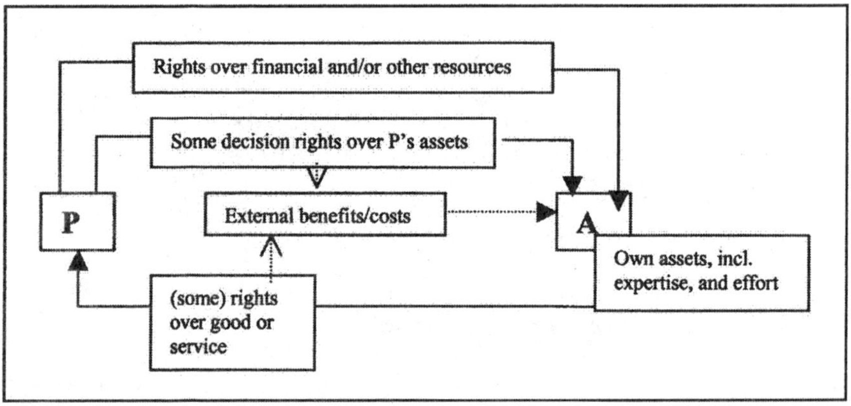

Consider for example the case of the firm X contracting with some specialised advertising agency. X would delegate the decision rights regarding how to find and produce a suitable advertisement for its product to the advertising agency, while probably keeping the residual rights of control, e.g. the right to set the theme and make the final decision. The rights of transfer would also be negotiated (e.g. can Andy Warhol or the producer of Campbell Soups sell the publishing rights for the picture?) The agency would receive a fee and possibly some right to a share of the residual returns, i.e. the profits from an increased turnover due to the advertisement. But on top of that the advertising agency could also profit significantly from external benefits, e.g. from reputation it has gained because X was famous or because X allowed it to develop an unorthodox way to advertise its products (e.g. the posters for Benetton). The agency could also benefit from an increase in knowledge, e.g. about how to deal with a big customer, the characteristics of customers for a certain product, or from recommendations of X etc. The value of its own assets would thereby increase.

Fig. 4.1. A customised exchange

Complying with the 'Resourceful, Evaluating and Maximising Man' model, all agents are assumed to have the general incentive to gain as much net benefit from the exchange as possible. As follows from above, they can pursue this: 1. by trying to increase the 'payment' they receive directly from the principal in financial or other form; 2. by cutting the costs they have, when they provide goods or services to the principal; and 3. by trying to obtain external benefits from the exchange.

With this conceptual framework the impact of organisational structures in a specific case can be analysed in a property rights fashion. It can be considered:

- which different courses of action are within the realm of each actor, given the respective decision rights they received from the principal?
- from which choices would they benefit most?
- what effect are these choices likely to have on the overall organisational goal?

The concrete decision rights, and the concrete impacts of different choices on the core organisation's goal, can only be judged in the particular empirical context. But the scenarios discussed in the organisational economics literature give an indication as to the type of choices actors may have, depending on the nature of the transaction, and which cost implications this has for the principal. The main points are summarised below (see 4.2.2).

Equally, the potential benefits for an actor of different choices can only be assessed in a particular empirical context. But to judge what actors are likely to do, because they want to benefit, one has to make assumptions about the actors' goals. Otherwise non-financial implications of the exchange cannot be interpreted as benefits or costs, or the interpretation could be tautological as argued in the previous chapter when introducing REMM (see 3.2.3). Therefore, the following section in this Chapter (see 4.3) will deal with establishing the 'generic' goals of the different types of actors involved in export support services delivery: individuals, private firms, public bodies and business associations.

4.2.2 Cost factors when aligning agents' choices to the organisational goal

In an exchange situation in which all actors have identical goals, anything an agent does for achieving the principal's goals has positive effects on his own. Such goal congruence is extreme, but weaker versions often exist. They underlie Williamson's argument of lower costs for asset specific transactions within firms, or explain cases of political alliances that fall apart once a major, mutual goal has been reached. In Simon's (1991) opinion the majority of employees identify to some extent with their employers' organisational goals, which is why they carry out their tasks even though they are not constantly monitored. Ouchi (1991 (1980)) argues essentially the same regarding 'clans', groups of actors whose goals have been aligned over time due to long-term relationships and the accompanying socialisation processes, as well as mutual dependency. They have co-operation advantages since costly protections against opportunism are not necessary. Chi (1994) studied business alliances and found that even though the goals of the actors were not the same, the subgoal for which they co-operated was mutual.

But agents may experience 'external benefits' from an exchange also, if their own goals are different from the core organisation's, but can be achieved in parallel. An example is the student, who does an unpaid internship with some blue-chip company, which improves his chances on the job market. Since the agent factors in this 'benefit' when negotiating the terms of the exchange, the principal can offer a lower direct compensation than he would have to offer to an actor with different goals.

Ideally then, not taking into account other factors, the cheapest exchange relationships for the core organisation are those with actors whose *goals or subgoals match*. In any other case, the principal has to compensate the agent fully for the effort undertaken on his behalf.

Regarding the choice of the 'best' agents, agency theory has alerted to the costs of *'adverse selection'* and the cost of protection against it (see Chapter 3). Since the problem stems from the *information asymmetry* regarding the future agents' potential contributions, attempts to increase the principal's information characterise one group of solutions. Another, or complementary option is to influence the expected pay-off from lying, for example by threatening to damage the actor's credibility in future negotiations with third parties, or by demanding warranties.

Once the agents are chosen, the challenge for the principal is to provide incentives so that agents use their decision rights to contribute to the core organisation's goal, while pursuing their self-interest.

The ideal option is to tie their compensation directly to the quantity and quality of their contributions. Not only will agents benefit from working harder, but they will also have an incentive to invest in their knowledge base, be it in the form of human capital or technology, so that they can do the same with less effort or cost. However, as agency theory in particular has discussed, the *measurability of agents' contributions* is often low. *Teamwork* might make it impossible to separate actors' inputs to the joint output and compensate them accordingly. In cases where *production functions are not known*, it cannot be rated to what extent environmental variables influence the output and to what extent it is the result of the actors' inputs. The *observability of output characteristics* may be limited. Finally, actors' contributions might be too complex to be measured, for example with regard to information sharing or innovation efforts (Nalbantian 1987:24f).

Under such circumstances actors' incentives to decrease their own cost, e.g. lowering the effort they put into carrying out tasks for the principal, or cutting back on input materials or input materials' quality, can impact negatively on the core organisation's goal achievement. Actors may also have the opportunity to gain benefits that are outside the exchange agreement, by misusing the delegated decision rights. 'Corruption' is the commonly used word describing the situation, e.g. when a public sector employee uses decision rights about building permissions to receive 'external benefits' in the form of bribes.

Monitoring and deterrence measures become essential to avoid negative effects on goal achievement, but the measures themselves are costly and cannot solve the problem fully. The principal has to weigh the cost of potential goal-adverse behaviour of the agents against the cost of protection mechanisms. These can again be grouped into those that try to reduce the information asymmetry by controlling inputs (e.g. monitoring, rules of procedure, programming of tasks) or outputs (e.g. proxy variables to measure outputs, competition, warranties to signal output quality), and those that aim to influence the pay-offs from cheating by increasing agents' identification with the core organisation, or by making it very costly in case it is discovered (e.g. 'creation of peer group spirit', demanding warranties, threat of dismissal).

The principal may also have to protect himself against agents' incentive to benefit from renegotiating contracts ex-post. As argued in transaction cost theory, this danger arises in the context of *dependency* of the core organisation on a certain agent. In order not to sacrifice the productivity advantage of asset-specific investments, core management can attempt to create organisational structures, which make the actor equally dependent on the transaction, and thereby align goals. They can also try to influence the pay-offs that actors can expect from behaving opportunistically, for example by demanding hostages in advance, or they can try to retain residual rights of control.

Hood (1996) points out that all the different protection mechanisms have their limitations. Since they partly exclude each other (e.g. creation of 'peer group spirit' vs. competition), efforts to reduce the limitations of each type of control by combining different approaches can only be partially successful. In a specific, empirical case it is necessary to establish what the agents want for themselves, and, if this does not match with the core organisations' goals, to what extent the organisational structures align the interests and at what cost.

4.3 Generic goals of the major actors

In the case of export promotion, like in many other organisational arrangements for public service delivery, managers of the core organisation deal with two types of actors: 1. individuals as employees with whom individual contracts are made within the remit of public sector employment practices; and 2. legal entities ranging from private firms and business associations to government bureaux. To judge which self-interested choices these actors would make in a given situation, it is necessary to make assumptions about their own goals.

While individuals', private firms' and public bureaux' goals have been discussed by other authors, as summarised below, assumptions about the goals of business organisations had to be developed (Hauswirth 2000).

In all cases goal assumptions are based on a perspective of methodological individualism, as presented in the previous chapter: Ultimately, organisational goals always derive from individual goals, and individuals try to maximise their utility. This notion is combined with Simon's (1964) notion of organisational goals as the sets of constraints that limit decision making. The strongest constraints for an organisation are its requisites for survival. Normally, these have to be met and therefore limit choices. Then top managers set further constraints by setting directions that satisfy their personal goals. Other stakeholders in the organisation might also have an impact, but normally management's access to information and its position as the co-ordinating and initiating agent give it a predominant role (Williamson 1963:37).

Thus the 'generic' goals of private enterprises, public bodies and associations are derived from assumptions about managers' utilities and the legal entities' requisites for survival.

4.3.1 Individuals' utilities in a work context

Organisation psychology's current state of knowledge about the utilities individuals derive from working is characterised by a multitude of theories, and failure of the theories to fit with research findings, or with each other (Kanfer 1992:7). The application of comparatively simple organisation theorists' and economists' assumptions regarding individuals' goals appears equally fruitful as more complex motivation theories.

According to Williamson's (1963:29) literature review *'a substantive consensus exists among those who have carefully studied the operation of the business firm on what constitutes the 'immediate determinants of behaviour''*: These are the pursuit of income, security, power, status, and prestige, as well as a feeling of professional accomplishment. Among these determinants 'income' stands out since it is not normally an end in itself. But as empirical surveys have shown (Gerhart and Milkovich 1992: 531,553) individuals treat income itself as very important, because of its 'unique instrumental capacity'.

In the forty years that have passed since this review, other writers have found no reasons to reject these assumptions, and have only added 'convenience' (e.g. Downs 1967) and 'feeling of being in control' or 'self-determination' (e.g. Evers 1995; Ondrack 1995) to the list.[2]

4.3.2 Private firms' goals

Mainstream economics has traditionally postulated that privately owned firms attempt to maximise their *profits*. This assumption has proven to be extremely useful for explaining and predicting aggregate firm reaction to price changes in competitive markets (see Machlup 1967). However, it has also been noted that profit maximisation is not a requirement for survival unless firms operate under perfect competition. In principle, decision makers have the discretion to pursue whatever might satisfy them, as long as they safeguard their firms' existence and attain

[2] Individuals' work-related utilities

	Income	Security	Power	Status and Prestige	Professional accomplishment*	Convenience	self determination**
Williamson 1963	X	x	x	x	x		
Marris 1963	X	x	x	x			
Downs 1967	X	x	x	x	(pride in performance)	x	
Niskanen 1973	salary + fringe benefits + perks		power and patronage	public reputation		ease of managing. the bureau	ease of making changes
Dunleavy 1991	X	x	x	x	work content		x

*see also McClelland 1976 (1953) — 'feeling of competence'; Herzberg 1974 (1966)
**see also the literature on 'intrinsic motivation' e.g. Frey 1997; Wiersma 1992

some minimum 'acceptable' rate of return.[3] (Machlup 1967; Marris 1963, 1992; Williamson 1963; Woehe 1986)

While it seems to be accepted that *owner–managers* are overall most interested in profit making, research has focused on establishing how *nonowner–managers* would use discretion, as they do not receive the residual profit.

The conclusion has been that managers who value income, power, prestige, status, and job security, are more likely to be interested in the size of their firm than in its profit rate (Marris 1963; Williamson 1963): There are many studies linking top management income to firm size (Pavlik and Belkaoui 1991; Lawler and Jenkins 1992; Gerhart and Milkovich 1992) while evidence shows only a very weak relationship between total compensation levels and firm performance (Jensen and Murphy 1990; Firth 1991; Lawler and Jenkins 1992; Evers 1995; Greenbury 1995; Sirower 1997). Status, power, and prestige are also perceived to be linked to company size, as is job security for top managers (George et al. 1992:43f; Marris 1992).

Viewed dynamically, this interest in size translates to an interest in company *growth*, particularly in terms of staff growth. Since managers are not perfectly mobile and cannot expect to move progressively from smaller to larger firms, they pursue the growth of the firm where they are employed (Marris 1963; Williamson 1963). The downsizing trend in the 1980s and early 1990s did not contradict these assumptions, but showed that they have to be placed in context of environmental constraints. For many companies downsizing was a last means to survive competition, and managers' pay often increased as a reward for cutting cost (The Economist 26.10.1996; 21.12.1996).

By asserting that managers like to have discretionary spending powers to finance their firms' growth, Marris (1963) and Williamson (1963) however reestablish the link with the initial profit maximisation assumption. Both point out that to assume managers' interest in management discretion and company growth, subject to a minimum profit constraint, does not mean they do not pursue profits, only that shareholders do not receive the full amount (see also Machlup 1967). In order to expand their firms, managers need to raise at least some of the capital internally, i.e. retain profits that were made beyond the minimum profit constraint. Growth and profit increases are also interrelated in that growth expectations lead to profit expectations and therefore higher share prices. Profit increases without growth are difficult to achieve over the long term even in uncompetitive markets.

The conclusion regarding firms' objectives is therefore that the profit motive is a major one, not only in competitive markets. It is a measure of achievement and success for both owner– and non– owner–managers and enables them to pursue other interests beyond profit making. However, particularly non owner–managers will tend to take into account the effects certain choices of action will have on

---

[3] According to Williamson (1963:34) the 'normal' rate of return is judged against rival companies, the firm's previous performance and special current conditions. To what extent shareholders can and will put pressure on management to maximise profits depends on their level of organisation and information (Pavlik and Belakoui 1991, George et al. 1992).

growth opportunities and their own discretion. To what extent they can, depends on the firms' environment, its ownership structure, and the internal penalties and rewards arrangements.

4.3.3 Public bodies' goals

'Public bodies', 'bureaux', 'departments', or 'agencies' are different terms, sometimes used interchangeably, sometimes with a more specific meaning in mind, to name organisational units within 'the public sector'. What constitutes them is not easily defined and depends on the perspective and purpose of the definition-maker (Dowding 1995:17ff; Rainey 1983:207ff). Here the terms 'public body' 'agency' or 'bureau' are used interchangeably for any government departments and their sub-units. Every bureau has to carry out specified tasks according to a set of rules, while at the same time it has considerable autonomy regarding policy decisions which relate to these tasks (Dowding 1995:113; Rainey 1983).

The perception of public bodies' goals was fundamentally shaped by Niskanen (1971). He argued that in order to survive, bureaux must produce services, which are broadly consistent with the purposes for which they received their budget, and that the services have to have some value to society. However, these constraints would still leave senior officials with a wide range of decision choices, which they would use to further their own interests by *maximising their budgets* (see 3.4.4).

Looking at the evidence for this argument, Dowding (1995) found nothing to suggest that Niskanen's behavioural assumption was false, yet plenty of evidence that budgets had not continually increased. The problem seemed to lie in an over-simplified model of bureaucratic organisation.

Dunleavy (1991) designed a more complex model of bureaucratic self-interest, 'the 'bureau-shaping' model, which could explain developments in the public sector, including those which contradicted Niskanen's budget maximisation prediction. In contrast to Niskanen (1971) he considered that different types of budget have different utility pay-offs, and that the pay-offs from budget increases vary for different levels of staff. The 'core budget' is the only part of a bureau's budget which is spent directly on the bureau's own operations. Its increase will benefit particularly lower and middle-ranking and highly specialised staff[4] by improving their job-security, their career prospects and the possibility of upward re-grading. Therefore, and because they can employ suitable resources, senior public officials will find the management of their unit easier with core budget increases. The 'bureau element', i.e. the part of the budget that is paid out to the private sector in form of contracts or transfer payments is also of interest, particularly for senior officials. They may be able to make discretionary decisions about large contracts or transfers, for which they may be rewarded by individual favours like post-retirement directorships (Dunleavy 1991:193). The programme element of the

[4] Breton and Wintrobe (1975) argue that highly professional staff who can use their skills only in specific jobs are therefore particularly dependent on the survival and expansion of their field of work.

budget, i.e. those monies which the agency receives but passes on to other public sector bureaux, is of comparatively little interest.

But even in those units where the 'core budget' and 'bureau element' make up most of the budget, only highly professionalised bureaux are likely to pursue open-ended budget maximisation. Dunleavy (1991) reasoned that since the opportunities to increase pecuniary income in their jobs were very restricted for senior public officials (pay and perks in the civil service are generally restricted according to clear formulas) and since people who placed a high preference on pecuniary income were not likely to enter those positions, it was likely that the focus was on *gaining utility from work content and the work environment.* This hypothesis is supported by Peacock's (1983) account of X-inefficiency in the public sector, based on his experiences as a government employee. Senior officials who enjoy job security and who can either expect automatic promotion or no further promotion after reaching a certain rank (e.g. under-secretary in the UK) derive utility in terms of status and prestige from the number of administrative grade officials working under their command and from 'on the job leisure'. *'On the job leisure'* according to Peacock (1983:128) involves attendance at official lunches, receiving overseas delegations, visits as a VIP to concerns in receipt of government funds etc.

Dunleavy (1991) elaborated and added to the point by suggesting that senior public officials would be more interested in *policy making and strategic management work* than in heading day-to-day routine, conflictual and low-status administrative duties carried out by a large number of low-grade staff. They would therefore engage in *bureau shaping*, i.e. try to transform their bureau into one which has the desired characteristics. Again, public sector development in the UK has been in accordance with these ideas, featuring, for example, no major opposition of senior officials against contracting-out of activities that are done by low-grade staff, or the transfer of routine functions into geographically separated special units with little senior management involvement.

4.3.4 Business associations' goals

4.3.4.1 Voluntary business associations – prerequisites for survival

Voluntary business associations are set up by individuals, firms, or others in order to carry out some form of joint activity. The members join voluntarily and can leave the association if they wish to. With exception of the leadership, there is no formal hierarchy in members' decision rights and, unlike in other bodies, associations' members constitute both input suppliers and customers of the outputs (Dunleavy 1991:14f).

Business associations perform a variety of functions, and offer a range of services. Based on Schmitter and Streeck (1981) these are often grouped into four categories (e.g. Bennett 1997; Lane 1997; Weber 1987):

- *Collective goods* arise from business associations' successes in influencing policy making as well as from improving supply and demand conditions for the interest groups they represent. The successes do not only benefit the associations' members but also outsiders, for example when cost increasing regulations are prevented, subsidies are granted, or customer awareness is increased by product promotion campaigns.

- *Selective goods* are characterised by the possibility to limit the number of beneficiaries. They can therefore be offered on a members-only basis, but may also be sold to non-members. They concern largely information provision, but also reductions on insurance fees or input materials due to bulk purchase, packaging, storage or transport arrangements.
- *Monopoly/enforcement goods* comprise those services and functions which are only provided by the association and/or for the provision of which associations have special rights. Examples are the setting of standards or certification services.
- *Solidarity goods* only come into being through members' active involvement and their interaction with each other. They encompass the knowledge, contacts, and social benefits gained in annual meetings, discussion groups, social events or leisure activities.

All larger voluntary business associations show this pattern of services, although the emphasis on single categories and the range of services within each varies.[5]

Since rational actors only demand services from associations if there is no better supply alternative, the existence of voluntary associations depends on having competitive advantages in each of the service categories they offer:

1) Collective goods

Pluralist, corporatist, as well as new right accounts of associative behaviour consider the pursuit of influence, mainly on public policy outputs, the major reason for business associations' existence (Dunleavy 1991; Cawson 1985). This is reasonably justified by empirical surveys of their activities, and by statements of associations' representatives (Bennett 1997, 1997b; Boleat 1996).

Compared with self-supply, i.e. the individual firm trying to advance its interests vs. the government, and compared with commercial lobbyists, associations can offer a more legitimate and cheaper pursuit of influence:

Only big firms have the weight and financial means to try to influence governments directly. But if acting on their own, or through commercial lobbyists, they face the difficulty that governments may have a political problem when perceived to be 'taking advice' from individual actors (Wilson 1990). Associations, due to their internal democracy, can claim to represent all members regardless of their financial potency, and to act as a voice for a segment of the business world. Doing so, their credibility depends on the recognition they receive as truly representing the respective group. Both a high mobilisation rate regarding the total potential

[5] See for example the descriptions of service provision by Weber (1987) for the machinery associations in Germany, Boleat (1996) for trade associations in Britain, Lynn and McKeown (1988) for US and Japan, Bennett (1997b) for British business associations, or the range of examples in Bennett (1997) for Germany and Britain.

membership and good, usually expensive, public relations work contribute to this effect. Besides, the potential marginal vote impact of the represented group is relevant (Dunleavy 1991:22f).

Apart from legitimacy, associations can also offer cost-effective representation vis-à-vis government, markets, and opinion makers for the individual member. Bennett (1996:663ff) points out that in order to have influence considerable intelligence is required. Policy processes, legal issues, factual data and relevant decision makers and their interests have to be known, and personal contacts are helpful. This type of intelligence can be highly specific, especially where legislation affecting a certain sector of industry or region is concerned. Associations, compared with private lobbyists or individual members, can benefit from economies of scale and scope regarding the employment of specialist staff, from learning effects, as well as from lower transaction costs due to little risk of hold-up[6] and frequent transactions. Additionally, transaction costs are lowered by associations' information advantage resulting from the inputs of different members. Compared with private lobbying firms, pursuing their collective interest through associations has further advantages from the members' point of view: Search costs are zero and other aspects of contracting costs can be shared. If members trust their association[7], monitoring and enforcement costs are also lower. Furthermore, the risk that representation on some policy issue might be needed, is covered by a fixed price. But to materialise these potential cost advantages, associations are dependent on their membership, funds and recognition. The number of members needs to justify a continuous involvement in different policy issues, and funds are required to cover the costs.[8] Members have to believe that their association can provide the required lobbying service.

Thus, associations' competitive advantage for collective good provision rests on recognition, funds and membership mobilisation. Yet as Olson (1971) showed, membership mobilisation by a voluntary association providing only collective goods, i.e. goods with positive externalities, is a big problem. In large groups of potential members, where nobody gains disproportionately or can be socially pressured to join, the only explanation of membership is that there are additional selective benefits, which are exclusive to those who join.

2) Selective goods

Selective goods can thus be seen as a remedy for collective action problems. But they can also be a reason for associations (Roepke 1992), or a source of income

---

[6] For a private lobbyist the information that needs to be acquired is highly asset specific, which causes hold-up risks.

[7] According to Bennett (1996:658) members of Chambers of Commerce normally offer a 'calculative trust', a self-interested trust which is upheld as long as it is rational to do so and which is based on previous experiences and the overall recognition associations enjoy. Keller (1988) argues that the parties co-operate initially and continue to do so as long as long as the other side co-operate as well.

[8] *'Lobbying, which is our core function, is expensive because you need high-quality staff, but it does not bring in money' (Hall 1997:113).*

(Boleat 1996). Either way, associations can only offer these selective goods effectively if they can compete with commercial suppliers.

A principal selective service is the provision of information, be it in the form of newsletters, trade statistics, or answers to enquiries (e.g. Boleat 1996; Weber 1987). The arguments for associations' competitive advantage in this field concern essentially cost, resulting from similar economies of scale and scope advantages, as described above. In order to represent their members adequately, associations have to collect data ranging from members' problems, their characteristics and development, to market developments and changes in the legislative and regulatory environment. Relatively little extra cost is involved if this information is offered to member firms as well, especially if several are interested. For private consultants the problem is again asset specificity, and they, as well as members on their own, are comparatively disadvantaged when trying to gather intelligence from other firms or from the government, e.g. for benchmarking purposes (Boleat 1996:106). With view to conferences, seminars or exhibitions, associations have lower marketing costs and preferential access to high-quality speakers (Boleat 1996:108). They can also customise the topics due to their information about business needs. Knowing that their association provides answers to enquiries, businesses on the other hand, can save on search costs. Bennett (1996:667ff) showed that the subject of the enquiries at British chambers of commerce is very broad, the average member uses the service infrequently (3.6 times p.a.), the questions can usually be answered briefly, and the individual members' need for certain information is highly uncertain. Considering the low annual membership fee, which covers the risk of needing some information on a multitude of issues and which promises a reliable service, membership can be attractive.

But again, economies of scale and scope depend on the number of members. Only if the association can sustain the provision of a range of different goods will advantages from their connectedness arise. This is linked to the availability of funds, which are needed to pre-finance services with high up-front costs like exhibitions, and sufficient demand for each of the information services offered. As to selective goods in the form of cost reductions on input factors, since they are based on associations' bulk purchasing power, membership numbers and density are equally relevant.

3) Monopoly/Enforcement Goods

In providing monopoly/enforcement goods, voluntary associations are not exposed to competition. But in order to do so, they have to be accepted as 'legislators' by the respective business community, and they rely to a great extent on government.

Even if the general application of rules, e.g. on safety standards, would benefit a profession or industry on the whole (see e.g. Lane and Bachmann 1996), an individual firm faces a competitive disadvantage if it follows the rules while others do not. This prisoner's dilemma can only be solved if enough agents participate from the beginning (see Lane 1997). If an association wants to provide for such rules, it needs to have some sort of enforcement mechanism. One means is compulsion – those members who break the rules are excluded from the association. This however presupposes that a violation can be easily observed and that the agent cannot easily do without other benefits of membership. It also presupposes that the associations' coverage is high enough, not to make members price themselves out of the market in which they compete with non-members. If this is not the case, the association has to convince government that the rules should apply for the whole sector. But as this strategy is only feasible if the association is recognised by government as a competent and informed representative, it is unlikely to succeed if the association has only a few members. Another or additional means is the certification of standards by the association and its parallel marketing to create customer demand, preferably also by the public sector. Pressure is thereby exerted on the firms, while making compliance profitable. This strategy, however, requires substantial funds for the advertising campaign and the certification facilities.

Complementing the enforcement goods initiated by the associations are those that are in demand by government. Government can give associations rights to represent it in executing quasi-public functions (e.g. certification or licensing), and can give formal access to policy shaping. Where this is practised, there is the view that it can be a pragmatic means of informed and cheap governance (e.g. Lane 1997; Lynn and McKeown 1988). Associations are expected to supply relevant information about business needs and market developments, to integrate heterogeneous or conflicting member interests into a singular business position, and to make sure that firms comply with negotiated results (Schoenig 1996; Weber 1987; Cawson 1985). They have to be recognised as capable of delivering, being big enough, well organised and run, and supported by the group they represent.[9]

4) Solidarity goods

Solidarity goods are created by members themselves through interaction with each other, resulting for example in increased knowledge, useful personal contacts, trust-based inter-firm relations (Lane and Bachmann 1996), or 'social status or social acceptance (Olson 1971:61). That their provision is important for associations is suggested by a number of references. Hall (1997:109) for example, states that *'to provide a meeting place, a club function for those who want it, where they can talk to people with common interests'* is a major function. Dunleavy (1991) argues from an academic viewpoint that solidarity goods are important to overcome collective action problems, by making members feel that their individual contribution is needed and by creating a feeling of unity.

Since members' time is scarce and social interaction is time-consuming, voluntary associations are in competition with all alternative types of forums, which give individuals the chance to obtain these 'social' goods. While associations have the advantage that they can present their members the chance to combine professional interests with a desire for social engagement (Hirschman 1982:85f; Lehmbruch 1994:375) the extent to which members identify with the 'group' and derive personal social prestige or acceptance benefits, is to some extent related to its public recognition, and to other 'relevant' actors taking part.

[9] In the UK these requirements were publicly stated by Michael Heseltine in his speeches to the CBI, (1993, 1995) and were also put in print in the 'DTI best practice guide for the model trade association' (see the list of desired features in Berry 1997).

In sum, voluntary associations can only offer collective, selective, and solidarity goods competitively, and monopoly and enforcement goods, if they have many members with a high coverage rate of the relevant businesses; are recognised by members, the markets and the government; and have funds to invest in service provision and opinion formation (see Table 4.1. next page).

These three requirements are inter-linked:

A *small membership* means low membership fee revenue, a low chance of benefiting from economies of scope and scale, and little or no recognition by government and markets. *Little recognition*, on the other hand, means little attractiveness for potential members. If there is no recognition by government, the motive to join in order to influence decision making and obtain first-hand information about policies and policy development (Bowen 1997:38) disappears. Also, in countries where associations are not formally recognised and supported by government, they have to pay taxes like any other business. No real recognition by members means that those competitive advantages, which are based on trust, disappear. It also means that the association will not be interesting for government as an intermediary. Lastly, if associations have only *small funds*, they find it difficult to offer enough competitive selective goods to attract new members. They will also find it difficult to engage in public relations work, which might increase their recognition. Resources and reputation also affect probability of attracting qualified and competent staff.[10]

Case studies on successful associations show that all of them owe their success to some external influence, which broke the vicious circle somewhere, be it an outside sponsor, unusual pressure on individuals to co-operate, or, in most cases, government support through personnel, institutionalised rights or even funds. The entrepreneurial qualities of founders and management were also very important.[11]

4.3.4.2 Management's preferences and goal impact

While voluntary associations are usually set up as representative bodies for their members, with participatory decision-making structures, their chief executives do have discretionary powers. There is also evidence that these discretionary decision rights are increasing (Boleat 1996; Bennett 1997; Braeunig 1997). The question in the context here is, how chief executives' preferences will influence the way in which the interrelated prerequisites for survival will be pursued and discretion will be used.

Associations' *funds* are very important for management. Not only will their own income depend on what the organisation can pay, but also availability and standard of office space, equipment, and the number and quality of staff. There is

---

[10] Anthony Parish, for example, complains that 'in Britain the lower status' (due to the associations' role not being formalised by government) *'makes it more difficult to recruit staff'* (quoted by Bennett 1997:7).

[11] See Schmid and Soroko (1997) for a review of case studies and an own case study, or Schoenig (1996) on the German government intervention to build up associations in East Germany.

Table 4.1. Voluntary associations' requisites for survival

Output	*Competitive Advantage*	*Preconditions for holding the competitive advantage*	*Requisites for survival*
Collective Goods	legitimacy potential vote impact lower costs of service provision lower transaction costs for members and for policy makers and market	membership no. and coverage; recognition membership no.; interest group size; pivotal position and preference intensity; publicity membership no.; recognition knowledge of services and trust of members based on brand name/recognition	*Members* *Brand name/ Recognition* *Funds for campaigns*
Selective Goods	unique services lower costs of service provision lower transaction costs for members	provision of information by members dependent on trust; provision of information by government and other sources dependent on recognition type of services (asset specific; connected); minimum no. of interested members; capacity of service development partly dependent on funds available; bargaining power vis-à-vis suppliers and customers depending on no. of affected members type of services (infrequent, uncertain); knowledge of services and trust of members based on brand name/recognition and on past performance; low subscription price	*Members* *Brand name/Recognition* *Funds for investing in service provision*
Monopoly/ Enforcement Goods - rule setting/negotiation right for members, or all firms/ individuals in the sector - monopolist in service delivery on behalf of the government	collective advantage cheap governance	role definition by the state – dependent on recognition, degree of interest integration and control of members (also history and cultural norms) - rights of monopolist service delivery can also depend on competitiveness compared with other potential service providers members complying to agreements, dependent on trust, history and cultural norms, attractiveness of selective goods adequate finances to initiate/run monopoly/enforcement goods	*Membership coverage* *Recognition* *Funds for campaigns*
Solidarity Goods	forum for interaction offering a combination of professional and social benefits	dentification of members with association, dependent on o public recognition o personal relationships o congruence of interests	*Recognition* *Members*

status and prestige attached to these features and managers' job security is directly dependent on the association staying solvent.

Unless associations receive donations, their income depends on membership fees and the profits made from offering selective goods and monopoly and enforcement goods. Focussing on income from goods rather than from membership fees provides management with the advantage that the motivation for and expectations of membership become directed to cost/benefit calculations regarding these specific goods. Management has more power vis-à-vis the members since they control access to what is in demand (Weber 1987:145). The type of members attracted by selective goods may also be less interested in participatory decision making. This can reduce internal conflicts and increase management's discretion. Threats to job security are also reduced because creating and managing high fee income makes the executives more difficult to replace. All cases reported in Bennett (1997) show attempts to shift from subscription income towards a higher proportion of service charges and fees income. An income from monopoly and enforcement goods brings attached cost-reduction effects for other services through connectedness and brand-name value. By managing a high number of monopoly goods, associations can make themselves irreplaceable and thereby transform the voluntary membership in a de facto compulsory one (Weber 1987). However, the precondition is associations' recognition.

Since especially *recognition* can suffer if membership numbers are low, voluntary associations' managers are expected to want to increase or retain membership. But if new members are to be actively recruited, big firms are a more interesting target group than small firms. They are less sensitive to membership fee changes, which means less conflict and more security of income. They are more likely to create publicity, which has positive effects on recognition and the attraction of other firms. Moreover, good personal relations with chief decision-makers in the industry enhance the chances of associations' managers to maintain a chance of an interesting career option outside the association. Small firms' membership is only useful to management in terms of the effects of high membership density on recognition. The easiest way to encourage SMEs to become members is the provision of selective services (Bennett 1997b).

Summarising, since membership, funds, and recognition are closely interrelated, any expectations of a positive contribution to either of these goals would be an incentive for management to take a certain action. But outcomes that enhance an association's competitive advantage in selective service provision, or opportunities to increase links with government in view of monopoly goods, have the most direct impact on management's own welfare. Managers can also benefit directly from the membership of large firms, which is why they would be inclined to emphasise such members' position in the provision of collective services.

4.3.4.3 Compulsory associations

The transition from voluntary associations to compulsory associations can be seen as a gradual one. With increasing institutionalised rights to provide monopoly and enforcement goods, the choice of firms whether or not to deal with the association is increasingly limited. However, a specific dividing point is where firms or individuals are forced by law to be member of an association. This applies for example to some professions, e.g. barristers in Britain, or to firms in countries where membership in chambers of commerce is compulsory, as in Germany.

Compulsory membership has a significant impact on the association. In the previous section it was shown how the three prerequisites for a voluntary associations' success, i.e. members, funds and recognition, are interconnected. Governments only force firms and individuals to become members of an association if they intend to take advantage of that body in the way described above. This means that for compulsory associations government recognition is guaranteed at the outset. By guaranteeing the association its members, government at the same time assures funds through enforced subscription. Consequently, the goals of voluntary associations do not apply as such to compulsory associations. As long as they can formally comply with governments' expectations, compulsory associations' existence is *de facto* guaranteed.

Management in compulsory associations has therefore no inherent restrictions that would narrow down their choice between different actions, apart from fulfilling their role vis-à-vis the government. They have to act within the constitution of the respective body and are submitted to the scrutiny of the supervisory body specified there, but to what extent this control practically comes into place, depends on the individual association. As there is a collective action problem for SMEs to make their voice heard, and as they cannot exit, small members' opinion can become irrelevant. This is what the protest movement against compulsory membership in German chambers of commerce and industry, the 'Interessengemeinschaft der IHK-Verweigerer' claims, being supported by two surveys in which up to 96% of German SMEs stated that they did not feel their interests to be represented by the chambers.[12] Bennett (1997b:23) suggested that *'...large businesses can extract special value or benefits in exchange for their involvement...'*

With their freedom not restricted by concerns about the associations' survival, there are two possible settings that could influence the direction managers are likely to take. First, if membership is guaranteed by law, the associations might be constituted as quasi-public units in which the employment rules and regulation of the public sector apply. If this is the case, compulsory associations' managers would be expected to operate according to the logic that was outlined for senior public sector employees, with the modification that their activities would be more directly scrutinised by members' representatives, i.e. big firms. In the case that a compulsory association is run under private law and chief executives can negotiate their contracts, they are equally likely to be interested in their work content and context. However, for income reasons, there might be a more pronounced focus on

[12] The German Section of the European Association of the Self-Employed (BVD) asked 827 SMEs whether they needed the IHK (98% answered negatively) and whether they felt represented (96.1% answered with 'No') (Frankfurter Neue Presse, 4.2.1998 – Verband wehrt sich gegen IHK-Zwangsmitgliedschaft). In an earlier survey by the business journal 'Markt und Mittelstand' 77% of firms stated that they would leave their chamber and 82% thought the services they received were not worth the money they had to pay for them (DIP-Drucksache 13/6063, 8.11.1996).

increasing the association's budget. Since the possibility of raising income through subscription increases is limited, more selective services and monopoly goods would have to be offered.

In German trade associations, where membership is de facto nearly compulsory (Lane 1997) there has been less emphasis on selective services than in Britain. But as the discussion in Bennett (1997) showed, chief executives have tried to expand these services. German chambers fought hard to obtain the right for issuing officially recognised certificates of origin.[13] Also, one major criticism of their work is their increasing involvement in activities in which they directly compete with private firms.

Overall however, the goals of compulsory associations are more difficult to establish than those of voluntary associations because there are hardly any structural constraints.

4.3.5 Summary

It has been argued that if actors' goals were fully compatible with the core organisation's, only decision rights would have to be delegated and no further reward–sanction structure would be needed. However, to the extent that this is not the case, the pay-off structures for each actor, as measured against his own goals are relevant. The less goals match, the less measurable individuals' actors outputs are, and the more relevant these outputs are to the core organisation, the costlier are the incentive structures that need to be put in place. One can conclude that assumptions about the effectiveness and efficiency of organisational structures must be influenced to a large extent by assumptions about the goals of the available actors.

The goals ascribed to the various actors are based on reflections on firms', public bodies' and business associations' requisites for survival, combined with assumptions about senior managements' utilities. It was argued that private firms would want to increase their profits and grow, and that public bureaux would aim to maintain or expand parts of their budget, and improve work content and work environment. Voluntary business associations would strive for members, public recognition and revenues, placing emphasis on bigger firms as members and on fee-based revenues, whereas compulsory associations' goals are more defined by the specific context.

This attribution of generic goals to actors necessarily involves generalisations and might not do justice to the single case. But, generalisations are the only means for model-building (see e.g. Machlup 1967; Riker 1990) and also for any situation where contracts have to be judged, designed or negotiated without knowing the exact individual utility function of the current or future agent. However, they can only predict a pattern of incentive processing, not the resulting behaviour as such. Even if modified with whatever additional information is available for specific cases, a multitude of situational factors will determine a specific outcome.

---

[13] see e.g. Deutscher Bundestag – Heft 4/06.0.3.96; Heft 2/07.02.1996.

4.4 Knowledge

The production of any goods or services requires some combination of inputs in the form of human effort, materials, finances, and legal rights. But regardless of the extent and configuration in which these inputs are used, in order to manipulate and transform them and thereby ad value, a further ingredient – knowledge – is required (Galunic and Rodan 1997:6). But although Marshall wrote more than a century ago that *'knowledge is our most powerful engine of production...organisation aids knowledge'*[14] (Marshall 1994 (1890):115), and although Taylor's (1997 (1912)) scientific management theory and Weber's (1997 (1992)) theory of bureaucracy are based on the notion of knowledge increasing organisational effectiveness and efficiency, neither the investigation of 'knowledge' nor of its relationship with organisation has found much attention until recently. In neoclassical economics 'knowledge' has largely been treated as 'given', with buyers and sellers knowing about markets and best prices, and producers having the knowledge of the technology of the time (Machlup 1980). While transaction cost theory and agency theory have highlighted the prevalence of incomplete and asymmetric market knowledge and its impact, they have not applied the concept of 'bounded rationality' to production knowledge as such.

However, if 'bounded rationality' is accepted as a general premise, knowledge is necessarily incomplete and likely to be unevenly distributed. If it is furthermore accepted that different decisions require different kinds of knowledge, the organisational problem from the 'knowledge perspective' is to bring the two together: Those actors who have the necessary knowledge to carry out certain activities should also receive the rights to make the related decisions, or, vice versa, those actors who have decision rights over certain assets should also obtain the knowledge to use them productively (Jensen and Meckling 1992).[15]

To assess an organisation's impact on the knowledge that is applied when producing outputs it is necessary to determine which knowledge the decision-making actors are likely to hold and use, and at what cost to the core organisation.

---

[14] In Chapter VIII Marshall discusses organisational aspects of knowledge, emphasising the productivity effects of a division of labour with regard to the development of special expertise, specialised machinery, and economies of scope *('Economies in production arising from division of labour can best be secured by the efficiency of specialised machinery or specialised skill, but also that when it is necessary to undertake different tasks, each of these tasks should be such as to call forth as much as possible of the skill and ability or machine capacity'(219f)*. He also discusses the positive effects of spatial proximity of closely related industrial activities (*'industrial districts'*) on knowledge transfer and transaction costs, and economies of scale arising from bundling certain activities within one firm, e.g. the continuous employment of specialised machinery.

[15] Demsetz (1992b) points out, that there might be issues of comparative advantage, e.g. the manager typing better than her secretary; and that there might be important factors like eyesight, or tenacity which have an impact besides knowledge.

4.4.1 Assessing actors' knowledge

'Knowledge' is usually defined as a structured and coherent stock of information, observations, impressions, and deductions, which have been accumulated and synthesised by an actor over time (Machlup 1983:642ff).

The type of knowledge which is of interest here is 'know-how' – knowledge which is related to carrying out a certain activity. It can be embodied in machines, and can be held by groups or whole organisations as 'competencies', or by individuals as 'skills'. It is based on a mixture of known 'routines' and 'principles', and an awareness of the relevant environmental conditions (Stinchcombe 1990).

'Routines' are those parts of knowledge that actors can use without conscious thinking. As a result they can do 'routine' activities fast, and due to the practise, which the development of routines requires, they can also do them well. Machlup's (1980:31) example of swimming illustrates the point. Someone who knows how to swim, does it subconsciously and semi-automatically while her mind may be occupied with other thoughts. Not accounting for differences in individuals' talents, it can be expected that the more practised the swimmer, the more efficient her technique. Regarding joint activities of various individuals or groups, routines imply that exchange processes have been so clearly structured that the exchanging actors neither have to make conscious decisions for each interaction, nor do they need higher authorities' case-to-case instructions for a coordination of the exchanges. An assembly line structure is an extreme example. In this case the different actors working in line are hardly required to make any discretionary decisions, to the extent their activities become so predetermined that they might as well be automated (Marshall 1994 (1890): 211). But routines can also develop subconsciously, e.g. within work groups, and there are routines where the interfaces between individual activities are standardised, but where some or all actors have to use considerable discretion when carrying out their part of the task. Grades, handed to exam boards by teachers are an example (Stinchcombe 1990, Ch.2).

In any of these cases, routines help to accomplish the activity faster and usually better than if conscious deliberation was necessary to make the adequate decision of 'what to do next and how'. They can be developed for production purposes, as well as for control purposes.

Since routines develop with practise and experience they depend on the respective activities to reoccur. This is more likely, the more specialised actors are. It is also necessary that the successful application of a routine is unaffected by the conditions under which the activity is carried out, or that those conditions do not change. As this is hardly ever the case, an actor also needs 'know-that' as part of her skill - principles which she can use to decide when a routine is applicable, and knowledge about the conditions in question.[16]

---

[16] Traditional assembly lines, for example, have been successful in mass-product markets where demand has remained relatively stable. But with an increasing variation in demands, improvements in technology have been used to develop machines with a range of 'subroutines' that can be chosen, depending on the product in demand. Firms also try to

'Principles' provide an actor with a view of the structure of a problem when making a decision, i.e. a list of possible actions and states of the world and a means–ends framework relating actions and outcomes (Langlois 1984). Again they can be based on experience, e.g. a window frame producer observing that some types of wood used for window frames last longer than others. They may also be based on deduction, or they may have been taught. Research has shown that skilled actors incorporate general, abstract knowledge into local, informal routines, 'freely adapting it as they work on actual problems in their particular social and physical circumstances' (Tyre and Hippel 1997:72). If the window frame producer knows the effect of humidity and temperature on wood of different figure and texture, she can choose the adequate type of window frames even for a country with different climatic conditions. With some experience, the principle might then be refined, for example to account for the impact of local insect or fungi populations. In short, principles offer a guideline for assessing the environmental conditions. The better they are in terms of identifying cause–effect relationships, the more effective the choice whether to apply a routine or how to modify one. With enough experience some principles might themselves be used subconsciously to switch from one routine to another, as for example in the case when people switch from walking on flat ground to walking upstairs. 'Information', i.e. a piece of news about the environmental condition flows in, and the routine is switched accordingly.

This definition of knowledge as a mixture of routines and principles, joined by information from the environment helping to decide which principle is relevant and which routine should apply, suggests that practical knowledge is not a static 'given'. As is implicit in the notion of experience, as well as in the link between knowledge and information about the relevant conditions, each 'stock' of knowledge is continually confronted and updated with new messages, and, when not updated may become redundant (Machlup 1993, 1980).

Which information or 'messages' reach an actor, and how fast, depends on his environment, including for example the tasks he is involved in or the people he deals with. But the decoding and absorption of information and observations depend also on an individual's stock of knowledge, since attention to messages and their processing are always undertaken on its basis. A daily piece of news regarding, for example, the exchange rate between Pound Sterling and the Guatemalan Quetzal will probably not be absorbed by the majority of newspaper readers, while it can contribute to the decision making of a British investor in Guatemala, or change a model of exchange rate development designed by a foreign exchange speculator. This example also shows that a third factor, aside from the environment and the existing knowledge, influences receptiveness to information, and thus to knowledge building – the perceived relevance of the information for the actor, based on its potential cost or benefit effects (Becker and Murphy 1992).

'buffer' routinised parts from fluctuations of the environment via standardisation at the points of exchange, as in the example of the processing of students' grades by exam boards (Stinchcombe 1990, Ch.2).

Such information that is valued as particularly important, is likely to be actively searched for.

Which skills and competencies can specific actors be concluded to hold? Routines depend on practise and can therefore only be developed by actors who have been active in the respective field. Principles can be learned in formal education, but can then be refined and improved with experience. Experience is in fact the absorption and processing of messages that question, reconfirm, or correct principles and improve routines. Which messages are received, depends on the environment in which the actor operates, his ability to interpret the message, and his interest in the message. All three are likely to be correlated with his current and recently undertaken tasks, while an individuals' understanding is also related to her education and training. Rough indicators for the practical knowledge individuals hold and how they update it are therefore their professional background and their daily field of work. Firms, public bodies and associations' competencies are similarly determined by their present and recent activities.

Such indicators may seem superficial, but are in fact commonly used due to a lack of alternatives. Stinchcombe (1990, Ch.7) finds that in selection processes seniority is roughly of equal importance to education. Due to the impossibility of measuring an individual's suitability for most jobs, seniority is taken as a 'certificate' for the individual's capability to perform the tasks that are crucial for doing the job. Regarding organisations, potential customers, for example, often base their decisions on reputation, or require a list of references, which prove that the firm has done similar work before.

4.4.2 The cost of knowledge to the core organisation

From the presentation above, it follows that the more routines actors can employ, the better their principles are, and the more relevant information about the environment they absorb, the more effective and efficient they are at carrying out the respective knowledge-related tasks. They are also faster at developing related knowledge. Becker and Murphy (1992) believe that greater knowledge raises the productivity of further investments in knowledge. Foss (1996b) states that related diversification is more profitable than unrelated diversification because it draws on existing knowledge bases, and that the more heterogeneous the activities are which are carried out in a firm, the greater the cost. Machlup (1980) points out that the clearer actors are about what they want to know, the more successful are they in their search, and the more receptive actors are towards certain issues, the cheaper new knowledge is, because any indications in the environment are realised. Thus, specialisation is advantageous from a 'knowledge' perspective. It can also bring 'economies of scale' as certain routines become worth developing if the respective activity reoccurs frequently (ultimately in form of machines), and certain information becomes worth collecting, if useful for a relevant share of decisions (Bolton and Dewatripont 1994; Madhok 1996). Projections of the future environment, which are often relevant for decision making, also tend to be more accurate.

Viewed from the perspective of the core organisation, holding decision rights over a range of assets, the optimal organisational solution from a 'knowledge perspective' would therefore be that all decision rights are handed over to specialised knowledgeable agents. This however, leads back to the delegation problems discussed previously, and the cost of overcoming them:

First, the 'knowledge gain' for the core organisation, when contracting out, is the bigger, the more unrelated and unfamiliar the activities are for which the decision rights are delegated. However, this is exactly the type of activities where the risk of 'adverse selection' and 'moral hazard' are the highest (Chi 1994; Foss 1996a; Madhok 1996). Monitoring does not help since the 'principal' does not know how the activity should be carried out, unless the outcomes are easy to measure. Otherwise the alignment of interests is essential (Cyert and Kumar 1996; Minkler 1993). Second, the more specialised actors become, being the only ones who have skills or competencies in exactly the area which is required, the more dependent core management becomes on them and exposes itself to the risk of 'hold up'. From the agent's perspective the asset specificity of knowledge is the higher, the less closely it is related to the knowledge that he can use for other purposes. Without some reassurance that his contract will be long term, an actor will be reluctant to invest in organisation specific knowledge. Third, due to their monopoly position, specially skilled agents can earn quasi-rents in the current set-up, which they will want to maintain. If they are the only ones who are in charge of searching new information related to their activity, they are likely to withhold information that could undermine their position. Cyert and Kumar (1996) explain for example incremental product-line innovations by this rationale.

It may therefore be better for the core management to retain decision rights if interests cannot be aligned or only at a high cost. This means that they themselves would have to obtain the necessary knowledge to make intelligent decisions: But in addition to the limits to acquiring knowledge that is unrelated to the knowledge a decision maker already has, and the time it takes to learn routines, the cost of knowledge acquisition rises with its tacitness, context specificity and its degree of dispersion (Galunic and Rodan 1997):

Tacitness of knowledge describes the difficulty of codifying knowledge, i.e. express it in words or numbers. Codification is necessary for knowledge transfer, unless it can be learnt by observation (Nooteboom 1992; Nonaka and Takeuchi 1995:8; OECD 1997). Tacitness therefore increases knowledge transfer costs, because it necessitates substantial investment in codification, or a prolonged or permanent interaction with the actor who holds the tacit knowledge (Galunic and Rodan 1997:14). *Context specificity of knowledge* also affects its transferability. If it is not completely clear which effects environment-specific factors have on the outcomes of certain actions, costly analyses are required to apply the knowledge successfully outside its context (Galunic and Rodan 1997). *Dispersion of knowledge* can pose a further difficulty. While skills are held by an individual, competencies reside with a number of individuals in groups, or even among groups. Short of transplanting the whole system, which may interact partly within tacit routines or in context specific ways, dispersed knowledge is difficult to transfer (Galunic and Rodan 1997; Madhok 1996).

But to stop here would still not give a complete picture of the difficulty, since there is also the problem of information. Even if a decision maker could acquire certain know-how easily at a given point in time, as the contingency theorists emphasised (Lawrence and Lorsch 1997 (1967)) he constantly needs to process information about new environmental conditions. The value of this information is determined by its recency, reliability, adequacy regarding detail, and is relative to its direct cost.[17]

The *recency* of information determines whether opportunities are lost or costly delays in decisions occur (Jensen and Meckling 1992). It depends on the closeness to the information source, in terms of physical proximity, personal contact and a shared background (Cornish 1997; Davenport 1997; Liebeskind et al. 1996; Stinchcombe 1990). Equally important is the *reliability* or *credibility* of information. Usually information is a conclusion derived from a number of observations, which are never complete or can eliminate uncertainty entirely. How adequate the conclusion is, and to which extent the degree of uncertainty can be assessed, depends on the expertise of the observer. But since even an expert might have an incentive to misrepresent information or its degree of uncertainty, or pass-on only selective information in order to deceive the recipient, reliability depends also on the interests of the observer (Cyert and Kumar 1996; Stinchcombe 1990; Milgrom 1988; Niskanen 1971). Thinking of a 'Chinese Whispers' effect, it is reasonable to expect that the reliability of information is also inversely related to the number of channels the information went through. The less knowledge the recipient has, the more difficult he will find it to distinguish good information from bad (Casson 1994). The *adequate detail of information* becomes an issue as soon as it is acknowledged that human beings can only consider limited amounts of information. Different degrees of detail and different temporal aggregations of data are relevant, depending on the specificity, complexity and time frame of decisions, and tacit elements are difficult to convey. Finally, the *direct cost* of information has to be weighed against its potential value. Jensen and Meckling (1992) argue that specific information is often a by-product of activities that will be performed anyway, and therefore comes at zero cost. But if this 'local' information has to be obtained, costs are involved, particularly if it is not precisely known which pieces of information might be relevant.

Considering these difficulties and that even the transfer of explicit knowledge and information incurs costs, one can agree with Picot, Dietl and Franck (1997) and Grant (1996) who argue that structures should make as little knowledge and information exchange necessary as possible. There have been several but compatible conclusions drawn by different authors, as to how this 'economising' on knowledge and information gathering and exchange can be achieved. Stinchcombe (1990) makes a strong case for his theory that successful organisations structure their activities in a way so that activities which rely on the same type of information are grouped together. This is a more specific version of Richardson's concept of similarity (Richardson 1972), which says that activities requiring the same ca-

[17] see Stinchcombe (1990:3ff). Apart from 'cost' he discusses all the characteristics listed here, but under different headings.

pability for their undertaking, are clustered. Dietl (1995) argues that an efficient delineation of activities chooses a 'knowledge maturity' criterion for the points of interchange. 'Knowledge maturity' means that the product of the activity can be used by the next actor in the chain, without having to have any knowledge about the previous production process. In cases where knowledge and information exchange between individuals with different expertise and backgrounds is essential, be it because new products need to be developed or the structure of interchanges needs to be redesigned, bringing the actors together physically for some time is essential to improve knowledge and information transfer (Nonaka and Takeuchi 1995).

4.4.3 Summary

Organisation determines what knowledge is available and used when decisions in pursuit of the core organisations' goal are taken. It was postulated that there is a trade-off between choosing specialised 'knowledgeable' actors, whose incentives have to be aligned via costly incentive mechanisms, and actors who have more self-interest in the organisational goal but have to acquire the knowledge that is necessary to employ their decision rights intelligently.

In reality there is always a mixture of the two, since any economic activity, except maybe subsistence farming, relies on a co-ordination of exchanges with other economic actors. Different structures imply different choices regarding the need of transferring knowledge and setting incentives.

When judging the solutions of existing organisations, the question of incentives can be addressed by employing the framework outlined in the previous section of the chapter. Based on this section, the questions, what knowledge is available and how expensive is the acquisition of additional knowledge and information, can be tentatively answered by an analysis of the following points:

- which tasks and decision rights do actors have within the structure?
- which principles, routines and information are relevant for an effective task fulfilment?
- what do the actors know, judging from their professional background and their major past and present activities?
- how much additional knowledge do the actors have to acquire and what type of knowledge is it?
- how recent, reliable, adequate and costly is it for the decision maker to get relevant information, judging from the actors position?
- which incentive do the actors have, to get it?
- which options are there to give the tasks to more knowledgeable and informed actors?

Any answers to these questions will not do justice to the high complexity of an organisation's knowledge and information environment. Describing what knowledge a decision maker has at the time of her decision, which of an unlimited number of information sources she has access to, or how the knowledge and information are used in the work process, are futile objectives. But in order to understand some of the knowledge aspects of organisational structures 'without insisting on measuring the non-measurable' (Machlup 1980:177), the outlined approach should provide a reasonable starting point.

4.5 Organisational adaptability

4.5.1 Conditions for adaptability

Organisational adaptability, or flexibility, refers to an organisation's ability to adapt its structures to a changed environment.

As discussed above, especially in the context of property rights theory, prevalent institutions, technologies, and scarcity conditions influence organisations. Together they form the framework within which choices for a delegation of decision rights and rights to returns are made. If any aspect of this framework changes, it possibly influences the cost–benefit characteristics of the previously chosen exchange conditions. In order to be effective and efficient in a dynamic sense, an organisation therefore has to be able to adjust to the new situation.

Again, the question is perceived from the perspective of the core organisation's management. A goal-oriented response to changes in the environment will only occur if:

- the relevant actors know that crucial environmental variables have changed, and that there is a need for adaptation
- they want to implement appropriate changes
- they have the decision rights to implement changes.

In the context of Chapter 3 and the discussion of 'incentives' and 'knowledge' above, ways to approach the first two questions in an empirical context were already presented. Major players may have an interest in keeping their entitlements when new conditions suggest that a different distribution of property rights would be more efficient, and they therefore may not report the information. Outsiders to the organsiation may also give wrong signals for rent-seeking purposes. It is therefore important to assess how the core management gets informed about changes in the environment. The next question is which incentives the management themselves have, when faced with a decision about changing structures and outputs. Sharfman and Dean (1997) have confirmed the relevance of this factor for flexibility empirically, and it can be assessed as outlined above.

Here, a framework for assessing the third aspect of adaptability features raised by OE theorists remains to be developed – the decision-making powers of the core management about adaptations in the organisational structure.

4.5.2 Aspects and dimensions of adaptability and managements' decision rights

Williamson's hierarchy vs. market argument is based on the notion that in cases of asset specificity a hierarchy is more adaptable. This is the case because of 'fiat' – the management of the core organisation can pursue sequential adaptations to changes without needing to consult or revise inter-firm agreements. But given institutions like labour law, the risk of sunk cost, etc. there are also grounds to argue that in many cases adaptability is easier in markets. It seems that the decision rights have to be considered within a specific empirical context, rather than assuming greater flexibility of one form of organisation per se (see 'A static approach', 3.5.3).

Several empirical studies regarding firm flexibility have been based on the 'model of the flexible firm', developed by Atkinson and his colleagues at the Institute of Manpower Studies (Atkinson and Meager 1986; Pollert 1989; Hewitt-Dundas 1997; Pinch et al. 1991). While it focuses on labour flexibility, postulating that a flexible firm has core workers who are functionally flexible and peripheral workers who are numerically flexible, the distinction between 'functional adaptability' and 'numerical adaptability' is useful as a more general concept.

Functional adaptability relates to an organisation's ability to adapt to changing tasks in pursuit of its goal, either by producing different types of outputs, or by producing outputs differently. Examples are export promotion activities relating to former COMECON countries, which had to be completely revised after the end of the Cold War; or the advance of information technology that has made it possible to publish information on the Internet instead of sending out printed documents. *Numerical adaptability* refers to an organisation's ability to change the quantity of its outputs, responding to changes in demand. Certain activities might become redundant and others may gain in importance. But the demand might also simply fluctuate without any clear trend, like for example the interest in Latin America as an export and investment market.

The question is, whether management can make decisions about restructuring and whether they have the decision rights over the use of resources that are necessary to implement the change. In addition, there may be provisions for 'automated' responses to some type of changes in the environment, in the sense that core management does not need to make an active decision about a change, but that respective other actors in the organisation would know about and have the incentive to respond appropriately, e.g. to fluctuations in demand.

Taking that the basic ingredients for any organisational activity are human effort, financial resources, and physical assets, core management and the other actors have to be able to make decisions about all three input factors. It is also relevant at what speed and financial cost the adjustments can occur.

Flexibility regarding labour and human capital inputs is determined by the freedom of choice regarding collaborators and subcontractors who have the required skills and competences, and by the freedom to allocate tasks. This is linked to the freedom of designing or altering the incentive structures for the actors, including the length of contracts.[18]

A second aspect of the freedom of reallocating tasks, cancelling redundant activities and introducing new ones, are the decision rights over financial resources. In the public sector this right is often limited, and regulations as to which other actors have to agree can slow down the re-allocation process.

For many manufacturing firms specific physical assets are a major constraint to flexibility because of their 'sunk cost nature' and the financial requirements of alternative physical inputs. Service production relies less on such inputs. The 'second best use' value of major physical assets like office space or office equipment is generally not much lower than for the original purpose. An exception might be purpose-designed software, databases and computer systems, the significance of which depend on their importance for certain activities. But despite of the low-asset specificity of most of the physical inputs, the question is still to which extent core management can make decisions about purchasing, selling or leasing such inputs.

Possible institutional constraints to all three types of decision rights are summarized in Table 4.2. (next page).

These considerations suggest that organisational adaptability increases if the core management and other actors have wide-ranging decision powers. But again, trade-offs with the two other variables, incentives and knowledge, seem to exist. Given actors' self-interest they might take advantage of their decision rights. For example, the inflexible procedures regulating public officials' discretion in spending were specifically designed in order to control the use of public funds. There may also be knowledge-related costs, since higher skilled actors are needed if directives cannot be used for a co-ordination of activities, and since constant changes prohibit the development of routines and the capacity to produce collective products of a given quality repeatedly' (Hannan and Freeman 1984:149). In addition Volberda (1996) states that too great a reaction capacity or too short a reaction time may lead to overreaction, excessive information search and wasted researches. He refers to Weick, who concluded that total flexibility makes it impossible for the organisation to retain a sense of identity and continuity and that flexibility must be the middle course between rigidity and overreaction.

---

[18] Maguire (1993) gives an overview about pay flexibility in the public sector. It is seen as a solution to problems in recruiting and retaining public sector staff as well as a managerial tool for structuring relative task-attached incentives.

Table 4.2. Aspects and dimensions of adaptability

	Functional flexibility –Type of output and production procedure		*Numerical Flexibility – Quantity of output*	
tasks and input factors	*allocation of decision rights*	*possible institution. constraints*	*allocation of decision rights*	*possible institution. constraints*
tasks	• decision rights regarding which outputs are the most appropriate for achieving the goal	• legal constraints on which task can/must be carried out • conventions	• decision rights regarding the quantities of service delivery	• prescribed quantities • prescribed prices
human effort and knowledge	own employees • decision right on whom to employ, whom to make redundant • decision right to allocate new tasks to employees and train them • decision right to vary the level of compensation for different tasks or qualifications • decision right on which activities can be outsourced other agents: • decision right to buy in expertise • decision right to choose agents • decision right to co-operate with other agents • decision right to terminate or re-negotiate contracts	• employees are allocated • permanent contracts • prescribed formal qualifications • job demarcation • fixed salaries and wage compression • type of contracts	own employees: • decision rights on whom to employ and whom to make redundant • decision rights in designing employee contracts, incl. options on overtime or short time other agents: • decision rights to subcontract work • decision rights in contract design	• lifetime employment (legal obligation as well as practical obligation or constraint, e.g. because of redundancy payments) • restrictions to contracts with limited work hours • long-term fixed contracts • general employment law
financ. resources (size and continuity of the budget)	• decision right to allocate budget • decision right to borrow/save • decision right to attract private sector funds	• rigid expenditure posts which cannot be transferred to other uses • public finance law	• decision right to allocate budget • decision right to borrow/save • decision right to charge for services or subsidise services • decision right to attract private sector funds	• public finance law
physical assets (e.g. office space, computer systems)	• decision right to rent, lease, rent out, buy, sell	• public administrative law • government/departmental regulations • contracts	• decision right to rent, lease, rent out, buy, sell	• public administrative law • government/departmental. regulations • contracts

4.6 An outline for assessing incentives, knowledge and adaptability

The structures of existing organisations determine how different tasks in pursuit of a goal are divided into activities, who the decision-making actors are, and which rights and obligations over residual results the actors hold. Organisation thereby links certain activities and decision rights with certain knowledge and certain incentives to act.

The previous sections have discussed which key questions need to be asked in an empirical context, to determine the impact of the links between organisational structures and the knowledge and incentives of actors on goal attainment, both at a specific point in time as well as in view of a changing environment.

- Which tasks and activities are undertaken to reach the organisation's goal?
- Who are the activities assigned to and which decision rights do these actors have?
- What do these actors know, judging from their major past and present activities and their ways of obtaining information in view of the respective task?
- Which different courses of action could they take, given their decision rights, and from which do they benefit most, taking into account their goals?
- What effect is this knowledge combined with these incentives likely to have on the attainment of the organisational goal?
- How is the organisation likely to respond to changes in the environment, given information flows, the incentives of the affected actors, and the decision rights of the core management and other actors in the organisation?
- For the core management, what are the costs of ensuring the relevant knowledge and its updating with information, given the characteristics of the knowledge and information required for the tasks?
- For the core management, what are the costs of providing the incentive structure, given the characteristics of the exchanges and the actors goals?
- For the core management, what are the costs of implementing numerical and functional changes to adapt the pursuit of the organisational goal to changes in the environment?

Throughout the chapter it is apparent that there are links between the different variables: What knowledge is acquired and is updated is related to incentives; which incentives agents have to 'cheat' is partly related to the knowledge of the principal; and the organisation's adaptability is linked to knowledge about the need for change and incentives to implement change. These links seem to work in some cases as trade-offs, e.g. efficient routines may counteract adaptability; highly adaptable structures may have negative implications for incentives; and those actors with the highest incentives to contribute to the organisational goal may not be those with the best knowledge of how to do it.

It has also become apparent from the literature review and the discussion that it is impossible to make quantitative cost–benefit statements, including quantitative judgements of trade-offs. Regarding the question of incentives for example, there is plenty of evidence that actors respond to incentives much as predicted by OE, but so far researchers have a poor understanding of the magnitude of incentive effects (Gerhart 1992; Lawler 1992; Macleod 1995). Even less is known about knowledge and adaptability, not to speak of trade-offs within and between the variables. Applied empirically, the model and this framework of analysis can therefore not produce any quantitative, or absolute results. Instead, the attempt will be to tightly integrate the available evidence into this conceptual framework, and by presenting the different arguments and conclusions transparently, give the reader the opportunity to judge how capable the approach is of providing coherent explanations for the relationship between 'organisation' and 'efficiency and effectiveness'.

Chapter 5: The research design

5.1 Overview

As set out in Chapter 1, many governments have shown increasing concern about their countries' international trade performance, and a growing interest in the contributions of small and medium sized firms to their economies. These preoccupations have triggered an enlarged interest in export support services for SMEs, and, as in other areas of public sector services, considerations of how to deliver them efficiently and effectively.

What underlies governments' reviews of their export promotion activities are the beliefs that:

- organisation matters for the efficiency and effectiveness of export support services delivery
- a restructuring of the export support services delivery will lead to higher efficiency and effectiveness, i.e. that an organisation A is better than an organisation B.

As stated in Chapter 1, the primary research objective here is to identify whether there is a causal link between 'organisation' and 'outputs', as well as 'costs of outputs', and then use the result to look also into the second assumption.

In Chapter 3 a theory-based model was developed which stipulates that there is a causal link, i.e. it supports the assumption that organisation matters. The model, and the subsequent discussion of its variables in Chapter 4 also suggests that different organisations might imply trade-offs in the factors that influence efficiency and effectiveness, and that organisational choices are framed by the environment, in particular by institutions. Consequently one organisation might not be more efficient and effective than another, and what is an effective and efficient organisation within one environment might not be the same when placed in another. In the following three chapters these propositions will be analysed empirically.

This chapter presents the research design and provides some contextual information about the organisations. First, it explains why a case study approach was chosen, and how a 'pattern matching technique' is going to be applied in the analysis. Then it puts forward the rationale for the choice of the two cases – the German and the British trade fair organisations – sets the cases into the context of the overall government export promotion efforts in the two countries, and explains in more detail the content and close similarities of the trade fair programmes.

Next, the benchmarks for 'effectiveness' are developed, followed by an overview of the information sources that were used to research the cases.

5.2 The research strategy

5.2.1 Comparative case studies

In the social sciences there are different strategies that can be employed when researching a topic, including: surveys, experiments, computer-based analyses of archival records (e.g. census data), and case studies. Each has its advantages and disadvantages and is more or less appropriate for a specific research question. According to Bryman (1995:173), case studies are a suitable means to investigate those management processes and aspects of organisational functioning that are *'not well documented and not amenable through fleeting contact with organisations'*. Other authors emphasise the potential of case study approaches to deal with complexity, to permit detailed examinations of processes, to capture context, to allow multiple sources of evidence, and to deal with events that cannot be influenced by the researcher (Orum et al. 1991; Yin 1994; Campbell 1998).

In view of the framework developed in the previous two chapters all these features are relevant. The units of interest are complex export support organisations set within specific institutional contexts. Their structures cannot be manipulated by the researcher to investigate cause–effect relationships, which makes a research strategy based on experiments impossible. The framework implies that to analyse the efficiency and effectiveness of the organisations, information about the participating actors and their specific roles is needed; their knowledge and incentives have to be assessed in relation to the tasks for which they are responsible; and information about the outputs of the organisations is required. Most of these issues are not documented. And although the framework implies the same themes for questions in each case, the specific questions that need to be asked differ with each actor and task, since actors' roles vary from organisation to organisation and task to task. Both surveys and analyses of archival records, therefore, did not promise to produce the required information. The case study strategy, which allows a variety of evidence to provide a full description of complex circumstances, appeared the most suitable for the topic.

Such a strategy implies that the analysis of a single case is resource intensive, which is why researchers often choose single case studies. Here a comparative research design was considered more suitable to investigate the second of the assumptions underlying public sector re-organisation, i.e. that one organisation may be 'better' than another one and to get a better insight into the relevance of institutions for organisations. A comparison of the evidence for two cases, whose analysis was structured by the same framework, also facilitates judgements about the validity of the framework, and makes generalisations more credible (Bryman 1995:171). Because 'government export promotion' in fact consists of many different organisations, each of which produce and deliver a specific programme, the case study research strategy required the selection not only of the countries of comparison, but also of the export promotion programme to be analysed. The rationale for selecting trade fair support in Britain and Germany is explained in section 5.2.1. below.

The case studies should be read as 'instrumental case studies' (Stake 2000:437ff). Government trade fair support in the UK and Germany is examined to provide an insight into the effects of export support organisations on the knowledge and incentives of its actors, the adaptability of the organisation, and in turn on the outputs and costs of outputs. The cases are used to investigate how the variables and the cause–effect links that Organisational Economics identified manifest themselves empirically. The objective is to draw conclusions about the assumptions underlying organisational restructuring.

5.2.2 The pattern matching technique

For Yin (1994:106), *'one of the most desirable strategies in case study analysis is to use a pattern-matching logic'* as promoted by Trochim (1989). An empirically-based pattern is compared with a predicted one to find out whether the patterns coincide. If they do, this supports the cause–effect propositions of the theoretical model on which the predictions are based. The approach also provides a certain rigor regarding the collection of evidence. Trochim (1989) acknowledges that all research employs pattern-matching principles, though seldom consciously. But for him *'the differences between pattern matching and more traditional hypothesis testing approaches are that pattern matching encourages the use of more complex or detailed hypotheses, and treats the observations from a multivariate rather than a univariate perspective'*.

In the case of this research, the template, against which the empirical results of two case studies are to be compared, is the 'model' that was developed in Chapter 3. It postulates that organisation, via its impact on actors' knowledge, actors' incentives, and the structure's adaptability, shapes the effectiveness and efficiency with which services are produced and delivered at a given point in time, and over time. In other words, the 'intermediary variables' of the 'model' are knowledge, incentives, and adaptability; the 'dependent variables' are effectiveness and efficiency.

To apply a pattern-matching logic requires the comparison of predictions with observations. Here, only relative – not absolute – predictions are possible. The 'model' can, for example, predict that deeper task-related knowledge of an actor leads to higher effectiveness and efficiency, all other variables remaining equal. But it does not allow the prediction that a certain quantity and quality of knowledge A, combined with incentives B, and adaptability C, lead to efficiency Y, and effectiveness Z. Equally, empirical observations regarding the variable 'knowledge' of an actor to do a certain task (see Chapter 4) allow only a relative value judgement, e.g. one actor has 'less knowledge' regarding a certain task than another. This means that a pattern-matching logic on the basis of this model is only possible in terms of comparisons.

In principle, there are three ways of comparing the effects of changes in the intermediary variables: 1. to compare two different organisations; 2. to compare the effects of modifications of one organisation by looking at all variables before and after the modification; and 3. to compare a real organisation with a hypothetical organisation.

The first two approaches are more difficult than the last, because of the richness of the data needed: The 'production' and delivery of trade fair support services consists of a chain of activities, each of which involves a number of actors that carry out different tasks. This leads to many variables, i.e. the incentives and the knowledge of all actors who are involved with regard to each task, and the efficiency and effectiveness with which each task is carried out. To compare two organisations' effects, 'data' has to be collected in a way that allows comparisons, i.e. the observations have to match each other. In the case of the chosen case studies, not enough empirical material is available to compare one country's solution at two different points in time, and the empirical material that is available about the two countries' organisations matches only in general, but not in detail.

Therefore, the third approach was chosen as a major component of the analysis. In Chapter 6 the German trade fair support organisation will be compared with a hypothetical 'ideal organisation', followed by the same approach for the British case in Chapter 7.

Based on the 'model', the ideal organisation is characterised by involving actors who have perfect knowledge of and commitment to their tasks, and carry them out in the way that contributes best to the overall objective of the organisation. The core actor knows when a changing environment requires the adaptation of the organisational structures, and is able and motivated to do this. The real organisations can then be characterised in terms of their shortcomings in comparison with the ideal organisation. On this basis a prediction can be made as to how the shortcomings regarding these 'intermediary' variables are expected to affect the 'dependent variables'. If the expected pattern corresponds with the observed pattern, the assumption that organisation matters for effectiveness through its impact on the intermediary variables is substantiated.

To use this approach in practise requires that the 'ideal' variables are defined in relation to the actual case. It is necessary to define the goal of the organisation to make statements about 'effectiveness'. It is also necessary to define the major activities that make up the service production and delivery. Each of the activities has an output objective on its own, which is necessary to achieve the overall goal. Each of the activities involves certain actors, whose ideal knowledge and incentives have to be defined in relation to the output objective. Once specified, the output objectives can be used as a benchmark for judging the effectiveness of the real organisations regarding that activity, and the 'ideal' knowledge and incentives can be used as a benchmark for judging the actors. In section 5.3 of this chapter, the overall goals, activities, output objectives and characteristics of ideal actors are developed, based on the trade fair programmes in Britain and Germany, and on the literature about successful trade fair participations. First, however, the rationale for choosing the cases and their setting in the export promotion programmes of the two countries are presented.

5.3 The units of analysis and their context

5.3.1 The rationale for the choice of the cases

Why trade fair support rather than another export support programme?
Both, preliminary desk research and a first round of interviews with government and business representatives showed the importance of trade fair support in government export promotion:

International trade fairs are a growing business. In 1990, for example, there were around 450 recognised trade fairs in Asia; six years later there were 1,100 (AUMA 1997a:29). Even in Europe and the United States trade fair markets grew by approximately 30% in both the 1980s and 1990s (Dekimpe et al. 1997:55). For manufacturers these exhibitions have become the most important marketing tool after direct sales, accounting for one-fifth to one-third of their marketing budget (Econ-Consult and ISG 1994; Herbig et al. 1996b).

This development is related to trade fairs' unique features as 'low-cost, high-density information exchanges under space–time constraints' (Florio 1994:267). They bring potential buyers and sellers of a product to one location at a given time and can thereby lower the search and contracting costs for both. This is especially relevant for SMEs that produce niche products, and, in an overseas context where communication with customers and potential customers is particularly expensive. Exhibitors can pursue direct selling and advertising objectives simultaneously. At a small per-contact cost, they have access to a qualified target audience, who usually have an influence on procurement in their firms. This gives exhibitors the opportunity to generate new high-quality leads, uncover potential customers, and introduce and test the response to new products. They can obtain a visibility, which SMEs in particular find difficult to get by other means. They can also get an overview of competitors and the market place, find business and distribution partners, and maintain personal contacts with existing customers (Rosson and Seringhaus 1991b; O'Hara et al. 1993; Meffert 1996; Herbig et al. 1996a;b; Dekimpe et al. 1997; Tanner 1997; Thoene 1997; Seringhaus and Rosson 1998; Shoham 1999).

Based on these arguments, and the fact that it is costly and requires knowledge to exhibit abroad, governments help firms to participate at overseas trade fairs (DTI and FCO 1996:41; Deutscher Bundestag 2001). Trade fair support programmes are probably the oldest form of official export support[1], and they are the most widespread central government export promotion tool[2]. The programmes receive the largest share of the export support budget in most countries (Nothdurft

[1] For example Louis XI planned to organise a trade fair in London in 1470 to promote French products (Thoene 1997). The German dukedom of Württemberg supported their firms' participation at trade fairs abroad in the middle of the 19th century (Zwonieck 1988).

[2] The Swedish government is the only EU government that does not subsidise trade fair participations abroad (Deutscher Bundestag 2001). Outside the EU, for example Poland, Switzerland, the Czech Republic, Hungary, Canada, the United States, Japan, South Korea, Singapore, and Thailand do provide trade fair support (Information from AUMA).

1992:51) and they are important to the business community (all interviewees). In policy discussions trade fair support, unlike other export promotion programmes, is not questioned (Engelhard 1992:91; Habuda, Hilpert et al. 1998b), and some research points to trade fair support as one of the more effective means of export promotion (Rosson and Seringhaus 1991b; Wilkinson and Brouthers 2000b).

But there are also voices that claim the explanation for the programmes' popularity lies mainly in their tangibility, not in their effectiveness. Nothdurft (1992:51) cited a Danish export promotion officer who thinks: "trade shows are weak, but they are very visible and politicians like them." Seringhaus and Rosson warned that there is an element of unquestioned faith in the usefulness of trade fair support. One of their own studies came to the conclusion that firms participating in assisted trade fairs often appear to do so ineffectively (Seringhaus and Rosson 1998:400). The British National Audit Office came to the conclusion that the British trade fair programme was effective in generating additional exports, but was not necessarily cost effective compared to other export promotion services (NAO 1996:32). So although there seems to be no question about the importance of trade fairs in the international marketing process, there are doubts whether the government trade fair programmes function well. Could this be related to the organisation of the programmes?

Why Germany and the UK?

The choice of Germany and the United Kingdom as case studies has been determined by the fact that in terms of public sector service delivery organisation, they are contrasting examples, whereas in terms of the role of exports and the role of SMEs in the economy, they are similar.

The United Kingdom has been one of the countries at the forefront of the New Public Management (NPM) movement. Over the past 20 years there has been a continuous programme of reforms in public service delivery. The emphasis has been on cost consciousness, higher quality services, improved accountability, 'downsizing' and 'delayering', which has resulted in a reduction of the civil service by over a third between 1976 and 1997 (Dowding 1995; Cabinet Office 1998). In Germany on the other hand, there have been no major reform initiatives at the federal level (Klages and Loeffler 1996). The country has therefore often been used as a contrast example in comparative discussions of public sector reform (Hood 1995; Pollitt and Boukaert 2000; James 2001).

The differences between the two countries have been reflected in the organisation of export support. Out of a group of industrialised countries – USA, Canada, Japan, France, the UK and Austria – the UK is the country that has changed its export support organisation structures most during the last decade (Habuda et al. 1998a:84). In Germany the organisation has remained the same. Trade fair support, as the particular service of interest here, is a case example (see below). Also, according to the literature, the United Kingdom has the most unified and centralised organisational structures for the delivery of government export support services (Habuda et al. 1998b). Germany, in contrast, has been described as a country where export promotion has been largely left to the private sector, with some assistance provided by different federal institutions (Seringhaus and Rosson 1990; Camino 1991; Deutscher Bundestag 2000a).

But even though there have been pronounced differences in the approaches to organising export services delivery, in terms of the 'target area' the two countries are similar. Both are among the five leading exporting nations whose economies depend significantly on overseas trade. Germany is the second-largest exporter of merchandise after the United States and the fourth largest exporter of commercial services. Britain ranks fifth for merchandise, and second for services (WTO 2000a). In both countries exports account for nearly one third of GDP, and in both countries about one-quarter of jobs depend on exports (BMWI 2001; DTI and Treasury 2001:151). Both countries are concerned about their trade performance. Although the UK increased its volume of merchandise exports from 110 billion in 1980 to 273 billion in 1998, its share of world exports dropped from 5.4% to 5.0%. Moreover, the country's negative trade balance for merchandise increased steadily from 5.4 billion in 1980 to 59.1 billion in 2001. The deficits could not be balanced out by the trade surpluses in services, which reached 19.9 billion in 2001 (WTO 2001b;c). Germany has kept a positive balance of trade throughout the nineties, but the balance of trade in services has been negative since 1990. An even stronger cause of concern has been the increasingly negative balance of trade in merchandise with some high-growth countries like China, Korea, or Taiwan (Deutscher Bundestag 1995a; BMWI 2001; Süddeutsche Zeitung 22.2.1996). Moreover, Germany has also lost global market share, which dropped from 9.6% in 1990 to 8.7% in 2000 (WTO 2001a).

Regarding SME involvement in overseas trade, neither of the countries produce statistics that relate their exports to firm sizes of the exporters (Bannock and Daly 1994; Deutscher Bundestag 1995a; BMWi 1997; Bank of England 1998:3). But in both countries SMEs play a more important role in the domestic market than as exporters: The German definition of 'SMEs' covers firms with fewer than 500 employees and less than 50 million Euro turnover (ca. £ 33 million). In 1999 3.3 million, or 99.6% of all taxable companies in Germany were SMEs. They accounted for 46% of gross investment, and 69.3% of employment. In the UK, of the entire business population of 3.7 million 99.9% had fewer than 500 employees. They accounted for 60% of all non-government employment, of which the majority (48.6%) was in firms with up to 100 employees (Deutscher Bundestag 2000c; Small Business Service 2001). Using VAT/HM Customs and Excise data, the DTI estimated that in 1995 the number of active British exporters was between 110,000 and 115,000, i.e. only about 3% of the business population (Bank of England 1998). Survey data indicated that about 40% were firms with more than 200 employees, and that the propensity to export rose with business size (DTI 1996). A study from the 1980s came to the conclusion that only 14% of manufacturing firms with a turnover of less than £1 million exported, while 72% of those with more than £100 million did (Bannock and Peacock 1989). For Germany there are no figures regarding the number and size of exporters, but export activity also declines with firm size. While in 1994 manufacturing companies with fewer than 500 employees contributed nearly 46% to overall turnover, their contribution to export turnover was only 30%. For companies with fewer than 50 employees the respective figures were 8% and 2.5%. The average export quota of manufacturing firms in Germany was 27.4%, whereas for firms with up to 50 employees it was only 8.9% (BMWi 1997). Both governments have been striving to improve the national trade performance by increasing SMEs' export activities (BTI 1999; BMWi 2000).

In conclusion, as far as such comparisons can go, Germany and the UK appeared to be suitable case study choices. They seemed to differ significantly regarding the topic of investigation, i.e. organisation, whereas the differences in the areas that are targeted by the organisations appeared not very large.

5.3.2 Export promotion in Germany and the United Kingdom

Having given the reasons for the choice of case studies, and some first comparative information, the next section describes the settings of the cases. It sketches governments' export support in the two countries to provide some information on the operational environment of the respective trade fair support organisations and to introduce the core actors of the two organisations.

5.3.2.1 Germany

The organisation of the German export support services is characterised by the involvement of multiple public and private sector actors, who offer export services that are not interconnected. The major objective is to help SMEs compete in international markets. SMEs are perceived to be disadvantaged in comparison with large companies, especially with regard to information about foreign markets, the establishment of overseas business contacts, and their experience in judging market risks and obstacles. Accordingly, trade fair support and the supply of information and advice are the key policy components. Some instruments to facilitate export finance complement them (Deutscher Bundestag 1995a; 2000a).

Trade fair support is the biggest federal government export support service. In 2000 DM70 million (ca.GB£23m) were assigned to it in the federal budget (Deutscher Bundestag 2000a). According to the Government, trade fairs play an 'outstanding role' in the development of new markets. By significantly reducing the cost of exhibiting at selected fairs abroad, and by facilitating the exhibition process, the government aims to encourage SMEs' use of this tool (Deutscher Bundestag 1995a). Trade fair support is the only service in which the 'Ministry of Economics and Labour' (BMWi) is directly involved, although the ministry is in charge of export promotion overall. A department within BMWi is the core actor in the trade fair support organisation (see below).

Information and advice is provided via the so-called 'three pillars' of German export promotion: the overseas chambers of commerce (Aussenhandelskammern – AHKs), the government agency for overseas trade information (Bundesagentur fuer Aussenwirtschaft – BfAI), and the diplomatic posts overseas:

The AHKs are a network of 115 bilateral chambers, 'delegation offices' and representations in 77 countries, where German firms sell 97% of their exported goods and services. All provide the same basic set of services: general enquiry services, market research and individual advisory services, as well as support with the legal, administrative, and financial procedures that exporters and investors are required to undergo in the respective host country. Clients for a service have to pay a fee. The AHKs are set up as independent, private sector bodies by the umbrella association of the German Chambers of Industry and Commerce (Deutscher Industrie- und Handelskammertag – DIHK). Their executive board and membership consist of business representatives from Germany and the host country (Deutscher Bundestag 1995a; 1998; 2000c). According to figures provided by the DIHK to the British Foreign Office, the federal government provided 40% of the total £55 million budget for the AHKs in 1998. The rest came from the private sector, mainly in the form of membership fees, and revenues from services (Foreign Affairs Committee 1999). In 2000 the government subsidy for AHKs was DM65 million (ca. £21) (Deutscher Bundestag 2000a).

BfAI, - the 'Federal Agency for Overseas Trade Information', is an executive agency of BMWi. It was created in 1951 to facilitate firms' export decisions with market- and product-specific information (Deutscher Bundestag 2000c). BfAI has its own network of 45 correspondents abroad, and 170 employees in Cologne. They produce newsletters, reports, and databases that are sold on subscription or individually. They also offer customised data searches, and publish sales leads. BfAI raises a small percentage of its income (ca 8% in 1995) from the sale of its publications, but the bulk comes from government, which provided DM41 million (ca. £ 14 m) in 2000 (Interviewees D-X; D-Y; Deutscher Bundestag 2000a).

A third source of export market information and advice are the German 'foreign posts'. The 150 German embassies and 68 general consulates provide businesses with a first contact point for general country information. They can support the concerns of German companies on a political level and can represent them, where necessary, vis-à-vis the foreign government decision makers. They also work on reducing entry barriers for firms. However, they stop short of providing detailed market analyses or legal information. Any such enquiry is handed to the AHKs. Budget information regarding their export promotion tasks is not available (Deutscher Bundestag 1995a; 1998; 2000c).

Export finance and finance for some investments abroad are facilitated by government-backed credits, insurances, and investment protection guarantees against political risk. The most important instrument is the export credit insurance scheme, where the government assumes responsibility for both political and commercial risks. Since its introduction in 1926 Hermes, the largest private credit insurance company in Germany, has managed the scheme in consortium with an accountancy firm. Subsidised interest rate export credits and overseas investments credits are scarce, and have usually development aid and foreign policy objectives. They are managed chiefly by the state-owned development bank 'Kreditanstalt für Wiederaufbau' (KFW) (Walzenbach 1998:138ff; Service Verbund Aussenwirtschaft 2001).

In addition to these export promotion programmes on the federal level, all German states have their own autonomous export promotion programmes and agencies, that cost around DM120 million (£40 million) (Ehrenfeld 1997). They provide similar and additional services (Interviewees in Baden Wuerttemberg and North Rhine Westphalia; Ehrenfeld 1997; BMWi 1995). Moreover, the Ministries of Economic Co-operation and Development, the Ministry of Education and Research, and the Ministry for the Environment, Nature Conservation and Nuclear Safety have their own little export promotion programmes. There are also private sector initiatives (Kiefer 1996; Habuda et al. 1998a).

This picture of German government export promotion efforts was essentially the same in the 1980s (Seringhaus and Rosson 1990; BMWi 1990; Engelhard 1992). The few small changes made were responses to persistent criticisms from the private sector and opposition parties. They have argued that the diverse export promotion activities have lacked a unified strategy and that the different actors have not been co-ordinated; they have criticised the non-transparency of support for the client SMEs; its inefficiency due to a fuzzy task distribution between the actors; too little interaction with the private sector; and a lack of political effort to influence foreign governments (BMWi 1995; Deutscher Bundestag1995a; 1995c; 1998; 2000b; BDI 1996; BGA 1996; Weidig and Ruprecht 1996; Habuda et al. 1998a). The government responded by introducing various new initiatives: an inter-ministerial committee for export promotion issues[3] in 1995; a federal government – states committee[4] in 1996; a federal government – states trade fair committee[5] in 1996; and an online-database 'IXPOS' (www.ixpos.de) about the available export support services in 2000. Also, over the 1990s, the diplomatic posts shifted their focus somewhat towards commercial work (Deutscher Bundestag 1995a; 1995c; Die Welt 17.2.1998) But despite these continuing criticisms, the government has not seen any reason to change the organisational structures for export promotion in general and trade fair support in particular (Deutscher Bundestag 1995a; 1998).

5.3.2.2 The United Kingdom

In the United Kingdom, similar and additional export services as in Germany are provided by the state. But in contrast to the German structure, with its variety of responsible parties, Britain has one government body with lead responsibility for export support:

'British Trade International' (BTI) was created in May 1999, following a Cabinet Office review of all government export promotion activities. The review had involved consultation with industry and business organisations, and had recommended far-reaching changes to the organisation of official overseas trade and investment support (DTI and FCO 1999). As a result all trade promotion work of the Department of Trade and Industry (DTI) and the Foreign and Commonwealth Office (FCO) was brought under the new BTI umbrella. In May 2000 the previously separate 'Invest in Britain Bureau' was also integrated into BTI. In the context of that expansion the name 'Trade Partners UK' (TPUK) has come to be used for the

[3] Interministerieller Ausschuß Außenwirtschaft

[4] Bund Länder Ausschuß Außenwirtschaft

[5] Bund Länder Ausschuß Auslandsmessen

BTI section that is responsible for trade support, as opposed to the other arm, now called 'Invest UK' (Hansard 2000; DTI et al. 2001).

BTI's chief executive is responsible for the performance of the entire organisation. He reports to the Secretary of State for Trade and Industry (DTI), the Foreign and Commonwealth Secretary (FCO), and to the Board of BTI, which is chaired jointly by DTI and FCO Ministers. The Board sets BTI's strategy and objectives, and decides about the allocation of resources across the organisation. Its other 17 members come from the private sector (7), the devolved administrations (3), local development agencies (2), and other government, or government related bodies. In addition BTI has industry-focused and geographically-focused private sector advisory groups. The services are provided by staff spread between the BTI offices and regional government offices in the UK (DTI staff), and over 200 diplomatic posts overseas (FCO commercial staff) (DTI et al. 2001).

The programme focus[6] – as in Germany – is on measures to facilitate market access, as well as on information and advice (DTI and FCO 1999). Recently, BTI stated the intent to dedicate more resources to 'export capacity building' programmes (DTI et al. 2001). Some BTI schemes involve partial financial support, while readily available information and general export advice are provided for free. BTI's 1999–2000 expenditure for export schemes and services was estimated at £62.5 million, excluding staff cost (BTI 2000). *Export finance* is facilitated by a separate government department, the Export Credit Guarantee Department (ECGD), which also reports to the Secretary of State for Trade and Industry. ECGD provides medium- and long-term guarantees, insurance and reinsurance.

Trade fair support is only one of the BTI programmes that aim to facilitate British firms' market entry –but it is by far the largest. About £20 million annually, i.e. one-third of the total programme expenditure has been spent on it (DTI and FCO 1997:32).[7] The programme is carried out in co-operation with the foreign posts and with intermediaries, and as in Germany, it offers grant support for exhibitors as well as administrative support. In addition to fairs, firms have the choice to market their goods and services at overseas seminars. The content of the programme is described in more detail below.

Other, but much smaller 'market access' programmes include the 'Trade Missions scheme', where the government subsidises groups of UK business representatives who travel abroad to promote their goods and services in organised meetings. The 'Inward Mission Scheme' matches industry funding to bring foreign prospective buyers and journalists into the UK; and 'training initiatives' subsidise

---

6 Unless other references are provided, the programme information is based on BTI (2000).

7 In 1995 the figure for trade fairs was £ 20.7 million, out of a total expenditure of 58.3 million for the 11 most commonly used export support services (NAO, 1996). The current figures have not been published by BTI. In its 2001/2 –2003/4 expenditure plan (DTI et al. 2001) the planned expenditure is listed according to the four TPUK operational objectives. The costs of individual programmes, which could fall under several objectives, are therefore intransparent. And as the BTI objectives were formulated differently in the previous year, it is not even possible to follow changes in the expenditure plan for groups of programmes.

the training of foreigners – potential future clients or joint venture partners – in British companies.

The *provision of information and advice* is a task carried out jointly by BTI's staff in the UK, the commercial officers overseas, and 'export promoters'. Export promoters are private sector executives seconded to BTI. Based on their backgrounds they provide advice on specific markets and sectors. BTI staff in the UK process and publish general background material, political and market information, often sector information, and advice on tariffs and export regulations for each overseas market. Much of the information is published on-line on the TPUK website (www.tradepartners.gov.uk), where firms can also find information about other support services, contact addresses, and market-specific signposts and links to other websites. BTI 'market desk' staff answer individual queries. In addition, BTI publishes newsletters and reports, and runs a self-service reference library in London where export-related printed information and databases are collected. Further services include information events in co-operation with local and regional development agencies, and help with accessing information on language and cultural issues, and technical procedures like export documentation. A new package, 'Export Explorer', targets first-time exporters and those with minimal experience. It offers general export training and export counselling before a group visit to an 'easy' export market, and advice on the next steps.

Firm-specific information can be obtained through a London-based market research scheme. Another source is BTI's free export sales leads service. The leads, identified by British embassies and a number of other sources, are matched to subscribing companies' requirements. The firms are informed automatically by e-mail, and they appear in the 'National Exporters' Database' on the Internet, free of charge. Intermediaries administer both services.

Abroad, FCO commercial officers provide companies with services such as market-specific information, tailored market reports, advice about the potential demand for specific products, and help in arranging overseas publicity or with finding an agent. They can introduce business representatives to senior local officials and ministers, and lobby on behalf of British firms' for major project contracts (FCO and DTI 1996,:45). Posts also work on particular promotional initiatives.

Two additional services that cut across the categories 'information' and 'market access' are 'project support' and help with 'aid-funded business', i.e. with obtaining contracts from multinational or bilateral donors. BTI aims to ensure that firms are aware of significant project opportunities and helps with lobbying in support of a UK bid, e.g. via the diplomatic posts, or ministers.

Although the BTI structure now presents a far more centralised planning and delivery mechanism for those services, 17 other Government Departments still provide some degree of export promotion as part of their work to promote particular industries. BTI aims to co-ordinate the activities via the inter-departmental forum for export support, the 'Government Group', but according to its own report the group (only) looks at 'cross-cutting issues such as making ministerial visits overseas more effective' (DTI and FCO 1999:19). In addition to BTI and the other ministries, each of the devolved administrations has its own export support agency. Scottish Trade International, Wales Trade International, and Trade International Northern Ireland are represented on the BTI Board and on the Government Group. They provide their own supplementary programme to suit local businesses, while also providing access to the national programmes. And as in Germany, a range of private sector export support organisations (e.g. Institute of Export, Export Houses, some Chambers of Commerce etc.) also offer export support services (interviewee UK-N; DTI 1998c; DTI et al. 2001).

The current structure is the result of several changes in the delivery organisation of British export promotion over the course of the past decade: In 1989, the belief that the quality of government services could be improved by privatisation motivated a re-organisation of export services delivery. Some services were outsourced, others introduced together with chambers of commerce; private sector competition was introduced into the trade fair programme, and attempts were made to make the services self-financing within three years. (The Independent 15.1.1989, 18.1.1989; Daily Telegraph 18.1.1989; Financial Times 18.1.1989; The Economist 11.11.1989) The results were mixed, and in 1991 a new trade minister introduced further measures to improve the organisation. Under the label 'Overseas Trade Services' a joint export promotion directorate (JEPD) between DTI and FCO was created and charged with providing a general policy framework for their export promotion work. The aim was to improve the co-ordination between the two ministries to ensure a consistent and coherent presentation and delivery of export services, as well as to make commercial work more central to FCO activities. (BOTB 1994; Financial Times 15.3.1991, 22.4.1991; The Economist 11.11.1989) Over the following years some further modifications were made, including the separation of trade policy from export promotion within the DTI in 1993, and the assignment of an extra 60 officials to export promotion. About 80 'Export promoters' with a private sector background were brought in on two year contracts to give 'hands-on' advice to business, and local access to the services was introduced via Business Links – local business development agencies. The 'professionalism in trade initiative' introduced in 1995 has focused on improving export knowledge of export promotion staff, and the 'Open Menu' put forward in 1996 organised information about export services according to markets, to make it more accessible to firms. (BOTB 1993; Financial Times 5.5.1994, 13.5.1993, 25.5.1995) The Foreign Office also increased its commercial activities, dedicating more resources to export support, and making commercial success more relevant to the career of senior diplomats (Interviewees UK-N, UK-R; Daily Telegraph 1.6.1994; The Times 4.3.1997; The Independent 11.11.1996).

But by the time a new election campaign started in 1996, businesses' continued dissatisfaction with the organisation of export support services was reflected in the statements of two major political parties. The Conservative government allegedly planned to give responsibility for export services to the Foreign Office. (Financial Times 17.2.1997) It also planned to re-organise trade fair support and allocate funds through a competitive bidding system called 'Sector Challenge' (Financial Times 4.2.1997). The opposition Labour party pledged in its 'Business Manifesto' to improve government backing for British exporters (Labour Party 1996:15,17).

When the Labour party won the 1997 elections it set up two major reviews of the services, both drawing on the opinions of the private sector. Responding to criticisms similar to those in Germany – unfocused support, confusion of exporters, significant duplication and waste of limited resources, not always sufficiently trained staff, inter-departmental rivalries between FCO and DTI (BCC 1997; CBI 1997; Institute of Export 1998; Financial Times 4.7.1998, 5.11.1997, 14.10.1998; International Trade Finance 17.7.1998) – the reviews identified the need for a more coherent delivery structure with a clear branding of the services (DTI and FCO 1997; DTI and FCO 1999). BTI was then set up in May 1999 as a unified DTI-FCO export promotion agency *'with internal coherence and external clarity of identity and purpose'* (DTI and FCO 1999).

5.3.3 Trade Fair Support in Britain and Germany

In both Britain and Germany, trade fair support consists mainly of assistance for a group of at least ten firms, who exhibit at a selected overseas trade fair. The group participants benefit from having the group event organised and marketed, and from a subsidy to the cost of exhibition space and stand. In both countries the group of exhibitors also benefit from a government financed 'information stand', which serves as a contact and information point for visitors and exhibitors, and may attract journalists and official delegations (DTI 1998a; 1998b; BMWi 2000; TPUK 2001).

In Britain, as a response to a DTI consultation and the Export Forum's report (DTI and FCO 1997), since 1998/9 a small part of the trade fair support budget has been made available for smaller groups. Under a separate programme, the 'Export Explorer' programme, export-inexperienced companies can receive funding for visiting selected trade fairs without exhibiting themselves. Also, in 1999 the small 'Overseas Seminar Scheme' (ca. £0.3-0.4m p.a.) was merged with the 'Trade Fair Support Scheme' to become 'SESA' – 'Support for Exhibitions and Seminars Abroad'. But despite these innovations, the group participations continue to receive the very largest part of the SESA budget (Interviewee UK-A).

In Germany group participations also dominate, constituting about 90% of all official trade fair participations. In some cases they are combined with seminars or demonstration events. The remaining 10% are either participations that consist only of government sponsored 'information stands', or 'information centres', the latter allowing firms to exhibit some small scale items, and to book cabins for meetings without setting up their own stand at the fair. They are chosen in cases where the government considers certain markets to be important, but where firms do not see enough current market potential to incur the costs of setting up their own stand at the fair. Occasionally, the German government, like the British, also finances national industry shows abroad. In Germany there have been no changes to the programme during the last decade (Interviewees D-A; D-B; BMWi 1992; BMWi 2000).

The budgets of the two governments for trade fair support differ, but not significantly. In 1997–98 the British Government spent £16.9 m, which was 33% of the Overseas Trade Services' non-staff export promotion expenditure (BOTB 1998). The programme supported over 5600 companies to exhibit at about 300 fairs and seminars abroad (DTI 1998b). The German federal government allocated DM64.5 million (£22.8 m) of its 1997 budget to trade fair support, which was roughly 38% of its non-staff export promotion expenditure.[8] There, 5047 firms received support for exhibiting at 158 fairs worldwide. The trends for expenditures and participation numbers in both countries can be roughly compared in Figure 5.1..

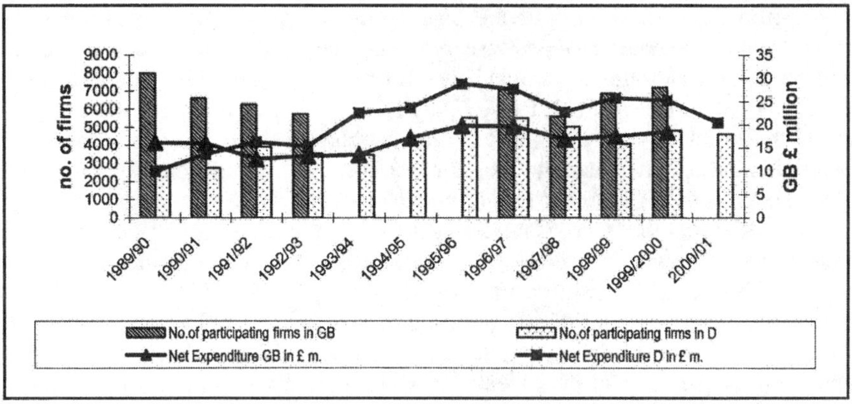

Calculations of the German government's expenditure in £ Sterling are based on the respective annual exchange rate averages £/DM and £/EURO according to Pacific Exchange Rate Service (http://fx.sauder.ubc.ca)

In Germany the budget year spans from 1.January to 31.December in contrast to the British 1.April to 31.March. Figures for Germany in the 1997/8 columns for example therefore represent in fact 1997.

Until 1999/00 the figures for Britain exclude the expenditure on 'overseas seminars', which amounted to £ 0.3-0.4 m p.a. From April 1999 the 'overseas seminar' programme has become part of the 'new' trade fair programme under the name SESA – Support for exhibitions and seminars abroad. The figures represent the no. of participating firms, not all of which received support. Figures for 1993/94-1995/96 were not available.

Fig. 5.1. Central governments' trade fair support expenditures and number of supported firms in the United Kingdom (GB) and Germany (D) 1989-2002

Sources: for data on Germany: AUMA annual reports 1992ff, for Britain BOTB annual reports 1989/90ff; BTI 2001, 2002

The German trade fair budget increased more steadily and faster than the British in the first half of the nineties, before it fell under the general budget freeze from 1996 onwards. Despite higher expenditures, fewer firms take part in the German programme. Note that it is not possible to draw conclusions about the comparative level of support per firm or the comparative efficiency of expenditure. Britain supports far more fairs in Europe, which are cheaper to attend. Germany seems to spend more on official support programmes for the trade fair par-

[8] The total expenditure was calculated as the sum of 1. the trade fair support budget; 2. the BfAI budget; and 3. the grant for the overseas chambers of commerce (BDI 1998).

ticipations (e.g. receptions), and more on the design of the group stands, the value of which are difficult to evaluate from the perspective of the individual firm. Also, in Germany the funding for events like World Expositions comes from the trade fair support budget and burdens it considerably (AUMA 1997). The level of support differs between West German and East German companies, and unlike in Britain it also differs from fair to fair (see Chapter 6). In terms of the development of the trade fair budget, the comparison is distorted by the changing exchange rate between £ Sterling and German Marks. Last, the figures do not include the overhead costs. 'Costs' and 'outputs' are therefore difficult to compare.

Regarding the 'outcomes' of the programmes, both the British and German governments have commissioned research which concluded that trade fair support encourages firms to attend fairs and increases exports (DTI 1994; Econ-Consult and ISG 1994; DTI and FCO 1997). They have been able to justify the expenditure to the taxpayer, as studies came to the conclusion that trade fair support creates higher tax incomes than the programmes cost and secures domestic jobs (DTI 1994; Thoene 1997; Deutscher Bundestag 2001).

But considering that there is no definitive academic research that shows how to measure the economic return on trade show investments these results need to be treated with caution: Measurement is difficult for a number of reasons: A firm's participation may result in direct sales, but also in attitudinal or cognitive effects like the creation of product awareness or interest, or in an increased image and reputation. Depending on the objectives of the firm, different firms might judge the same outcomes differently. And depending on the industry and the country in which a fair takes place, the primary function of the fair differs. Even if only the direct sales effects are measured, it is not straightforward. Usually, there is a time lag between the visit of the prospective customer and her actual purchase, during which other marketing techniques interact with the effect of the exhibition. And a third of all companies never attempt to measure the costs and effects of their trade fair participations, and are therefore unlikely to give precise information when interviewed (Gopalakrishna et al. 1995; Dekimpe et al. 1997; AUMA 1998a; Shoham 1999; Wirtschaftswoche 2.1.1997).

But even if it were established that the trade fair programmes have the claimed positive effects, this would still not necessarily imply that the support is delivered effectively and efficiently. For example, Legeler et al. (1994) found that individual exhibitors reported significantly stronger successes from a trade fair participation than exhibitors who were part of a group participation. The objective of the next three chapters is not to judge whether firms in Britain and Germany should receive trade fair support or not, but whether the current organisation of the programmes has an impact on how well the support is provided. First, the benchmarks on which these judgements will be based need to be developed.

5.4 The benchmarks for the analysis

5.4.1 The goals of trade fair support in Britain and Germany

In Chapter 1 'organisation' was defined as a purpose-directed activity. An organisation is chosen to produce outputs that can be expected to achieve the goal for which the organisation was set up. The effectiveness of organisations has been defined as the extent to which it produces the goal-oriented outputs. To judge the effectiveness of the German and British trade fair support organisation it is therefore first of all necessary to establish what the proclaimed goals of the organisations are, and then with which outputs these goals can be accomplished within the framework of trade fair support.

In the British case, they are clearly stated in the government's description of 'SESA' – Support for Exhibitions and Seminars Abroad' – (DTI 1998a; TPUK 2001). They are:

- to assist new exporters to become established in markets abroad
- to help more experienced exporters enter under-exploited and newly emerging target markets.

These objectives of SESA,[9] which was announced in December 1997, are in line with the operational objectives for TradePartnersUK as a whole. In order *to enhance the competitiveness of Britain's companies through overseas sales and investments,* it has two objectives: to facilitate market entry for new, inexperienced and occasional exporters on the one hand, and for experienced exporters on the other. Two further objectives are to provide firms with useful information, and to provide more focused help in those markets and sectors that have strong potential for British business (DTI et al. 2001:11). Obviously there are overlaps between the four objectives, and trade fair support can contribute to all. But if the TPUK budget is taken as an indication of the relative importance of the two SESA objectives, the focus is on the first. According to the BTI Expenditure Plans Report 2001–02 45% of the total budget is dedicated to help 'inexperienced and occasional exporters', with an equally large share planned for the subsequent three years: 22% goes to experienced exporters, with the remainder of the budget split between the two other objectives (DTI et al. 2001:10). In a different publication TPUK stated that *'Trade Partners UK has a special remit to identify and support new exporters'* (TPUK 2000).

In the case of Germany the identification of the government's trade fair support goals is less straightforward. Although the Ministry of Economics has now published its fourth edition of the booklet 'Trade Fair Support Policy for the Federal Republic of Germany' (BMWi 2000), the objectives of the organisation have not

9 A third listed objective – 'providing support for smaller groups of exporters at niche events' – does not have the same quality as the other two, but appears to be rather a means than an end in itself.

been explicitly stated.[10] Pieces of text that can be interpreted as objectives appear in the first part of the booklet, but they are not entirely coherent. It seems that the general objectives are similar to those of the British government. The objective is *to secure employment and markets in the long run* by facilitating firms' use of 'one of the most effective and important export marketing instruments' (BMWi 2000:10). In relation to this, two issues are stressed. First, SMEs are the target group. They are perceived to be disadvantaged because for them a trade fair participation incurs proportionately higher financial cost, risk, and management effort (BMWi 2000:11).[11] In the government's statement about the general aim of its export promotion programme this focus is reinforced: *'It remains the prime objective of the federal government's overseas trade promotion, to strengthen the competitive position of small and medium sized enterprises on overseas markets'* (Deutscher Bundestag 2000a). Second, the government is concerned with creating a positive image of the 'enterprise Germany' ('Unternehmen Deutschland'), because this would entice foreigners to buy German products (BMWi 2000:8,9).[12]

The two aspects 'SME focus' and 'country image' were also raised in the British context, though not directly in the context of trade fair support. In 1998 the government staged the 'Cool Britannia' initiative with an exhibition that was timed to coincide with the Asem 2 summit of Asian and European leaders in London; British Diplomats spoke of the 'UK.plc agenda'.[13] And two of the objectives, which British Trade International inherited from the joint DTI/FCO overseas trade promotion, were *'to encourage more businesses, especially SMEs, to take an active and professional approach to business opportunities overseas'* and *'to enhance the image of Britain as a reliable and innovative supplier of goods and services'* (DTI and Treasury 2000). Although these objectives were rewritten in February 2000, and are now the ones described above, 'SME support' still features

[10] After German reunification the government published the brochure 'Auslandsmessepolitik fuer die Bundesrepublik Deutschland' (BMWi 1992) which is now in its forth edition (BMWi 2000). The text has remained largely unchanged.

[11] 'SMEs are without government help seldom in the position to resolve the financial and organisational problems of a trade fair participation abroad... The fixed cost of an acceptable exhibition is high and therefore affects SMEs more.... The trade fair policy takes the special needs of SMEs into account as far as possible, to alleviate the competitive disadvantages of this firm size compared with large firms.'

[12] 'For the success in the competition of countries, not only the success of single firms and products count. It is also decisive, which ideas the potential customers and competitors of German products and services have, or form, about Germany's productivity, its infrastructure, people, political importance, and its role in global policy'..... 'Trade fair policy can be restricted even less than before to provide merely the frame for the presentation of individual products of different firms. What it is about is to present the whole performance spectrum of Germany with its political, cultural and economic elements. ...Accordingly, (such a type of presentation) has to be at the forefront of trade fair policy considerations' (8). '... the financial support is a politically justified government task. Trade fair policy fulfils herewith an important, public function in the political and economical relations of Germany with foreign countries. (9)

[13] Sir David Gore-Booth: British Diplomacy in the new Millennium. Speech for the 'European Atlantic Group', 25 October 1999; http://www.eag.org.uk/Gore%20speech.htm

as the key commitment in the National Strategy for International Trade Development and Promotion: *'There will be a special emphasis on helping smaller companies to develop their capacity and ability to tackle overseas markets'* (BTI 1999).

Based on these statements about the purpose of export support in general and trade fair support in particular, the following analysis will focus on the impact of the trade fair support organisations on the achievement of the following two goals:

1. the promotion of successful trade fair participations of inexperienced and potential exporters, with special regard to SMEs
2. the promotion of successful trade fair participations of experienced exporters in new, high potential markets, with special regard to SMEs.

The impact of the organisation on promoting a positive 'country image' will also be considered. But since in Britain this objective is not an explicit concern for the programme, and since the German government has pursued this aim only by setting up information stands (see above) and by using a logo 'made in Germany' at all group participations, the 'country image' objective is treated more as a side issue, rather than a main goal in itself.

5.4.2 The major activities in the process of delivering trade fair support, their operational objectives, and the ideal organisations to accomplish these

Given that the governments provide their trade fair support in the form of subsidising group participations, the process of delivering trade fair support can be separated into three major tasks. First, the fairs for which groups of exhibitors receive government support are selected. Second, groups of exhibitors are recruited to participate at the selected fairs. Third, the actual support is delivered to the group participants.

Each activity can be carried out by the government trade fair agency on its own, in co-operation with other actors, or entirely by other actors. But whoever the actors are, to accomplish the overall goals of the trade fair support organisation, each activity implies that certain output objectives are met. The following section describes what the activities involve and defines these objectives in relation to the overall goals. Based on the output objectives of an activity the characteristics of 'ideal organisations' for carrying out the respective activity can be specified in a generic way.

5.4.2.1 The selection of fairs

The task

More than 10,000 trade fairs take place every year (AUMA 1997a:19), and the number has grown continuously (Motwani et al. 1992; Herbig et. al.1996a). Given that the German or British trade fair support budgets currently stretch to fund only some 150–400 group participations, both governments face a ranking problem.

Based on the trade fair support objectives, they have to select those fairs that promise to best help inexperienced and potential SME exporters establish themselves in foreign markets, and experienced SME exporters in new, high-potential markets. This is not easy. Trade fairs differ from each other regarding several characteristics: the markets in which they take place; the visitor profiles; the industries which are served by the fair, and the degree of specialisation of the trade fair theme. And little is known about the determinants that make one fair better than another (Dekimpe et al. 1997):

From the perspective of an individual firm, the question of the 'right' market and type of fair depends on the motives for participating. For example, there is a difference between exhibiting primarily to attract new customers, or to maintain contact with existing customers. But even if the 'best' market location is determined only in view of the opportunities it gives firms to break into a new market, the choice is not definite. Each market has both entry costs and potential benefits that depend on a variety of factors, and have to be weighed against each other. Potential sales depend on the size of the market for the product, purchasing power, the growth rates of demand, and the market shares, strength and weaknesses of main competitors. Entry costs are related to language, distance, tariffs, standards and regulations, need for modifying the product, costs of storage and distribution etc. (AUMA 1998a, 1998b). Limited resources of participating firms combined with the risk of a wrong market assessment can make the initial costs of some market entries prohibitive. So even for one specific product and one specific firm a considerable amount of information is needed to rank the possible target markets in view of the net-benefits they promise.

It is much more difficult to rank the markets and subsequently the fairs that are on offer for the whole variety of British or German firms. What adds further to the complexity is that in some markets exhibiting as part of an 'official' government participation is believed to have more of an impact on sales than in others. But there are no studies that could support this assumption or give indications about the size of the effect. Another factor is that what constitutes a 'new' market and the difficulty of entering it are different for new and occasional exporters compared with experienced ones. So choices between the two target groups have to be made. Furthermore, the role trade fairs play in the marketing mix varies in different countries – European shows attract more chief executive officers with purchasing power, who are geared more toward in-depth dealings, while North American trade shows are normally used by visitors to get an initial overview of the products that are available in a specific sector (Dekimpe et al. 1997). Exporters have rated the value of trade fairs in South East Asia highly, because personal contacts and relationships are particularly important there (NAO 1996:51). Trade fair support is therefore likely to have a more direct impact on exports in some markets than in others.

Aside from the decision about markets, decisions have to be made about the type of fair. The few studies that have been carried out on trade fair effectiveness (Dekimpe et al. 1997) and the experience of trade fair support organisations (Michigan Small Business Development Center 1998; AUMA 1998a, 1998b) and consultants (Goodsell 1996; Borenstein 1999; DePasquale 2000) suggest the following: The quality of the trade fair company plays a role, e.g. because good marketing has an impact on how many attendees with purchasing power attend. Firms are also advised to look for fairs in which their line of business has a captive audience. For example, providers of television services with niche content for lawyers are advised not to exhibit in broadcasting-related events but at law-related trade fairs (Borenstein 1999). It also appears to be unanimously agreed that firms with niche products or services are usually better off attending small, focused trade fairs: floor space at small fairs is usually cheaper; the shows require less expenditure for marketing; and because the audience is smaller there is more time to get to know potential customers. Focused trade fairs, i.e. trade fairs that represent a narrow segment of a market, also make it easier to attract the target audience. Large trade fairs provide image, but they also diminish the chance of meeting and selling to qualified visitors (Rosson and Seringhaus 1991b:166; Motwani et al. 1992). One comment on CEBIT, the largest IT-related trade fair with 26 exhibition halls is for example that it 'is too unfocused, too expensive, there are not enough local buyers, e.g. from Southern Germany, and too many other exhibitors so that the individual message gets lost' (DePasquale 2000). However, if small, focused trade fairs are on average more effective than large ones, this means that the selection of 150–400 government-subsidised fairs becomes even more difficult. The more specialised the events are, the fewer firms can benefit from exhibiting there because their products and services do not fit. The task of selecting fairs thus also involves deciding which industries might benefit more from participating than others.

The 'ideal selection organisation'

The complexity of the issues to consider when selecting the 'best' trade fairs for the two target groups places high demands on the knowledge of the selecting actors. In an 'ideal' organisation those with the decision rights to put together the list of supported fairs need to have or obtain: the knowledge about the market prospects for different industries; the relevance of 'official support' for sales; which fairs take place in these markets; the fairs' focus and profile of attendees; the quality of the trade fair companies; and differences between the markets and between industries regarding the effectiveness of the tool 'trade fairs'. Furthermore, they must know how to weigh these factors in order to rank the worldwide fairs.

Table 5.1. Features of the ideal trade fair selection organisation

Output objective: Selection of those fairs that offer the best opportunity for a successful market entry of new/occasional and of experienced exporters	
Knowledge of the actors with the decision rights to select the fairs	*Incentives* of the actors with the decision rights to select the fairs
▪ market potential for different industries ▪ trade fairs worldwide and their characteristics ▪ relevance of official support ▪ relative usefulness of exhibitions in different markets/industries	▪ benefit from choosing impartially according to highest impact of trade fair support on market entry success ▪ benefit from cater for both inexperienced/ potential exporters and experienced exporters entering new markets

To ensure that they select the 'best' fairs based on this knowledge, actors in the ideal organisation have the incentive to choose impartially between different fairs, and, assuming that the 'best' fairs differ for the two target groups, have the incentive to cater for both of them. Table 5.1. (previous page) summarises these features.

5.4.2.2 The recruitment of participants

The task

Once the trade fairs have been selected, the next task is to recruit group participants. To reach the goal that successful trade fair participations of inexperienced, potential and experienced exporters are promoted, it is indispensable that all suitable firms are aware of the opportunity.

In principle there are two ways of doing this: One is to inform every firm that would benefit from exhibiting at one of the selected trade fairs directly; the other is to inform all firms, and let the firms decide themselves whether they 'fit' a selected fair.

To follow the first approach the recruiting actors would have to know or find out about not only every single one of the 3–4 million firms in their respective country, but also their exact production profile, their resources, their strategy and their potential markets. Only then could they judge which firms to contact. Moreover, they would have to be completely unbiased in their information collection and choice of whom to contact.

For the second, comparatively easier approach, the actors can use general information channels that reach large numbers of the business population at once, as long as they know which channels fulfil this function. But informing all firms is not enough on its own. Among the companies that receive the information are firms who would have exhibited at the trade fair without government support. They are not the target group. The other firms can be sorted into four groups: 1. those who could enter a new market by exhibiting at the trade fair and, as a result of the information about the government support, decide to participate; 2. those who could not exhibit successfully, and do not participate despite the subsidy; 3. those who could exhibit successfully, but do not realise it and do not go; 4. those who cannot exhibit successfully, but do not realise it, and do want to participate.

Table 5.2. Groups that require specific attention in the recruitment process

		Are the firms able to exhibit at the fair successfully?	
		Yes	No
Do the firms join the group participation?	Yes	1	4
	No	3	2

With the recruitment of the first group, part of the target group has been reached. But the target group also includes the third group who still underestimate their potential net benefits. According to research on SMEs export attitudes, wrong perceptions of exporting risks, and insufficient information are the biggest obstacles for firms (Miesenbock 1988; Bannock and Peacock 1989; Sharkey et al. 1989; Axinn et al. 1995; Leonidou 1995a, 1995b; CBI 1996). One of the main justifications for trade fair support is 'information market failure': Firms are thought to 'lack the information required to assess whether it is worth attending a particular trade fair' (DTI 1994:31). These problems also affect the fourth group, for whom a trade fair participation is detrimental. Legeler et al. (1994:45) found, for example, that some participants in Lower Saxony's trade fair programme did so unsuccessfully, not because the firms were as such unable to benefit from a trade fair participation but because they chose the wrong country and type of fair. In advice booklets for firms on how to select a fair, they are recommended to visit a fair before deciding to exhibit there (AUMA 1998a, 1998b). Other potential pitfalls for exhibitors have been that firms did not have enough staff to follow-up on leads after a participation, or that they did not have the resources to service the business they attracted, and could therefore not benefit fully from their participation (Yuhas 2000).

For these reasons, informing the firms about the opportunity is not sufficient. Firms need to be in the position to judge rationally whether participation could help them enter a new market, and whether it constitutes the best use of their limited resources. Seringhaus and Rosson (1998:410), who found that almost 60% of trade fair support programme participants did not recover their participation costs, go further. They suggest that the recruitment process should include a screening process, which establishes that prospective exhibitors are export-capable (i.e. have the requisite product and technological capability), are committed to export market development and expansion, and will acquire valuable international trade fair experience.

The 'ideal recruitment organisation'

Thus, the actors who are responsible for recruiting participants ideally know which information channels to use to make all exporters and potential exporters aware of the support for the selected fairs. But as many firms are not aware of the potential benefits of a trade fair participation or of the potential cost, in order to improve firms' decision-making the actors must also know what additional information they need to provide and how. The ideal actors have the incentive to do so. They do not favour specific groups by focusing their information delivery on them, and they benefit from optimising firms' decision making.

Table 5.3. Features of the ideal recruitment organisation

Output objective: Recruitment of inexperienced, potential and experienced exporters who can successfully exhibit at a selected fair to enter a new market	
Knowledge of the actors with the decision rights to recruit participants	*Incentives* of the actors with the decision rights to recruit participants
▪ suitable information channels to inform all firms ▪ information that is relevant for firms to judge whether the fair can be useful for them, and sources for such information	▪ benefit from informing all firms that could participate and for which it is a new market ▪ benefit from providing sufficient information to allow firms to make rational choices

5.4.2.3 The support for the exhibitors

Trade fair support is given to promote firms' participation at trade fairs, because exhibitions can be an effective step into a new market. The underlying assumption is that by lowering the cost of exhibiting, firms can be enticed to participate in a fair. Governments justify the subsidy on the basis of information market failures, inherent competitive disadvantages of SMEs, and positive external effects of exporting (DTI 1994; Thoene 1997).

By supporting trade fair participations through organised groups, the objective of exhibitor support – to reduce the net cost of a trade fair participation – can be pursued on five levels: 1. with direct subsidies to each participant; 2. through group discounts on exhibition related services; 3. through reductions of marketing costs; 4. through reductions on search, information, contracting and monitoring costs; and 5. through reducing the net participation cost by increasing the trade fair returns.

Firstly, the most straightforward way of reducing exhibitors costs is to pay a lump sum subsidy to an exhibiting firm. But this form of support could also be given to individual exhibitors. The design of trade fair support in form of group participations is based on the notion that it allows additional forms of cost reduction.

Given that support is provided for normally ten or more exhibitors at the same fair, the costs for the individual firm can secondly be reduced through negotiating price discounts for the group on the basis of 'economies of scale'. For example, firms could benefit from more favourable shipping terms for exhibition pieces, or from joint advertisements.

Thirdly, being part of an 'official' group can raise the profile of the exhibitors. To get the same degree of attention from trade fair visitors, they have to spend less on marketing their stands. This 'image factor' might be very important, since studies show that exhibiting firms have approximately only seven seconds to capture the interest of those passing by (Michigan Small Business Development Center 1998). Increasing efforts have been necessary to attract visitors to a trade fair stand (Wirtschaftswoche 2.1.1997). An official participation attracts attention and can convey the effect of a 'quality seal' for the exhibitors (AUMA 1983). Moreover, aside from the cost reduction for exhibitors, the 'official image' is relevant from the wider perspective of the government, if group participations are also supposed to function as a more general advertisement for the country's products.

Fourthly, a trade fair participation can become cheaper if the demands on firms' management and staff capacity, two of SME's major bottlenecks, are reduced (Econ-Consult and ISG 1994). Exhibitions usually require that an exhibitor deals with a whole range of issues outside the 'normal' business processes. According to the booklet 'Successful Trade Fair Participations' (AUMA 1998a) requirements concern, for example, the registration for the fair, transport and storage of goods, insurance, customs clearance, travel planning, stand planning and design, as well as stand construction, cleaning, and security. For inexperienced and potential SME exporters in particular, 'technical help' can considerably reduce the costs of finding out about the procedures, about prices and sellers, and of negotiating with, and monitoring the contractors.

Lastly, the relative cost of participation can be reduced by making the participation more successful: There are four factors that are believed to have a major impact on trade fair results: strategy, marketing, the stand personnel, and follow-up (Rosson and Seringhaus 1991b; Gopalakrishna et al. 1995; Dekimpe et al. 1997; Tanner 1997; FAZ 1998; Seringhaus and Rosson 1998; AUMA 1998a, 1998b; Wirtschaftswoche 2.1.1997). Successful exhibitors have clear objectives for their participation that match the fair's visitor profile. They plan their whole presentation according to these objectives. Good marketing (e.g. pre-show promotion, receptions, stand design and location, presents for visitors) drastically improves the exhibition's effect on sales leads (Gopalakrishna et al. 1995; Tanner 1997; FAZ 1998). Which marketing measures are most effective depends on the exhibition objectives, but also on the business culture of the country where the fair takes place. The overall success then depends critically on the staff at the fair, and on the follow-up and speed of follow-up on leads after the fair (FAZ 1998). Like the procedural knowledge described above, the knowledge about the critical success factors, the best options for a specific fair, and how to put the information into practise is costly to acquire, especially for first-time participants. A survey on trade fair support among East German firms in 1997 showed that 99% of exhibitors considered financial support to attend trade fairs as very important, or important. Many, but fewer, perceived advice regarding market analysis/marketing concepts (73%), distribution (65%), stand construction and design (46%) and training of stand personnel (41%) as very important or important aspects of support. Potential exhibitors on the other hand, while also appreciating financial support most (100%), valued advice even more than exhibitors (market analysis/marketing concepts: 86%; distribution: 85%; stand construction and design: 77%; training for the stand personnel 72%) (Habuda et al. 1998b:35). Given that even a subsidised trade fair participation is costly if it is unsuccessful, efforts to increase the benefits of participation can be essential to reduce relative costs.

The ideal organisation of exhibition support

Ideally, the actors who are responsible for 'exhibition support' have a wide range of knowledge with which they can provide all the above-mentioned forms of exhibitor support. They know the best way to provide the direct financial subsidy, they know how to negotiate with different suppliers for group discounts, and how to contract for services and monitor the suppliers to save participants' management time. They are also aware of the appropriate marketing measures in a country, and of the critical success factors in exhibitors' performance, and can transfer that knowledge. In addition they can judge which combination of support measures is the most cost reducing, given a specific fair and given the recruited participants, and the budget limitations. The ideal actors also want to provide export support in the most suitable ways, and do not neglect some forms of support over others.

Table 5.4. Features of the ideal exhibition support organisation

Output objective: Cost reduction of a successful trade fair participation in a new market for inexperienced, potential and experienced exporters	
Knowledge of the actors with the decision rights for exhibition support	*Incentives* of the actors with the decision rights for exhibition support
▪ best ways of providing direct financial support ▪ know-how to negotiate with, contract with and monitor suppliers and subcontractors ▪ know-how to make official participation attractive for visitors and how to market the group and the whole German/British sector in the host country ▪ critical success factors for specific fairs, and how to alert firms to the issues ▪ mix of the above approaches that is most suitable for a specific fair and for participants	▪ benefit from using their knowledge to provide adequate support, considering all forms of support as equally valuable ▪ have no incentive to favour specific participants over others

5.4.3 The perfectly adaptable trade fair support organisation

Organising the trade fair support along the lines of the described 'ideal' organisations is insufficient if the conditions are fulfilled only temporarily. The knowledge of the actors has to be continuously up-to-date, incorporating changes in the respective fields. For example, some trade fairs abroad might have deteriorated in quality, or some new industry could benefit more from being supported than an industry for which a trade fair was selected previously. The same applies for the 'incentives' side where ideal actors keep benefiting from making those choices that match best with the organisations' objectives.

In addition, the organisation needs to adapt to changes in demand for trade fair support services, be they numerical or functional changes (see Chapter 3). Numerical changes imply a higher or lower demand for support from the side of the target firms in general, or for specific regions, industries, or types of fairs. Ideally, the organisation can easily accommodate these changes in demand, and is not restricted by finances, human resources or physical assets.

Functional changes in demand can be triggered, for example, by new laws that change how trade fair support can be delivered or new technologies that create alternative options for exhibiting products. Ideally, the core actor, who is responsible for delivering the government's trade fair support policy, can then adjust the types of tasks actors have to fulfil, or the organisation structure as such, if it no longer meets the organisation goals. To do so, the core actor ideally knows when changes in the organisation are required and has an incentive to implement them.

Table 5.5. Features of the perfectly adaptable trade fair support organisation

1. Actors are receiving up-to-date information *and* make decisions based on up-to-date information

2. The organisation is numerically adaptable to a changing environment in terms of total numbers of selected fairs, as well as in terms of markets and industries
   - numerical adaptation is in-built into the selection process, or
   - the core actor knows when the output of the organisation needs to be adapted and
   - the core actor can effect numerical changes (has decision rights regarding the allocation of finance, assets and human inputs)
   - the core actor wants to effect numerical changes

3. The organisation is functionally adaptable to a changing environment in the type of exhibition support that firms can benefit from
   - the core actor knows when the output and/or the structure of the organisation need to be adapted functionally to respond to external changes
   - the core actor can effect functional changes (has decision rights regarding the allocation of finance, assets and human inputs)
   - the core actor wants to carry out functional changes

5.5 Information sources

To analyse the effects of the German and the British trade fair support organisations according to the suggested research framework, three questions had to be researched:

1. How is each activity organised? This involved finding out which actors play a part, what their tasks and decision rights are, and whether that structure had changed over time.
2. What incentives and what knowledge do the actors have when they carry out their respective tasks, and which decision rights, knowledge and incentives does the core organisation have to adapt the overall structures?
3. What are the actors' joint outputs in each of the activities?

Each of these questions was investigated by reviewing a wide range of case related information sources:

Printed information

As already mentioned, academic research on the topic has been very limited. To find more printed, publicly accessible information, especially regarding question one and three, the following sources were searched systematically:

- Government official publications, covering
  - parliamentary debates
  - committee reports
  - command papers
  - annual reports
  - audit reports
  - press releases
  - brochures for the export support clients

For the UK, the databases UKOP (United Kingdom Official Publications), HANSARD (House of Commons and House of Lords debates), and COI (Central Office of Information) were used as search tools; in Germany's case DIP-Parliamentary documentation (covers minutes of 'Bundestag' and 'Bundesrat' debates; 'Drucksachen', i.e. parliamentary questions to the government and government answers; press releases); OPAC, the catalogue of the parliament's library; and BMWI's catalogue of publications. The government publications provided the most useful and richest source of printed information for both case studies.

- AUMA's library

AUMA, the German umbrella organisation for the trade fair industry and main player in the German trade fair support, runs a 'trade fair issues' library. There, official documents, books and articles, as well as 'grey literature' like theses or AUMA surveys are collected. Relevant publications were studied on site in January 1999.

- Newspaper articles

All major British and German newspapers were searched for articles on export promotion in general and trade fair promotion and its actors in particular, starting from 1990 (where the database allowed it). For Britain, the databases 'FT-Profile' and FT.com were used. The findings were particularly useful to trace the changes in the delivery of export support. For Germany, the information provider 'newscan.de', and a search service for journalists were used, but with fewer results.

- Trade journals and management journals

To find trade-fair-related articles that have been written for a 'practitioner' audience the databases 'ABI-INFORM' and 'Business and Industry' were used. The information was mainly relevant for determining what is known about trade fair success criteria.

- Websites

To find out more about the single major actors, their websites were visited. The amount of information they published varied, but apart from contact details they usually provided an overview of their activities, and often press releases or position papers. In the cases of British trade fair sponsors and German trade fair organisers, both large groups of actors, the websites were used to do some quantitative evaluations of the actors' features. The websites of major representative bodies for exporters and for SMEs were also consulted. In addition the Internet was searched for particular information, e.g. information about specific fairs, with the search engine 'Google'.

AUMA's on-line trade fair database with its reports about previous official trade fair participations and its profiles of trade fairs proved a further useful, web-based resource.

Interviews

Despite these extensive searches for printed information, the information in secondary sources was not detailed enough to get a full picture of the organisations. Starting with the most obvious actors, i.e. government and the major business associations, interviews were carried out to get more information about the structures. Once it was established how service delivery was organised, representatives of all involved parties were interviewed. Some were recommended by previous interview partners, others were approached independently. The 48 interviews were semi-structured. The research framework determined a clear, general structure. The main focus was on answering question one and two. All actors were asked about their role in the respective activity, their decision rights, their motivation to be involved, the knowledge on which they draw to make decisions, and what they thought could be improved in trade fair support. But since the tasks of the actors differed with each actor and activity, the questions had to be phrased slightly differently in each case. Also, during the first interviews more emphasis was on getting information about the general structures and processes, whereas these questions did not need to be repeated with subsequent interviewees. Rather, in the later interviews particular issues could be brought up that had evolved during previous conversations, and if interviewees appeared especially co-operative, they were asked in more detail about problems of the organisation.

Some of the interview partners provided additional printed material that is not publicly available, which contributed mainly to answering question three. To ensure confidentiality, the references to interviewees are coded. For interviewees in Germany, the codes start with D-, for those in the UK with UK-.

5.6 Summary

This chapter has presented the research approach that will be applied in the following three chapters. The units of analysis are the German and the British trade fair support organisations. They are set within different public sector management traditions and within different government export support organisations, but share the same prominence as an export support tool, similar target groups, and comparable goals.

The chosen analytical method is pattern matching. Starting from the goals of trade fair support, and the activity chain in the production and delivery of it, characteristics of a hypothetical 'ideal' trade fair organisation have been developed on the basis of the theoretical model, and professional as well as academic literature on trade fair exhibiting. The next two chapters analyse, for both Germany and Britain, how trade fair support is organised and how far the two cases diverge from the 'ideal case'. Then expected theoretical outcomes can be defined, given the differences, and it can be investigated whether the evidence either complies with or contradicts these predictions.

Chapter 6: The organisation of trade fair support in Germany

6.1 Overview

The German federal government's trade fair programme is run and financed by the Ministry of Economics (*Bundesministerium für Wirtschaft und Technologie* – **BMWi**).[1] Which fairs are officially supported depends mainly on trade associations, representatives of which sit together with government representatives on the **'Committee for Trade Fair Participations'** (*'Arbeitskreis für Auslandsmessebeteiligungen'*). The committee meets biannually and is co-ordinated by **AUMA**, the umbrella association for the German trade fair business. Once the Committee has agreed on a list of trade fairs that should receive support, and the BMWi has approved the list, BMWi select a trade fair company (*Durchführungsgesellschaft* - **DFG**) for each event. The DFGs are then responsible for recruiting firms to participate at 'their' event, and for providing exhibition support to that group of participants. They also have to co-operate with a trade fair architect, chosen by the BMWi to design the stands for the group participation.

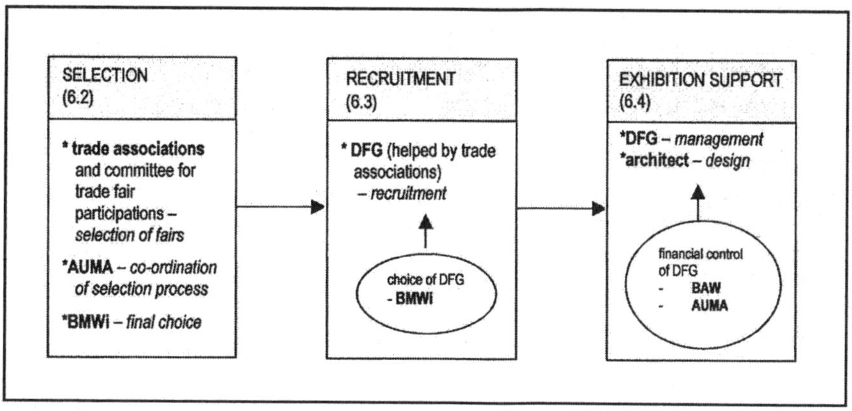

Fig. 6.1. The actors and their tasks in the German trade fair support organisation

---

1 Some trade fairs selected by the Ministry of Agriculture, Food and Forestry (BML), at the BML's own discretion and cost, supplement the programme.

According to the AUMA representative, D-B, this structure has not changed for many years. The only detail that has changed is that in 1996 the responsibility for financial supervision of the DFGs went from the BMWi itself to an executive agency of the BMWi, the Bundesamt fuer Wirtschaft (BAW).

The following sections describe the selection, recruitment and exhibition support organisation in detail. For each step the combination of the different actors with their respective tasks is described first. Then each actor is characterised, and their incentives and their knowledge are discussed in view of the task for which they are responsible. Comparing the actual organisation with the ideal organisation for that activity concludes each section. The 'pattern-matching technique' (see 5.2.2) is used to predict consequences of the differences, and the evidence for the expected consequences is established. An analysis of the adaptability of the organisational structures follows.

The overall interest lies in establishing whether 'organisation matters' for effectiveness as suggested by the model. Can the organisation's outputs be traced back to actors' knowledge and incentives as implied in the distribution of decision rights and rights to returns, and to the adaptability of the organisational structures?

6.2 Trade fair selection

6.2.1 The allocation of tasks and decision rights

As mentioned, the major actors in the selection of the Government's annual list of trade fairs are trade associations, most of them represented in the 'Committee for trade fair support', AUMA, and the BMWi.

On paper the process is the following: The 'Committee for Trade Fair Participations', consisting of government and industry representatives, discuss which fairs should receive support. In two annual meetings they produce a ranked list, which is presented to the BMWi. The BMWi then makes the final choice (BMWi 2000:12).

In practice, AUMA and the trade associations have a more important role than is suggested by this description. AUMA collects all the requests for trade fair support, the very large majority of which come from trade associations. Chambers abroad or diplomatic posts can also make recommendations, but not individual firms. AUMA acts as a 'clearing' office, collects and provides information on specific fairs, communicates with the associations' representatives, and puts together a list of the suggested fairs. AUMA also hosts the meetings of the Committee for Trade Fair Participations (D-B).

The Committee, established in 1949, has 51 members. Most of them (37) are representatives of umbrella associations and individual trade associations, which cover the range of German export-oriented industries. On the whole, they are the same associations that suggest trade fairs to AUMA. Besides, the Committee includes representatives of BDI and DIHK, the top umbrella associations of the German industry, representatives of five industry-led 'promotion societies' for economic relations with different world regions (e.g. Afrikaverein), and representatives of seven government bodies.[2] At the Committee's first meeting in May a preliminary list of official trade fair participations is drafted and subsequently published; at a second meeting in November the list is finalised with replacement options (D-B). But unlike the formal description of the process suggests, the Committee's major function is that of a consultation and information forum for strategic trade fair policy decisions. As two meetings per year would not be sufficient to discuss and rank more than 200 trade fairs, and in addition discuss other issues, de facto over 90% of fairs are selected beforehand (D-C; D-J; D-I; AUMA 1993). A kind of informal 'quota' system operates, so that the associations know roughly how many fairs their industries can expect to 'get'. Their trade fair choices within this quota are usually accepted (D-C; D-J; D-I).

The final numbers then depend mainly on the trade fair budget for the coming year, and in some cases industries might be favoured for cyclical or structural reasons (BMWi 1998a). The BMWi makes decisions about 'political participations' and consents to the final list (D-B).

This means that it is largely the trade associations who choose the fairs, with AUMA ensuring that different industries get their share, and that compatible wishes are linked up.[3] The Committee is a forum that brings representatives from export-oriented industries together with government representatives and gives the different parties the opportunity to discuss general trade fair policy issues. It is only marginally involved in the actual selection of fairs. Therefore, and because it is largely the trade associations in the Committee who influence the choices, the Committee is not discussed below as a separate actor in the selection process.

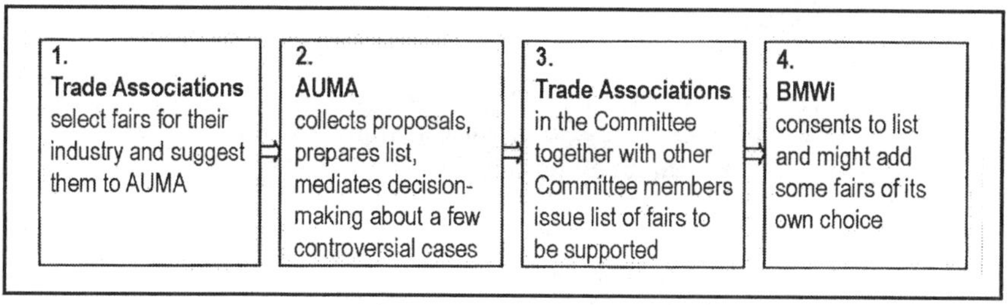

Fig. 6.2. The selection process

For this division of tasks to meet the characteristics of the ideal organisation for the 'selection' activity, the different actors would have to have the following features: The suggestions from trade associations cover the whole spectrum of indus-

---

[2] These are the ministries of economics (BMWi), agriculture (BML), foreign affairs (AA), the BfAI, the ministry for economic co-operation and development (BMZ), a representative of the Länder governments and the press and information office (List of members provided by D-B, AUMA).

[3] D-A, BMWi , stated that AUMA's role was to co-ordinate the interests of the trade associations.

tries. Each association knows which fairs offer the best opportunities in their sectors for inexperienced exporters and for those exporters that want to enter a new market. They also know where official support is most important and have the incentive to select fairs according to these criteria. AUMA mediates impartially and has the knowledge to advise BMWi and the Committee about the relative merit of different fairs for different industries. BMWi knows enough to decide about priorities between industries and to reject fairs that do not promise to meet the government's trade fair support programme objectives. It also wants to make decisions accordingly.

Do trade associations, AUMA and BMWi have such knowledge and incentives?

6.2.2 The trade associations' selection knowledge and incentives

Characteristics of trade associations in Germany

Germany has a complex network of trade associations, whose voluntary members cover on average 70–90% of the production volume in an industry. The high level of membership is not least due to the fact that German trade associations have a constitutionally-defined role as consultation partners for the government. They are organised in an orderly, hierarchically-integrated way, with little competition or overlap within, or between, sectors. The Federation of German Industry (*Bund Deutscher Industrie* – BDI) is the over-arching umbrella association, with 35 umbrella associations as members. These are internally differentiated into *'Fachgemeinschaften'*, i.e. groupings that represent subsectors or specialist products within a larger industry. In addition, each of the large German associations has geographically decentralised sub-groupings. Generally, the associations are well resourced. The VDMA for example, the largest German association, employed 360 full-time staff in 1995. And due to their hierarchically-networked structure even small associations can pool resources. (Bennett 1997; Kohler-Koch and Quittkat 1999).

Trade associations of industries with high export quotas are represented on the Committee for Trade Fair Participations. Thirteen are large umbrella associations that are members of BDI. The others are some smaller umbrella associations, and associations for niche industries that historically have had high export quotas, for example the 'Federation of the Gem and Diamond Industry' or the 'Federation of the German Musical Instruments Producers'. A third, but minor group are representatives from umbrella associations representing farmers, the 'free professions' (*'Freie Berufe'*), and the crafts and trades (*'Handwerk'*). The latter two are not actively involved in the selection process, judging from the names of associations that represent an industry at the selected fairs, which are usually the associations that suggested the fair. Also judging from the names of representing associations, in 1999 there were only four trade associations that were not represented on the Committee but that successfully suggested fairs for their industries. All four had a strong focus on providing trade fair services to their members.

This means that those associations that select fairs represent the majority of firms in their industries. They do not have to compete with each other and are well enough resourced to engage in the selection process. The fact that hardly any associations besides the Committee members have suggested fairs successfully can mean either that all industries with export potential are represented on the Committee, or that 'outsiders' find it difficult to take part in the selection process.

Trade associations' knowledge about suitable fairs

The associations are in charge of selecting the best fairs for their industry, which are then put forward to AUMA. The selection process can therefore only be effective, if the associations have knowledge about the trade fair opportunities for their industry. They need to know about the range and quality of the fairs, and in which markets the official trade fair assistance makes the biggest difference. They also need to know about the export capabilities of the SMEs in their industry to judge which fairs might be the most suitable.

German umbrella associations have staff who are specialised in trade fair issues, as have the larger associations on the tier below. They have internal trade fair committees for information exchange with the members, and for working with German trade fair organising companies (Negelein 1992). Many have foreign trade committees, which shape the associations' approaches to export issues. In the process of providing export services like the common export market information or trade missions services to their members, the associations acquire information about overseas markets, and about client members' export interests and capacities.[4] However, large firms with 1000+ employees use these export services more than smaller firms and therefore presumably influence the information pattern disproportionately.[5]

The knowledge about specific trade fairs abroad stems from members, from previous official participations, from trade fair organisers who contact the associations directly and, in some cases, also from AUMA. The judgement of the quality of a new fair is based on associations' experience, mainly regarding the trade fair organisers and the associated sponsor organisations (D-J; D-I; D-K).

Compared with the government or with private consultants, trade associations are therefore likely to be more knowledgeable about the global trade fair market for their industries and their members' export support demand. But as D-J from the umbrella association A pointed out, associations' size matters, since it largely determines to which extent they can afford to employ experts for export-related issues. A's member associations, for example, are small and are not actively involved in looking for suitable trade fairs. They might only take up suggestions from members. Only D-J in the umbrella association does trade fair market research. In the case of the umbrella associations B and C, their sub-groups make their own suggestions (D-I; D-K).

---

4 Committee members' websites show that such services are provided

5 Ruprecht and Weidig (1996:73) established in a survey for BMWi that while only 18.9% of exporting companies with fewer than 250 employees use the services of trade associations, 34.4% of firms with more than 1000 employees do.

The information about firms' needs and preferences for trade fair support stems from the members themselves (D-J; D-I; D-K). But a survey on the ways in which associations acquire information on firms' expectations and needs suggests that this information is usually selective. 'Personal contacts with members' is cited by 52% of association managers as a means of information acquisition, and 22% are informed through member response to activities of the association. The third largest information source is meetings and committees (19%). All three sources share the problem of not reflecting all members, the more so the larger the association (Eser 2000). Export specialists in the associations are less likely to have personal contacts with non-exporters, and non-exporters do not take part in export-related events. Small firms usually do not have the personnel to staff committees in their association.

In conclusion, trade associations are likely to be comparatively well informed about the exporting activities, needs and capacities of their active, exporting members, especially of larger firms. These members are also a major source of information about trade fairs abroad, which supplements the trade fair knowledge that associations have built up through their own involvement in trade fair activities over the years.

Trade associations' incentives in the trade fair selection process

Presuming that the trade associations know the world-wide trade fair market for their industry and their members' export potential to specific markets, it is still questionable whether associations' have an incentive to choose those fairs which offer the best opportunities for a successful market entry of new, occasional and experienced exporters.

Their choice is framed by several rules. A participation will normally be cancelled if it fails to attract a minimum of ten firms. According to D-I, it is an informal 'rule' that those fairs for which more than one association applies to AUMA are definitely going to be supported. He can also expect fairs for which he has more than ten binding participation applications in advance to be included in the programme.

In Chapter 4 it was argued that the management of voluntary associations would be interested in maintaining and increasing the association's membership, its public recognition, and its finances:

Here, government recognition is already granted. Associations have a formal role as advisors, which gives them a strong influence on government decision-making. But they are supposed to suggest fairs only if the support entices their member firms to participate (D-C; D-J). If an association repeatedly chooses fairs that do not attract the minimum number of ten participants, it loses credibility and may have its quota reduced. To be taken seriously as advisors, trade associations also have to acknowledge that the government's resources are finite. Asked whether the organisation of the selection process would not lead to long lists of suggestions by each association and quarrels in the Committee about whose needs are to be served first, D-C from AUMA stated that the associations were very co-operative and overall made only reasonable requests. This is supported by the informal, rough consensus about how many fairs each association can 'expect'.

Among the members and non-members it will be mainly the active exporters who pay attention to the association's trade fair activities. They will consider the selection of fairs at which they want to exhibit a good service from their association. If the association consults members about which fairs to select, it will be these active members who will suggest fairs they want to attend. The large umbrella associations then have to mediate the diverging interests of different industry subgroups to keep all parties content.

The need to satisfy members, the need to find a consensus, and the need to ensure that at least ten firms are interested, means that associations are inclined to suggest those fairs in which many actively exporting members are interested. This is more easily achieved if fairs have a broad, rather than a very specialised, theme. Further advantages are that another association might apply for it as well and that enough firms might commit to exhibit at the fair even before the association contacts AUMA.

Another issue that can influence the selection of a fair is the fact that associations sometimes derive an income from certain trade fairs. If they participate, for example in advertising a fair, the organiser pays them. For some German fairs, they themselves are the organisers or co-organisers. The closer an association is linked to a certain fair, the more this fair may constitute a source of income (BOERNER 1989). Associations are therefore unlikely to support overseas fairs by suggesting them for official participations, if these fairs stand in competition to the event in which they are stakeholders. D-K from an umbrella association supported this assumption. D-I from a different umbrella association argued that it was in the interest of the industry to avoid visitor numbers and attention being divided between many fairs of the same type.

In sum, the organisational structure implies incentives that incline associations to comply with the government rules, select fairs that attract many of the actively exporting members – preferably from different sub-sectors – and not to choose events that may erode their own incomes.

6.2.3 AUMA's selection knowledge and incentives

AUMA, the German trade fair industry association

Once the trade associations have made their choices, they pass the information on to AUMA. AUMA is the umbrella association of the German trade fair and exhibition industries. Its members are the trade fair organising companies and their federations, as well as industry, commerce, and agriculture associations, who represent the interests of trade fair exhibitors and visitors (AUMA 1983; AUMA 1995). The tasks of AUMA's 36 employees are varied, but reflect the organisation's statutory purpose of being a neutral promoter of German trade fair affairs. They include lobbying the EU, the federal and the Länder governments; marketing Germany as an international trade fair centre; reconciling the different interests in the German trade fair market and ensuring fair competition; collecting and disseminating information about trade fair matters, and, since 1949, co-ordinating the government's trade fair support programme (Boerner 1992; AUMA 1995). AUMA is consulted by government departments on trade fair related issues, and serves in the trade fair committees of the Federation of German Industry (BDI) and the umbrella association of the chambers of commerce and industry *'Deutscher Industrie- und Handelskammertag'* DIHK ('German Industry and Commerce Chamber Summit').

AUMA's whole existence therefore hinges on its credibility and success as a neutral mediator and promoter of all German trade fair related interests. Considering that AUMA has the role of a clearing office for trade fair support suggestions, manages around 90% of the decisions before the Committee's meetings, and then co-ordinates the meeting – this is vital. Both BMWi and the associations must be able to trust its competence and impartiality.

But AUMA also needs sufficient knowledge of the worldwide trade fair landscape to qualify as an advisor when it comes to ranking fairs and to prepare the discussions of the Committee. These requirements appear to be met to a large extent:

AUMA's knowledge about trade fairs

One major role of AUMA is to disseminate information about trade fair related matters. Besides supporting and surveying training activities, and commissioning research about the industry, AUMA collects information about ca. 5000 trade fairs worldwide 'which are important for German industry' (AUMA 1995:7). It is published in the 'AUMA Handbook International', which is updated twice a year and can be accessed on-line. AUMA provides information about dates, organisers, product ranges, and exhibitor and visitor statistics. AUMA also collects and publishes information about individual countries and exhibition centres, and co-operates with other national and international trade fair associations (AUMA 1995). It communicates regularly with the representatives of the major German industry sectors and with representatives of those industries that have long been involved in exporting and in the Committee (Reuther 1982).

AUMA is therefore in a good position to know about developments in the international trade fair markets, about trade fair policy issues, about specific events, and about the needs of the industries it deals with. No other body has a comparable breadth of trade fair related information.

But even for AUMA, the growth of the trade fair market, especially overseas, has been too fast to let it keep track of all fairs. So far, the information in the AUMA database on international trade fairs is based predominantly on information provided by the trade fair organisers themselves. The database provides no information on many of the fairs that are in the official trade fair programme for the first time, with the comment that the organisers do not provide any data. That there is a 'knowledge' gap is also suggested by the fact that in 1997 AUMA ran a project with five German chambers in Asia, which involved the chambers in drafting trade fair reports according to a standardised questionnaire (Kresse 1997:29). Faced with a situation in which AUMA has to judge the relative merit of two particular fairs that had not been in the official programme before, AUMA is unlikely to have its own trade fair specific information from which to make the choice. The decision would have to be based on the short justifications that trade associations provide on form sheets when they suggest a fair, and on the reputation of the trade fair organiser and alternative events for the industry. Given that in many cases AUMA relies on trade associations' judgement (D-I), given that AUMA's market research is focused on foreign fairs 'which are important for German industry' (see above), and given that AUMA is in regular contact with 'important industries', it appears likely that AUMA is more familiar with the problems and interests of established industries.

AUMA's incentives in the selection process

As described above, the centre of AUMA's activities is very much the provision of collective goods for the German trade fair industry, with AUMA being recognised as the representative body by both government and industry. Its purpose as a neutral mediator of the different interests in trade fairs is re-enforced by the statutory requirement that the composition of its board of directors' reflects visitors, exhibitors and organisers. It is also enforced by AUMA's major source of revenue, a 'tax' on trade fairs that amounts to ca. £0.7 per each square metre of exhibition space at trade fair events in Germany (D-C). A contribution from the BMWi and membership fees are other, but less important, income sources.[6]

AUMA has no incentive to endanger its credibility, and consequently its existence as an impartial mediator, when co-ordinating the trade fair support programme. In the selection process there are only two possible reasons for being impartial: First, due to its main source of finance and its statutory objective, all other things being equal, AUMA can be expected to disfavour a fair that could stand in competition to a similar event in Germany, rather than a fair that does not (e.g. one that is organised by a German trade fair company abroad as an advertising event for a similar German fair). This assumption was supported by D-A from BMWi, who perceived it as being in the German interest to favour fairs that strengthen the German trade fair industry. Second, AUMA is in regular contact with, and partly directed by, representatives from the major sectors of German industry. These established trade associations are also likely to be the 'opinion leaders' regarding AUMA's usefulness as a representative of exhibitors' and visitors' needs. AUMA's personnel might therefore be more susceptible to their arguments in favour of certain fairs, and regarding the trade fair programme in general, compared with less established or niche associations.

In sum, AUMA can be expected to act as a well-informed impartial mediator and clearing office, which does not abuse its powerful position as information broker, key assessor of fairs, and spokesman to the BMWi. Its knowledge and interests are likely to be skewed to some degree in favour of established industries, and in favour of fairs that are connected with the German trade fair industry. But these influences on decision making appear to be limited to cases where the trade associations suggest more fairs than can be supported and it has to be decided which fairs should be taken from the list.

---

[6] The BMWi contribution is not for AUMA's activities in the trade fair support programme, but for its initiatives to market Germany internationally as a trade fair location (D-A, BMWi). It was not possible to obtain exact figures or even only percentage figures of the AUMA budget. They are also not published in the annual reports.

6.2.4 The BMWi's selection knowledge and incentives

The Federal Ministry of Economics and Technology (BMWi) is the ministry responsible for the federal government's trade fair support programme.[7] One of its units, the *'Referat V A4 – Internationales Messewesen, Beteiligung an Messen und Ausstellungen im Ausland'* (International Trade Fairs, Participation at Trade Fairs and Exhibitions Abroad) is in charge of this task. This unit is one of seven belonging to the division Va 'General Issues of Foreign Economic Policy and Trade Policy', itself one of four divisions of the Directorate General V 'Foreign Economic Policy and Development Co-operation'.

The *Referat V A4* has seven employees including the head of the section and a secretary. Day-to-day business is concerned with the current trade fair programme, but also to a great extent the time-consuming planning and management of German participations in world expositions, and of German industry trade shows. Regarding the standard trade fair programme the tasks involve financial planning, and the approval of the design for each official group participation. Until 1996 the financial control of the trade fair programme was also part of the section's task, but was then handed over to the Bundesamt fuer Wirtschaft (BAW), an agency of the BMWi. This was done at the initiative of the head of the section, who wanted his section to focus more on the strategic issues. The change has reduced the number of employees by four (D-A).

Regarding the selection of trade fairs, the *Referat V A4* has the ultimate decision rights. To select the final list of supported fairs according to the stated goals, the BMWi would need to know which trade fair participations could benefit German firms most, and would need to have the incentive to choose accordingly.

However, as all interview partners stated, the BMWi usually agrees with the list that was drafted by AUMA and the Committee on the basis of the different bids. The head of the section sees this as demand-oriented work of his unit. The knowledge of the other actors, which is embodied in the list, is not questioned, and the BMWi therefore does not need to spend resources on building up its own worldwide trade fair and industry knowledge. To the large number of fairs, which thus effectively have been settled by the trade associations with AUMA, and the small number, which have been discussed and decided during the Committee's meetings, the BMWi may only add a few trade fairs for political reasons. Normally these participations take the form of information stands or information centres (14 in 1999), i.e. firms do not participate with their own stands.[8] According to D-A the section tries to keep the number of 'political participations' low. They are chosen in response to suggestions from the country sections in the BMWi and to suggestions from the diplomatic posts.

From the discussion about public sector senior officials' goals in Chapter 4, it is understandable that the *Referat V A4* does not have any incentive to disagree with

---

[7] As mentioned, the ministry for agriculture (BML) has its own small trade fair programme with ca.10–15 agriculture-related fairs per year.

[8] While D-I from an association stated that some group participations take place for political reasons, e.g. in Africa, D-A from the BMWi said this was hardly ever the case.

the choices of the trade associations and the Committee. On the contrary, it is very useful to have AUMA and the Committee deal with potentially controversial ranking decisions. If it wants, the BMWi can nevertheless influence the choice by setting the number of fairs that can receive funding, or by deciding the extent to which a fair is subsidised. For example, an industry in recession might receive funding for more fairs or higher funding for each fair than it would normally get (m+a 1986; BMWi 1992). The BMWi can give instructions to that effect to AUMA, but does not itself have to decline the wishes of another industry, and the choice does not even have to be stated openly. Keeping in the background, the BMWi can additionally benefit from the other bodies' expertise, cut the work they would otherwise have to do, and present itself as being a supporter of the private firms own stated needs.

6.2.5 Consequences of the selection organisation

To summarise, in Germany the actual distribution of tasks in the selection process leads to the expectation that established associations of exporting industries dominate the choice of trade fairs. Associations' export staff deal with those members on a regular basis, who are involved in export-related committees, and who initiate, and take up the association's export services. Thus associations' export officers are bound to know more about the trade fair support wishes and export target markets of these active members than of others. The active members are on average larger and export-experienced firms. Association staff are also inclined to respond to the explicit wishes of those members who make their preferences known, which would also be in the former group. One output prediction for this selection organisation is therefore that *fairs will be chosen which suit experienced, larger exporters but not necessarily novices.*

The framework within which the associations make their choice pressurises them to select fairs that attract at least ten participants. This, and the incentive to pick fairs that are interesting for different sub-groups within the association, make a second output prediction plausible: *The choice will be pushed towards fairs that have successfully attracted participants in previous years, and/or fairs that have a broad, rather than a specific, exhibition theme.* Big, established industry fairs are also better known than small, specialised events. AUMA and the BMWi strengthen this bias towards broadly themed, popular events as they 'guarantee' funding for fairs in which more than one association is interested, and for which firms have booked in advance.

For trade associations, a further aspect to consider, is their shareholder interest in specific trade fairs. To strengthen a competing fair by attending it with an official group is detrimental. They, and AUMA are also better informed about trade fairs that are connected to German trade fair organising companies, who inform them about their overseas events. Where AUMA as a mediator has any preferences between two otherwise equal fairs, it is for fairs that are linked to German trade fair organisers. The third expectation is therefore that *of the selected trade fairs abroad, a disproportionately high percentage are fairs that are linked to the German trade fair industry.*

BMWi, though it is officially the actor with the right to select the fairs, only adds 'political' participations to the list. The prioritising between industries is effectively done via quotas. Firms that are not represented by a trade association involved in making suggestions for the programme lose out.

Table 6.1. (next page) summarises the differences between the ideal and the real organisation of the selection process, and the predicted consequences.

There is some evidence that these predictions match the actual output pattern:

1) Selection bias towards the needs of active, larger members

As indicated above, larger firms tend to be more active in trade associations, and exporting firms are much more likely to be involved in export-related committees, and use the associations' export services.

Regarding the size of the participating firms, the AUMA evaluation of the 1997 official trade fair programme (AUMA 1998d)[9] found that 57% of the firms had up to 100 employees (35% up to 50), 28% between 100 and 500, and 15% more than 500. But the overall share of firms in Germany with from 100 to 500 employees was only 1.6% in 1996 and only 0.3% had more than 500 (BMWi 1998b). (As mentioned in Chapter 5, there are no export statistics related to firm size.) Though the two sets of figures cannot be directly compared, since for many small firms export activities are not feasible, and since the trade fair programme is predominantly oriented to the manufacturing sector, it seems that larger firms which are more likely to export anyway, are better represented than smaller firms. Prognos' survey supports this (Weidig and Ruprecht 1996:90). They found that the highest percentage of firms, who knew of the trade fair programme and used it, was in the size category '1001 and more employees' of their sample. A survey of the Rhineland-Palatinate export promotion programme, where in contrast to the federal programme individual firms can get support for fairs which they select themselves, found that smaller firms were much better represented – 51.1% had fewer than 50 employees (Hemmersbach 1993:304).

Regarding the experience of participants, the available data confirms that the fairs are selected in favour of experienced exporters. Firms that participated in 1997 attended on average between five and six trade fairs outside Germany in that year, only two of which were supported by the federal government (AUMA 1998d). Both figures and their quotient rose with the size of the firms, but even for companies with up to ten employees the share of individually organised participations was over one third. In many cases the participating firms already had a partner firm in the respective country (AUMA 1998d). Of the 1997 participants nearly 40% would have participated independently, had the fair not been included in the official programme, which is a very high number considering that the firms were asked directly at the trade fair. Fifty-seven per cent had exhibited at the same fair before (AUMA 1998c).

---

[9] In the beginning of 1998 a questionnaire was sent to all firms that participated in the 1997 group participations, and 26.5% (1.374 firms) responded.

Table 6.1. The German trade fair selection compared with the ideal organisation

Ideal selection organisation	*German selection organisation*

Ideal knowledge of the actors with the decision rights to select the fairs
▪ most promising markets for different industries
▪ trade fairs worldwide and their characteristics
▪ relevance of official support
▪ relative usefulness of exhibitions in different markets/industries
	Real knowledge on which selection is based
	within an industry – *trade associations*
	▪ market knowledge based on
	  o info from active members
	  o info gained when providing other export services (which active members use)
	  o info gained at previous trade fair events
	▪ trade fair knowledge based on
	  o previous participations
	  o trade fair organising companies
	  o active members
	▪ knowledge about relevance of official support based on
	  o previous participations
	  o active members
	▪ knowledge about relative usefulness of exhibitions in different markets based on
	  o previous participations
	  o active members
	between industries – *AUMA, BMWi* knowledge based on
	▪ suggestions from trade associations
	▪ involvement in trade fair matters
	▪ no. of associations applying for a fair
	▪ no. of pre-booked participants
	▪ information from other parts of BMWi and other ministries
	▪ quotas

Ideal incentives of the actors with the decision rights to select the fairs ▪ choose impartially according to highest impact of trade fair support on market entry success ▪ cater for both inexperienced/potential exporters and experienced exporters entering new markets	*Real incentives which influence the selection* within an industry – *trade associations* ▪ to cater for active members (who are already exporting, and who are tendentially larger firms) ▪ to attract at least ten participants, the more the better ▪ to satisfy different member-associations/subgroups ▪ not to support events that may compete with fairs in which they are shareholders between industries – *AUMA, BMWi* ▪ to leave choices to the private sector ▪ to provide more support for industries in recession ▪ to choose some trade fair locations that are important for political reasons ▪ bias towards fairs that support German trade fair organisers
Ideal output selection of the fairs that offer the best opportunities for a successful market entry of new/occasional and of experienced exporters	*Predicted real output pattern:* 1. suggested fairs are biased towards the needs of active trade association members 2. suggested fairs are likely to have a broad trade fair theme and/or have attracted a large group of participants previously 3. disproportionately, many fairs have links to German trade fair organisers

A further indication that experienced exporters are the main focus group for the associations is a rule concerning trade fair locations (see figure 6.3): Supporting a trend that had already begun in the 1980s (Schellkes 1987) the Committee agreed in 1997 to focus on fairs outside Western and Central Europe when faced with a budget cut for the 1998 participations (VDMA 1997). Now any suggestions for fairs in Western and Central Europe are treated as controversial and are subject to the approval of the Committee (D-J).

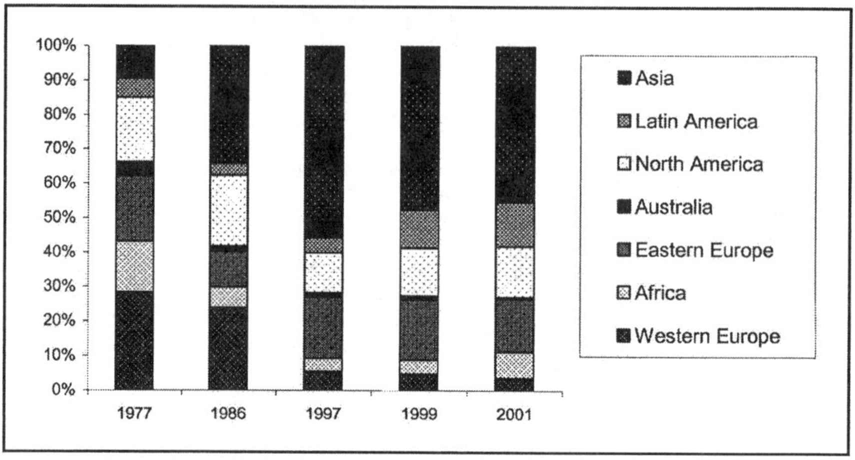

Fig. 6.3. Distribution of official trade fair participations according to location 1977-2003
Sources: Schellkes 1987; AUMA 1998; AUMA 2001, 2003

This agreement was initiated by the larger associations (D-I). BMWi justified it subsequently with the growth opportunities and the relatively more difficult market entry in these countries (BMWi 1998a). AUMA (1998d:17f) found that the firms participating in the government's trade fair programme exhibit in Western Europe without government help, and used it as an argument for the agreement. But AUMA itself wrote *'even for the participants in the official programme, the EU and the rest of Europe are their main focus of export activities with 88.65% or 76.20% being engaged there.* ***This is not surprising, since firms open up close markets first, before they explore destinations further away.'*** (1998d:18, emphasis added). Weidig and Ruprecht (1996:91) came to the conclusion that small firms have to concentrate their trade fair activities on a few events and many would choose events in the major industrialised countries. Considering that the main motive for participating in the official trade fair programme is financial support, mentioned by 88% of all firms,[10] it is not far fetched to assume that it was the larger, export-experienced association members who were interested in the coun-

[10] This figure is based on an evaluation of more than 10.000 questionnaires, which were filled in by official trade fair participants between 1987 and 1992 (Econ-Consult & ISG 1994). In the AUMA survey (1998d) 66% stated that the financial subsidy was the major reason for them to participate.

try rule. The German governments' financial subsidy for the participants is not fixed, but is higher the more 'difficult' the market is considered to be (D-A). Firms that exhibit in Western and Central Europe, but also in Asia or Latin America, benefit more from support for farther away trade fairs.

2) Selection of fairs that are likely to attract many participants
Asked whether they would rather choose trade fairs in which they know many members want to participate, or fairs through which 'new' markets could be initially explored, all interview partners answered with the former.

As mentioned above, repeat participations by the same firms are prevalent.[11] One of the cost-cutting attempts for the 1998 programme was to introduce lower financial subsidies for firms after their fourth participation at the same fair, which suggests that this occurs frequently (VDMA 1997). Trade associations can assume that a fair that was popular previously would attract many firms again. And the data confirms that fairs where many firms participated in the past are suggested again. Of 195 fairs scheduled for 1999 only 20 were in the programme for the first time (D-B) and 18 have been visited for ten or more years. Of the 14 trade fairs outside Europe, which were not included again in the 1999 programme, 12 had 17 or fewer participants, five of them fewer than 12. The other two were a book fair in Tokyo and a universal fair in Cairo. Both had shown a continuous decline of exhibitor numbers (AUMA 1998f; AUMA database - http://www.auma.de).

As to the broadness of the trade fair themes, 17 of the 164 group participations in 1999 fairs were general, investment or consumer goods fairs, i.e. any such product may be exhibited there. Other fairs are listed under various product group headings in the AUMA list of official trade fair participations, have titles like 'International Machine Tool Exhibition', or 'Interior Lifestyle', and the information stands of the previous participation were manned by representatives from two different associations (AUMA 1998g; AUMA database – http://www.auma.de). In Econ-Consult and ISGs (1994) survey on SMEs' view of the programme, one of the negative aspects in participants' view was that the trade fairs exhibits were too diverse. D-J, asked about the selection of fairs with broader rather than special themes, agreed that he would rather choose the former. He argued that otherwise the risk of not attracting ten exhibitors would be too high, a point confirmed by the other trade association representatives. D-J agreed that this could be a problem for small, very specialised firms, since their trade fair budget did not allow them to exhibit at many fairs and they had to choose those that most closely matched their product profile. It also meant that for markets that interest only few firms no fairs were suggested. Another indication that the selection organisation results in a trade fair list with a bias towards broad trade fair themes is a recommendation by BDI: Based on a survey in 1995 they recommended to improve the trade fair support programme by cutting back support for general fairs in favour of participations at more specialised events (BDI 1996:14).

[11] Repeated participation at the same trade fair is usually necessary since building customer relations takes time and it is a sign of commitment to a market. However, one of the major arguments for trade fair support – to overcome 'information failure' – does not apply to firms that have already participated at a trade fair several times.

3) Selection of fairs that are connected to the German trade fair industry
The data on trade fairs with official group participations in 1999 show that 28% were either organised by a German trade fair company, or had German trade fair companies as representatives for the foreign organiser (AUMA trade fair database). It was not possible to establish the market share that German trade fair companies have in the trade fair business abroad, and thus to establish precisely how skewed the choice is. But the figure appears to be large: German trade fair companies organise only approximately 160 fairs each year abroad (AUMA 2001) while many thousands take place. At the German Trade Fair Forum 2001 German trade fair companies' presence abroad was characterised as 'relatively minor and fragmented' (AUMA 2001a).

6.3 Participant recruitment

6.3.1 The allocation of tasks and decision rights

In Germany the so-called *'Durchführungsgesellschaften'* (DFG) are the principal actors in the recruitment activity. They are trade fair companies (*'Messeveranstalter'*) who are registered as official trade fair participations organisers. Recruitment is supported by AUMA, who publish and distribute the official trade fair programme on the Internet (since 1998) and on paper. The trade associations who have suggested the respective fairs also support exhibitor recruitment. Firms who hear about the opportunity from sources other than the DFG have to register with the DFG if they want to be part of the group.

As specified above, the recruitment activity involves informing the firms that belong to those industries represented at the fair. The firms need to receive enough information to judge whether a participation might benefit them. If additionality is to be avoided, the objective must be to convince those firms that would not go on their own, but who nevertheless have a realistic chance to benefit from the participation. The question is whether the DFG know enough about the industries and markets to be able to do so, and whether they benefit from attracting the right type of firms.

6.3.2 The 'Durchführungsgesellschaften's' recruitment knowledge and incentives

Who are the Durchführungsgesellschaften?
DFGs are German trade fair companies who are registered as 'official trade fair participation organisers'. Only they are entitled to bid for a contract with BMWi to lead a specific group participation abroad. This involves recruiting the participants, as well as providing exhibition support. In exchange for their service they receive a management fee from BMWi.

To become a DFG, a trade fair company has to apply to BMWi, showing that they have experience in arranging trade fair participations abroad, that they have sufficient personnel, and that they are based in Germany (D-B). There are no formal benchmarks, as the community of trade fair companies is considered to be small and transparent enough to allow AUMA to judge the suitability of an applicant (D-G). While in 1970 only five trade fair companies had DFG status (m+a 1970), the number has increased since, especially over the last decade. In 1999 there were 17 DFGs and in 2001 there were 21, reflecting not only the growth in the trade fair programme, but also the growth in the number of trade fair companies, and their interest in DFG status (D-B; D-F).

The majority of the DFGs have been in public ownership, which mirrors the ownership structures of German trade fair companies. The ten leading German trade fair companies, all of them DFGs, are publicly owned[12] and the six largest of them cover 80–90% of the German market (Groth 1992; AUMA 1997a:30). But there are also smaller, privately-owned companies with DFG status (four in 1999, eight in 2001). A further two DFGs are owned by trade associations. These two are exceptions in that they only bid for participations in their respective industries, the book and the toy industry. As their cases are not representative for other industries, they will not be discussed further.

The motive for trade fair companies to become a DFG is not directly financial. All interviewed DFG representatives affirmed that the fee they receive for organising a participation barely covers their costs. This is supported by other evidence: D-C from AUMA, as well as D-A from BMWi stated that unless there were selection criteria in addition to price, large DFGs would make offers below their costs. Small organisers could not compete because they could not cross-subsidise events. According to the AUMA annual report 1997/98 (AUMA 1998:47), AUMA has had talks with the BMWi regarding the low fees of the DFGs. And in an interview about overseas activities of trade fair organisers, the director of unMiller Freeman (Deutschland) GmbH, the German subsidiary of the British owned, largest trade-fair organiser worldwide, said that his company was not interested in becoming a DFG, because there was hardly any money in it.[13]

But the DFGs do not lead official participations for altruistic reasons. Their motives can be traced to the weak position of German trade fair companies in the global trade fair business. Their big Anglo-Saxon competitors responded to the growing demand for regional trade fairs in Asia and Latin America as early as the 1970s, while the major German trade fair companies concentrated on their Ger-

[12] The local authority where the trade fair company owns an exhibition site holds between 50% and 100% of the shares; the respective Land holds up to 50%. It is also common that the local chambers of commerce, the crafts' chambers and other local or regional business organisations own a small amount of the shares, usually 1–5% together (Busche 1992).

[13] The interview with Walter Jung, the director, was carried out in 1997 by Mr. Hans Werner Reinhard in the context of a research project on globalisation trends in the trade fair business. The interview was transcribed and printed in Reinhard (1997).

man sites.[14] Finally, in the nineties, they were forced to change their business strategy in the face of overcapacity in the Western European trade fair business, and Western producers' increasing exhibition engagement in growing markets overseas (Groth 1997:15; AUMA 1997a:25). Business abroad is now perceived as a means to hold or to improve a company's market position, to advertise for fairs in Germany, to take a share in growing markets, and to diversify risk.[15] In 1998 German trade fair companies held a total of 180 fairs outside Germany (AUMA 1998:48) in contrast to only 44 in 1991 (Kresse 1997:21). However, compared with British competitors like unMiller Freeman or Reed Exhibition Companies, each of which organise far more than 300 exhibitions annually (AUMA 1998:48), the German 'newcomers' to the overseas trade fair business are disadvantaged. The competitors entered the new markets while they were still uncontested. They have more flexibility because unlike the big German companies they do not have the fixed cost of their own exhibition sites, and they have big media concerns behind them, which give them marketing advantages.[16] Moreover, they have been able to raise money on the capital market and from their holding companies[17] to buy up established trade fair themes, and to buy up established foreign trade fair companies. In these respects they also hold a big advantage over the German private DFGs, who have neither the media link nor a comparable financial power. What all the German trade fair companies therefore need foremost is to gain expertise and a platform to market their own services.

This is reflected in the replies of interviewed DFG representatives, when asked why they were interested in organising official trade fair participations. All four

[14] The public shareholders of the main German trade fair companies shied away from the risk of overseas engagements. Moreover, to organise fairs abroad was seen as taking clients away from the home market, where the companies own their exhibition sites. And for the public owners socio-economic and regional policy aspects of trade fairs are more important than profit aspects of their trade fair companies: Just the regional trade fair related expenditures of organisers, visitors and exhibitors reach approximately five to six times the turnover of the exhibition organiser, not to speak of trade fair related employment and of tax income (Groth 1992; AUMA 1998e).

[15] Deutscher Bundestag 2001; AUMA 1998e:5; Kresse 1997:21; W. Lenarz, General Manager, Hannover-Messe International GmbH, 28.1.1997 and W.Dornscheid, Company Secretary NOWEA International GmbH, 15.1.1997 in: Reinhard 1997:XXXIIIff, XXXVIIIff; M.Wutzelhofer, Director Messe Muenchen GmbH, in: AUMA 1997:25.

[16] H. Krausmann, Director of the department 'Trade fairs abroad', Messe Frankfurt GmbH, 29.1.1997; S. Osthues, Company Secretary and Managing Director Reed Exhibition Companies (Deutschland) GmbH, 30.1.1997; W.G. Jung, Managing Director unMiller Freeman (Deutschland) GmbH and executive board member unMiller Freeman London, 30.1.1997 in: Reinhard 1997. Mr. Jung specifically pointed to the huge address database to which his company has access, because of its media link. They can target the subscribers of business journals and the companies that advertise in these journals.

[17] Nearly the entire business assets of the ten leading German trade fair companies consist of their exhibition sites in Germany (AUMA 1997:30). The public shareholders of the major German trade fair companies are not inclined to provide capital for buying up overseas companies (H. Krausmann, Director of the department 'Trade fairs abroad', Messe Frankfurt GmbH, 29.1.1997, in: Reinhard 1997:XLIIIff).

interviewees responded that it gave them the opportunity *to gain knowledge about new trade fair locations or new industries*, and that they use their DFG status *for advertising purposes*. The answer was the same regardless of whether the interviewees worked for a public or for a private company (2 and 2). As an official organiser a DFG has the opportunity to work closely with the respective trade association. The DFG can develop new contacts and new sector expertise. This 'networking' aspect was particularly emphasised by the managers of two young private trade fair companies, who were interviewed. They need to develop close relationships with industry and a reputation, so that their own events attract exhibitors and visitors. The contacts are particularly important in the context of the German trade fair culture where the business associations have always worked closely with the trade fair companies (Negelein 1992). The private companies also stated that in addition to the advertising opportunities that come with a specific participation, their DFG status served them as an official 'seal of approval'. This made it easier to find other customers for their trade fair organisation services, like Länder or trade associations (D-G; D-H). The motive was confirmed in that all but one of the privately-owned DFGs with a website (seven out of eight in Nov. 2001) advertise their DFG status there. For the publicly-owned DFGs with their own exhibition sites the synergy and advertising effects for their own fairs play an important role. One interviewee pointed out that the BMWi allows the DFG to distribute advertising material during the group event (D-E).

DFGs also apply for participations where they can make profits despite of the low management fee. This can be the case where they have subsidiaries abroad, where they have already organised that particular participation before, or where they themselves are the trade fair company that is running the fair abroad (D-G).

These motives of DFGs have consequences for their knowledge and incentives regarding the recruitment task.

The recruitment knowledge of the DFGs

DFGs depend on trade fair marketing knowledge to make their own events profitable. Therefore it can be expected that they know the general trade fair advertising channels. But they find it particularly easy to promote an event if they know the respective industry. In that case they have lists of addresses, and know which firms act as 'crowd pullers' that convince others to participate (D-F). However, some DFGs deliberately apply for fairs through which they get to know an industry and can develop new contacts (D-E; D-G).

That DFGs know the industry for which they become an official event organiser is not a precondition set by BMWI. D-A from BMWI said they, in consultation with AUMA, consider the price of a DFG's bid, and the DFG's competence regarding markets and/or industries. In addition, having a position close to that of a monopsonist, BMWI aims to make contracts with various DFGs.[18] But once chosen, a DFG usually gets to organise the same trade fair event from three to five

[18] While D-C from AUMA confirmed this, the answers from the DFGs differed, when asked for the selection criteria. One stated it was just a question of price, the others thought it was a mixture of the issues mentioned.

consecutive times (if the fair is selected that often). Then BMWi chooses another DFG as a matter of principle (D-C; D-J).

To get a rough picture of the number of trade fair participations where the DFG does not know the industry, the trade fair database for 1999 was analysed in conjunction with the web-pages of the DFGs. The industries for which DFGs organised events were compared with the sector expertise which the DFGs list on their website. The same was done for the countries in which the events took place, to judge the extent to which DFGs could advise firms about the respective markets and help them with their exhibition (see 5.4. below). Data was available for nearly three-quarters of the events. The missing data concerns five DFGs that did not have a website.

As Figure 6.4 shows, in 24% of the cases the DFG arranged the official participation for their own fair abroad, i.e. they knew the industry and country well enough to run their own business venture on that basis. In a further 18% they had expertise regarding both the industry and the country where the event took place, even though the fairs were not their own. Another 31% of events were organised by DFGs who did not know the country, but had expertise in the industries attending the fairs.[19]

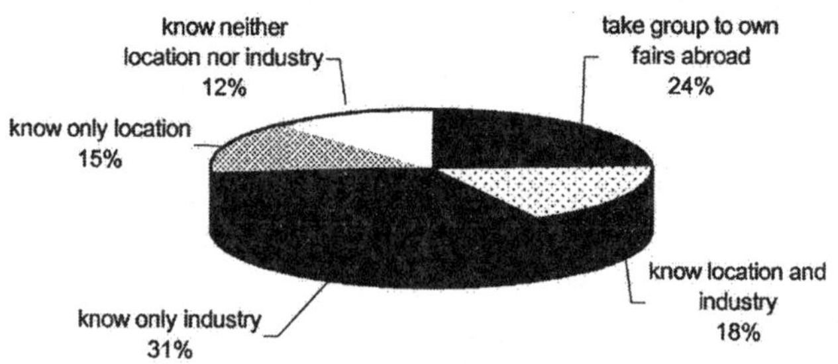

Fig. 6.4. Industry and location expertise of DFGs for participations they led in 1999
Source: compiled from AUMA's official trade fair participations database for 1999 (www.auma.de) and websites of DFGs.

This data suggests that only about one-quarter of the participations are organised by DFGs who do not know the industry. If one takes into account that the missing data concerns mostly the small private trade fair organisers, who might

[19] A DFG was defined as '*knowing an industry*', if they either run trade fairs for that industry themselves, or if they organised participations for that industry in 1999 independently of the central government's official participations. To '*know a location*' means either that the DFG have subsidiaries there, or that they organised trade fairs or participations in the respective country in 1999 independently of the central government's official participations. Obviously this definition of 'knowledge' is flawed, since it cannot reflect whether the DFG have gained other industry or country expertise in previous years or dealt with them for the first time in 1999.

have a smaller range of experience with different industries, the actual figure could be slightly higher. But even in the quarter to third of events where DFGs do not know the industry from their other business activities, they often have some knowledge from leading a previous participation to the same fair. Of all official participations, 64% are 'repeat organisations'.[20]

For the remainder of official participations DFG's 'industry' knowledge is not as crucial for recruitment, as it is for their own independent events. The business associations help out since, as argued above, they have their own interest in attracting members to participate. D-K reported that when he started his job in association C, his superior explicitly pointed out to him that to support DFGs in their recruitment efforts was an important part of his role. For example, the associations supply address lists to the DFG, advise them, might contact firms directly, and advertise the fairs in their publications (D-I; D-J; D-K). They know who suggested the fair, and who went to previous or alternative fairs.

Furthermore, the DFGs are supported by AUMA, which publishes and publicises the group participation programme in print and on-line. For AUMA this is a routine activity, which is part of their role. Due to its activities as the central body for promoting German trade fair interests, AUMA is known to firms and other organisations with trade fair experience. Their information services are good, prompt, and free,[21] and experienced firms can therefore easily find out which trade fairs are included in the official programme. Those firms then directly approach the DFGs.

In summary, DFGs are therefore likely to know, either by themselves or with the help of trade associations and AUMA, which firms are likely to be interested in the group participation. They are also capable of using general marketing channels to inform more firms in the industry.

But this does not mean that they know whether firms' choices are based on reasonable assumptions, nor that they know those details about the fair and market that might be relevant for an individual firm's decision. Their own business expertise is a different one, and as shown above, in a large number of cases they do not know the market where the event takes place. As a representative of the trade associations confirmed, the DFG cannot assess the suitability of the firms who register for participation (D-I). Consequently, neither can they assess which of the firms that do not register would be suitable, nor convince them with detailed knowledge why they should.

The recruitment incentives of the DFGs

Although AUMA formally supports the DFG in their recruitment activity, and the trade associations informally do so, the DFGs are meant to make an active recruitment effort. This is part of the service for which BMWi pays the management fee (D-H).

---

[20] For each of the 148 'old' events the summary report of the previous participation was available on-line, and it could be traced whether the DFG led the participation the previous time.

[21] This was experienced when asking for printed information and interviews, and while working in the AUMA library, observing responses to other visitors and phone enquiries.

DFGs have various reasons to comply. Large groups are attractive for the DFG, not only because they can advertise their company to many firms, but also because the DFG can earn an additional income by selling extra services to the participating firms. Moreover, since 1997 they have received a bonus for each firm beyond the minimum number of 10 (D-A). They have the negative incentive that an event is cancelled if not enough firms have applied by the given deadline. In such a case the appointed DFG receives only a small compensation fee (D-H). Furthermore, trade fairs that attracted only low participant numbers are most likely to be dropped from the programme in the following year (see 6.2.5. above). Since DFGs usually get to organise a fair several times and its profitability increases with DFG experience, this is another incentive for recruiting participants.

Yet the benefits of recruiting a large group have to be seen in relation to the costs. The DFGs receive a flat fee from the BMWi, and marketing costs can be high (D-H).[22] D-I from the umbrella association B stated that in some cases DFGs had tried to cut marketing costs by relying on the associations' interest in recruiting participants. But since building or keeping good relations with associations was in the interest of DFGs who wanted to stay in business, they were normally likely to make an acceptable effort. They advertise in trade magazines, on their websites, and send out brochures to firms on their address lists. Also, if trade associations had reasons to be particularly unhappy with a DFG they could insist on not working with them again.

Thus the DFGs appear to have incentives to try to recruit participants for the group events. But all of these incentives are connected to the quantity of attracted firms, regardless of their capabilities to win export orders or to otherwise benefit from a participation. The cost of recruiting firms that are uninformed about potential trade fair benefits or that are indecisive, are higher than for firms that want to participate anyway. It is therefore unlikely that DFGs would approach firms directly and try to convince them that exhibiting could be beneficial for them, when they can get enough interested participants through AUMA, the trade associations, and through their standard marketing channels. It is also unlikely that the DFG would spend resources on collecting detailed information that might help to convince firms of the benefits of exhibiting at the fair. Giving firms advice about their suitability as exhibitors is also not seen as part of the DFGs' task (D-I).

The trade associations that support the DFGs in recruiting firms do not benefit from targeted information provision either. As argued in the section on trade fair selection, for the trade associations it is also the number of members that counts, especially the number of active members. The associations' benefits are not reduced if the firms would have participated at the respective fair anyway. On the contrary, their members would value the subsidy even more. The interviewed representatives of associations did not see it as their role to approach indecisive firms with detailed information. They were of the opinion that firms could get information from the Federal Agency for Overseas Trade Information (BfAi) and the

[22] Asked whether DFGs might be able to receive a 'top up' if the organisation of a participation proved to be more expensive than anticipated, D-H answered that in rare cases they could. He gave the example of very high marketing costs.

chambers of commerce. If they wanted to, they could make telephone enquiries to the association.

6.3.3 Consequences of the recruitment organisation

Having considered the recruitment knowledge and incentives of the DFGs and how AUMA and the trade associations support them, it has become evident that this organisation corresponds only partly with the ideal organisation. The task of information provision beyond mere event marketing is not formally assigned to any actor, nor do they have any incentive to do it irrespectively. The responsible DFG has neither the knowledge nor the incentive to target those inexperienced exporters, and new exporters to a market, who could benefit from exhibiting with the group. However, the DFGs want to recruit at least the minimum number of participants, and they know how to use information channels that reach interested firms. This is reinforced by the interests of the trade associations, and helped by the work of AUMA.

It is possible to draw the following conclusions on how the actual organisation would affect the recruitment outcomes: First, it ensures that the number of firms who receive information about the trade fair programme is relatively high. Second, although all firms can get the information about the opportunity, and many will come across it, the experienced exporters and prominent firms are most likely to be directly targeted for recruitment. They are the ones that are personally 'known', and/or that are on the mailing lists of all three parties. They are the ones that are easiest to convince, or those of whom it is known beforehand, that they want to go. Third, firms that do not source the relevant information themselves, be it due to a lack of experience, a lack of understanding of the potential benefits, or due to time constraints, will not receive sufficient information for a balanced judgement of the costs and benefits of the group participation. The DFGs are neither capable of providing them with the information, nor do they have an incentive to try. This will lead to some firms participating although the fair is not really suitable for them, and to some firms not participating although they could benefit from exhibiting with the group. The points are summarized in Table 6.2. (next page).

Again, to provide direct evidence for this expected pattern is difficult. But the available evidence supports the conclusions:

1) Many firms receive the information about the trade participation programme

The overall number of firms who know that the trade fair programme exists is high. According to Prognos' survey (Weidig and Ruprecht 1996:90) 65.7% of firms know of the central government's trade fair programme, and in BDI's survey (1996) the result was even higher with 77.9%.[23] These figures have to be seen in the context of the general criticism that Federal government's export promotion

[23] BDI took its sample from Germany's major exporting industries.

Table 6.2. The German recruitment organisation compared with the ideal organisation

Ideal recruitment organization	*German recruitment organisation*
Ideal knowledge of the actors with the decision rights for participant recruitment ▪ suitable information channels to inform all firms ▪ information that is relevant for firms to judge whether the fair can be useful for them, and sources for such information	*Real knowledge* of the DFGs ▪ re. knowledge of suitable information channels o know major general information channels o know industry specific information channels in three-quarters of cases o receive firm specific distribution information from trade associations o benefit from AUMA and trade association advertising channels ▪ re. knowledge of information that is relevant to firms o know only in some cases about trade fair details, exhibiting in that market, and industry in the market
Ideal incentives of the actors with the decision rights for participant recruitment ▪ inform all firms with equal prospects equally ▪ provide sufficient information to allow firms to make rational choices	*Real incentives* of the DFGs benefit from high number of participants/lose out with low number of participants ▪ re. to inform all firms equally o firms known to be interested are cheaper to recruit than firms that need to be convinced ▪ re. to provide sufficient information for rational choices o recruitment benefits unrelated to success of exhibitors o information provision not expected by BMWi nor trade associations o information provision is costly
Ideal output recruitment of inexperienced, potential and experienced exporters who can successfully exhibit at a selected fair to enter a new market	*Predicted real output pattern* 1. a high number of firms receive information about the trade fair opportunity 2. only firms known to DFG and trade associations are recruited directly 3. many participants and non-participants do not receive enough information to make a rational choice about participation

services are not widely known among the SME target groups (Habuda et al. 1998a:34).

2) Only firms known to DFGs and trade associations are recruited directly
Some evidence about the type of participants was already presented in 5.2.5. above, when the effects of the selection organisation were discussed. It can be argued that the organisation of the recruitment activity does nothing to make the participants more likely to be inexperienced firms or small firms. It is too expensive and without particular benefit for the DFG, and they lack the knowledge to target that group and convince them. EconConsult (1994), and the BDI (1996) and

Prognos (Weidig and Ruprecht 1996) surveys concluded that the bigger the firms, the more likely they are to know about the trade fair programme. In a survey about the sources from which group participants obtained their trade fair information, most firms mentioned trade publications, which would include journals or newsletters of trade associations and ads placed by DFGs in trade journals ('Fachpresse': 54%). The next most frequently mentioned were 'own sources', which would include direct contact with the trade associations or DFGs ('eigene Quellen': 48%), and AUMA (42%). 'Other associations and organisations' (which would include mail shots from DFGs) were mentioned by 33%, while newspapers (5%), commercial directories (9%), or 'other sources' (13%), were of little importance (AUMA 1998d). Interestingly, the survey showed that large firms receive information predominantly from 'own sources', while small firms rely most on trade publications.

3) Firms do not receive sufficient information to judge the costs and benefits of participation adequately

Although over 80% of the participating firms stated they were content with the information offered on trade fairs abroad, these statements seem to cover predominantly the information about the events as such, not necessarily information about how to assess whether a participation would be useful or how to make a participation successful. All interviewed DFG representatives stated that there were always a number of badly prepared firms, and all four editions of the BMWi trade fair policy proclamation (BMWi 1992:6; BMWi 1993:15; BMWi 1998a:15; BMWi 2000:15) mention the problem of inadequately prepared firms. Questioned directly after the fair, only 55.8% of the firms intended to participate again (AUMA 1998c), which indicates that for a large number of firms the event did not work as well as they had anticipated.[24] In a representative sample of exhibitors AUMA came to the conclusion that there are quite a few firms that participated with unrealistic expectations (AUMA 1998d:7). Legler et al. (1994:53) found that experienced individual exhibitors make far more intensive use of different information sources before participating at a fair than group participants who seem to rely on the 'selection wisdom' of the programme organisers. Stating their problems with trade fair preparation, firms mentioned most frequently the time constraints of the owner manager or senior manager, but information problems regarding new or difficult markets followed suit (ECON-CONSULT and ISG 1994).[25]

As to non-participants, information seems to be a problem as well. BDI (1996) found that although 78% of their survey group knew of the programme, only 25% used it. Prognos (Weidig and Ruprecht 1996) had a similar result (23.1% compared with 67%). When EconConsult and ISG (1994) questioned more than 700

[24] This can certainly have a variety of reasons other than insufficient knowledge about the fair and/or the market, e.g. an unexpected change in exchange rates.

[25] BMWi commissioned the survey. It was based on an evaluation of over 10.000 questionnaires filled in by participants of official trade fair participations between 1987 and 1992; direct surveys at a number of trade fairs in 1993/94, and a questionnaire sent to 7.300 firms all over Germany, of which more than 700 responded and about 100 gave in-depth interviews.

randomly selected SMEs, firms stated that their major reasons for *not participating* at a trade fair were costs, followed by information deficits and staff shortages. However, in subsequent questions it became evident that a large number of those firms made their judgement without any knowledge about exhibiting abroad (19%) or without knowing which fairs would be suitable for them (37%). Another 31% said they received very little information about potentially interesting markets.

In their research on German SMEs' (non)-activity in Asia, Borrmann et al (1996) found that firms lack information, not because it is not available, but because they are not open to absorb it. In addition, SMEs perceive the cost of information gathering as high, especially in terms of time and opportunity costs. These firms would need to be approached directly with tailored, specific and reliable information, before they respond to opportunities. BFAI experience confirmed this. They found that SMEs are increasingly inundated with easily accessible information that they cannot evaluate and use. More and more firms only collect information if they have a very concrete reason for doing so (Deutscher Bundestag 2000a).

6.4 Exhibition support

6.4.1 The allocation of tasks and decision rights

In the previous chapter it was argued that the direct output aim of trade fair support was to improve firms' real and perceived net benefit of exhibiting abroad. Ideally, the responsible actors know how to provide the various forms of exhibition support that can reduce firms' costs of exhibiting, and increase their benefits. They know which is the best mix of the different types of support, and have an incentive to provide the ideal mix.

In Germany, firms receive *'complete participation support'* (Deutscher Bundestag 2001) from the DFG that has been appointed to lead the group. This does not include the direct financial support. The subsidy is not paid out to each exhibitor, but is integrated into the support 'package' in form of a reduced participation fee. 'Complete support' neither includes services that aim at increasing exhibitors' returns. In Germany no actor is responsible for this task.

DFGs 'exhibition support' consists of the other three approaches to reducing exhibitors' costs. They are formally appointed to reduce costs by negotiating group discounts related to the exhibition space purchase and to stand construction, to reduce cost by arranging an attractive design for the entire group, and by lowering some exhibition transaction costs before and during the participation. They rent the exhibition space in bulk from the exhibition organiser and offer it to participants on a square metre basis. The price also includes stand construction, security, cleaning, etc., access to communication facilities, and entries in the catalogue of exhibitors. The DFG has the task of arranging all these services either by itself or through subcontractors and has to work with an architect who is responsible for the stand design. At some trade fairs, additional services are included in the price as well, for example, advertisements in local papers, or receptions with the German ambassador (BMWi 1998a). The DFGs are also the contact partner for any queries and problems before and during the fair, e.g. when a ship with exhibition goods does not arrive (D-F; D-G; AUMA 1983). On top of this BMWi funded 'package', DFGs may offer participants the joint shipment of exhibition pieces, services regarding paperwork, additional stand design services, support with receptions, organisation of translator services, advertising, etc. on their own account.

The trade associations, overseas chambers, and diplomatic posts can be supportive, but do not have any formal responsibility within the organisation. The only support for exhibitors who seek to increase their returns from exhibiting is an AUMA brochure on how to manage trade fair participations effectively.

6.4.2 The DFGs's exhibition support knowledge and incentives

The knowledge of the DFGs

To provide for cheaper exhibition costs in terms of negotiated group discounts, savings on exhibitors' transaction costs, and an attractive design, DFGs need to know about the relevant exhibition procedures, about suppliers of exhibition-related services, price levels, payment, and negotiating and monitoring techniques for the subcontractors who are often based abroad.

As to the availability of this knowledge, the picture is mixed: Since all DFGs are trade fair organisers in their own right and, by definition, have experience in arranging trade fair participations outside Germany, all are familiar with the general organisational aspects of a trade fair participation. Their own profit margins depend on how successfully they contract with exhibition-related service providers, so they are likely to have built up expertise in these matters. Since 1977 participants have had to fill in a questionnaire, which has also helped DFGs to improve their exhibition support services (Schellkes 1987:50).

But as it was pointed out in DFG interviewees, and in an article in a trade fair industry journal, specific country knowledge increases the effectiveness of exhibition support. Knowledge about issues like the local trading customs, advertising channels, the particularities of the exhibition site, as well as contacts with the exhibition organisers, diplomatic posts etc. facilitates the participation (m+a 1970). Particularly in countries with erratic and strong bureaucracies, e.g. in China or India, it is important to know 'who is who', for example in customs or transport (D-F). As demonstrated in Figure 5.4. above, the DFGs often do not have that local knowledge. D-G from a private DFG emphasised that the BMWi does not pay for the travel of DFG officers to the location before the trade fair, only in very rare cases if the sites are 'exotic' (e.g. Tashkent).

Knowledge of the industry is another requisite for smooth organisation, which is also not always given (see Figure 5.4.). Here, familiarity – for example with the exhibitors' need for specific transport arrangements, storage room, or stand equipment requirements – improves the service the DFG can offer (D-G). But the trade associations can give advice and, as mentioned above, the majority of group participations are 'repeat participations', which were led by the same DFG before. They are therefore often familiar with the most important country and industry features.

When it comes to marketing support for exhibitors, the German trade fair support programme offers them a pre-constructed stand that is part of an attractively designed official 'German' group of stands. The appearance of the 'German group' is specifically planned for each fair, except for a unifying logo – the colours black red and gold combined with the slogan 'made in Germany' -- which has been used for all official participations since 1992 (AUMA 1992; BMWi 2000). Regarding this form of support, the DFGs do not have the decision right to provide it as they consider best. They are required by BMWi to work with a selected German trade fair architect, since the official group display is a 'public construction project' for which an architect must be employed by law (D-B). The architect prepares design plans, which have to be approved by the BMWi. More recently the trade associations have won some influence on the design, in that they are asked their opinion and wishes for 'their' fairs. DFGs can suggest architects, but they have to be approved by BMWi. He/she must be a member of the pool of 'official trade fair architects' to ensure his/her competence to design for fairs abroad (D-F). Thus, DFGs themselves do not need any design knowledge, and are helped in their 'designer choice' by the availability of a qualified list.

To summarise, compared with an individual inexperienced exhibitor, the DFGs in co-operation with the architects have extensive knowledge that can reduce the transaction costs of exhibiting, and of attracting visitors to the stand, and can also lead to group discounts.

The incentives of the DFGs

DFGs have mixed incentives to reduce exhibitors' direct costs where they work as agents of BMWi. But where they work on their own account, they can only sell their services if they have something to offer and if participants demand them.

The exhibition support services for which BMWi employs DFGs consist mainly of dealing with the trade fair organiser, and of contracting with, and coordinating the architect and other service suppliers involved in stand construction and maintenance. For this work, the DFG receives the initially arranged management fee. The fee is fixed, and completely unrelated to a DFG's subsequent results in reducing the direct and indirect exhibition costs of participants.

For a DFG the direct costs, for example the fees of the subcontractors, are costs that are passed on to the exhibitors and BMWi. A DFG does not benefit from negotiating good prices, e.g. for exhibition space, which is the most important cost factor (D-H). On the contrary, they would have extra costs in terms of the time spent on searching for cheap suppliers or on negotiating good contract conditions. The only indirect incentive, which D-G from a DFG pointed out, is that it is easier to recruit the minimum ten participants if costs are low. Where many firms want to participate anyway, this is a very weak incentive.

When it comes to the trade fair architect, the DFGs are not even involved in the price negotiations. As far as the architects are concerned, the more elaborate the stand design, the better. They are paid according to the rules for architects' compensation *(Honorarordnung für Architekten)*, which basically means that they receive a percentage of the project costs. Over the years this has led to increasingly costly designs (D-A).

But DFGs' lack of positive financial incentives for keeping the costs down is partly offset by control provisions and negative incentives against bad organisation or fraud. The DFG has to provide the cost calculations for a fair to AUMA and BMWi's agency BAW (Federal Agency for Economics)[26] for approval. It also has to present all bills and final accounts, which BAW audits (D-C). Regarding prices, the information asymmetry between DFGs and their subcontractors on one side and AUMA and BAW on the other is not big. There are many official participations, and in many locations several take place and are organised by different DFGs. Therefore, AUMA and the BAW can directly compare the financial claims of a DFG for a certain location. Due to the recurring nature of the events and the change of DFGs after between three and five times, they can also compare cost developments over time. DFGs have to fear that they will receive fewer contracts in the following year or are ultimately excluded from the pool if their bills are unusually high.

However, this does not imply that they would try to push costs below some acceptable or defensible level. Since a major objective for DFGs is to advertise their services to participating firms and to the respective trade association, their primary interest is to ensure reliable, good quality services. The DFG would get blamed for problems whereas not they but the BMWi would be credited for cheaper participation prices. It is safer to employ reputable or personally known subcontractors, rather than experiment with cheaper providers. While the costs can be monitored by comparison, the quality of the DFGs' services is evaluated through the participants, and the trade association representative who mans the industry information stand. D-A stated that BMWi went to court in one case over unsatisfactory DFG contract fulfilment. D-I from an association has refused to work with a DFG, with which he had had bad experiences.

Summarising, as far as their exhibition support services for BMWi are concerned, it is in the self-interest of DFGs not to enter into unfavourable contracts with suppliers and not to provide low quality services. The DFGs do not have an incentive to minimise exhibitors' costs, but to keep them within reasonable levels.

Regarding other forms of exhibition support that DFGs provide on their own account, they also have an incentive to provide good quality, reliable services if they want to keep participants and their trade associations as future customers. But for these non-subsidised services the price is also relevant, especially if DFGs want to sell these services to experienced exhibitors who can compare prices. DFGs are therefore likely to make an effort to negotiate group discounts and organise those exhibition necessities for the group, which even experienced partici-

[26] The BAW is a '*Bundesoberbehörde*', founded in 1954 and in charge of foreign trade, energy, and economic development promotion. Its activities cover the monitoring of rules, for example regarding exports or the issuing of licences, and the management of all major government subsidies, for example SME programmes, regional development, coal (http:www.bawi.de).

pants would find more expensive to arrange on their own, as long as the DFG can make a profit or at least cover their costs. On the whole, it is more profitable to offer 'cost reducing' rather than 'benefit increasing' services. EconConsult & ISG (1994) found that companies do their trade fair calculations based on absolute costs rather than based on the net benefits or the opportunity costs of a participation. Only 11% of firms sought external advice, i.e. only a very small number of participants would pay DFGs for such services. Information events, which some DFGs had offered to participants before a fair, were visited by fewer than 20%.

6.4.3 Consequences of the exhibition support organisation

Of the five approaches to 'cost reduction' for exhibitors that were outlined in Chapter 4, the German organisation of trade fair support provides for four. Participants receive a direct subsidy in the form of a price reduction on the participation costs, and an indirect subsidy in the form of the DFG services and the architect's stand design for which BMWi partly pays. But these services do not include measures that aim at reducing the net cost of exhibiting by increasing the participation benefits. As a result of the organisation it is expected that participants receive good quality exhibition support services from the DFGs at moderate prices, that the design service is expensive due to the incentive structure of the architect, and that some exhibitors do not benefit fully from a participation (see Table 6.3., next page).

1) Good quality services at moderate prices

On the whole, it appears that the organisational structures for exhibition support should result in the provision of some good quality support services. The DFGs are more experienced in arranging exhibitions than the average participant, and they do not want to dispel potential future clients. Even though the DFGs often lack the knowledge and the incentives to negotiate the very best prices, the costs of the BMWi subsidised stand-related expenditures should be kept at a reasonable level with the help of the available control mechanisms.

This positive judgement is supported by some pieces of evidence, though overall the information on 'exhibition support' by the DFGs is sparse.[27]

Of the programme participants between 1977 and 1987 only 15% were not satisfied with the organisation of the participation (Schellkes 1987:54). To date, the high satisfaction rate has not changed. The Prognos survey (Weidig and Ruprecht 1996) found that exhibitors are usually very content with the services they receive. Respondents specifically mentioned the lower cost of services like exhibition piece shipments as one of the benefits of the programme. Another survey (EconConsult & ISG 1994) also came to the conclusion that firms had no complaints

[27] Although each participant is asked about their satisfaction with the DFG support, the answers do not appear in the annual AUMA evaluation of the participant questionnaire. The results of all other questions are summarised (e.g. AUMA 1998c). The comments about DFGs of the industry representatives at the information stands, who have the duty to write a report about the fair, are not included in the reports either.

Table 6.3. The German exhibition support compared with the ideal organisation

Ideal exhibition support organisation	*German exhibition support organisation*
Ideal knowledge of the actors with the decision rights for exhibition support ▪ know best ways of providing financial support ▪ know how to negotiate group discounts, and join up participants to share fixed expenditures where possible ▪ know how to make official participation attractive for visitors and how to market the group and the whole German/British sector in the host country ▪ know how to reduce participation 'transaction costs' for firms ▪ know critical success factors for specific fairs, and how to alert firms to the issues ▪ know which mix of the above approaches is most suitable for a specific fair and for participants	*Real knowledge* of the DFGs ▪ BMWi decides about financial support; DFGs know how to collect reduced participation fee ▪ know how to negotiate and join up participants to share fixed expenditures ▪ know which architects are competent to deal with group stand design/architect is experienced with designing trade fairs abroad ▪ general, not always market- and industry-specific knowledge on how to reduce transaction costs and advertise group ▪ do not always have market- and industry-specific knowledge; 'training' of participants is not part of their role ▪ do not have the right to decide about size/mix of support
Ideal incentives of the actors with the decision rights for exhibition support ▪ benefit from using their knowledge to provide adequate support, considering all forms of support as equally valuable ▪ have no incentive to favour specific participants over others ▪ have no incentive to make deals with suppliers / contractors at the cost of exhibitors or funding body	*Real incentives* of the DFGs ▪ benefit from using their knowledge to provide BMWi subsidised forms of support and some other services ▪ cannot favour specific participants. Fixed management fee to DFG and reduced participation price for all on a square metre basis ▪ disincentive to commit fraud through fake contracts with suppliers ▪ real incentive of architect to provide an elaborate, expensive design
Ideal output reduce the costs of a successful trade fair participation in a new market for inexperienced, potential and experienced exporters	*Predicted real output pattern* Costs are reduced, but with the following pattern: 1. support services for arranging exhibition are usually good quality at medium price 2. expensive design which is over-proportional in mix of support 3. lack of attention on increasing participants' benefits

about the DFGs' services. Participants who were interviewed informally at the trade fair 'MIDEST' (Paris, November 2000) were of the same opinion. Their only complaint with the exhibition set-up was that the French organisers (always) allocated a remote section of the exhibition hall to the German group.

When the trade association interviewees were asked what problems might occur regarding the DFG's exhibition support, they confirmed that it normally worked well. When firms had problems, they had often caused them themselves. The interviewees also supported the judgement that, for the DFGs, smooth operation would be a higher priority than low costs. D-I thought it was sensible for a DFG not to take risks with cheaper but unknown providers. D-J pointed out that DFGs were forced to demonstrate their good organisational capabilities because they earned their money with selling unsubsidised services, not with the BMWi management fee.

However, in both surveys mentioned above, and in AUMA's review (1998d), it became evident that, despite praising the simplification of organisational matters and the representativeness of the official design, participants saw the chief benefit of trade fair support in the financial subsidy. That this is the prevalent perception, in spite of the general claims of a complete 'support package' for SMEs, was confirmed in the Committee's 1997 discussions. When it agreed to raise participation costs for firms that had already visited a fair four times, the largest association VDMA, supported by others, insisted that the firms would still enjoy some financial subsidy (VDMA 1997). It can be argued that because participants are predominantly experienced exhibitors, the savings on transaction costs are not as significant as they could be for new and inexperienced firms.

2) Expensive stand design

As far as the German government is concerned, visitors of a trade fair perceive the official group participation as a 'visiting card' of Germany (D-A). Therefore there is a strong emphasis on providing a representative design for the group stands. The DFG has to deliver the design on the basis of a trade fair architect's work and cannot decide to what extent the design element is more or less important than other forms of support. For the architect, the more expensive the design is, the better. He/she is paid a percentage of the total costs.

Such an organisation suggests that firms will receive a lot of 'design support', even though they might value other forms of support more. Exhibitors' comments, and the recent development of BMWi's design-related rules support this assumption. Firms complained that the 'German design' was overpowering their own corporate identity (AUMA 1994; Schlitt 1997). There were even complaints that a place in an official participation was more expensive than a participation organised through a local representative, due to the cost of elaborate German stand designs (AUMA 1994; Weidig and Ruprecht 1996:91; Schlitt 1997). At the end of 1997, when it became evident that fewer resources were available for 1998 than anticipated, BMWi required that construction costs would have to be lowered by 20% at each fair (VDMA 1997). This was apparently possible without major difficulties, confirming the view that unnecessarily high design costs were incurred before.

According to D-A, the BMWi is now cost-aware, and emphasis is placed on keeping construction costs low, e.g. by insisting on local construction elements. Where the associations were content with the design of a particular participation, they can suggest the same architect with a repeated design in the following year. Of the year 2000 participations apparently 50% were planned with repeated designs. However, the architects' basic incentive structure has not changed.

3) Lack of attention to increasing participants' returns

Although it is acknowledged that the right selection, the preparation and the follow-up of fairs are essential for a firm's participation success (see 5.4 above), the German trade fair programme does not assign responsibility and resources to ensure these preconditions. Just recently the German government re-affirmed its position and declared that subsidies for trade fair related training and information measures were not necessary; the promotion and provision of these services could be left to trade fair companies (Deutscher Bundestag 2001).

But while the DFGs offer some exhibition services on their own account, these are mainly services that are directly related to the exhibition, e.g. logistical arrangements. It can therefore be expected that many exhibitors' do not accomplish full returns:

In a 1994 survey, suggestions from firms for programme improvements concerned mainly information provision before and after the fair (EconConsult & ISG 1994). More than half of the firms saw significant problems with the follow-up process, e.g. language difficulties or problems with judging the quality of sales leads. Compared with individual exhibitors, group participants seemed even less inclined to acquire the necessary information by themselves, and relied fully on the DFGs and trade associations' services. While individual exhibitors had a trade fair participation 'failure rate' of 24%, official group participants' was 44% (Legler et al. 1994:53).

In 1996 the government was asked by the opposition party to expand the trade fair support for SMEs by offering management help, in order to improve participants' preparation, market information, gathering of sales leads, and follow-up (Deutscher Bundestag 1996). References to the insufficient information levels of participants were also given in summary reports written by information stand representatives at the fair: An example is a statement about the fair 'Konsumexpo' in Russia 1998 which reads '*...as to the other exhibitors who were not as successful, it was usually due to insufficient preparation, which itself could be related to a poor knowledge of the Russian market....*' (AUMA trade fair database).

When the head of the trade fair section at the BMWi, was asked about this issue and the fact that all four editions of the BMWi trade fair programme proclamation (BMWi 1992, 1993, 1998a, 2000) and the report of the parliamentary committee on economic affairs (Deutscher Bundestag 1996:5) stated that measures should be taken to help SMEs with the preparation and follow-up of fairs, he mentioned a pilot programme that was set up in 1998. Firms who registered for participation at some fairs were invited to attend free preparatory meetings. However, according to D-A the take-up of the offer was too low to continue with the programme, probably due to management time shortages and travelling distances. No other approaches were therefore planned. The interviewed trade association representatives said they sometimes offered participants information to facilitate preparation, but not on a regular basis. Firms could always ask their chamber, and the number of participants of a fair was too small to offer specific preparation (D-I). Associations did not get involved in any follow-up activities. Considering these answers, it is unlikely that a commercial provider would have filled the gap.

6.5 The adaptability of the organisation

So far the consequences of the current organisational structures were investigated by looking at their impact on the knowledge and the incentives of the decision-making actors. But the extent to which the organisation allows adaptation to environmental changes is also relevant. The ideal organisation ensures that all actors' decisions are based on up-to-date information, and that the core actor can and wants to effect numerical and functional adaptation, knowing when it is necessary.

6.5.1 'Up-to-date decision making'

Looking at the information on which actors' decisions are based in each stage of the delivery process, the key information appears to be up-dated regularly:

In the selection process, trade associations rely on the information that the export officers receive on a recurring basis from members, through trade fair participations, and through other export services in which the association is involved. AUMA and BMWi receive new proposals from trade associations every year. BMWi also receives 'political' information that may be relevant for trade fair selection from diplomatic posts and other ministries, while AUMA stays informed about developments in the trade fair markets by doing its other business. The only aspect in the selection process, which does not undergo 'automatic' updating, is the distribution of industry 'quotas'.

Regarding the recruitment of participants, DFGs need to keep informed about new developments in trade fair advertising, to stay competitive in their independent business. They get fair-specific information from the trade associations, based on associations' latest knowledge about potentially interested firms. The more they deal with the respective industry independently, the 'fresher' their own information will be.

Looking at the exhibition support services, the same applies. The general knowledge in contracting and negotiating, with which DFGs have been credited, is their business asset. The less informed they are, the lower the profits they make in the medium and long run.

On the whole, decision making appears to be based on reasonably up-to-date info, except where the industry quotas are concerned.

6.5.2 Numerical adaptability

Numerical adaptability of trade fair support organisation refers to its capacity of adjusting to a growing or declining need for support. It may involve changes in the overall number of supported trade fairs, or their numerical distribution between markets and between industries. An organisation is expected to be numerically adaptable, if the core actor, as the ultimate decision maker, becomes aware of the need for changes, has the necessary decision rights about the financial, physical and human resources to implement numerical changes, and wants to do so.

In Germany, BMWi as the core actor learns about the need for numerical changes through the trade associations' applications for exhibition support, as mediated by AUMA, and through the data on participant numbers at each fair. If trade associations were to bid according to the target groups' current exhibition needs, the organisational structures would ensure that BMWi automatically became aware of changes in demand. Given the described bias of trade associations, to represent the needs of their active members, it can still be assumed that BMWi learns about experienced exporters' shifts in demand for trade fairs in different markets. The 'quota' system, however, suggests that shifts in the needs of different industries are not reflected as clearly.

Once BMWi has learnt of a quantitative shift in the need for support, the question is whether the organisational structure allows BMWi to adapt its programme. With the existing organisation this does not seem to be a problem. BMWi has the decision rights over the number and distribution of supported events, and is hampered relatively little by inflexible *financial, human* and *physical* assets:

Referat V A4 can set the number of fairs that will receive support in the following year, and can decide to support fairs in whichever markets or industries are requested by the trade associations. Although the total number depends largely on the budget, which is outside the decision remit of *Referat V A4*, some flexibility is granted by the way in which fair participations are funded. BMWi pays the DFG a fixed amount, and finances the information stand; but the contributions to the exhibitors' costs are set for each fair. What is then advertised as the square metre price for participants includes this element of subsidy. On average the support amounts to 65% of the costs for stand construction and space, but it varies significantly between the trade fairs and can range between more than 90% and less than 40% (Thoene 1997).

Since information gathering, co-ordination, recruitment and exhibition support are carried out by outside actors, and since the remaining very small workload per fair in the *Referat V A4* does not vary substantially between fairs, numerical adaptability is not impeded by an inflexibility of staff hours either. The DFGs only have contracts on a 'per event' basis, and AUMA, the trade associations and members of the Committee work for free and without a formal contract. They would not object to increases in the numbers of supported fairs or changes in markets because of their self-interest in the programme. However, BMWi has to work with the Committee when trying to reduce the number of supported fairs, or when trying to re-distribute the subsidies between industries to avoid confrontation. Formally though, BMWi alone has the final decision rights, and it could impose such changes.

Adjusting physical assets to numerical changes presents no difficulty either, since the few pieces of equipment, like the trade fair database or the offices for the Committee's meetings are not provided by the BMWi, are used for other purposes as well, and are fully adaptable to changed trade fair numbers, sectors or markets.

The last question is whether BMWi would want to adapt the trade fair numbers. As argued in section 5.2.4 above, BMWi does not have any incentive to disagree with the choices of the trade associations and the Committee. As argued in Chapter 4, BMWi does have an incentive though, to oppose a reduction of its trade fair budget. It has done so successfully to date, judged on the development of the budget at times of cutbacks in most government departments, and on the cross-parliamentary support for export promotion and trade fair support (D-A, BMWi; Deutscher Bundestag 1996).

This makes numerical adaptations likely as long as they are in the interest of the established trade associations.

6.5.3 Functional adaptability

Functional adaptability of the trade fair support programme refers to the adaptability of the way in which trade fair support is given.

Regarding the details of each participation, there is a large degree of flexibility. Trade associations can apply for a framework programme as they see fit (e.g. they might offer seminars for product presentation), and the design of the group stands can be modified for each fair (D-I). But the issue is whether environmental changes that call for changes in output can be accommodated, and whether alterations in the organisational structures are possible to ensure that the desired outputs continue to be delivered.

BMWi's major information sources regarding the functioning of the trade fair programme are AUMA, the associations on the Committee, and the data on participant numbers. In addition, they receive information from the Ministry of Finance about the budget plan, and from other parts of government and parliament about political concerns related to the trade fair programme. Occasionally other bodies carry out surveys that produce information, but BMWi itself has not commissioned regular, systematic, independent reviews of the programme. This means its perception of the need for (non-politically determined) changes is predominantly shaped by AUMA and the trade associations on the Committee. These bodies cannot be expected to suggest any need for changes that would threaten their own role in the trade fair programme.

Should BMWi nevertheless learn about significant changes in demand, supply, in technology, or in institutions, *Referat V A4's* decision rights are limited. Unlike decisions about numerical changes, decisions about the nature of outputs, or ways of producing them, are not in its remit. According to the head of *Referat V A4*, they cannot alter how they use the budget in any way without being allowed to do so by the budget commission (*Haushaltsausschuss*). Even when he only wanted to introduce the recruitment-linked bonus for the DFGs, it took him a long time to convince the budget commission of the value of the idea. A more fundamental change, for example dedicating part of the trade fair budget to support firms participating in electronic trade fairs, would be even more difficult.

But this limitation of decision rights is not only tied to the control function of the budget commission. The political dimension of the subsidy programme makes functional changes difficult as well: Since it has always been emphasised that the programme is designed for and according to the needs of the private sector, decisions about fundamental programme changes cannot be made without the Committee. As much as they are unlikely to suggest changes that would threaten their own role in the trade fair programme, they are unlikely to agree with them. On the contrary, AUMA and the trade associations on the Committee have attempted to expand their role in the organisation (D-A). In 1995 the Committee passed a resolution with which it tried to convince the government that instead of passing the rights of financial control to the BAW, AUMA and the associations should take over most decisions about trade fair support, and the budget control.

This means that the core actor, BMWi, can neither easily modify the organisational structures, nor the organisational outputs. And like the Committee members, BMWi itself does not have any incentive to reduce its own role. If it made, for example, subsidies to individual firms possible, this would reduce the *Referat's* activities to a routine application-processing agency. If it tried to make changes against the wishes of the Committee, it would have to engage in confrontations.

It seems BMWi would only be likely to question the role and opinion of the current actors if the pressure from outside parties to effect changes were even more challenging than confronting the Committee members.

6.5.4 Consequences for the adaptability of the German trade fair support organisation

It has been argued that the organisation allows actors to make decisions on the basis of information, which is updated regularly. Also, the numerical adaptability of the organisation appears to be high with regard to increases in numbers and their distribution between countries. Regarding the trade fair distribution between industries, it is expected to a much lower degree. Concerning functional adaptability, the organisation seems to present an obstacle. The organisation and its outputs are unlikely to change significantly over time. The comparison with the ideal organisation is summarized in Table 6.4. (next page).

1) High numerical adaptability
Some evidence for the trade fair support programme's *numerical adaptability* has already been presented. Figure 6.5 (next page) shows the degree of flexibility in terms of the total number of participations, given an externally determined trade fair support budget.

The interviewees agreed that the programme's flexibility regarding the *number* of supported trade fairs was fairly high. In the 1980s, when demand was increasing but the budget did not, the average subsidy per fair was reduced (D-A). It is also possible to use the funds of fairs that were cancelled to increase the support for others (D-B). In 1997 the government unexpectedly announced that the German stand on the World EXPO Lisbon and the German KONSUGERMA in Shanghai would have to be financed out of the trade fair budget. This meant that the remainder would have covered only half of the already advertised 195 official participations. BMWi, in co-operation with the Committee, decided to increase the cost contributions of participants on average by 10%. This, combined with the introduction of higher prices for exhibitors participating the fifth or more time, and

Table 6.4. The German organisation's adaptability compared with the ideal

Ideal trade fair support organisation	*German trade fair support organisation*
▪ Actors make decisions based on up-to-date knowledge	▪ Actors make decisions based on up-to-date knowledge
▪ Core actor o *knows* when the output of the organisation needs to be adapted 'numerically' to respond to increasing or decreasing needs in terms of the total number of fairs, number of fairs in each market, number of fairs in each industry o *can* provide for numerical changes o *wants to* respond to changed needs	▪ BMWi o finds out about increased or decreased demand through the applications of trade associations o can provide for numerical changes – it is flexible regarding finance per fair, human and physical assets o wants to respond to changed needs of industries with established representation
▪ Core actor o *knows* when the output and structure of the organisation needs to be adapted 'functionally' to respond to external changes o *can* provide for functional changes o *wants to* carry out functional changes	▪ BMWi o learns about requirements for functional changes mainly from trade associations and AUMA. Information is filtered o decision rights regarding functional changes are very limited o has no interest in confrontation with Committee and AUMA;
Ideal result	*Predicted real output pattern*
perfect numerical and functional adaptability of outputs and organisational structure	1. numerical adaptability is high, especially regarding total numbers and geographical distribution 2. functional adaptability is low; changes that reduce the influence of current actors are unlikely

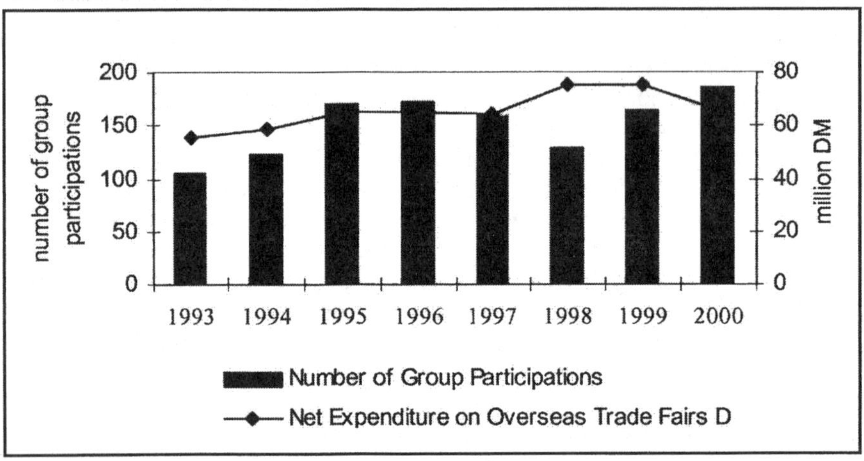

Fig. 6.5. Adaptability of group numbers to changed budgets
Source: based on data provided by AUMA

with the decreed 20% reduction in construction costs, made some 20 extra participations possible (D-A).

Figure 6.3 above gave a picture of the adaptability of trade fair support to changing needs regarding the *location* of the fairs. The share of fairs in Asia for example increased from less than 10% in 1977 to more than 55% in 1997, following the expansion of the market. It could then also be reduced to respond to the reduced demand in the aftermath of the Asian crisis.

Trying to follow up on changes in the distribution of fair support for different *industries* has proved more difficult. Only data for the years 1999–2002 was available, and for these years the evidence looks supportive, but is not fully conclusive. AUMA categorises the German industry into 57 'sectors' (excluding agriculture, forestry, animal husbandry and fishery, for which the ministry of agriculture is responsible). Checking the fairs that were supported for each of the sectors in the four years showed that in 25% of cases the number per sector did not change at all. In a further 37% of cases the numbers changed by one or sometimes two, plus or minus, but this change could be related to the trade fair cycle (many fairs take only place every second year). For the remaining third there were only two sectors ('books, printed products, libraries' and 'music') that appear to have had their 'quota' cut by three or four fairs. Five sectors gained up to four fairs, while 11 gained and lost fairs over the years and this could not be related to the trade fair cycles. Only two of the ten sectors that did not have any supported fair in 1999 obtained funding in subsequent years. These were 'gastronomy, shop-interiors', and 'security, rescue services'. Other sectors like 'banking, investment, real estate', or 'art and antiques' did not have any supported fairs throughout the period. There was also a slow response to the developments in the information technology sector. The sector category 'information technology, telecommunications' was only introduced in 2000, while until 1999 this industry group was grouped under 'office equipment, data processing, and telecommunications'. These observations seem to support the argument that the organisational structure would result in less adaptability to changes in demand between industries than to changes in demand for geographic markets in which fairs take place.

As far as *functional adaptability* is concerned, organisational structures and outputs are basically the same as 30 years ago (m+a 1971). For example, outputs have not responded to the growth of the service sector, for which seminars abroad would be a more adequate marketing tool than fairs. Although the government itself, maybe overenthusiastically, acknowledges that *'traditional trade fairs are challenged by the new economy. E-commerce and trade fair web sites, communication forums and virtual market places provide the communication function of a trade fair within seconds and without time consuming travelling'* (Deutscher Bundestag 2001), there has been no attempt to provide support for such virtual fairs, unlike for example in Australia.

6.6 Summary judgement

This chapter has described and analysed the German trade fair support organisation along the lines of the framework developed in the previous chapters. The objective was to investigate whether there is empirical evidence for the assumption that 'organisation matters' for effectiveness, as predicted by the theory-based model. The German organisational structures for the delivery of the trade fair programme were compared with the ideal organisation, and predictions were made how differences would affect the outputs of the actors. The validity of most of these predictions could be supported by evidence from interviews with participating actors, compilations of data from actors' websites and databases, evidence from previous empirical surveys on participant satisfaction, from annual reviews of the trade fair programme, and from other printed sources. Although, because of the scarcity of research and of transparency in this field, the evidence is not as extensive as one might wish for, every piece that was available supported the model.

Judged against the two goals of trade fair support (see 5.4.1. above) there are clear implications of the organisation on goal attainment:

The German trade fair support organisation promotes trade fair participations of experienced exporters in new, high potential markets, but not always directly, and not with an emphasis on small firms. Experienced exporters that have enough resources to be actively involved in their trade associations can influence the selection process in favour of fairs at which they want to exhibit. Although these will be major fairs for the industry, with broad exhibition themes, the support they receive when exhibiting there frees up resources to take part in additional, individually chosen fairs. There is at least the possibility that experienced exporters will use these 'freed-up' funds to experiment with new, promising markets. For other exporters, who have considered testing one of the markets that are in the programme, the official support can tip the balance in favour of going.

Small exporters' influence on the selection of fairs is limited. Considering that they often serve only a specific market niche, small firms are likely to find the chosen fairs too general. Considering that the value of one product often constitutes a significant share of the firms' assets (e.g. a custom-built specialist machine), the 'difficult' markets chosen for the programme may also be too risky. And although the fairs in the trade fair programme are subsidised, a participation is nevertheless expensive for a firm. Combined with little support for evaluating the fair, preparing it and following-up, small firms often make the investment without being able to make most of it.

However, if a fair in the official programme meets small firms' needs they receive good quality exhibition support and a representativeness, which they could not attain otherwise.

The goal to promote successful trade fair participations of inexperienced and potential exporters is also met with little success. To expect an average new exporter to exhibit at fairs in 'difficult markets' is unreasonable and potentially detrimental to their business success. Moreover, they are unlikely to be able to judge the potential net benefits fully, and to use the opportunity to their best advantage.

The organisational structure, which bases the programme on the active demand of industries, brings with it that non-exhibitors who will not raise their voice get neglected.

The combined knowledge and interests of the current actors make it unlikely that inexperienced and potential exporters are likely to benefit from redesigns of the organisation or programme by the core actor.

In conclusion, the assumption that 'organisation matters' because of the suggested cause–effect relationships could be confirmed. The way the German trade fair support is structured leads to ineffectiveness in supporting small and first-time trade fair participants. Should major changes in the trade fair landscape occur, the organisational structures would hinder fast responses. But the structures are currently effective in supporting 'main-stream' experienced exporters.

Chapter 7: The organisation of trade fair support in the United Kingdom

7.1 Overview

The British government's overseas trade fair programme is run and financed by British Trade International (BTI) with their programme 'Seminars and Exhibitions Abroad' (SESA). Within BTI, TradePartners UK (TPUK) is responsible for SESA. In a similar way to the German programme, TPUK choose the fairs and seminars for which a government subsidy is made available via bids that UK business support organisations submit on an annual basis. TPUK then appoint the business organisation that submitted a chosen proposal as the 'sponsor' for the fair or seminar. Each sponsor is responsible for the recruitment of participants for 'its' fair, and for the exhibition support. In contrast to the German case, BTI pays out the subsidy to each eligible exhibitor through the sponsor. The sponsors are also supposed to run an information stand at their events. In return, they receive a fixed grant, normally £ 4300 per fair, from TPUK. In contrast to the German DFGs sponsors can cover any additional costs by charging group participants a 'management fee'. TPUK, apart from selecting the supported events, only monitor sponsors' activities.

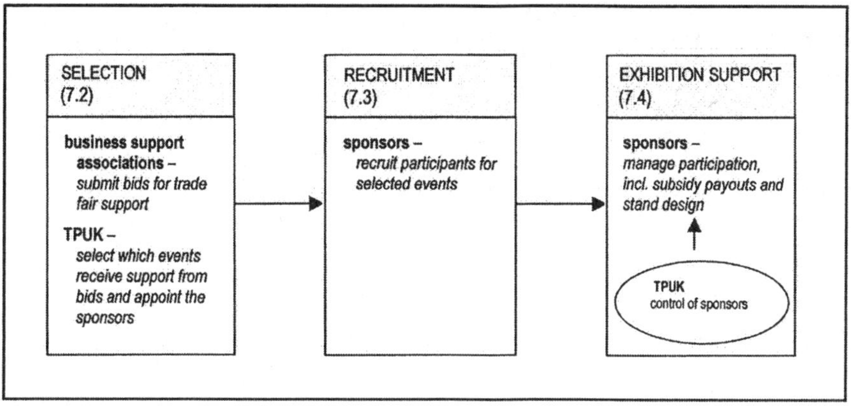

Fig. 7.1. Overview of the actors and their tasks in the British trade fair support organisation

This chapter describes and evaluates the British selection, recruitment and exhibition support organisation and its adaptability, in detail, using the same framework as in the German case.

Again, the purpose of the chapter is to evaluate the consequences of the differences between the British and the ideal organisation of trade fair support. While major differences to the German organisation are pointed out, the focus is on the British case. A direct comparison of the two different organisational structures is presented in Chapter 8.

7.2 Trade fair selection

7.2.1 The allocation of selection tasks and decision rights

In the UK, TradePartnersUK (TPUK) and British business organisations are the two major actors in the trade fair selection process. Each year, defined by a deadline in June, British business support organisations can suggest up to 25 'supportworthy' events each, ranked according to their preferences. Since 1999, these events could be either overseas trade fairs or seminars. From these suggestions TPUK choose the events for which a subsidy will be made available. Out of the over 1000 bids, which were received for the programme 2001–02, TPUK chose 479 trade fairs and 66 seminars (TPUK 2000a). The selection process for trade fairs, on which this chapter concentrates, is thus divided among the bidding sponsors, who narrow down the choice from the thousands of trade fairs taking place worldwide, and TPUK.

With this division of labour, the bidding business organisations must ideally represent all sectors of industry. Otherwise, as argued in the German case, those industries that do not have bidding sponsors are automatically excluded in this selection process. Sponsors have to know the trade fairs for their industries, the market potential of different regions in the world, and the relevance of the official support in each market. They have to choose impartially according to the highest expected support impact and cater for both experienced and inexperienced SME exporters.

TPUK decides how to distribute the subsidies between the industries. Its staff must know which events promise the highest value added for the two target groups of British SMEs, and must have the incentive to choose events on this basis.

7.2.2 The sponsors' selection knowledge and incentives

Who are the sponsors?

The government requires sponsors to be 'business support organisations'. Among business support organisations they favour 'trade associations representing a defined sector of industry' and only choose *'broader-based bodies such as a Cham-*

bers of Commerce or Business Links ... where no relevant industry sector body exists or seeks to be involved' (TPUK 2001). A look at SESA sponsors shows that trade associations do indeed form the large majority. In the 2001–02 programme (TPUK 2000a) only two fairs (0.4%) were sponsored by Business Links and only 35 (7.3%) by four Chambers of Commerce and Industry.[1] Government agencies and regional business associations sponsored 9% (e.g. the China Britain Business Council), however over half of those events were not regular trade fairs but 'British' shows, or 'universal' fairs. Except for the British Council, with 21 education-related shows, none of these agents managed a large number of events. Given trade associations' predominance as sponsors, the following analysis concentrates on them.

Compared with Germany, the range of British trade associations that could bid for events is wider because the British programme allows sponsors to bid for seminars abroad. Thus more industries, especially in the service sector could benefit from the programme.

But of the many British trade associations only a small number are trade fair sponsors. TPUK requires business organisations bidding for an event to have *'adequate staffing and financial resources to recruit and organise effectively the group'*. In their application they have to submit the last two annual reports and audited accounts, or information on turnover, pre-tax profit, current liabilities, and assets (DTI 1998d; DTI 1999; TPUK 2001a). Since most British trade associations are small in terms of membership, and have staff numbers that reflect their 'meagre resources' – between 14% and 25% have no staff at all (Boleat 1996:21; Bennett 1997a:15) – this requirement effectively precludes many from becoming a trade fair sponsor:

In 2001–02 only 100 trade associations out of the *'well over 1000 trade associations in the UK'* (Boleat 1996:12) sponsored events. Figure 7.2. on the following page shows their size distribution in comparison with the size distribution of the whole population of trade associations. Although the numbers are only approximations,[2] they clearly illustrate the proportionately larger size of sponsors. None is without employees or with only one. And an additional calculation

[1] These were the Birmingham, London, Liverpool and Mid Yorkshire Chambers of Commerce and Industry. Birmingham is the most active one, sponsoring 27, i.e. 75% of the Chambers' events.

[2] The 707 large sample for the overall figures appears to be biased towards the larger associations. Bennett, who based his survey on the entries in the Gale Directory 1994, found 14% of associations had no staff. A questionnaire survey carried out by Manchester Metropolitan University in 1994 (494 responses out of 1300) found 25% of associations without staff (BOLEAT 1996, p.21). Moreover, very small associations are not only less likely to be listed in a directory, but they are also less likely to answer a questionnaire. The data on sponsors' staff numbers are based on the entries in the Trade Association Forum's online directory. Of the 100 trade associations that sponsor events only 72 were listed with staff numbers. It is likely that there are more small associations that do not advertise their staff numbers than large ones. Presumably the sponsors' size distribution is therefore biased towards larger ones as well.

showed that even if only associations with two or more employees are considered as a comparison group, sponsors are still better staffed.

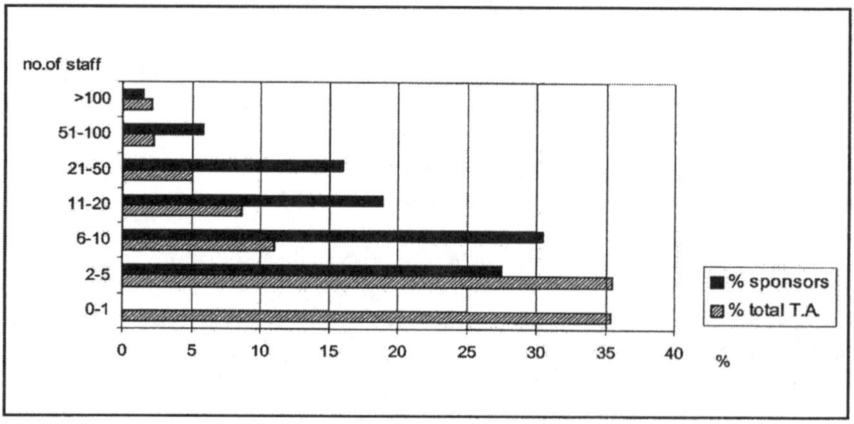

Fig. 7.2. Size distribution of trade associations and of trade association sponsors
Sources: Based on TPUK (2000a) and Trade Association Forum (2001) for the size of the 2000/1 sponsors; Bennett (1997a) for the size distribution of the British trade association population.

The graph also illustrates the differences among the sponsor associations regarding their resources and the number of services they can offer, as these factors correlate largely with the number of staff (Kohler-Koch and Quittkat 1999).

Better-resourced sponsors appear to bid for more events, or to be more successful in the bidding process. Comparing those 35 (35%) who sponsor only one fair with those who lead more events, the latter are bigger (see Table 7.1). If one excludes one exceptionally large 'one-event sponsor', the Chemical Industries Association with 60 employees, the mean staff number of the other 'one-event sponsors' is only 6.7.

Table 7.1. Number of events per sponsor and sponsor size distribution

No. of events organised by one sponsor	*No. of sponsors (total: 100)*	*No. of sponsors for whom data on staff is missing*	*Mean no. of staff*	*Median no. of staff*
1	35	15	9.6	5.0
2 or 3	27	5	12.1	8.0
4, 5, or 6	18	3	20.6	12.0
7, 8, 9, or 10	11	3	23.8	14.5
11 – 27	9	2	27.3	29.0

Sources: Based on TPUK (2000a) for distribution of events among sponsors; Trade Association Forum (2001) for the size of the 2000–01 sponsors

The impression that resources of trade associations matter when it comes to bidding for trade fair support was confirmed by a look at sponsor's websites.[3] Of the eight sponsors without a website only one sponsored more than one fair.

This means, broadly speaking, that the more resources business organisations have, i.e. the better organised their industries are, the more successful they are at obtaining trade fair support. On the other side of the spectrum are disorganised sectors, which have no sponsors who bid for events. Trade associations that cannot or do not want to become sponsors can only suggest fairs through another business organisation that is willing to become a sponsor for the desired fair (UK-A).

Sponsor's knowledge about suitable fairs

Asked how they know which fairs to pick, the interviewees from British trade associations gave similar answers as their German counterparts. Their major sources of knowledge are experiences from previously visited fairs, members' views, and notifications from trade fair organisers.

The trade fair officers UK-L and UK-M from associations W and X reported that they could easily keep track of the fairs that take place worldwide, because there were few for their industry. Both would not bid for a fair in its first year. They formed their opinion about a fair they had not yet attended on the basis of previous experiences with the organiser, based on the opinion of members who had exhibited there before. Representatives of association W have also visited specific fairs before deciding whether to bid for them.

The umbrella association Z has a more difficult task. In contrast to the previous two associations with narrowly defined membership bases, Z represents a heterogeneous group of firms for whom many trade fairs could be interesting. Z collects information by inviting all 6500 firms on their database, including their 192 members (large companies, associations), to make suggestions for fairs. They also ask participants at 'their' fairs directly. Of the approximately 50 different suggestions that they normally receive, they then choose the 25 fairs for which one sponsor can bid. Some events have proven popular year after year and will be put on the list. Others are selected according to their perceived relevance for firms' product strategy (e.g. Internet, e-commerce), and/or geography (e.g. China). They also consider where the government subsidy would have the highest impact, e.g. in the defence industry trade fairs are so expensive that the maximum government grant of £2300 to an exhibitor would make little difference. To choose between fairs that would interest only some members, the proposals are sent to the respective member associations who then have to put forward arguments for 'their' event. But the decision about the final ranked list, and its justification to the members, is nevertheless difficult (UK-J).

From these two examples, a general point can be made. The more homogeneous an association is, the easier it is for the association to know the 'best' trade fairs. If all members produce a similar product, the sponsors only have to research

[3] To find out more about the export support activities of the sponsors as a group, 48 were selected randomly and their websites were analysed in January 2001. 35%, i.e. the same percentage as for the whole group of sponsors, happened to be sponsors with only one event.

the worldwide demand regarding that product. If all customers for the industry fall into a particular group, the sponsors can look for fairs with such a customer profile. Clearly defined products and markets thus also reduce the number of trade fairs that are relevant. Conversely, the more diverse an industry or its markets are, the more resources are required to gather information about all subgroups' trade fair opportunities and about their relative merits.

Whether these resources are available depends on the size of the trade association, and on members' interest in dedicating the association's resources to export development. At W, which with six staff was the smallest of the associations interviewed, the officer in charge of export matters has several other responsibilities. He was not as well informed about some aspects of the trade fair programme as the other interviewees, and his first response to the question about how fairs were selected, was that it was based on historical precedents. At association Y on the other hand, with three more staff, one of four units is dedicated to export matters. Members' interest is strong, and seventy members (i.e. nearly one third) pay a top-up membership fee to be part of the association's 'export group'. This is reflected in a range of export services that Y offers to its members. Information collected in the course of providing these services supports the trade fair selection process (UK-K).

For the purpose of getting a more general picture of sponsors' export services beyond SESA, a sample of half of the trade association sponsors for the 2000–01 trade fair programme was taken, and their websites were analysed.[4] Of the 83% with a website,[5] more than half (57%) did not indicate that they provide any other export services (e.g. host 'Export Clubs', invite guest speakers on exporting, or offer information material on foreign markets). Only 37% provide lists of overseas trade fairs, and 5% of these are out-of-date. Ninety per cent do not sponsor trade fair participations outside the SESA programme.

This indicates that the majority of sponsors do not engage in export support activities or trade fair research beyond the government financed SESA and trade missions programmes. Thus their selection of events cannot benefit from cross-information. Taking only the trade associations that sponsor one event, the figures were worse. Of the sample of 15 (total 34) 40% did not have a website, indicating the lesser resources available to the average sponsor. Of the nine sponsors with a

---

4 Presumably most sponsors who can afford it would try to advertise their services, and/or keep their members informed. Also, one would expect associations that want to keep up with international trade developments and promote their industry abroad, to have a website.
Association's websites were analysed regarding the following criteria: 1.Does a website exist? 2. Does the association mention export support in their mission statement or trade fair sponsorship as a service to members? 3. Does the association offer other export services? 4. Are other international fairs that are relevant for the industry listed? 5. Are the SESA 2001–02 fairs that are sponsored by the association listed on the website? 6. Is SESA explained and/or a link to the TradePartnersUK website provided? 7. Are further details about the fairs provided?

5 Of those, 5% had not been updated for more than a year.

website only two list other trade fairs and only one (11%) offers another export service.

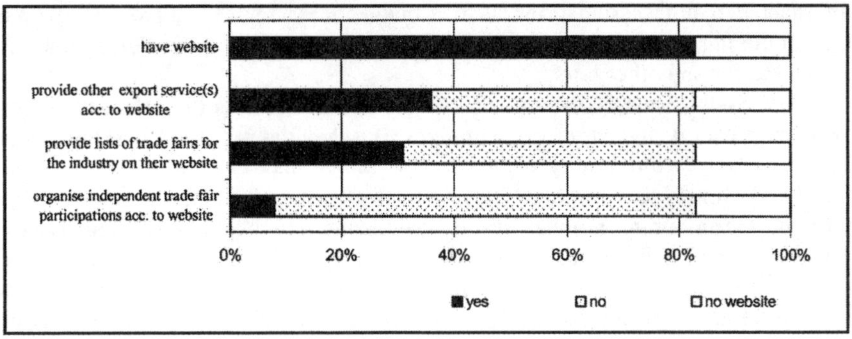

Fig. 7.3. Other export support activities of trade association sponsors according to their websites
Source: websites of 48 randomly selected trade association SESA sponsors

Overall, it can be concluded that only few sponsors are likely to have the ideal selection knowledge. Their knowledge seems to vary significantly, depending on members' and their markets' homogeneity, their export interest, and the sponsors' size. Judging from their staff numbers, the websites, and interview responses, many do not have the resources to actively find out about and rank the possible events. This corresponds with the conclusion KPMG drew after their survey (DTI 1994:75f): *'A significant number of sponsors appear to lack the resources to undertake a comprehensive scanning of their markets and therefore rely heavily on exhibition organisers direct contact to make them aware of new trade fairs (...) The majority of sponsors indicated that a large number of their trade fairs were repeat events which are automatically proposed for support on the basis of historic participation'*. Those associations who do spend resources on obtaining detailed information spend it mainly on finding out about trade fair wishes from interested members, i.e. largely from firms that visit fairs already.

Sponsors' incentives in the selection process
To find out how much the incentives of bidding trade associations differ from the ideal, all interviewed trade association representatives were asked why their association was interested in sponsoring SESA events, and which considerations guided their selection. As expected, 'government recognition' and 'attracting and serving members' were the two important objectives, though associations differed in their emphasis on either. As in the German case, the minimum number of participants framed the sponsors' choice.

Government recognition: For association X and W their profile as industry representatives was the major issue. Both felt it was essential to show presence at the international flagship trade fair for the industry. To strengthen their position vis à vis government, the two associations co-operate at the fair, demonstrating that their sector is united. Each year they jointly invite the minister for Culture, Media and Sports to a day with the exhibiting members and to an 'intimate dinner', which makes the fair an important annual lobbying and advertising event. It is so important that both associations have a budget for a representative information stand at the fair, the cost of which exceeds participant fees and the TPUK grant. X did not bid for any other fairs.

Associations Y and Z also considered the sponsor role as important for being perceived as active industry representatives. But they did not stress it to the extent the others did, nor did they perceive specific fairs as major lobbying events. However, like W and X they felt that TPUK would give them 'bad marks' if they failed to recruit the minimum number of ten participants. This would have negative effects on their bids in the following year. Although they could apply for 'niche events', i.e. events which need not attract ten participants, they did not see them as equal to 'regular' participations. They felt that the probability of getting a 'niche event' application approved was much smaller, and that the net cost of organising such a small group was higher.

Since more than half of all sponsors with a website advertise their good relations with the DTI, it can be assumed that for most other sponsors 'government recognition' is a factor considered in their choices as well. As UK-J pointed out, the British government has been trying to establish 'lead associations', on which it wants to concentrate its relations with different industry sectors. For associations that compete for this status with other associations covering the same industry it is important to show that they can provide export support to members, and that their services are taken up. This makes the probability with which a fair attracts the minimum participant number a major issue in the selection process.

Membership: The Y association representative UK-K emphasised the 'member service' aspect. He puts all fairs that are popular and relevant for all members on the annual list of bids. He then chooses a mix of focused events, which are interesting for those sectors that have active exporters among the members. Thereby, he commented, he lowered the risk that not enough firms participated at a selected fair. Both Y and Z had recruited new members by being a sponsor, and like W and other sponsors they also presented 'their' trade fairs as a selective service to members, by charging them a lower participation fee. The websites sample showed that the large majority of sponsors (78%) either advertise explicitly with trade fair sponsorship or with export support as members' services in their mission statements.

Finances: The financial aspect, which was identified as a third goal of trade associations in Chapter 3, was also mentioned, and was until some years ago a major bidding motive. KPMG (DTI 1994) reported that many trade associations cross-subsidised other activities with the profits they made as trade fair sponsors. To prevent this, the government introduced much tighter accounting rules for the sponsors. But according to UK-J, sponsors can still make a profit if they recruit enough participants. The break-even point can be reached with 10–18 participants, depending on the level of services the sponsor offers and on the management fees charged. In UK-J's case, he has to demonstrate to his association's board that the trade fair sponsor role does not burden the association's budget, and he tries to balance out loss-generating participations with profit-generating ones. 'Niche events' with only from six to eight participants cost the sponsor and are therefore not attractive. According to UK-C from TPUK the average number of SESA trade fair participants is 22. Asked about niche events, he informed that TPUK does not collect data on how many bids for niche events have been made in the past few years or how many have taken place.

In associations where many members do not support export-related activities, or in associations that cannot subsidise a sponsor role, finance can thus be an important deterrent for seeking sponsorship for fairs that might not attract many participants. At Z, most members are large enterprises with a limited interest in supporting non-member SMEs (UK-J). In other associations, many of the members have no interest in exporting, with the effect that the associations' management cannot dedicate resources to this activity (TPUK 2000b).

It follows that sponsors' incentive structure would not lead them to choose fairs primarily because of market entry impact considerations, with an equal emphasis on the possibilities of inexperienced SMEs as on active exporters. As for their German counterparts, a fair's potential to attract participants is the major selection issue. Apart from reducing the risk of failing to meet the minimum participant number, it increases the chances of satisfying the association's (potential) members, and it is better in financial terms. Given a choice between experimenting with a new fair and suggesting an 'old' popular event, the interviewees would choose the latter. After choosing fairs that can appeal to any member, they choose those events in which their export-active members are interested. There are no incentives for sponsors to select according to the needs of inexperienced exporters.

7.2.3 TradePartners UK's selection knowledge and incentives

TradePartners UK

Having received business associations' bids by a deadline in summer, it is then up to TPUK to make the final selection, and to announce the list in autumn. Usually the number of bids is about twice as high as what the SESA budget can support (UK-A). TPUK is expected to choose those events, which promise the highest value added for British SMEs trying to export to new markets.

To understand the selection arrangements within TPUK, an overview of TPUK's structure is necessary: TPUK is divided into three core groups – the international, the regional, and the business group – and two administrative support groups. The international group consists of 'market directorates' that deal with specific markets or regions, and interact with the diplomatic posts. The small regional group at the headquarters in London co-ordinates the delivery of the government's trade promotion programmes in the English regions, and it liases with the devolved government administrations. SESA, the trade fair programme, is run by one of the five directorates within the 'Business Group'. The Business Group brings together all parts of TPUK that are sector oriented. It co-ordinates SESA and the trade missions scheme, and it is responsible for liaising with other Government departments (see Figure 7.4). The 'International Business Schemes & Engineering' directorate, which runs SESA, and the 'Oil & Gas' directorate are located in Glasgow. All other TPUK directorates are based in London.

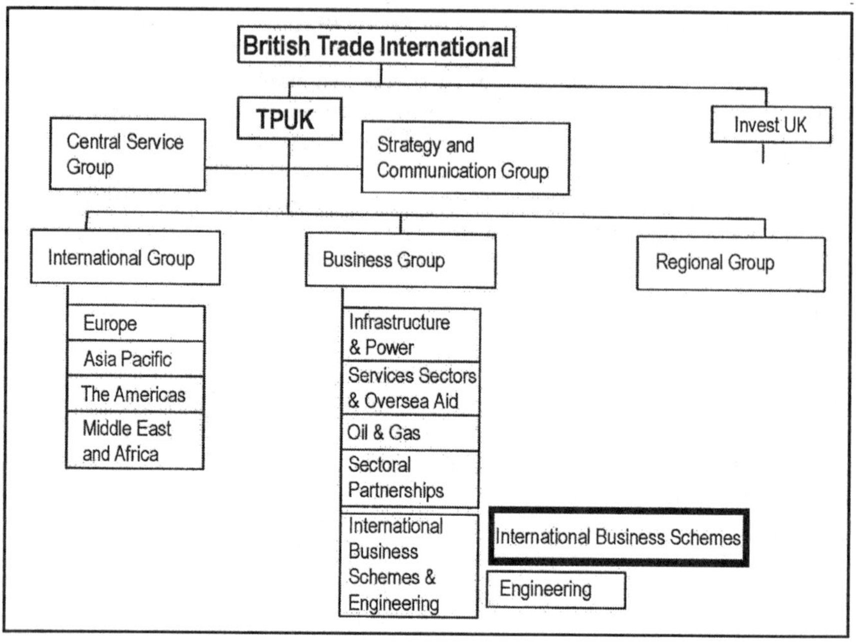

Fig. 7.4. SESA administration within BTI-TPUK
Sources: Interviews and Stationary Office (2000)

The selection procedure within TPUK is the following:
'International Business Schemes' (IBS) receives all bids from the business organisations. First, the cost of 'core events' is estimated and set aside from the total SESA budget. Core events are well established, large, international trade exhibitions, which have in the past attracted groups of at least 20 UK exhibitors. If an event is categorised as a 'core event', funding is guaranteed for at least three years. Sponsors can bid for particular exhibitions to receive 'core event' status. Until a review of core events was carried out in 1998, they took up half of the total trade fair budget (DTI and FCO 1997:34). Since, their number has been cut from 140 to 59 in the 2001–02 programme, and only about a quarter of the total SESA budget is now spent on them (TPUK 2000a).

Second, a small allowance[6] is set aside for the 'niche events' – groups with fewer than ten participants that want to exhibit at an untested fair, in a difficult market, or in a specialised sector.

6 It is not a fixed percentage of the budget, but depends on how many bids there are for niche events (UK-B, TPUK).

The third group of fairs – the non-core, non-niche, 'standard' events – receive the large remainder of the SESA budget:

The budget is apportioned to the regions in the world, in the same relation as sponsors have bid. For example, if 25% of non-core bids, by value, were for Western Europe then 25% of the budget would be allocated to that region (DTI 1999; TPUK 2001). Within each group, all bids are then ranked. According to the head of the SESA administration, the IBS rank on the basis of the market directorates', sector groups', and UK diplomatic posts' judgements. Each of them ranks the fairs that fall into their field of expertise. The different ranked lists are then computer-processed by IBS, giving all opinions, including that of the sponsors, equal weight. IBS itself does not put forward its own opinion. Those bids with the highest aggregated priority within the bounds of the available budget are selected. Interestingly, none of the interviewed sponsors knew about this process, or could predict which of their bids would be successful.

TPUK's selection knowledge

From the description of the selection system it has become clear that IBS selects the fairs mechanically, following the choices of the International Group directorates, the sector groups, the diplomatic posts, and the sponsors themselves. The idea is, that via their ranking, the different parties pass on their specific knowledge about the relative merits of individual fairs in certain markets and sectors. All the different aspects of expertise are then combined by IBS to choose the best fairs. The questions are therefore, on what knowledge are the choices of the government-related parties based, and whether that knowledge is adequate to choose the 'best fairs'.

From the interviews with TPUK staff (UK-A; UK-B; UK-E; UK-D; UK-F; UK-G), and with other government sector sponsors (UK-I; UK-H), from government papers (DTI and Treasury 2000:prg.5.23; TPUK 2001) and from an analysis of the 2001/2002 programme (TPUK 2000a), it became evident that the different contributors base their choice predominantly on the current list of *'target markets'* and the *'sector-market matrix'*.

The following describes what the target markets and the sector market matrix are, and how they are chosen, before assessing their usefulness as a blueprint to select the 'best' fairs.

The target markets and the sector market matrix

The list of *target markets* was developed after the Export Forum's review of British trade promotion services in 1997. The Export Forum, supported by contributions from interest groups (e.g. CBI 1997), had criticised a lack of strategic focus in the government's promotional activities. It was agreed that a new approach was needed, one that would focus export support expenditure on far fewer markets than the previous 80. Based on a number of indicators, which reflected market growth potential and market barriers, the Export Forum suggested 12 'target markets'. Two of them, Western Europe and the US, were designated for new and inexperienced exporters, while the others were selected as presenting particularly good opportunities for experienced exporters (DTI and FCO 1997:25,65ff). In

1998–99 the list was revised to include five new markets and to remove Russia and South East Asia (BTI 1999a).

The *'sector market matrix'* was created to supplement and integrate the list of target markets, and took effect from April 1999. The matrix is meant to provide an overview of all markets and sectors where government export promotion can add most value. British industry was grouped into 27 sectors. Then, for each market (country/region) – sector combination, it was determined whether British products were 'in demand' – with 'high priority', 'priority', or 'no priority' for Government export promotion services – or whether there were 'niche opportunities', or a 'low level of demand' (BTI 1999a).

The first update of the matrix, including designated campaign markets, took place in 2001. Senior TPUK staff manage the process, but the BTI board have to approve the new matrix, and the final decision lies with ministers (House of Commons 2000:prg.73; DTI et al. 2001:33). The new campaign markets were chosen according to the Export Forum's criteria and on the basis of suggestions from the market directorates, service take-up, and economists' assessment (House of Commons 2000:prg.73; UK-D; UK-E; UK-F; UK-G). The market-sector assessments were based on market directorates' and sector groups' opinion. The former categorised each of the 27 product groups within their markets according to priority status. The sector groups rated the market priorities for their product groups. Where opinions differed, the parties met for discussion (UK-G).

The value of the sector market matrix is therefore largely determined by the knowledge of the market directorates and the sector groups.

The market directorates' expertise lies in following the economic development of specific markets, processing the information and passing it on to UK firms. Each of the 16 sections operate help desks, which provide general market information, information on tariffs and export regulations, and signposting, for individual countries or regions. They draw on a wide variety of information sources such as foreign embassies in the UK, private sector advisors, and export research. They also receive information from the commercial officers in the UK's diplomatic posts (see 5.3.2.2). Based on all these information sources market directorates are in a good position to assess market developments and firms' demand for support, particularly as the quality of their staff has improved significantly over the past years (UK-T; UK-S).

Sector specific work is carried out by the directorates in the TPUK 'Business Group', each of which is responsible for some of the 27 sector-market matrix sectors. They are in the process of developing an export strategy for each sector, and have made their assessment for the new sector-market matrix on the basis of the collected information. To obtain the information, the sector groups work with the relevant industry representatives,[7] and with the Whitehall department that sponsors the industry (DTI et al. 2001:39). In some cases this is the DTI, but in many it is other government departments, their agencies and sponsored bodies, or several of those. Governmental sector sponsorship involves knowledge gathering about

[7] Interestingly the interviewed trade association representatives did not know how the sector market matrix was constructed, and said they did not have an input.

the sector, relationship building with the sectors' representative bodies and firms, information and representational roles vis à vis other government directorates and the industry, and the delivery of specific programmes meant to raise the competitiveness of that sector (Booth di Giovanni 2001).

Thus, the sector-market matrix with the campaign markets is based on market as well as sector expertise and on the comparative assessments of economists and the other parties involved in the final decisions. This should be an ideal combination for judging the relative market opportunities for British products. However, there are problems with aggregating and transmitting knowledge in such a format:

- The knowledge comprised in the matrix cannot be up-to-date. The list is to a large extent reactive, following trends that the parties have observed in the previous years. It is only reviewed every two to three years, and reviews get delayed (e.g. an update was due in 2000 but only accomplished in the second half of 2001 (DTI and Treasury 2000: prg.5.2.3.)). As Sir David Wright admitted in his answer to the House of Commons Foreign Affairs Committee, the removal of campaign markets from the list is 'extremely tough' for political reasons. He also admitted that BTI has had problems with responding to changes in the economic environment of markets that are not on the list. This was shown in the case of South East Asian countries, which were removed from the list in 1998, but then experienced a recovery (House of Commons 1999).
- It is questionable to what extent the market opportunities for products within each of the 27 groups can be reasonably generalised. The sector 'creative and media industries' contains for example both 'lighting and sound technology' and 'books and published materials'. The categorisation presupposes that the demand for the two types of products would be the same.
- To select fairs only according to product and markets, presupposes that there are no quality differences between fairs. But this is not the case (see Chapter 5).
- Considering that the sector groups consist of few people, often responsible for several sectors, that the trade associations they might co-operate with have the described research constraints, and that the other Whitehall sector sponsors concentrate on the British market, it is questionable whether the sector groups can get enough high-quality information about more than 80 markets, and their relative merits. It is likely that they are mainly guided by past performance. As to the governments' private sector advisors for export promotion, who are in contact with the market and sector directorates, criticisms have been raised that they rarely represent SMEs (BCC 1998; UK-T).

The knowledge for choices outside the sector-market matrix and ranking the fairs
While the sector-market matrix is supposed to be the key tool guiding government's trade fair expenditure decisions (DTI and Treasury 2000:69; TPUK 2000:20; DTI et al. 2001:34), BTI management recognise the need for flexibility, and thus give all parties the freedom to favour other events (House of Commons 2000:prg.73). Moreover, the market directorates, foreign posts, and sector groups need to rank all those events that match the matrix. Therefore, additional decision criteria have to be used to assess the relative merits of fairs.

Sponsors provide the different parties with event-specific information. They submit their bids on forms, which require them to give information about their organisation, and details such as an estimate of the number of participants that will be recruited, how many would be likely to qualify for grants, and how many would be first time exhibitors. If the event is not in a market that was identified as high priority in the sector-market matrix, additional justification for support is required (TPUK 2001).

However, when the representatives of market and sector groups were asked how they rank the fairs apart from using the SMM, this information was not mentioned by them. The unanimous statement was that they judge according to the past performance of the sponsor. What counted was that the sponsor had managed to attract a large group of participants in previous years (UK-D; UK-E; UK-F; UK-G). For UK-E it was also important that the trade fair was international, e.g. an event for the whole Middle East rather than just Abu Dhabi.

Compared with the ideal knowledge of TPUK in the selection process, one can conclude that there are discrepancies. As the sector-market matrix dominates the choice, the knowledge is likely to be out-of-date. The sector knowledge is too general, and the final choice between fairs is led by a criterion that has little to do with the organisation objective.

TPUK's incentives in the selection process

What are the incentives for the parties in TPUK to make 'good' choices? As discussed, IBS is formally responsible for the SESA programme. But they do not choose, and the list of selected fairs is based on an aggregation of judgements from four different parties.

In the discussion of public bureaux (Chapter 4) it was argued that they are constrained by rules, that the lower tiers in particular have an interest in increasing their budget, and that further 'benefits' might be on the job leisure and strategic policy making. The activity of ranking trade fairs does not give much freedom to pursue these goals. It does not involve policy making, especially since the selection is not done by one party. In order not to burden their budget with a task for which the respective directorate will not receive credit, and in order not to jeopardise on the job leisure, it is rational for the parties not to spend much staff time and other resources on the ranking. This is somewhat confirmed by the CBI complaint regarding export support, that 'activities should not be pursued just because they have always been there' (CBI 1997). Following the sector-market matrix is easy, as is the subsequent ranking according to a straightforward criterion like sponsors' past recruitment success.

This tendency has been reinforced by the government's increasing emphasis to focus on 'target markets'. In 2000 BTI management dedicated ca. 65% of the programme budget, and 50% of the running costs to promote exports to selected markets (House of Commons 2000:prg.73). For most of the target markets (except for the 'easy markets' designated for the inexperienced exporters), supplementary SESA grants are available, which increase the maximum support of normally £2300 by up to £1200. In 2001 BTI announced that *'the future strategy will con-*

tinue to tighten the targeting of activity in those markets and sectors with most potential' (DTI et al. 2001:34).

To do the 'fine-tuning' of the selection according to expected participant numbers with specific sponsors also makes sense. The success criterion pronounced by ministers in their press releases and interviews is the number of firms that benefited from the SESA programme (e.g. DTI 1998). This suggests the same conclusion regarding the TPUK decision making as KPMG reached in 1994: 'The main factor behind the decision to support an event was clearly the ability to raise a viable delegation' (DTI 1994:76).

7.2.4 Consequences of the selection organisation

The previous sections have tried to establish what knowledge and incentives sponsors and TPUK have to select trade fairs. It was argued that a large number of trade associations de facto could not become sponsors. Of those who can and do bid for fairs, many do not have the resources to assess the whole range of fairs that are available in combination with market opportunities for SMEs. And in their own interest sponsors are well advised to bid for fairs that can attract many participants, whether or not these are best for the target SME groups. TPUK, choosing from the bids, base their selection mainly on the categorised knowledge incorporated in the sector-market matrix, and on their knowledge about the number of participants that sponsors have been able to recruit previously. Table 7.2. (next page) summarises the major findings in comparison to the ideal selection organisation.

From an organisation that operates the selection process with such actors under the given rules it can be expected that the list of selected fairs shows the following characteristics:

1. it does not contain events for all sectors, as not all sectors have bidding trade associations
2. fairs that are suggested are mostly well known, large and/or repeat events with broad themes that do not require much research input and can attract many participants
3. the final list is likely to consist of fairs in predetermined markets, with little responsiveness to new market prospects, or specific opportunities for sub-sectors.

There is some evidence, which supports the expected consequences of the SESA organisation:

1) Neglect of sectors that are not represented by strong business associations
To judge the validity of the first prediction, a TPUK study looking at the strength of export support through trade associations in nine different industries was used, and two extreme cases were picked. In this study (TPUK 2000b) the sector 'metals' is described as 'fairly fragmented', with fragmented associations. None of the

Table 7.2. The British trade fair selection organisation compared with the ideal

Ideal selection organisation	*British selection organisation*
Ideal knowledge of the actors with the decision rights to select the fairs ▪ most promising markets for different industries ▪ trade fairs worldwide and their characteristics ▪ relative relevance of official support ▪ relative usefulness of exhibitions in different markets/industries	*Real knowledge* on which selection is based within an industry – *trade associations* ▪ highly variable knowledge ▪ market knowledge based on o info from active members o knowledge gained when providing other export services (which only some do, and only active members use) o knowledge gained at previous trade fair events ▪ trade fair knowledge based on o previous participations o trade fair organising companies o active members ▪ knowledge about relevance of official support o previous participations o active members ▪ knowledge about relative usefulness of exhibitions in different markets based on o previous participations o active members between industries – *TPUK* knowledge based on ▪ suggestions from trade associations that decide to bid ▪ sector-market matrix ▪ no. of participants recruited previously by the sponsor
Ideal incentives of the actors with the decision rights to select the fairs ▪ choose impartially according to highest impact of trade fair support on market entry success ▪ cater for both inexperienced/potential exporters and experienced exporters entering new markets	*Real incentives* which influence the selection within an industry – *trade associations* ▪ to attract at least ten participants, the more the better/not take participant number risks ▪ to cater for active members/subgroups (who are already exporting, and who are often larger firms) between industries – *TPUK* ▪ to choose impartially between bids according to sector-market matrix; (sector-market matrix caters for both inexperienced and experienced exporters) ▪ to select according to sponsor's past performance
Ideal output selection of the fairs that offer the best opportunities for a successful market entry of new/occasional and of experienced exporters	*Predicted real output pattern* 1. selected events do not cover all sectors or subsectors 2. selected fairs are mostly large and/or repeat events with broad themes, that make recruitment easier 3. selected events are in predetermined markets with little responsiveness to new market prospects or to specific opportunities for sub-sectors

trade associations within the sector have dedicated export staff, and there is no single sector focal point for export. None of the associations have sub-sector export strategies. And there is little support from many metals-sector companies for trade associations to be proactive in export trade development (TPUK 2000b:17ff). The trade fair programme 2001–02 does not include a single event for 'Metals & Minerals', which is one of the 27 sectors in the matrix. This is the case even though the sector is classified as 'priority' in 15 markets, five of which are target markets, and as 'high priority' for government export promotion services in a sixth target market. Aerospace, on the other hand, is an industry with a highly consolidated representation, which provides dedicated export resources to its firms (TPUK 2000b:13ff). Its sponsors have managed to bid successfully for 20 aerospace-related events.

Of the other 27 sectors, some are better represented than 'metals and minerals' but sub-sectors lose out. One example is the chemicals sector. It is the UK's largest manufacturing sector, which exports around 48% of its turnover. Many large multinational companies operate and manufacture in the UK, but 80% of chemical companies employ fewer than 50 people (TPUK 2001b). The study cited above (TPUK 2000b) found that the representation of sub-sectors differs. Only two associations, both of which do not represent the whole sector, provide mentionable export support. Looking at the SESA 2001–02 programme it is these two associations (the Chemical Industries Association and the British Plastics Federation), which sponsor three events. The other five events that are classified as 'chemicals events' are sponsored by GAMBICA, a strong trade association for the instrumentation, control and automation industry. They have bid for fairs that cover analytical instruments; and 'analytical services' are sub-grouped under the chemicals sector. Thus, the fair themes on offer for the chemicals sector cover only 'rubber and plastics' (2), 'speciality and fine chemicals' (1), and analysis, diagnostics, etc. (5). Producers of 'coatings and paints', 'detergents and soaps', 'photomaterials' and many more subgroups have no specific supported events.

Talking to the Minister for Small Business and E-Commerce, the editors of the trade journal 'Printing World' complain, *'how can the sector achieve greater prominence in the bidding process for funding when Printing Machinery is sub-categorised under 'Production Machinery & Engineering'?'* (Printing World 29.5.2000).

The problem that some subsectors de facto do not have access to SESA is probably worsened by TPUK's budgeting. As it is done according to the broad sector descriptions, TPUK or auditors cannot keep track of an uneven distribution of funds (HANSARD 2000a).

2) Selection of broad themed, large fairs

To some extent the representation problem of sub-sectors remains hidden, as funds are allocated to broad-themed events, where many sub-sectors can exhibit. As argued above this is the expected result of an organisation that has actors who bid for well-known events that are likely to attract many participants, and TPUK also defining successfulness in terms of participant numbers.

In the 2001–02 programme, 11% of the events are 'core events', defined as well-established events that attract large groups of exhibitors. Funding is guaranteed. But before the Export Forum's criticism of their large number, there were nearly three times as many, and their number has already risen again from 66 in 1998 to 77 in 2001 (DTI 1998a; TPUK 2001). The interest of sponsors in these profitable large events was shown in a consultation process preceding the Export Forum. Many trade associations, were strongly in favour of retaining core events, even though participants were against this (DTI and FCO 1997:33).

To judge the focus and size of non-core events, a random sample of 30 fairs was taken from the 2001/2 programme (see Annex 1). The AUMA trade fair database (www.auma.de) was used to obtain comparable data on the selected fairs. On a scale of 1–6, where 1 are 'universal' fairs without any sector focus, and 6 are very specific events, most fairs were classified as 2 or 3, and none as 6.[8] The degree of focus was determined according to how many product categories were listed as 'predominantly exhibited'.[9] Thirteen (43%), including 3 niche events, were very broadly themed events categorised as '2'. This group included, for example, the fair 'MEDICA' in Germany, where 20 types of healthcare-related product groups from pharmaceuticals to hospital beds to computer software is on offer. A further five (17%) were broadly-themed fairs – '3'. These included, for example, the American International Toy Fair, where books, dolls, baby-products, crafts materials etc. are shown. Only three events (10%), two of which were niche events, were classified as 'considerably focused' – '5'. One example was the 'IPC Expo', where mainly circuit boards are exhibited.

The point about the broadness of the selected trade fairs is also made in the cited article in 'Printing World'. The authors criticise the *'continuing trend to support wide-ranging bodies like engineering industries federations when they try to recruit printing and other suppliers to take part in general engineering shows which are of no relevance to them. We need more focus on specifics, not generics to support SMEs.'* (Printing World 29.5.2000).

In terms of size, it is difficult to make a precise judgement about the distribution, because, depending on the industry what is considered to be a 'big' fair will vary. However, the tendency towards selecting large events is shown to some extent by the figures: According to the AUMA database 27% of the fairs had over 1000 exhibitors with an own stand, 13% between 501 and 1000, 33% between 201 and 500, and only 16% between 101 and 200 in the previous years. For the remaining three fairs no data was available. For comparison, a major manufacturing industry fair in the United States had on average 400 exhibitors in 2000 (Industry Week 24.1.2000).

---

[8] Several 'universal' fairs, e.g. the 'Havana International Fair', 'or the 'Industria' in Hungary, were in the programme but not in the sample. Government-related bodies with a geographical focus sponsored them.

[9] This is by no means an exact measure, as the preciseness of product labels varies. But the evaluation was done to get a rough idea about the product ranges of selected trade fairs.

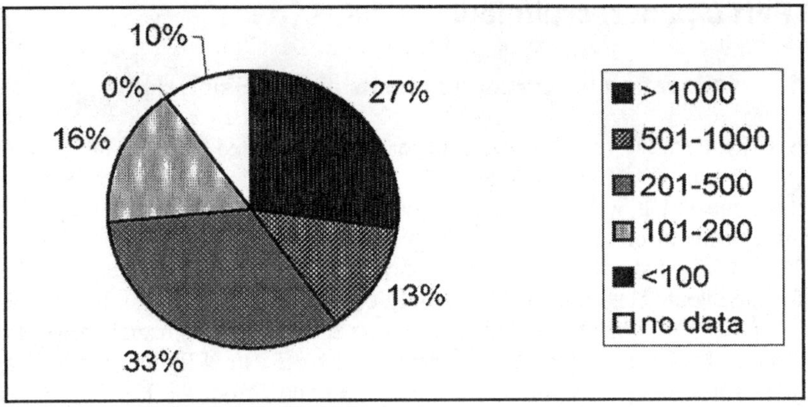

Fig. 7.5. The size of trade fairs in the 2001/2 SESA programme
Source: AUMA database (www.auma.de) for a randomly selected trade fair sample (see Annex 1)

3) Little responsiveness to new market prospects

To establish the real extent to which the sector-market matrix (and sponsor and group size considerations) predetermines the selection of fairs, one would need to compare the list of bids with the list of selected events. Because the former could not be obtained, the assessment is based on the 2001–02 programme only. But as all of the interviewed trade association representatives said that they did NOT choose the fairs according to the sector-market matrix, the bids should not have been very biased towards sector-market matrix fitting events.

It was found that of all 555 supported SESA participant groups in 2001–02, 85% visit one of the 15 campaign markets. Of the remaining 15%, only 21% (that is 3% of the total) visit fairs in sectors and markets that have not been categorised as 'high priority' or 'priority' for government export promotion services in the sector-market matrix. A look at these 17 SESA groups shows that one third visit core events with broad themes that attract visitors from beyond the country, e.g. 'The Big Five Show', the major construction industry fair for the Middle East. Another third visits large, regional shows that are not classified as 'core event', like the 'Food & Hotel Asia' in Singapore. Three groups exhibit at 'universal' fairs, or at a 'British' show, which makes the sector classification largely irrelevant. Another two concern seminars that are part of a seminar series by the respective sponsor. Interestingly, all sponsors for these events are sponsors that organise several fairs. On average, they organise 8.6 events, compared with the total average of 4.5. This confirms that in the few cases where TPUK supports events outside the matrix, the sponsor's capacity is an important factor in that decision.

7.3 Participant recruitment

7.3.1 The allocation of recruitment tasks and decision rights

In the UK the task to recruit participants has been allocated solely to the sponsors (TPUK 2001). TPUK assist sponsors' recruitment by publishing the selected events on the TPUK website, in their magazine, and in a brochure. But they do not recruit firms themselves.

The sponsors have to recruit at least the number of participants stated in their bid for the event. They must collect a fully completed 'SESA Trade Fair Exhibitors' Application Form' from each firm, advise the firms on their grant eligibility, and submit the forms to TPUK by a specified cut-off date. Eligibility criteria are that the firm is UK-based and that it intends to export from the UK. Since 1991 trade fair grants have been restricted to three participations per firm in any one country (or five in Japan, China, Russia and USA), and to two in a core event. But even if firms are not eligible for a grant they are counted towards the minimum group size as long as they participate as members of the group (TPUK 2001a).

7.3.2 The sponsors' recruitment knowledge and incentives

Sponsors' recruitment knowledge

As argued in Chapter 5, the ideal organisation of participant recruitment ensures that the responsible actors know how to inform all those firms that produce relevant goods and services about the event; and has relevant information to enable firms to make a rational choice.

Regarding the first point, there is reason to assume that sponsors' knowledge is patchy:

The mean membership size of 84 trade association sponsors for the 2001–02 SESA programme was 420, with a median of 200.[10] Assuming that the other 16 trade associations, for which no data was available, were of a comparable size, roughly 42,000 enterprises were members of a sponsor trade association. In addition several thousand firms were members of one of the four chambers of commerce, or were linked to the two business links, or to the other agencies that acted in some cases as sponsors. But the figure of, at best, 50,000–60,000 firms stands against a total of about 3.7 million businesses in the UK (Small Business Service 2001). British Trade International therefore requires sponsors to have *'a willingness and ability to recruit businesses which are non-members…'* (TPUK 2001).

Sponsors recruit some non-members 'passively'. All sponsors mentioned in the interviews that trade fair companies refer interested British firms to them. Firms might also find out from the TPUK publications, or from other bodies, which disseminate the information, e.g. some chambers of commerce. Whichever source

[10] Calculations are based on the membership figures published by the Trade Association Forum (http://www.taforum.org.uk/). Not all members are necessarily firms.

firms receive their information from, they all have to contact the sponsor and apply for a grant through them.

But the problem for sponsors is how to reach those non-members who do not approach them on their own. KPMG and A.D. Little (DTI 1994; TPUK 2000b), which both looked at trade associations in different industry sectors, found that sponsors vary greatly in their knowledge of firms within their sector. In the interviews with trade associations, differences in their capacity and willingness to collect contact details became evident. Z, a well-resourced sponsor, has built up a database of 6500 firms, which it uses for recruitment purposes. The other interview partners only added those non-members to their mailing lists that had participated at previous fairs or appeared in exhibitors' catalogues. The firms on the mailing lists are informed with mail-shots. In addition, members receive the membership magazines in which advertisements for the fairs are placed.

Since the users of trade associations are predominantly larger firms (> £1m turnover) (Runiewicz 1997), and since the non-members on the lists are existing exporters, sponsors are less likely to know the small and non-exporting firms in the industry. The problem is exacerbated by the broadness of many selected trade fairs, which cause the group of potential participants to go far beyond the circle of firms with which the trade association normally deals. A passage in the DTI's 'Sponsors' Handbook' demonstrates the extent of the difficulties for some sponsors: The DTI advise trade associations to check with the DTI market branches, whether the civil servants could give them names of companies! (Export Publications Unit 1996:27). At the same time, the NAO (1996:44f) reported, that the DTI did not have high quality information on businesses, and was poorly placed to capture information on firms that had not already used a government export service. It found that the lack of high quality information on businesses prevented those firms that were most likely to benefit, from being reached.

Regarding the second component of knowledge, which the recruiters should ideally have – to be able to provide firms with sufficient information so that they can judge whether a participation is likely to be beneficial – many sponsors' knowledge appears to be patchy too.

Sponsors are obliged to give exhibitors *'all relevant information'*, before the firms have to commit themselves to participating. But 'relevant information' is only defined as consisting of *'space and stand costs, management fees, services provided by the sponsor, other costs, DTI grant details, and exhibitor's terms and conditions'* (Export Publications Unit 1996:25). To give details about the fair, and to help firms assess whether exhibiting at a particular fair could be a good investment for them, is not part of the duty. However, the relevance of this information is acknowledged. Sponsors are asked to *'...strongly consider including a brief summary of why the market and the fair are likely to present attractive business opportunities'* (p.26); and they are told that *'it is good practise for sponsors to confirm where possible that the company's products are appropriate to the event'* (p.31).

But just over one quarter of the sponsor trade associations describe 'their' trade fairs on their Internet pages. Most list only the title and date of supported events.

TPUK do not supply any information either, except for the country, industry category, and which sponsor to contact. This means that firms will only find out more, if they actively seek further information.

The extent of sponsors' knowledge, from which firms could benefit if they contact them, depends on three factors. First, whether the sponsors have had previous experience with the particular trade fair, second, whether they acquired relevant knowledge about markets and exporting through other activities, and third, whether they make a determined effort to obtain the information they lack.

Many of the selected events have been in the programme before and most have been organised by the same sponsor. Some sponsors also visit fairs before they bid for them (MPI). But fewer than half of the sponsor trade associations with a website offer some export support service in addition to the trade fair support. Many do therefore not have other sources of knowledge regarding different markets and exporters' difficulties. Again, it is easier for associations to gather focused information, if they deal with a homogeneous group of companies. Where the fair has a broad theme, or where industry is fragmented, the sponsor is unlikely to know enough about the market opportunities to advise each potential participant about the suitability of a participation.

To which extent the respective officer is inclined to try, is a question of incentives.

Sponsors' recruitment incentives

Ideally, recruitment should be organised so that sponsors have a net benefit from informing many firms about the SESA opportunity, especially those SMEs that are new to exporting, or new to the market in which the trade fair takes place and could benefit from exhibiting there. Sponsors should also be able to provide sufficiently detailed information so that firms can better judge the benefits of participation.

As mentioned above, it is important for the sponsors to recruit the minimum participant number, to stay credible with BTI. Also, the costs of sponsoring an event are mostly fixed, while each participant pays the management fee. Furthermore, the more members participate, the more appreciate the sponsors' SESA involvement, and every non-member participant might join the association as a result of getting to know them.

But sponsors derive these benefits from all participants, whether they are new to the market or not. And as for the German DFGs, active recruitment is costly for them, because it requires staff time, or funds to contract-out the recruiting. As discussed above, the staff time that can be dedicated to trade fair organisation is often restricted, and most associations are not well resourced. It is not surprising therefore that, of the recruitment methods which have been suggested in the 'Sponsors' Handbook' (DTI 1996) (it was written to improve the performance of sponsors), only the 'low cost' options were mentioned by all interviewees. Asked how they advertise the events, all stated 'articles and advertisements in the trade press'. They also tell participants at 'their' fairs about their other events, and respond to inquiries from firms that approach them independently. Other, more resource intensive suggestions in the Handbook, like 'telesales initiatives', 'approaching trade fair organisers to agree a recruitment programme and promotion budget', or 'using a mail house' were not mentioned. While all send the information to firms on their mailing lists, only Z has made a major investment in developing the list into an extensive database of firms in their industry. According to UK-J this was done at considerable cost. Z also uses seminars about specific markets to advertise events. However, with 34 staff Z is one of the wealthier associations, and they believe that the database is an asset that makes them an interesting industry representative for government. Moreover, Z is in competition with several other trade associations that service firms from within the same industry group and also seek to sponsor fairs and attract firms as members.

For business association sponsors in general, tied to the deterring cost factor of broad advertising campaigns, is members' overall negative attitude to incurring these costs. Even in associations where many members are in favour of using part of the budget for export support services, they are unlikely to support large participant recruitment expenditures. Interested members would get informed in any case through the cheap channels of notices in members' magazines and through direct mailing. Many would not see why they should vote for additional recruitment expenditures that largely benefit non-members. As UK-J pointed out, and UK-A confirmed, TPUK does not take into account the marketing efforts of sponsors, when they choose among the bids. So although sponsors are interested in recruiting participants, not many will be inclined to spend more resources than necessary for recruiting the minimum number. In many cases the necessary number of interested firms has been identified before the application.

The lack of an incentive to do broad advertising was reflected in the Governments' Quality Management Survey Satisfaction Reports (TPUK and Taylor Nelson Sofres Harris 2000; 2000a; 2001).[11] Although sponsors turned out to be the largest single source of information for participants, they reached only a small number. In the sample of SESA trade fair participants between July and September 1999, only 16% found out about SESA trade fairs from sponsors. In the following two periods (October '99 to March '00, and April '00 to September '00), the respective figures were 10% and 22%. Trade fair organisers were the second biggest group, informing 15%, 11% and 15% of the respective participants, followed by a variety of other sources ranging from government promotional literature to chambers of commerce to personal contacts. Given sponsors' central role in recruitment their actual role thus appears very limited.

Their overall limited interest and/or resources in advertising the events was also reflected on the websites. Of those sponsors with a website, 43% did not use it to advertise trade fair events, and a further 10% did, but had not updated their pages within three months after the list of 2001–02 had been decided. Only 47% of those

[11] A consulting firm carries out the Quality Management Surveys for TPUK. Twice or three times a year a very small sample of trade fair participants is phoned to answer several questions regarding the event and firm characteristics. The three reports which could be obtained from TPUK after several months of pleading covered the period from July 1999 – September 2000. Sample sizes for the three reports were 30, 62, and 61. The quality of the reports is doubtful. Figures do not add up, and for many questions there are only one or two respondents, so that the percentages presented are meaningless.

who put the events on their website describe the support that is available, sometimes without mentioning that the grant comes from BTI. Only 10% provide a link to the TPUK website, where the interested firms could find out about additional government export support programmes which are available to explore specific markets.

If the cost of advertising as such is a constraint, it is unlikely that sponsors focus their recruitment activity on new exporters, or those who have to be convinced about the opportunities in a particular market. This would be more expensive than a blanket approach like advertising in trade magazines. The extra £ 20, which sponsors have received since 1998 for each first-time exporter they recruit, is unlikely to cover the additional cost, especially as these firms also need more support with the exhibition. But the question, whether sponsors have an incentive to actively recruit firms in the target groups, is also related to the question of what attitude they have towards 'convincing' firms. BPI for example advertise their event through direct mailing and articles in the trade press. Asked whether they tried to recruit first-time exhibitors directly, UK-L answered, *'If people have not exhibited before, you won't get them over the phone... It is not our role to sell exhibitions.'* None of the others thought it was their role either, but all of them said they would try to answer questions about a fair if asked.

Given that it is not a duty for the sponsor to advise firms, or provide information beyond the mentioned cost factors, and that many do not consider it their role; given that it is a risk for a sponsor to persuade a firm that might later be dissatisfied with the exhibition results; given that despite the three times rule, all firms are counted towards the minimum size of the group, rational managers would behave like the interviewees. They would use low cost information channels, even though they reach predominantly experienced exporters, and would not spend resources on gathering more than the basic knowledge than is necessary to give firms broad advice and information.

7.3.3 Consequences of the recruitment organisation

As described above, there are discrepancies between the sponsors' knowledge and incentives and the knowledge and incentives that the ideal recruitment organisation should provide. Far from knowing all firms that could exhibit at the event, sponsors' knowledge is usually limited to members, large companies, and previous exhibitors. Among those firms that the sponsors do not know are predominantly small and inexperienced firms. In addition, as in Germany, the sponsors do not have an incentive to focus their recruitment efforts on these target groups. Also, they do not have an incentive to advertise with many different means, or target inexperienced or potential exporters. Information is mainly disseminated via cheap information channels like advertisements in trade journals, which only reach firms that have the capacity to study such sources, and are receptive to the information.

Although SESA is based on the assumption that firms underestimate the benefits of exhibiting at a fair and therefore need a subsidy that rectifies their wrong calculation of net benefits, the programme appears to assume otherwise fully informed, rational decision-makers. None of the actors in the organisation are formally obliged to, nor benefit from providing information about market opportunities and about the necessary conditions firms have to meet to exploit these market opportunities. As in the German case, interested firms therefore have to source the relevant information themselves. If they do not know how to do that, or are not motivated to do so, their choices about exhibiting or not will be unbalanced.

Table 7.3. The British recruitment organisation compared with the ideal

Ideal recruitment organisation	*British recruitment organisation*
Ideal knowledge of the actors with the decision rights for participant recruitment ▪ suitable information channels to inform all firms ▪ information that is relevant for firms to judge whether the fair can be useful for them, and sources for such information	*Real knowledge* of the sponsors ▪ re. knowledge of suitable information channels o know how to inform members and participants at previous exhibitions o may know general and targeted information channels to reach non-members o benefit from TPUK , Chambers of Commerce, and other business organisations' advertising channels ▪ re. knowledge of information that is relevant to firms o know only in some cases about trade fair details, exhibiting in and exporting to that market, and supply and demand in the market
Ideal incentives of the actors with the decision rights for participant recruitment ▪ inform all firms with equal prospects equally ▪ provide sufficient information to allow firms to make rational choices	*Real incentives* of the sponsors benefit from high number of participants / loose out with low number of participants ▪ re. to inform all firms equally o firms known to be interested are cheaper to recruit than firms that need to be convinced o advertisements in trade and member magazines are cheaper than active recruiting ▪ re. to provide sufficient information for rational choices o recruitment benefits unrelated to success of exhibitors o information provision not a specified duty o information provision is costly
Ideal output: recruitment of inexperienced, potential and experienced exporters who can successfully exhibit at a selected fair to enter a new market	*Predicted real output pattern* 1. Not all firms hear about the opportunity 2. Inexperienced exporters and small firms, especially non-members are less likely to be aware of the opportunity 3. Many participants and non-participants do not receive enough information to make a rational choice.

As a result, the following outcomes are to be expected:

1. Not all firms hear about the opportunity

2. Small firms and inexperienced exporters are less likely to be aware of the opportunity
3. Many participants and non-participants do not receive enough information to make a rational choice.

1) Not all firms hear about the opportunity
Although the government's instructions to sponsors are clear (*'Sponsors should aim to make all UK companies within the relevant industry or industries aware of the fair.'* (Export Publications Unit 1996)), not all firms hear about the opportunity.

In a survey the National Audit Office found that only 47% of SMEs are aware of the trade fair programme's existence (NAO 1996:42), not to speak of being aware which fairs are currently being funded. In the same year even among exporters, 20% did not know that the service existed (Runiewicz 1996). When the CBI looked at SMEs and export promotion services they found that *'in essence, many companies who need and would use the services are unaware of them...'* (CBI 1996:7).

However, compared with other government export promotion programmes SESA and the trade mission programme, i.e. those programmes that are promoted through sponsors, are better known (NAO 1996:42; Runiewicz 1996). This can be explained by the fact that SESA is the biggest export promotion programme, but also because SESA and the trade missions are advertised by the sponsors, in addition to being advertised in the regular TPUK marketing publications. As the Quality Management Surveys showed, around 20% of the participants heard about SESA through the sponsors. So although the sponsors do not reach the whole target group, their efforts make a difference.

2) Inexperienced exporters and small firms, especially non-members, are less likely to be aware of the opportunity
Although in the NAO sample of British SMEs, only 47% of firms were aware of the programme, in the NAO sample of exporters 84% were. Firms with fewer than 20 employees were less likely to know than larger companies (NAO 1996:42ff).

Looking at the characteristics of exporters to South East Asia, NAO found that the number of new exporters to SE Asia, which could be attributed in whole or in part to export support, was the lowest for the Trade Fair Service, in absolute as well as in relative terms. Only about 15% of the participants in the SE Asia trade fairs intended to export to that market for the first time (NAO 1996:21).

In KPMG's qualitative interviews, a number of firms, which were not members of their sponsoring organisation, stated that they often felt out of touch with the scheme and were often not aware of what future events were being supported (DTI 1994:75).

The results of TPUK's Quality Management Surveys also indicate that existing exporters and larger firms are much more likely to be recruited. However, as the results also show that the samples in these surveys were too small to be reliable (there is no indication of how the samples were selected), the surveys were not summarised. Their results are presented separately in Table 7.4. (next page)

Table 7.4. Firm characteristics of SESA trade fair participants

	July'99-Sept'99 (sample size 30 firms)	*Oct'99-March'00 (sample size 62 firms)*	*April'00-Sept'00 (sample size 61 firms)*
Number of employees			
not stated	*1%*	*4%*	-
0-19	**43%**	16%	**41%**
20-50	30%	16%	26%
51-250	13%	27%	28%
251-500	0%	5%	2%
500+	13%	**32%**	3%
Turnover			
<1 million	10%	11%	**33%**
1-5 m	26%	**19%**	24%
5-20m	**34%**	14%	24%
20-100m	6%	16%	5%
100m+	7%	5%	0%
Percentage of turnover made up of export sales			
None	3%	3%	3%
1-4	0%	2%	0%
5-15	13%	15%	16%
16-25	13%	5%	8%
26-50	**30%**	16%	25%
51-75	7%	**18%**	**28%**
76-99	17%	13%	8%
100	3%	5%	2%
Years of exporting			
not stated	*7%*	*6%*	-
None	0%	8%	11%
1 – 5	17%	6%	15%
6 – 10	20%	19%	20%
10 – 25	**33%**	**35%**	**34%**
over 26	23%	26%	20%
Average previous use of SESA	*3*	*11*	*5*
% of firms that would exhibit without support from TPUK	*63%*	*63%*	*56%*

Sources: TPUK and Taylor Nelson Sofres Harris 2000; 2000a; 2001

The information that was collected at the MIDEST subcontractors' fair in Paris, November 2000, suggests that the QMS might even underestimate the size and experience of the average exhibitor. Paris is *not* in a difficult, expensive to visit, overseas location, and the subcontractors fair covers a field in which many British SMEs are active. But of the ten British firms that participated, the smallest in number of employees had 75 (mean 521), and the smallest in turnover had £ 4.6 million (mean £42 m). All were active exporters operating in several international markets, and half of them had subsidiaries abroad. Three were members of international groups.[12]

3) Insufficient information for rational participation choices

Recent surveys confirm that there is an export information problem that affects SMEs. According to the Bank of England's report, the availability of focused information and advice has been the single, most important, enduring issue facing smaller exporters. Firms without exporting experience often do not know who to approach. If they identify sources, they do not always receive tailored information and advice, and they often do not know the right questions (Bank of England 1998:23). The British Chambers of Commerce found that 54% of SME exporters had experienced failure in previous export ventures. The two leading causes were insufficient time/resources put into the failed venture (45%) and poor research and preparatory work (30%). Of SME exporters, 55% thought there should be more up-to-date information on markets and 39% would like more assistance with research (BCC 1997a). Considering that all respondents were exporters, who presumably know more about how to obtain export-related information than non-exporters, it is reasonable to assume that potential first-time exhibitors have difficulties making a balanced judgement.

So although sponsors argue that the high financial contribution that programme participants have to make to the cost of exhibiting (about 85% of the real costs, according to UK-J), would ensure that only firms who benefit attend, this is probably not the case. Of the 25% of participants who told KPMG that they would not have attended the trade fair with a grant of 10% less, many had developed this attitude because of the disappointing results they had at the last fair (DTI 1994). The CBI put forward the opinion that small firms sometimes receive export assistance when it is not in their best commercial interest. '*... A clearer analysis therefore needs to be undertaken of a company's capabilities and suitability for assistance in international market. ... There is a concomitant need to move away from broad numerical targets for new exporters. Such targets do not judge export success, viability or benefit to the UK economy*' (CBI 1997).

But the organisation of recruitment with its lack of information provision also leads to the situation in which firms do not take advantage of the assistance, although they could benefit. Over half of the SMEs (53%) that do not export state that this is because they do not consider their product/service suitable, and 22% feel that they lack the knowledge. Asked what would motivate them to consider selling abroad, 64% would like some evidence that there is demand (BCC 1997a). It seems that the target group of new/inexperienced exporters could be reached better, if recruitment was organised in a way that took the information need of firms more into account.

---

[12] The company information is based on the fair itself, on firm profiles in the TradeUK database of British Exporters (http://www.tradeuk.com), and on information from the firms' webpages.

7.4 Exhibition support

7.4.1 The allocation of exhibition support tasks and decision rights

In Britain, it is the sponsors who are responsible for providing exhibition support. But TPUK has specified few tasks, which sponsors are obliged to do:

Their major duty is to administer the government grants, which are paid out directly to each exhibitor. Besides, they must run an industry information stand *'with appropriate facilities to function as a support and meeting point for the exhibitors, and an information point for visitors, unless agreed otherwise with BTI'* (TPUK 2001a:prgs.5.6, 5.8, 5.10). Unlike DFGs, the information stand does not need to be part of a British group stand. Sponsors only have to appoint a contractor for setting up the stands, but can leave everything else, including the space booking, to the individual participants. They can also allow individual exhibitors to arrange the stand construction on their own. The participants do not have to exhibit in a group, but can exhibit anywhere at the show. Sponsors must only distribute a list of all group participants among the relevant government bureaux, and hand out evaluation questionnaires to the participants at the end of the show (TPUK 2001a: pgrs.5.12, 5.16).

Whether sponsors offer other services to the participants, e.g. book the exhibition space with the trade fair organisers, offer a travel package, or preparatory and follow-up meetings, is their own choice. They can charge participants a management fee, as long as they specify clearly which services the firms can expect in exchange, and they can subcontract the service provision (TPUK 2001a: pgr.5.4).

TPUK monitors whether sponsors fulfil the specified duties. To help sponsors fulfil their role the government published a 'sponsors' handbook' in 1996, which describes the tasks in detail and gives advice and recommendations to the sponsors (Export Publications Unit 1996).

7.4.2 The sponsors' exhibition support knowledge and incentives

The knowledge of the sponsors

'Understanding how to organise trade fairs requires intensive resourcing and substantial investment (from the sponsors)' (BCC 1997).

Sponsors must fulfil the duties specified in the SESA 'Terms and Conditions' as summarised above, and are encouraged to offer additional support services described in the Sponsor Handbook (Export Publications Unit 1996). Together, these services broadly cover the five different forms of exhibition support that were outlined in Chapter 5. As argued there, to provide the full variety, sponsors should ideally know about the relevant exhibition, logistics, and payment procedures for the respective market and industry; about effective exhibitor marketing; about how to negotiate with, and monitor suppliers and contractors; and about the specific factors that can make an exhibition more or less successful for the individual participants. Furthermore, they should know what is the best combination of services.

But if one looks at the obligatory exhibition support services in comparison with the recommended, voluntary ones, sponsors need far less knowledge for the former: The compulsory task of administering payments to eligible exhibitors basically involves transferring money and checking invoices. In contrast to the German system, the exhibitors initially have to pay the full price for exhibition space and stand construction. After the fair they can claim back 60% of that expenditure, up to a maximum of £2300. (In some target markets a supplementary grant is available.) The sponsors have to collect evidence that the exhibitors actually incurred the expenditure (i.e. they have to look at invoices), they have to calculate the specific grant amounts, and submit the claim to TPUK. TPUK then forward the total sum to the sponsor, who pays it out to the participants (TPUK 2001a, pgrs.5.17, 5.18). Any sponsor who is used to dealing with accounts and with members can perform this task, though it demands staff time and becomes easier with practice.

The second obligation of sponsors – to run an information stand at the fair – does not require much specific knowledge either, if done according to the Handbook: Sponsors are supposed to make sure they know what the exhibiting firms sell. The information stand should be equipped with a UK industry trade directory so that sourcing contact information can be provided. 'Support for the group' is specified to be about acquiring practical information before the beginning of the fair, such as the location of delivery points in the exhibition hall, shops for office items, opening times of the halls etc., and about liaising with the trade fair authorities, e.g. in the case of complaints (Export Publications Unit 1996).

The third obligation, to select contractors for stand construction in a tender process, is more demanding. Many sponsors are not used to contracting with other parties in an international context. Of the sampled 48 trade associations, only two had a bilingual website, and only five led exhibitors' groups abroad outside the SESA programme. The government has acknowledged the general lack of expertise in this respect, and has provided a guideline and a blueprint for tender documents in the Sponsor Handbook (Export Publications Unit 1996). But in terms of the skill requirements, all those other services, which may reduce exhibitors' costs through bulk purchasing, or through saving them the time to deal with contractors by themselves, fall into the same knowledge requirement category. To enter good contracts for the group and monitor them, sponsors need market overview, negotiation skills and contracting and monitoring knowledge in the different fields of service provision. They need to know what the exhibitors need. This knowledge comes with experience, and/or with the resources to research the matters and buy in experts. As argued in the sections above, sponsors' experience and resources vary widely.

Lastly, there is the list of recommended sponsor services, which essentially aim at improving exhibitors' returns through information provision. The array of suggestions in the Sponsors' Handbook, is striking. Listed are, for example, newsletters that are to be circulated to exhibitors before the event, information packs *'in accessible format with all the information that exhibitors can reasonably be expected to need....'*, and briefing meetings two to three months before the event. Sponsors are advised to obtain the information that companies are likely to need to develop a pricing policy; they should counsel exhibitors on advertising material that is most adequate for the country *(e.g. regarding colour, quality, paper size, languages)*; advise on appropriate means to get exhibits into the country; provide services such as on-line buyer credit checking facilities at the fair; etc. (Export Publications Unit 1996: sect.11). It is pointed out that *'even experienced exhibitors sometimes fail to understand how to manage a stand to full effect'*, and that they might have *'no grasp of the fact that certain techniques can be successful in one market and not in another'* (pgr.11.8).

It is difficult to see why a small sponsor trade association, which is unlikely to have a single full-time trade fair officer, should be more knowledgeable about this than an experienced exhibitor. Especially if the fair takes place in a new market, the time and other resources that would be required to fulfil these 'best practise' guidelines were considerable. The Sponsor Handbook advises sponsors to think of subcontracting the work, but also points out that the contract issues may be complex and that sponsors are liable (sect.16).

In sum, it appears as if only those sponsors with experience, or with the resources to buy in experience, have the knowledge to provide services that go beyond the minimum obligatory ones. But even those sponsors who have led many SESA groups previously have not learnt as much over time as they could have, had they received full feedback on their services. Although sponsors distribute and collect TPUK's detailed exhibitor questionnaire and can therefore check 'their' participants' comments, TPUK does not provide them with aggregate data.[13] They therefore do not have a benchmark against which to compare their own performance. UK-J from a trade association also raised the criticism that the TPUK questions were very broad, and not co-ordinated with the sponsors' feedback need. Moreover, the sponsors do not get to see the reports from diplomatic posts, which are sent to TPUK on each supported event in their market, and which include an assessment of the sponsor's performance.

---

[13] In the interviews it was suggested by sponsors that TPUK collects the exhibitor questionnaires, but does not evaluate them. In the course of the research this assumption appeared less and less far-fetched. Over 7000 firms participate in SESA each year, and most of them fill in the extensive questionnaire. But no data is available from the questionnaires in any of the government papers. Any references to evaluations refer to the Quality Management Surveys, which, as mentioned above, cover only samples of 30–60 exhibitors, of which not all answer each question. Several 'aggregate' answers are based on samples of one or two respondents! Also, the range of questions is smaller, and the choice of respondents is up to the private consultants who do the telephone surveys. Sponsors who have inquired for benchmarking data from the questionnaires have not received any. And when TPUK was asked repeatedly over several months to provide access to the data, they finally sent some Quality Management Survey reports. UK-J reported that he asked TPUK to make it possible for participants to fill in the questionnaire on-line (which would also make the evaluation much easier). The reply was, that TPUK had just recently spent money on scanning the questionnaire, and could not spend more now. When TPUK was asked what happened with the data from the questionnaires, the answer was '*We don't use this data externally because figures we quote in the public domain need to be independently and externally gathered.*' (UK-C, TPUK)

Sponsors' incentives

Looking at sponsors' incentives to minimise exhibitors' costs it is also useful to distinguish between the obligatory services, which sponsors must provide to keep their sponsor status, and the voluntary exhibition support services. The question is how trade associations' own goals – government recognition, sound finances, and contented current and future members – may affect the service provision.

- Obligatory services

To maintain government recognition, sponsors must fulfil their contractual obligations. They receive a fixed fee of £4600, and in some target markets a top-up sum of £500, £800 or £1200. TPUK can easily monitor whether they perform. They can immediately observe the distribution of participant lists, as well as the existence of an information stand and meeting point. The contracts for stand design and construction must be copied to TPUK. Requiring sponsors to submit an annual accountant report controls sponsors' grant administration. It needs to certify that the claim for grants was appropriate, that the sponsor has maintained adequate records, and that all eligible businesses received their grant. TPUK might also spot-check sponsors' books (TPUK 2001a). Where a sponsor has in TradePartners UK's opinion performed unsatisfactorily, TPUK may decide not to appoint the sponsor again (TPUK 2001). It is therefore unlikely that a sponsor would not fulfil their obligations.

Nevertheless, as sponsors' past performance has shown, their own interests influence how they carry out these compulsory services: In the case of grant administration, sponsors pursued their financial interests by keeping the government grants for several months before paying the participants. Some deducted the management fee as well as other outstanding debts of the firms (DTI 1994). Now sponsors have to pay the full grant amount within three weeks of receipt, unless they have a formal offset agreement (TPUK 2001a: 5.18).

In the case of the information stand design, TPUK has not defined any norms or minimum quality levels, except that the stand has to be staffed throughout the event. The sponsor is only advised to '*bear its representational role in mind*' (DTI 1996:53). In the interviews it became evident that sponsors have different approaches, depending on their main objective and the type of the event. As stated above, W's and X's major objective at the flagship fair has been positive publicity. They spend far more than the government subsidy of £ 4600 on their information stand, viewing the extra cost as 'marketing' expenditure (UK-L; UK-M). Other sponsors have to pay attention to cover their costs. UK-J felt that in comparison with other national stands, British Pavilions had been less representative since sponsors only received the fixed contribution, which did not allow for expensive designs.

- Voluntary services

Looking at sponsors' voluntary exhibition support services, the incentives for providing them vary depending on the service. Overall, sponsors have to take into account that costs beyond the fixed TPUK grant can only be recovered from the exhibitors. On the other hand, government puts some pressure on sponsors to provide voluntary services. The interviewees felt that sponsors who did only the very minimum were less likely to be appointed in future. TPUK had become more demanding. They were also aware of the government's efforts to foster the development of lead associations for each sector, and saw their performance as sponsors as being important for reaching or keeping that status. Sponsors therefore have to consider which 'voluntary' services they should provide, considering how the different services can contribute to their own goals.

To keep exhibiting association members content, and to attract non-member participants to the association, sponsors have to provide the services they offer well. And unless they are prepared to subsidise their sponsor activities, they can only provide services that participants consider 'value for money'. This means that sponsors either have to be able to negotiate better prices than participants could obtain themselves, or help them save on management time, by not having to find and deal with all the different providers (space booking, stand construction, freight, insurance...). However, the size of the discounts that a sponsor can negotiate is likely to depend on the size of the group, the frequency with which the sponsor deals with the service provider, and his or her negotiating experience. The extent to which companies save on management time, and consequently the perceived value of a 'package offer', depends on their (in)experience.

The 'cost saving services' all have in common the fact that group participants can 'see' what they get in return for the management fee, and that they would have to spend money on services like shipping or stand construction, whether the sponsor provides them or not. In contrast, expenditures for activities that aim at increasing the returns from exhibiting are not inevitable, and their value is not as easily judged. For example, it is difficult for a firm to assess how much they might gain from an exhibitor training session. Also, the perceived value of information services will vary between participants. Again, inexperienced exhibitors are more likely to benefit from general information than experienced exhibitors. And the more firm-specific information needs to be valuable, the more expensive it becomes for the sponsor to provide. Moreover, unlike the 'cost saving services' the 'benefit increasing services' bear the risk that participants do not credit the sponsor with positive results, but blame them for high fees. The Handbook warns sponsors for example that many exhibitors are reluctant to take advantage of the pre-event information offers (Export Publications Unit 1996), and UK-M remarked, *'most people know how to do it. They want to get on, on their own. If they need advice they can ask us.'*

In addition, apart from the risk that members do not value a service enough, a sponsor has to consider the financial risks of service provision. If a firm's application for a trade fair subsidy has been approved, the firm does not have to use the sponsor's services. The only exceptions are stand booking and stand construction services, the take-up of which the sponsor can make obligatory (UK-J). The fewer companies share the cost of the sponsor's services, the more expensive the services become for those who do. Given that most of the participants have trade fair experience and often prefer to exhibit in the exhibition area that is relevant for their product, a sponsor can, for example, have difficulty getting enough firms booked into a pavilion. Sometimes firms even look for locations next to the British pavilion as 'independents' and thereby save on the management fee, while still benefiting from visitors' interest in the British stand (UK-J). Adding to the financial risk and the complexity of providing voluntary services are sponsors' exposure to the full exchange rate risk when dealing with providers abroad (TPUK 2000:5.6),[14] and the necessity to plan their cash flow carefully as *'in some cases sponsors will need to expend on-site large sums of money for service provision'* (Export Publications Unit 1996). Considering the limited management capacity and resources of small sponsors, for whom even fulfilling the compulsory tasks constitutes a burden, these are relevant issues.

Considering these factors, sponsors on the whole would not want to provide many voluntary services. As there is nevertheless some pressure to offer them, they have an incentive to pick those services that are relatively cheap to provide, that are visible to members and the government, and that allow some protection against financial risks. 'Visibility' is an issue not least because TPUK do not systematically collect information on what sponsors offer for their management fees. They only ask participants whether the fee represented value for money, and receive the reports from the diplomatic posts (UK-C, TPUK).

7.4.3 Consequences of the exhibition support organisation

Sponsors' knowledge and incentives for providing exhibition support services are, in summary, the following: In contrast to the ideal organisation, where actors know how to provide all forms of exhibition support, and have an incentive to choose the combination that is best for exhibitors, sponsors' focus is first of all on the few, narrowly specified, compulsory tasks. All sponsors have sufficient knowledge to fulfil TPUK's basic expectations. But regarding 'good' contracts with subcontractors and suppliers, and regarding voluntary information services, sponsors' readily available knowledge varies. It depends on their experience with the respective trade fair and market, and on the exporting and exhibiting expertise of the associations' staff. The incentives for offering voluntary services are not the same for each service, both in terms of how much they cost the sponsor to provide, and in terms of how much providing them can contribute to the sponsor's own goals. The relative costs also differ between sponsors. The less experienced sponsors are, the more resources they need to acquire the missing knowledge. The fewer resources sponsors have, the higher the relative financial risk becomes. If these threats cannot be mitigated without alienating participants with high management fees, or very unflexible contract terms, sponsors are unlikely to provide the services. Overall participants are better prepared to pay a fee where they see concrete cost-savings for themselves.

Therefore, it is to be expected that the range of exhibition support services provided depends to a large extent on the experience and resources of sponsors, and that sponsors only offer those voluntary services that are visible, do not require ex-

---

[14] Cost-savings from favourable moves of the exchange rate must be passed on to the exhibitors. Unfavourable changes can be passed on (TPUK 2000, 5.4.).

tensive expertise, do not involve financial risks, and reduce direct exhibition expenses.

Table 7.5. The British exhibition support organisation compared with the ideal

Ideal exhibition support organisation	*British exhibition support organisation*
Ideal knowledge of the actors with the decision rights for exhibition support ▪ know best ways of providing financial support ▪ know how to negotiate group discounts, and join up participants to share fixed expenditures where possible ▪ know how to make official participation attractive for visitors and how to market the group and the whole German/British sector in the host country ▪ know how to reduce participation 'transaction costs' for firms ▪ know critical success factors for specific fairs, and how to alert firms to the issues ▪ know which mix of the above approaches is most suitable for a specific fair and for participants	*Real knowledge* of the sponsors ▪ Amount of financial support has been fixed by TPUK; sponsors know how to process grant applications, check invoices, and transfer money ▪ Sponsors' negotiation and contracting knowledge, as well as marketing knowledge differs with trade fair experience and resources ▪ Sponsors' knowledge that could reduce 'transaction costs' for the participants differs with trade fair experience and resources ▪ Sponsors' knowledge about success factors differs with trade fair experience and resources ▪ Sponsors do not have the right to decide about the size of direct financial support, and they set up the composition of the 'support package' in their participants' contract before they know which firms will sign the contract
Ideal incentives of the actors with the decision rights for exhibition support ▪ benefit from using their knowledge to provide adequate support, considering all forms of support as equally valuable ▪ have no incentive to favour specific participants over others ▪ have no incentive to make deals with suppliers / contractors at the cost of exhibitors or funding body	*Real incentives* of the DFGs ▪ Benefit/avoid problems by providing compulsory exhibition support services; net- benefit of some services higher than of others, considering provision cost, financial risks, representational effect, and participant appreciation; cost reducing services are more attractive than benefit increasing services; ▪ For inexperienced/'poor' associations relative costs/risks of service provision are higher; ▪ Disincentive to commit fraud due to tendering obligation and TPUK monitoring of contracts
Ideal output: reduce the costs of a successful trade fair participation in a new market for inexperienced, potential and experienced exporters	*Predicted real output pattern* Net costs are reduced due to direct financial subsidy, but other forms of support shows the following pattern 1. support provided varies, depending on sponsors' experience and resources 2. visible, cheap, low-risk 'tangible' services are more often provided than information services

1) The range of exhibition support services varies with the trade fair experience and resources of the sponsors

When KPMG investigated the British trade fair support programme in 1994, they found a '*considerable variation between the sponsors as to the level and breadth of services ... offered*' (DTI 1994:73). The size of a sponsor appeared to have a substantial impact.

To find out whether this was still the case, and to find out whether there were variations depending on group size and participants' experience, TPUK was asked for information about the services offered at different fairs. UK-A confirmed that the services on offer differ widely. However, it turned out that the strategy unit of TPUK do not collect fair-to-fair data on services offered, nor data about management fees. They only ask participants in the exhibitor questionnaire,[15] whether the fee represented value for money (UK-C).

In the interviews differences between sponsors became evident. Y book the exhibition space in the majority of cases, and take either stand shells available from the organiser, or employ a designer and constructor for a British Pavilion where they have many participants or where a unified UK presence is important. They always appoint a freight and travel agent, which they find through tender. Exhibitors receive a briefing at arrival and a reception may be organised with the local Foreign Office post (UK-K). W and X, even though they place a lot of emphasis on the design of the information stand, have a 'minimalist' approach. They provide only the compulsory services – a meeting space in conjunction with their information stand, and a brochure about the group. According to UK-L and UK-M, those participants who needed help could phone, or ask the sponsor personnel at the fair. Z has some fairs where they organise a pavilion, might make shipping and travel arrangements, and help with publicity (e.g. they organise a promotion in local journals and press photographers, publish a brochure, organise a reception). In other cases they only do the minimal duties. The differences in the extent of services are reflected in the management fee (UK-J).

To widen the sample of sponsors, information about exhibition services was collected from the websites of all sponsors that describe their exhibition services there. Obviously, it is not a representative sample because it covers only those sponsors with the resources and interest to maintain a detailed website. Trade fair activities must also be relevant enough for the association to specify them on their website. (For example, one result of the detailed analysis of 48 sponsors' websites was that just over 10% organised exhibition services independently of SESA. In this sample over two-thirds do). But this bias means that the services provided by those sponsors rather overstate than understate the available support. The majority of the other 82 sponsors are likely to offer fewer voluntary services.

The results are summarised in Table 7.6. (next page). It can be assumed that many of the boxes that were left blank stand for services that are not offered, as 'no' was only put where the sponsor explicitly denied offering the service.

[15] see footnote 13 of this chapter

Table 7.6. Range of voluntary exhibition support services provided by the sponsors

Sponsor	No. of events 2001/2	Size (no. of staff)	Own indep. Trade fair groups	Space booking	Stand shells/ stand construct.	British Pavillion	Display only option if firms do not want own stand	Freight	Travel+ accommodation	Insurance	Export – Import licenses/ customs clearance	Pre-event meeting	Pre-event printed information	Post-event information
CSSA *)	20	29	Yes	Yes	Yes – obligatory	Yes		Suggest agents	Suggest agents					
TIA *)	19	5												
SBAC	15	60	Yes	Yes	Yes – voluntary if stand > 35m2	Yes – shell scheme + self build option for large stands (>35m2)		May appoint agent	May appoint agent	No	No			
FEI	14	34	Yes	Yes – For some fairs – optional	Yes – For some fairs – optional	Yes – For some fairs— optional		Appoint agents	Appoint agents	yes		Yes		Distribution of visitor attendance statistics
EIC	11	19	Yes	Yes	Yes – obligatory	Yes		May appoint agent	May appoint agent	No				
BESA	7	9	No	Yes	Yes	Yes – For some fairs		Appoint agent	Appoint agent			Yes		
FMCEC	5	80	Yes	Yes – optional	Yes – optional	Yes – optional	Yes	Appoint agent						Distribution of visitor information
PLASA	5	16	Yes	Yes										
SMMT	4	105	Yes	Yes	Yes									
DMA	4	25	Yes	Yes	Yes – optional	Yes – optional	Yes	Appoint agent	Appoint agent	No			Exhibitor's manual	
BEDG	4		Yes	Yes				For some fairs – optional	Advice on good flight deals, names of travel agencies		For some fairs – optional	Yes, one month in advance	Newsletters with exhibition information	
Publish. Assoc.	3	18	Yes	For some fairs	For some fairs	For some fairs	For some fairs							
Gardenex	3	7	Yes		Yes				Yes – optional					
MPA	3	4	Yes	No	No	No								
PPMA	2	15	No		For some fairs	For some fairs								
BPF	2	22	No					Information	Information			yes		
BPI	1	24	No	No	No	No	Yes			No				
Sports	1	11	No	Yes				Negotiates group rates	Negotiates group rates					

*) use joint trade fair company Trade Fair Support Ltd. to manage participation'
Source: Associations' websites, Jan 2002.

The table shows a clear tendency of experienced sponsors, with scope to negotiate prices for a large number of exhibitors, offering more contract services. Negotiation scope and experience are indicated by the number of TPUK supported events. They are also reflected by sponsors' engagement in trade fair services outside the SESA programme. The two trade associations who bid successfully for the largest number of events – the Computer Industry Association (CSSA) and the Telecoms Industry Association (TIA) have set up their own company 'Trade Fair Support Ltd.' which specialises in providing trade fair services. The company advertises on its website: *'As we are bulk buyers for space at all major shows, we obtain the best prices to pass on to you.... Again, through partnerships with our service providers for construction, freight and travel, we are able to obtain economies of scale and keep these costs to a minimum'* (www.tradefair.co.uk).

The table also suggests that sponsors with fewer resources (as measured in staff numbers) tendentially offer fewer services, if compared with other sponsors who lead a similar number of events.

2) Few voluntary services are on offer, and some forms are more likely to be available than others

If table 7.6 shows the voluntary services that the most active sponsors offer, SESA participants overall are a long way from receiving the exhibition support recommended in the Sponsors' Handbook (see 7.4.2.1 above). It appears that despite the instructions in the handbook not much has changed since 1994, when KPMG found that only 25% of participants were offered a stand construction service (DTI 1994:70). The principal reason for participating in SESA has been the direct financial support, not the other forms of exhibition support (DTI 1994:25ff). But participants are usually content with those services that they do receive from sponsors (TPUK and Taylor Nelson Sofres Harris 2000; 2000a; 2001; NAO 1996:60, DTI 1994:70).

The table not only demonstrates that sponsors provide a limited range of services, but also that some services are more likely to be offered than others.

The most common services are the booking of space, arranging for stand shells and organising a British Pavilion. These are 'tangible services', and the stand and pavilion construction are highly visible. They are also the only services that sponsors can oblige participants to take up. Applicants for the group participations had to sign for example that they would take a stand shell provided by the sponsor, and they had to pay a 100% space deposit up to six months in advance, where sponsors booked exhibition space. Sponsors also reduced their financial risk by specifying that the management fee (which ranged between £ 150 and £ 600, and was in nearly all cases cheaper for members) is non-refundable. SBAC, the association for the aerospace industry, specified that the TPUK grant could be offset against any outstanding debt (websites of Trade Fair Support Ltd, of EIC, SBAC, SMMT, DMA).

But sponsors cannot oblige exhibitors to use other services. As the table shows, with one exception (BEDG) travel, accommodation or freight forwarding services are not provided. What sponsors do instead is appoint agents with whom they may or may not negotiate a preferential rate. The exhibitor deals directly with the agent, but saves the time to identify a suitable company. For an experienced sponsor the identification is not costly, but with this arrangement they do not have any financial risks or liabilities vis à vis either agent or participants. Services regarding insurances, and export and import licences, or help with customs clearance are – in contrast to travel or freight arrangements – much more case specific. They cannot be negotiated or arranged as a blanket agreement, which means that they would cost the sponsor far more to provide.

When it comes to information provision, the table also clearly shows that little is on offer. This stands in contrast to the government statement that *'exhibitors need a wide range of information to make full use of opportunities presented by events'* (Export Publications Unit 1996). However, apart from the table there are other pieces of evidence, which suggest that the current organisation results in the neglect of information services:

In the 1994 review of the trade fair service exhibitors pointed out that one service to match their needs better, would have been the provision of a preparatory checklist; and a number of participants wanted general advice on exhibiting (DTI 1994:70). Although sponsors were subsequently advised to prepare information packs for the participants (Export Publications Unit 1996) again in 1997 the Export Forum recommended that the government should do more to help firms prepare for participating in trade fairs (DTI and FCO 1997).

TPUK has tried to respond. They devised a 'Help for Exporters Exhibitors checklist', and obliged sponsors in the 'SESA terms and conditions' to make sure that participants are aware of the advice and information that is available from BTI (TPUK 2001a). TPUK also *'compile and research'* a free *'structured package of info and advice'* for first time participants. *'It contains general background information about the sector and market, incentives to use export information services, ...and guidance on the promotion of their attendance at the overseas event'* (TPUK 2001).

However, the fundamental issue, that the organisation of exhibition support results in insufficient information services, still seems to be valid. Respondents in the Quality Management Survey (2000b) who found the service lacking said their 'needs had not been understood', and there were 'opportunities they had not been told about.' In its 2001 expenditure plan BTI announced about the trade fair and seminar programme: *'These exhibition schemes are of long standing and continue to be popular with UK industry. But as work on performance measurement and trade development proceeds, TPUK is reviewing them with the intention of ensuring that they support company and sectoral strategies more closely and that companies taking part are better prepared and their participation more systematically followed up.'* (DTI 2001:29)

7.5 The adaptability of the organisation

Having looked at the impact of the organisation from a static viewpoint, how the organisation might affect the adaptability of British trade fair support remains to be analysed. The adaptability of the organisation is assessed from the perspective of TPUK's top management. An ideal organisation ensures that all actors' decisions are based on up-to-date information, and that the core actor can and wants to effect numerical and functional adaptation, knowing when it is necessary.

7.5.1 'Up-to-date decision making'

In the trade fair *selection process*, British trade associations' decisions are informed by members' opinions, experiences made at previous trade fair visits, and information gathered while providing other forms of export support. The more engaged sponsors are in export activities and the more members export, the more comprehensive and recent is the incoming information. Trade associations that sponsor only one specific event and that are not otherwise involved in export support activities are least likely to know whether that fair continues to be the best choice for their industry. TPUK relies for its selection choices on the sector-market matrix with the specified target markets. As argued above, the decisions may therefore be based on out-of-date information.

In the *recruitment process*, sponsors rely strongly on their mailing lists, which active sponsors update regularly to include new members and exhibitors at previous fairs. Sponsors also receive referrals from the trade fair organisers with each new event. In terms of the 'general' marketing channels, it is in the interest of trade associations to keep up-to-date with the information sources that firms in the industry use, even if they would not do so just for participant recruitment.

Regarding *exhibition support*, sponsors learn with each participation. But unless they are engaged in other exhibition support activities or in other business fields that involve contracting, monitoring etc., no other sources will 'automatically' assist them in updating their knowledge.

On the whole, there seem to be few overlaps between the information that trade associations require in their position as sponsors, and that which the majority receive when they pursue their other activities. How up-to-date their trade fair related information is, will therefore depend on the extent to which sponsors put resources into fulfilling their role. TPUK's crucial decisions in the selection process are not always based on recent information.

7.5.2 Numerical adaptability

As argued above, numerical adaptability refers to the trade fair support organisation's capacity to adjust to changes in the need for support, be it in overall numbers, or in demand-shifts between markets or industries. An organisation is expected to be numerically adaptable, if the core actor becomes aware of the need for changes, has the necessary decision rights about the financial, physical and human resources to respond, and wants to do so.

TPUK as the core actor becomes aware of the need for numerical changes through the bids from sponsors, and by observing the development of participant numbers in the selected events. As argued above, the sponsors' bids do not represent the whole business population, and TPUK will not easily find out about changing needs in sectors without strong trade associations. Also, as argued above, the bids are biased towards large, previously successful events. However, taking these limitations into account, and considering also that its sector- and market-based units receive additional information from other sources, TPUK does learn about major changes in demand.

The existing allocation of decision rights allows numerical adaptability with some restrictions. TPUK is bound most by the SESA budget. As they promise exhibitors a fixed percentage contribution to their space and stand construction costs they do not have the flexibility to adjust the number of supported fairs by changing the subsidy per event. Having said that, BTI does have the decision rights to review the allocation of its total budget to its different trade support programmes (House of Commons 2000). With a time lag of a year, management could increase or decrease the SESA budget.

Within the boundaries of the budget they can freely decide over the number of supported fairs and their distribution, once they have provided finance for the 'core events' (DTI et al. 2001:29). Changes in demand for different continents are automatically taken account of as the budget allocations are made in proportion to applications. However, for the market allocation within continents the sector-market matrix is generally decisive. And the matrix, like the core events, has not been reviewed on a perpetual basis.

In contrast to finance, fixed assets are no impediment to flexibility since the few assets used – for example the TPUK offices in Glasgow – are not affected by changes in trade fair numbers, markets or industries.

Regarding human resources, higher numbers of bids affect the workload of TPUK staff in the selection process. But decisions are made mainly on the basis of the sector-market matrix and then by computer, and consequently do not take much time per case. Therefore, it is unlikely that the number of TPUK staff is a serious bottleneck for dealing with varying bid numbers or changes in requests for locations or industries. Most human resources required by the programme have to be provided by the sponsors.

It remains to be asked, whether TPUK would want to adapt the number and distribution of events. As in the German case, TPUK does not have an incentive not to respond to businesses' changing needs within the rules it set itself. Political preferences for certain markets or industries can be pursued via the matrix, and via the ranking, which is given to individual SESA bids. But as argued above, the incentives to comply with the matrix are strong, so the response to changing numerical demand would be triggered by a change in the matrix, rather than directly by a change in the focus of the bids. It is unlikely that the overall budget would be increased significantly at the cost of other programmes, as this would create tensions with the recipient clients of other programmes.

To summarise, numerical adaptability appears to be somewhat restricted by the limited information transfer from weakly represented industries, by the existence of a fixed subsidy and of core events, and by the sector-market matrix.

7.5.3 Functional adaptability

Functional adaptability means adaptability in the way trade fair support is delivered, i.e. adaptability regarding the delivery structures and the outputs. While for each individual fair functional adaptability is high – sponsors can decide freely on suitable forms of exhibition support – this does not necessarily entail that trade fair support, as a whole, is functionally adaptable. For this, TPUK have to know about the need to adapt trade fair support, have to be able to make changes happen, and have to want to do so.

Looking at the organisation of trade fair support since the restructuring of the British overseas trade services under the roof of BTI, it is unclear to what extent the organisation accommodates all these requirements. The major problem seems to be the information about the need for functional changes:

In contrast to Germany's BMWi, TPUK does not have one unit that manages all aspects of SESA. IBS deals with the administrative side, but all other parts of TPUK, i.e. the sector-oriented units, the market-oriented units, as well as the diplomatic posts are to some extent involved in the programme delivery. Decisions about 'strategic' changes lie with the top management of TPUK (UK-A). This means that the decision makers are removed from the programme, and are therefore less informed about the functioning of the programme. They have to gather information from IBS and from the other units and the private sector. But as already argued above, the information that is collected as part of the management information system does not seem to be extensive. According to UK-C from the 'strategy unit', TPUK have not even collected data on the geographic distribution of events over the past years, on the number of repeat events, or on the distribution between 'core, niche and regular events'. Moreover, it is unlikely that top management would be concerned with investigating SESA development on a regular, frequent basis, unless they felt the programme was not working.

But on the other hand, there is competition for resources within BTI and top management has the decision powers to allocate the trade support resources as they see fit. It is likely that those sections that believe they could use the funds better, will argue their case. There may also be requests from the private sector representatives on the board or in the advisory groups, to use the resources in a different way. This may trigger-off an in-depth evaluation of the programme, or an investigation into specific aspects. And since the top decision makers do not have vested interests in any one of the BTI programmes, and do not see SESA in isolation of the other programmes, it can be expected that changes will be made if they are perceived to be beneficial for the trade support objective on the whole.

7.5.4 Consequences for the adaptability of the British trade fair support organisation

It has been argued that the British trade fair support organisation limits numerical adaptability by relying on potentially weak sponsors – the actors that are supposed to represent firms' needs – by depending on a fixed budget, part of which is taken up by previously selected 'core events', and by relying on an infrequently updated sector-market matrix. Functional flexibility appears to be only somewhat limited, due to the fact that top management does not have an information system in place with which it could continuously monitor the successfulness of SESA (see Table 7.7.).

Table 7.7. The British organisation's adaptability compared with the ideal

Ideal organisation	*British organisation*
▪ Actors make decisions based on up-to-date knowledge ▪ Core actor o *knows* when the output of the organisation needs to be adapted 'numerically' to respond to increasing or decreasing needs in terms of the total number of fairs, number of fairs in each market, number of fairs in each industry o *can* provide for numerical changes o *wants to* respond to changed needs ▪ Core actor o *knows* when the output and structure of the organisation needs to be adapted 'functionally' to respond to external changes o *can* provide for functional changes o *wants to* carry out functional changes	▪ Some actors have up-to-date knowledge, but the limited information search and absorption capability of many sponsors, and an out-of-date sector-market matrix can be a problem ▪ TPUK o finds out about increased or decreased demand through sponsors' bids, but there is little information transfer from weakly represented industries o can provide for numerical changes only to some extent – they are bound by the annual SESA budget, core events, designated target markets, but not by human and physical assets o TPUK wants to respond to changed needs of industries, but only via the sector-market matrix ▪ TPUK o top management learns about the need for functional changes from different units and from business representatives on the board and in the advisory groups; continuous systematic monitoring is limited o has extensive decision rights regarding functional changes o top management sees SESA in context with other programmes. Decision makers have no vested interests in keeping the programme as it is at present.
Ideal result:	*Predicted real result*
perfect numerical and functional adaptability of outputs and organisational structure	1. numerical adaptability is limited, unless there are changes to the lists of core events and sector-market matrix 2. functional adaptability is potentially high, but only once top management perceives a need for changes

One would therefore expect an output pattern over the years where group participations fluctuate with the SESA budget, not with export opportunities abroad, where there is no significant shift in selected markets unless the sector-market matrix has been reviewed, and where the attended fairs do not reflect changing export opportunities for different segments of the economy. Functional changes would only take place after major reviews of the programme, or when there is a 'top down' political decision that the programme has to be changed.

Evidence for or against the predicted pattern is very limited. The current structures have only been in place since 1999 and no functional changes have taken place since. Also, as already stated above, TPUK does not keep statistics about fair locations, types or industry focus, and the 'sector' classification has changed with the introduction of the matrix. It is therefore difficult to trace numerical changes.

Regarding this type of adaptability only two points can be mentioned again: In 1997 the Export Forum levelled the criticism that 'core events' impeded the flexibility (and additionality) of the programme (DTI 1997:34). As a consequence the number of core events was reduced, but the system of guaranteeing resources for pre-selected events over several years was kept. In section 7.2.3.2 about the sector-market matrix, Sir David Wright's admission of the difficulties in responding to market changes was referred to. But despite good intentions of frequent updating, the evidence so far has shown that updating gets delayed.

Regarding functional adaptability, past changes in the programme were always initiated at the top. One can argue that this gives some indication of the impact of the current organisational structure: even though the SESA delivery structure was not integrated into a unified export support structure like BTI, what has been identified as a central feature of the SESA organisation – that responsibility for the trade fair programme is shared between different TPUK units – was similar. The decision rights about the programme design were held at the top level of DTI and then in the Joint Export Promotion Directorate (see Chapter 5), while several directorates participated in the delivery. Monitoring was even more underdeveloped than now (NAO 1996:63).

Between 1989 and 1992, after several internal reviews and pushed by a changed political perception of government service production, the DTI's Fairs and Promotion Branch was dissolved. It had employed 103 career civil servants, who were in charge of trade fair stand design, graphics, and construction, and had carried out the 'on-site' work for the sponsors. Sponsors were gradually given the right to contract these services on the free market (DTI 1991, DTI 1994, UK-R). After the KPMG review of the trade fair support services in 1994 (DTI 1994) controls of sponsors' grant distribution and the handbook for sponsors were introduced to improve sponsors' performance (NAO 1996:43). In early 1997 another major change in programme delivery was planned, as the Conservative government had decided that funding for all sectoral business support activities – including trade fair support – should be allocated through a competitive bidding process, to encourage new ideas and provide for more flexibility. This triggered off coordinated protests by the biggest sponsors, who were backed by BCC, CBI and the

Institute of Export (DTI and H. M. Treasury 1997:11; HANSARD 1997; Financial Times 18.1.1997, 4.2.1997, 8.7.1997; The Times 13.2.1997, 25.2.1997).

However, the new organisation was never implemented since the Labour party won the elections in May 1997 and immediately reversed the decision (DTI 1997). A public consultation was carried out and considered by the Export Forum, which had received the task to make recommendations on the effectiveness of public trade promotion (see Chapter 5). Regarding the trade fair programme the Forum successfully recommended that the grant process should be streamlined, that the trade fair support scheme should be combined with the seminar scheme, and that the possibility of 'niche events' should be introduced. It was also recommended that inexperienced exporters should be given a 'taster visit' to a major fair in their sector before they commit themselves to the full cost of exhibiting, and to ensure that firms are better prepared (DTI and FCO 1997). But instead of integrating these issues into the existing trade fair programme, an additional programme 'Trade Fair Explorer' was set up (DTI 1998e). It enables SMEs with minimal export experience to visit a key trade fair in Europe as part of a guided and prepared group, without having to exhibit. The fact that the responses to the consultation from the business community (including the active sponsors) were negative, when they were asked whether part of the trade for budget should be reserved for alternative ways to support participation in the events, may have played a role in the decision to have a separate programme.

The 'Wilson Report', the follow-up review on the trade promotion delivery structures, resulted in the creation of BTI in 1999, into which the SESA organisation was integrated. Apart from the unification of decision rights at the top level, the division of labour between units was not changed for the trade fair support delivery.

Since, TPUK has identified a gap in the provision of effective support for new exporters with the main concern that there has been insufficient emphasis on preparation and follow-up in export support. The declared future strategy, supported by the BTI board, is to put more emphasis on trade development, rather than trade promotion (DTI et al. 2001). It appears that considerations regarding functional changes in the trade fair support programme are again shaped by this wider agenda at the top. What has been announced regarding envisaged functional changes is that BTI will review the programme with regard to these two aspects (DTI et al. 2000:29).

7.6 Summary judgement

Using the same framework as for the German case, this chapter presented a description and analysis of the British trade fair support organisation. As in the previous chapter the aim was to compare the 'real' organisational structures with the 'ideal' ones, and to establish how the discrepancies would influence the outputs, provided the model was correct. Then it was checked whether the existence of the predicted pattern could be supported by empirical evidence.

To do both description and analysis, information from interviews, website analyses, and government documents was brought together. Since little has been published about the organisational structures of the British trade fair support and about its actors, and since the evaluations of the programme have not been systematic and regular, some of the evidence has inevitably been 'anecdotal', and some has not been as precise or exhaustive as one could wish for. But as in the German case, the combined weight of the evidence is in favour of the proposed explanation, why organisation would affect the effectiveness with which services are delivered.

The conclusion that can be drawn is that organisation does matter. The British trade fair support organisation's impacts on the service's effectiveness are the following:

The promotion of successful trade fair participations of experienced exporters in new, high potential markets is achieved to some extent. As the case of the fair MIDEST in Paris, and the data on SESA participant characteristics showed (Table 7.4 above), the majority of group participants have many years of exporting experience and a large share of their turnover is made up of export sales. Since they can only receive the SESA grant three times in the same market, they have to exhibit in new locations to benefit fully from the programme. And because of the sponsors' interest in recruiting viable groups, they are more likely to be aware of the SESA opportunities than of other TPUK export promotion programmes. But due to the significance of the sector-market matrix and its categorisations in the selection process, the SESA programme offers them only delayed responses to new market prospects or to specific opportunities for sub-sectors.

Regarding SMEs in particular, the major problem with the organisation is that it results in the choice of fairs with broad exhibition themes. This reduces the effectiveness of the programme, as small focused trade fairs promise better results for SMEs (see 5.3.2.1 above).

When it comes to promoting inexperienced or potential exporters' successful participation at trade fairs, the SESA organisation has perhaps the most detrimental consequences for effectiveness.

First, in industries where few firms export, trade associations do not engage in export support activities. They are unlikely to become sponsors, which means that those industries that have the highest number of firms in this target group are also those that are most likely to be underrepresented in the programme.

Second, of the trade associations who do put in bids, few have the resources for evaluating the available fair options in depth, and for providing extensive exhibition support, from which inexperienced, small exhibitors would particularly benefit. Again, the relationship between the extent of the service that sponsors can offer and the size of the group of biggest beneficiaries, is inverse. In an industry where few firms export and where representation is not well organised, the sponsors' are less informed about trade fair related matters, have fewer resources and fewer incentives to provide services.

Third, due to the comparative cost, even in those industries with active sponsors, inexperienced and potential exporters are the least likely to be recruited as group participants.

Fourth, sponsors overall have no incentive to invest in their capability of giving detailed trade fair selection and procedural advice. This affects the exhibition success of inexperienced or novice exhibitors more than that of experienced firms. It also affects SMEs more than large firms with more capacity for information search.

TPUK has tried to remedy some of these problems by introducing an extra programme, 'Export Explorer', outside the SESA structure. This confirms that the organisation of SESA itself has adverse effects on achieving what it claims to achieve ('*SESA helps new exporters establish themselves in markets abroad*' (DTI 2001:28)). TPUK has also started to put more emphasis on developing export skills, and with its 'Sector Partnership programme' on developing trade associations' export-related service capabilities.

As can be seen from the references that were used as 'evidence', several of the listed problems have been recognised before. The contribution of the model was to explain why SESA shows these weak points, and to put them in context.

Chapter 8: Organisation matters

8.1 Overview

In the preceding chapters I have sought to make an original contribution to a larger debate: the relationship between organisation of public sector services delivery and output effectiveness and efficiency.

The topic arose in the context of government export support services. Different countries have chosen different organisations for delivering export support services, although nominally the services are the same. But there have been doubts about the choices. Governments have tried to learn from studying their competitors' organisations, and some have re-organised their service delivery to improve it. While this suggests that there is a relationship between organisation and outputs, the nature of this relationship has not been clear. Why should the ubiquitous attempts to re-organise public export support services have any impact on effectiveness and efficiency? Why should a 'new' organisation cause 'better' results than its predecessor?

Framing these considerations into two research questions, this thesis set out to explore the issues: 'Does organisation matter for effectiveness and efficiency?' 'Can one organisation unambiguously be identified as being 'better' or 'worse' than another?'

The purpose of this concluding chapter is to draw together the findings of the previous chapters and, by means of comparison, fill remaining gaps. Before the respective evidence and conclusions are presented in sections 8.3 and 8.4, the main arguments developed in the previous chapters will be recapitulated. The chapter closes with section 8.5, assessing the contributions that have been made to the research in this field, but also assessing critically what remains to be questioned, and to be researched further.

8.2 A review of the previous chapters

Having identified the subject area of the research: export support services delivery, and the main research interest: the causal link between 'organisation' on the one hand, and 'effectiveness' and 'efficiency' on the other – the first objective in Chapter 2 was to define these terms in the context of the thesis. Organisation was defined as the goal-directed co-ordination of different actors by a formal structure. The concepts 'efficiency' and 'effectiveness' proved to be more ambiguous. I showed that the boundary between the two – one of which is taken to be more associated with costs, the other with results – is blurred. Neither can be measured in a way that would allow direct quantitative comparisons between most public sector organisations' performances. Consequently, in practice, audit offices have judged the effectiveness or efficiency of public bureaux by using 'checklists' on organisational characteristics. Such an approach requires that the relationships between the observed characteristics, and the conclusions on efficiency and effectiveness features are valid. But this validity has not been demonstrated; the underlying cause–effect assumptions have neither been clarified nor proven.

Organisational economics was identified as the most promising theoretical field to provide insights into possible causal links. The use of this set of deductive theories required accord with its foundations: 'methodological individualism', and the model of 'Resourceful Evaluative Maximising Man', in view of the research purpose. Then, a sympathetic appraisal of property rights theory, agency theory, and transaction cost theory revealed that each of these schools has provided important insights into the cause–effect relationship between organisation and effectiveness and efficiency, but none has offered a complete theorisation. Based on the findings and the criticisms of the three theories I concluded that a more comprehensive model could specify the relationship. It implies that organisation affects effectiveness and efficiency because it impacts on three key variables: the actors' knowledge to fulfil their different tasks, their incentives to do their tasks, and the adaptability of the structures to change with the environment. These variables, which are not fully independent from each other, cause differences in the shape, quantity and quality of organisations' outputs, and in the cost at which the outputs are produced.

The following two chapters, 4 and 5, dealt with operationalising the model for the purpose of studying export promotion services' delivery. In Chapter 4 the three variables were discussed one by one, to design ways of assessing the incentives and the knowledge of the actors in an existing organisation, and of assessing an organisation's adaptability, given its formal structures. The result was a list of questions, another 'checklist' to assess organisational structures. Since the model is based on the assumption of maximising actors, it was also necessary to define what actors would seek to maximise. Following the literature on this topic I argued that the behaviour of private companies would reflect their chief executives' strive for both company growth and profits, while managers of public bodies would want to be engaged in policy making and strategic management, rather than in routine, conflictuous and low-status administrative duties. As regards business associations, I concluded that their management would be interested in increasing membership, revenues, and the association's influence on government decisions.

Chapter 5 provided context information about the German and British export promotion systems, and further operationalised the model in view of the particular research subject. Due to the complexity of each export support services delivery organisation, the fact that these organisations are hardly documented, and the need to validate the model, 'instrumental', comparative case studies appeared most suitable. German and British trade fair support delivery organisations were selected, because the German and British cases are similar in many aspects, apart from the organisation itself. Trade fair support is by far the most important government export support service. To validate the model, I chose a pattern matching technique. The model would be used to generate predictions of outcomes of organisational structures. Similar to methods used in statistics, the reference case for both the British and the German case would be a hypothetical 'ideal' organisation, with perfectly knowledgeable and motivated actors, and fully adaptable structures.

In Chapters 6 and 7, based on information collected through interviews with participating actors, website analyses, surveys carried out by other organisations, government documents, and reviews of the annual trade fair programmes, I described and analysed the German and the British trade fair support organisations. I predicted the effects of the differences between the real organisations and the ideal one according to the model, and compared these predictions with the evidence. The objective was to assess for each case and each step of the trade fair services delivery process, whether 'organisation matters' for effectiveness due to the postulated impact on the three variables. In both cases, the match between model-derived predictions and available evidence could support the validity of the model.

Going beyond this detailed analysis of the two individual cases, the following two sections review first the evidence for 'organisation matters' by comparing the two cases directly. The major similarities and differences in organisation are highlighted, and the consequences are compared. Then, it is asked whether it can be established if one is better than the other.

8.3 'Organisation matters'

The model developed in Chapter 3 postulates that organisation matters for effectiveness and efficiency, because it implies a distribution of decision rights, and how an actor may 'be benefiting or be harmed by his own decisions' (Alchian 1965: 130). The selection of actors and the distribution of rights and responsibilities define not only the knowledge each actor has to do his assigned tasks, but also which task-related decision he is likely to prefer, compared with other options. Moreover, organisation defines how actors can respond to changes in the environment, and to what extent the core actor can and is likely to change the organisation itself, when the environment changes.

The previous two chapters on trade fair promotion in Germany and Britain have shown that for the same overall goal the two governments have employed organisations that are partly similar and partly different. It could be shown, as highlighted with examples below, that similarities in the organisations led to similar results, and that differences between the organisations were reflected in different results. As will be outlined hereafter, the cases also show the impact of organisation on cost.

- Similar organisation has led to similar results

In the context of the selection process, among the various organisational features discussed, it was shown for both countries that trade associations' returns depended on selecting fairs that attracted at least ten participants. It could be observed in both countries that large fairs with broad themes, and fairs that had previously attracted large groups of participants were chosen, irrespective of their suitability for the target groups. Highly specialised firms or firms interested in 'exotic' markets were little served in either country. Moreover, due to the fact that effectively only fairs of industries with an active representation could enter the selection process, in both countries some sectors or subsectors were not assisted.

Both in Germany and Britain, the recruiting actors had no incentive to focus on the two target groups for trade fair support. They were also unlikely to have much knowledge about non-exporting SMEs. In both countries this led to a choice of relatively cheap, general advertising channels for trade fair participation. No resources were spent on ensuring that those firms, who may have underestimated the value of a trade fair, participated, and that those firms that may have overestimated it, did not. As a result, the target groups – SMEs new to exporting, or new to a promising export market – were little represented in both cases. Where they did participate, not few of them were disappointed with the results.

In the process of providing direct exhibition support, neither side focussed on increasing participants' net benefits through increasing their returns from the participation. They only assisted, to some extent, in reducing the participation costs for firms. This was due to the fact that in both cases the actors had limited knowledge to achieve the former, and incentives only in favour of the latter. It was cheaper and less risky for the German DFGs and British sponsors not to engage in capacity building, especially in view of many participants belonging not to the target groups but being experienced trade fair exhibitors. The vast majority of firms mentioned the financial support (government subsidy) as their main reason to participate in the programme, not the help they received in exhibiting at the fair.

- Different organisation has led to different results

While in both countries trade associations played a major role in selecting fairs within industries, the organisation of choices between industries differed. In Germany the umbrella organisation for the trade fair industry, AUMA, was largely responsible for co-ordinating the selection process, being helped by an informal quota system. In Britain, the choice between industries was made by TPUK, via a computer programme and guided by the sector-market matrix. These differences in turn implied differences in the knowledge used as a basis for making choices. In Germany, the trade associations selected their preferred markets, knowing roughly how many subsidised fairs could expect for their industry. AUMA as a trade fair market specialist could mediate in those remaining cases, where decisions about the relative merits of different fairs had to be taken. As a result of this selection organisation, the trade fair programme adapted well to changed market circumstances for given industries, but less well to the development of new industries. AUMA's and also BMWi's interest in supporting the German trade fair industry was reflected in a large proportion of fairs being linked to German trade fair organisers.

In the UK, the rigidity of the German 'industry quotas' was exchanged for the rigidity of predetermined choices in terms of sectors and markets: A large part of the budget was used for 'core events'. In addition, although TPUK asked diplomatic posts, sector groups and market groups to rank the bids for support, all three parties were pressured and inclined to use the sector-market matrix, especially the current list of target markets. Only 3% of events did not fall within the matrix, and in those cases, the choice was determined by the track record of the sponsor. Thus, due to the way the selection was organised, in spite of the bidding process, the industries AND the markets on which trade fair support funds were spent, were, in effect, chosen by the government. One consequence was a time lag in adapting the sector-market matrix to market developments.

In the recruitment process, the major difference was between the actors. On the German side, paid, professional trade fair organisers, the DFGs, undertook advertisement for the trade fair participations. Both the respective trade associations and AUMA backed them. On the British side, the trade associations themselves, many of which did not have resources, nor many members or advertising experience, were in charge. They were supported by TPUK, advertising its trade support programme. While in both countries the trade fair support programme was more widely known than other export support programmes, the percentage of firms who knew about the trade fair programme in Germany was higher. Also, the British sponsors, who according to the organisational structure were in charge of recruitment, represented only 20% of the information sources from which participants had learned about the opportunity.

With regard to direct exhibition support, organisation mattered as well. The main difference was again the actor, who the task was assigned to, and his or her obligations. In Germany, the DFGs had to provide ready trade fair stands with all facilities to the participants, and could offer other services for sale. Government appointed trade fair architects, who had the task of making the German group look 'representative', and who earned a percentage of the total stand construction cost, designed the stands. In Britain, apart from the management of the financial subsidy, sponsors were only obliged to set up an information stand, and to appoint a stand construction contractor for voluntary use by the participants. According to the German participants, the DFGs provide highly satisfactory services, but focus on flawless management of the participation rather than on its low cost. The stand designs were perceived as disproportionately costly by trade associations, due to the architects' incentives for receiving a high commission. UK-J commented that the German designs were overall far more elaborate than the British ones. In Britain sponsors' financial resources, and their experience in negotiation and contracting, in marketing, and in other areas relevant for the exhibition support task varied widely. The support participants received thus varied widely too. Those sponsors with experience and resources offered far more services than the others, and the satisfaction with the quality of services varied.

Looking at trade fair support programmes' and organisations' adaptability to changes in the environment, organisation seemed to matter as well. It appeared that in Germany, the information that was available to different actors when making their task-related decisions, was generally more comprehensive and recent than in Britain. This was due to the actors' larger involvement in similar tasks, in the course of their other business activities. But in Germany, the core actor, BMWi, could neither modify the organisational structures of the programme easily, nor the definition of its organisational outputs. BMWi's Referat V A4, only responsible for the German trade fair programme and German national exhibitions abroad, had no independent information system about the functioning of the programme, relying on the evaluations of the other actors. In TPUK, by contrast, IBS dealt only with the administrative side of SESA, while decisions about strategic changes lay with TPUK's top management. On the one hand, this meant that the decision makers were removed from the programme, and, given the poor management information system, were not informed in detail about its functioning. But unlike in Germany, there was competition for resources within TPUK and top decision makers did not see SESA in isolation. Independent evaluations were carried out. In Germany, hardly any changes in organisational structures and outputs had taken place for decades. For example, there was hardly any response to the growth of the service sector, or to new opportunities related to the development of information technologies. In Britain, major modifications of the programme had been implemented over the past 15 years, all of them initiated at the top.

- *Organisation has had an impact on efficiency*

In Chapter 2 (2.3.2) it was demonstrated that the distinction between efficiency and effectiveness is not clear-cut. For the purposes of the thesis, the two terms were conceptually differentiated by defining 'effectiveness' as referring to goal attainment, in contrast to 'efficiency', which refers to the cost incurred in goal attainment (Hannan and Freeman 1977:110). In Chapter 5, the annual cost of the trade fair programmes for the governments of both countries, and the numbers of firms participating in the programmes, were presented (Table 5.1). But this did not allow conclusions about the comparative efficiency of the organisations, nor whether organisation impacted on efficiency. As it was argued (5.2.3), the figures did not convey how many firms were actually helped to export or to what degree. On the input side, the figures included different types of cost but no overhead costs. It could therefore not be established in numbers, how efficiently each of the organisations produced its results, how they compared, and how or whether this was related to the organisations.

But the model developed in Chapter 3 suggests that organisation does affect efficiency. Again, the effect can be investigated by comparing the cost at which real organisations match the ideal: Ideally, actors' goals overlap with that of the core organisation, which therefore does not need to construct cost-involving positive or negative incentive and control systems. Also, all actors know exactly how to best perform their tasks, so that no costs are incurred by training, failure, or suboptimal decision-making. These two conditions are fulfilled at any given point in time as the organisation can automatically adapt to any changes in its environment.

How do the German and the British trade fair support delivery organisations compare with these characteristics? In the trade fair selection process both governments work with trade associations. Compared with the core organisations doing the work internally, or contracting it out to private consultancy firms, the trade associations provide information on preferred fairs for free, and prevent the core organisation from having to settle disputes within an industry. The knowledge of trade associations with export-oriented members about their industry's overseas markets and exporters' demands for trade fair support is regularly updated in the course of providing other export-related services. But the cost advantage, which the two governments derive from drawing on the 'free' knowledge of business associations, is diminished by the factors that not all businesses are represented, nor all associations equipped to have the expected level of knowledge. These factors seem to be more pronounced in Britain than in Germany. As to the choice of fairs from those suggested by trade associations, the British organisation also seems to be more expensive. While the selection is made entirely by TPUK, based on advice from within TPUK and the Foreign Office, creating corresponding staff time costs, in Germany AUMA does most of the work for free, inputting its knowledge on the global trade fair market.

With regard to recruitment and exhibition support, both Governments rely on the interest of their chosen actors to participate in the trade fair programme. TPUK pays sponsors a maximum of £5800 (normally £4600) for their expenses, giving them the option to collect more money from the participants. The BMWi contracts professional trade fair organisers, the DFGs, but pays less than 'market rates'. (It could not be established how much exactly they receive to compare it with the British rates). Relative to the sponsors, and considering that the German trade associations help them, the DFGs have more knowledge about marketing the trade fair participations. Their contracting and negotiation skills in preparation of trade fairs are important business assets. Also, in the British case, TPUK relies on a time-consuming subsidisation system in which firms must collect and produce invoices, sponsors must examine the receipted invoices and calculate specific grant amounts, apply to TPUK for the funds, which in turn has to check the sponsors' statements, pay the sponsors, who then have to transfer the money to each participant. In Germany, participants do not have to do any paperwork and DFGs do not need to transfer money, as the subsidy is given in the form of a reduced square metre fee. However, on the German side, high expenses are incurred by employing trade fair architects who benefit more, the costlier their designs.

Without having been able to quantify the efficiency or effectiveness of either organisation, it could nevertheless be demonstrated that organisation has had an impact on the cost at which outputs are produced, and on the shape, quantity and quality of these outputs. Organisation matters, and the model defining cause–effect relationships between organisation and effectiveness and efficiency was supported.

8.4 Is A better than B?

Re-organisation on the premises of efficiency and effectiveness improvements suggests that the 'new' organisation is considered more efficient and effective than the old one. As described at the outset, many countries have compared their organisation of export support services with that of other countries to gain inspiration on how to improve their own.

Having compared the German and the British organisations, should one advise either of the two core organisations to copy the organisation of the other? In addition to the hypothesis that 'organisation matters', which was confirmed in the previous pages, such advice would imply that one organisation is clearly better than the other. But the model suggests that there may be trade-offs between the variables, and that the institutional context matters.

8.4.1 Trade-offs between knowledge, incentives, and adaptability

The model developed in Chapter 3, and the subsequent discussion of its key variables 'knowledge', 'incentives' and 'adaptability', suggest that organisational structures imply trade-offs:

From a knowledge perspective, specialisation of actors is beneficial. Specialised actors can develop routines and fine-tune principles with positive impacts on efficiency and effectiveness. But the more specialised an actor, the more difficult it becomes for the core organisation to judge his inputs. This may have negative effects on the actors' incentives, or may make costly incentive systems necessary. Also, the more specialised an actor, the more the returns of his knowledge are tied to the specific context in which it is used. Therefore, less specialised actors may be reluctant to invest in their task-related knowledge unless they have specific incentives to do so. Highly specialised actors may try to gain monopoly rents, and they have an incentive to block organisational adaptations that would challenge their position. High adaptability, if shown in the form of constant changes in organisational structures, in turn undermines the development of knowledge. It may also undermine actors' identification with the organisation and its goals. From an incentive perspective, the ideal actors are those whose goals precisely overlap with those of the core organisation. However, these actors are not necessarily those who know how to do the task most effectively and efficiently.

Therefore, a 'new organisation', which compared to the old organisation has a positive effect on any of the variables, may not bring any 'net' improvements. It is likely that the change incurs a negative effect on one of the other variables. This could explain why organisational structures introduced as an 'improvement' in one country are at the same time discarded in another country (e.g. outsourcing versus vertical integration, consolidation of local authorities versus increased segmentation of local authorities). It would also be in line with De Alessi's (1990:15) statement that *'Two systems of property rights may yield different consequences, but it is not obvious, without adopting Pareto criteria or some other set of value judgements to provide a frame of reference, why one system is better than the other.'*

In the context of the case studies, it is not easy to validate this part of the model. It was argued that in Germany the main actors – trade associations, AUMA and the DFGs – were more knowledgeable than their respective counterparts in the UK, even though none of the actors was fully specialised on its role in the trade fair support organisation. In the German trade fair selection process, the BMWi had actually passed most of the decision rights to the trade associations and

AUMA. There seemed to be a reliance on these actors controlling each other and on matching goals, even though this was not the case as regards SMEs new to exporting. On the positive side, this delegation of decision rights lead to a relatively high adaptability to new market opportunities for the average exporter in the represented sectors. But it also appeared that the 'Arbeitskreis' was a somewhat 'closed shop', where certain industries were represented and pursued their interests, but into which new industries entered only with difficulty and changes in the design of the group of beneficiaries were not pursued. In the UK on the other hand, the core organisation, TPUK, kept all essential decision rights for the fair selection to itself. The procedural efforts required and the political difficulties in changing the basis for the selection, led to choices that were based on outdated information. However, keeping decision rights centralised within the core organisation enabled it to be less exposed to the subjective interests of the sponsors and more flexible to functional changes. Germany does not have options for the service sector, no niche market events, and no trade fair explorer programme option.

In the recruitment and exhibition support organisation Germany has used the trade associations to control the DFGs. It seems that the BMWi has had to pay more to DFGs for their expertise, as they had some self-interest in recruiting participants and taking them to overseas fairs, but not as much as the British trade associations. In return, it appeared that the outputs of DFGs and architects were more evenly professional than those of British sponsors. If some resource-poor sponsors do not need these skills in any other context but one or two government sponsored trade fair events per year, for which they may or may not bid successfully, it is hard to imagine that they would try to develop their expertise in this field.

Thus there are some indications that trade-offs exist. However, the evidence is vague and the trade-offs would need to be analysed in more detail in a context where more data is available.

Does this mean that an organisation cannot be improved or cannot learn from the example of others? Clearly there are some aspects of both organisations, which should be reconsidered in both cases in view of the goal: For example, does it make sense to recruit SMEs, which may not be sufficiently prepared to participate in a trade fair abroad? Does it make sense to specify ten participants as a benchmark? Is the advantage of paying every single British participant directly, months later, big enough to warrant the administrative costs compared to simply asking for a reduced price per square metre as the Germans do? Should not Germany, follow the British example and change its trade fair support rules so that the programme can better accommodate the service sector?

In conclusion it seems that, since organisation affects efficiency and effectiveness, specific organisational aspects can be improved in view of a goal. But fundamental structural changes may imply trade-offs, and it depends on the preferences of the core organisation which of the variables influencing efficiency and effectiveness is considered the most important in the current set of circumstances. Seringhaus and Rosson (1990) were right to question *whether one organisation is more efficient and effective than another.*

8.4.2 Institutions

In Chapter 2 institutions were defined as the framework within which organisations operate: They are formal and informal structures that have developed over long periods of time and cannot be changed purposefully in the short or medium term.

Britain and Germany differ in many institutions, many of which may have some influence on how the trade fair support organisations function. Here, only three institutional differences with a direct impact on service delivery will be highlighted.

The examples will underline the argument that organisations are affected by the specific institutional framework within which they are placed. As a consequence, what is an efficient and effective organisation in one country may not be the same in another.

- Different trade associations
In both Germany and Britain the organisation of the trade fair support services relies on trade associations. But even though the name is the same, the 'actors' 'trade associations' represent institutions that differ considerably.

German trade associations have a recognised role as business representations in a corporatist state. They are structured in an orderly, geographically and hierarchically integrated pattern with little competition. Britain, in contrast, has a very fragmented system, with gaps and multiple overlaps in sector coverage, and a lack of systematic regional organisation. The associations have traditionally not worked together, and in many cases they have seen each other as enemies. They have a less formalised role and a lower status in the political and economic system. As described in Chapter 7, most of them are small and inadequately resourced, and they have fewer staff with lower qualifications than their German counterparts. Since they do not co-operate, functions are duplicated and few economies of scale are developed. As a result, the majority of British trade associations can offer few services beyond a single focus on representation (Boleat 2000; Bennett 1998:12ff; citing Parish; Lane 1998:24f).

For the organisation of export support services this means that the knowledge and incentives of the actor 'trade associations', to represent and co-ordinate business demand for the services, differs. The difference cannot be eliminated in the short term, as has been shown in the UK, where a government initiative to strengthen the trade association system has been ongoing for more than a decade.

Organisational structures involving this actor cannot simply be copied into a different country context. Or, if they are copied, the 'same' organisational structure will have different effects.

- Different trade fair industries
The trade fair industry in Germany is fundamentally different from the trade fair industry in Britain. In Germany all large trade fair companies are owned by local and regional authorities and combine the roles of trade fair organiser and exhibition site owner. As discussed, this structure has had an impeding impact on the German trade fair companies' overseas activities (BUSCHE 1992, p.72). German

firms have had a relatively small choice of trade fairs abroad, where organisers have had an office in Germany and close relations to the respective industry. Given that the international language is English, and that the biggest global trade fair organisers (Reed and Blenheim) are British, British firms have had an advantage over German firms in this respect.

On the other hand, because of their unified role as organisers and owners, and because of the public owners not being profit driven, German trade fair companies have been independent from the exhibiting and visiting industry. They have aimed to balance the different interests by developing close links with representatives of both groups and a culture of co-operation has developed (Groth 1997, Kresse 1997). Trade fair concepts have been designed and executed jointly with the concerned industries' trade associations (Negelein 1992, Busche 1992, Boerner 1989). The aim to balance the interests of all trade fair stakeholders has also been reflected in the industry's umbrella association AUMA, which represents organisers, exhibitors and visitors. Because of these structures the German government has always had an acknowledged representative body to consult where German 'trade fair' interests and any other trade fair related questions have been concerned. In Britain such a 'neutral' strong body with its own income could not develop. Fair organisers and site owners are separate companies, each with their own interest representation. Britain could not copy the German trade fair support organisation if it wanted to, since there simply is no AUMA equivalent.

Possibly due to the strong and co-operative structures, Germany has evolved as the largest trade fair venue in the world. Two thirds of all leading international fairs are hosted in Germany, and over two million foreigners visited the fairs in 2002. This means that German SMEs, in contrast to British SMEs can, to some degree, reach an international audience without exhibiting abroad. It also puts into perspective the fact that the British programme subsidises a large number of events in Western Europe, whereas the German programme includes very few.

- *Different administrative traditions*

It was argued that the British trade fair support organisation was more functionally adaptable than the German one. But, restructuring the German organisation according to the British model, would most likely not lead to an equally high adaptability. It is also affected by different administrative traditions:

Political scientists who have investigated 'New Public Management' approaches and administrative reform projects in a comparative context, have tended to use Germany and the UK as opposing examples of 'reform capability' (Loeffler 2000; Peters 2000; Knill 1999).

Knill (1999), based on an extensive literature review, summarised three major institutional differences that affect the scope and scale of administrative change. He argues, first, that in Germany, in contrast to Britain, there is a very *restricted scope for executive leadership*. It is impeded by the federal administrative system, requiring inter-governmental bargaining, and by the German electoral system, which usually leads to coalition governments. Britain knows no judicial review, subjecting the laws passed by the legislature to scrutiny as to their constitutionality, whereas in Germany the Federal Constitutional Court can be used by opponents to block or delay reforms. Also, the German tradition of corporatism increases the government's need to bargain with various societal interest groups, and the Chancellor has less influence on his ministers, who are autonomous hierarchical heads of their departments. Second, Germany's *administrative structures and procedures are legally entrenched* in the German Basic Law and in public law. Furthermore, the German model emphasises legalism as the basic principle of administrative rationality. This blocks comprehensive reforms and makes even small adaptations in a specific area difficult. In Britain, with its principle of the supremacy of parliament, and neither a written constitution, nor a comprehensive legal system for the public administration, the government of the day can impose structural changes. Third, although formally decision-making competence lies with the political level, the German *bureaucracy has considerable influence to shape programme formulation and implementation.* Their procedural and specialist knowledge of the civil service is a crucial factor. In contrast with Britain, German civil servants do not regularly change their positions and they therefore accumulate expert knowledge over time. Political leaders are dependent on the specialist knowledge, and the legalist culture increases the importance of procedural knowledge in policy making. In Britain, from 1979 there was a move away from dependence on bureaucratic advice. The government has increasingly relied on external 'think tanks'. Accordingly, the role of the civil service shifted from advising the minister to implementing ministers' wishes.

As a result, the organisation of trade fair support services delivery and the impact of the observed impact of the organisation on adaptability, have been influenced and reinforced by the administrative traditions. In Germany, reform generally means *self-reform* with incremental adaptations rather than radical change. Long-established structures, principles and procedures persist. In Britain, sufficiently committed leaders face hardly any constraints in putting through restructuring initiatives.

8.4.3 Summary

In a nutshell, it has been argued that organisation affects outputs in a fairly predictable way. Nevertheless, usually an optimum solution cannot be established since each organisational structure implies trade-offs in how it affects the variables that influence efficiency and effectiveness. Choices depend on preferences and the situation. The options available are limited by institutions. Learning from others is possible but copying is not.

8.5 Summary of the research contribution

In its widest sense, this thesis has been an experiment. It has started with observing governments' quests for an effective and efficient delivery of their public sector export support services because of a perceived link between countries' economic development and export performance. A closer look at the questions involved in restructuring export support services' organisations to improve efficiency and effectiveness, and in learning from other countries' examples, quickly revealed that concerns about public administration research in general (Peters 1988) have also been valid in this field: 1) A dearth of academic research on export support organisations, an absence of systematic data collection on services delivery, and problems with the intercomparability of different public sector data have prevented inductive analysis. 2) The lack of a clear theoretical understanding of how organisation is related to effectiveness and efficiency has inhibited deductive analyses of existing export support organisations, as well as targeted approaches to their improvement. 3) A lack of systematic approaches to comparing administrative structures in general, not unrelated to the previous two problems, has made it difficult to draw on insights from research in other fields of public management.

Dealing with all three aspects, this thesis has been the first to interrogate the empirics of government export support services' delivery organisation based on a theoretical and comparative framework. It has proposed answers to the two research questions set at the outset of the thesis: yes, organisation matters for the effectiveness and efficiency of service delivery; but no, it may not be possible to identify one organisation indisputably as being more efficient and effective than another, unless priorities among the different aspects of efficiency and effectiveness are set. Moreover, the relevance of institutions makes it difficult to copy organisational structures and achieve the same effect in a different environment, even if the availability of public funds for the service delivery, and of technology, e.g. ICT, is comparable.

In developing these answers, this thesis has offered the first detailed account of trade fair support services' organisation in the two countries, placing them in the wider context of German and British export promotion services, and delineating which organisational aspects may be crucial for the success of the services. It has assembled primary and secondary information on the most common and best-financed government export support service from sources of which most are not, or not easily, accessible to the public.

Combining different approaches in organisational economics, a new, theory-based approach to examining organisations, and indeed a new hypothesis for explaining why organisation matters were developed. By identifying incentives and adaptability as the key parameters underlying the arguments in the three OE theories, rather than trying to assess either agency or transaction costs as indicators for efficiency, it has become possible to combine the theories' insights as to the effect of organisational structures. Moreover, including 'knowledge' in the framework, not only because of its effect on transaction costs, but also because of its major importance for production costs, has allowed the theories' weaknesses to be overcome, in acknowledging the trade-offs between the two.

The suggested model for the causal relationships between 'organisation' and 'effectiveness and efficiency' was supported, in that it provided coherent explanations for the outputs of the German and British trade fair support organisations. Accurate predictions of the shortcomings of the respective trade support services could be given and confirmed with empirical evidence. The model has also emphasised the importance of goal-directed organisation and, in view of the case studies, it has allowed the demonstration of the problems which multiple, declared and undeclared goals can have for efficiency and effectiveness: Organisational structures that were overall effective in view of experienced exporters needs, were far less effective in targeting potential exporters; structures that strengthened British sponsors or German DFGs were not those that provided for the most effective or efficient trade fair service delivery in view of the SME target clients. The dependency on goals as a reference point for the assessment of a particular organisational structure, and the trade-offs between the key parameters, have also demonstrated that judgements about the 'best' organisation are largely normative.

The analysis of case studies with a pattern matching technique – along a theoretically underpinned catalogue of questions that investigated incentive, knowledge and adaptability aspects of the organisation – was a successful experiment of how to systematically assess and compare different public sector organisations in cases where not enough quantitative data is available to undertake statistical comparisons. The approach allowed interpreting the particularities of specific organisational contexts, and assessing which features of alternative organisations may be copied to bring the desired results, as opposed to those that only work in the particular institutional context in which they are placed. Aucoin's (1990:135) appeal, *to search 'for conceptual frameworks with which to determine what factors in organisational design and management deserve analysis' was responded to.*

But in spite of the listed accomplishments of this work, it is evident that it has had a number of limitations. Due to the lack of a 'tried and tested' model for assessing public service delivery effectiveness and efficiency, the thesis followed two strands in parallel: the development and 'testing' of a model, as well as the description, assessment and comparison of a major export service in two countries. On the one hand, the suggested new approach to assessing organisations itself is not without weaknesses, a fact which has impacted on the results of the German–British comparison; on the other hand, by applying it to the German and British trade fair support services, it has not been tested in an ideal context. Both aspects will need to be addressed in future work, if the proposed new framework for exploring the impact of organisational structures on efficiency and effectiveness is to become more than a working hypothesis.

Regarding the weaknesses of the framework itself, two are substantial: First, by defining organisations as goal-directed constructs, and then specifying a goal and the core actor, the boundaries of the organisation are drawn. However, particularly in the public sector, but also in the private sector, goals are usually part of a hierarchy of goals. If an organisation is analysed according to the suggested framework, it is analysed in the context of a specific goal from within this hierarchy. This is the equivalent of treating the goals on different levels of the hierarchy like the layers of a Russian Doll, and, also, of ignoring the 'neighbouring' goals on the same level. It suggests that regarding organisation, they were all independent from each other. In the case of this thesis for example, the case studies dealt with trade fair promotion, and made statements about the strengths and weaknesses of the organisations with regard to the goals of trade fair support. However, these organisations are placed within the wider organisations of export support, SME support, industrial policy etc. The interplay of the structures, e.g. the positive impact which the sector-market matrix may have had on co-ordinating various types of export support services' delivery, remained neglected. If a goal higher up in the hierarchy had been taken as a starting point, the analysis would have been far more complex, even though the same analytical framework could have been applied. This thesis, for example, started out with looking at government export promotion in general, but in view of the limited research capacity of an individual, and the amount and type of information required to apply the framework, the focus was limited to trade fair support and trade information support. Later, in view of the sheer volume of information, the thesis was reduced to only presenting the cases of trade fair support, even though the results in the field of trade information provision were also fully supportive of the model.

Secondly, as critics of Organisational Economics have pointed out about OE theories, the variables are not precise. This applies here as well. Their assessment is based on a chain of reasoned, but simplifying assumptions. First, there are simplifying assumptions about human nature, then there are simplifying assumptions about firms', public bureaux' and business associations goals'. Next, simplifying criteria about what constitutes incentives and knowledge, and how they interact, are used.

It is in the nature of models to simplify a complex reality in order to highlight its most important features in view of a specific question. But the problem here is that variables about which relatively little is known, which have many facets and depend on the context, are used in combination with each other. This creates a significant danger of interpreting reality in such a way as to conveniently 'prove' the model. And since the precise impact of a given organisation on incentives, knowledge and adaptability, and in turn on efficiency and effectiveness, cannot be specified, lengthy qualitative evidence needs to be produced, to argue for the attribution of ordinal values to each variable. The impact of alternative forms of organisation remains debatable. Williamson's (1998:43) 'remediableness criterion', according to which an existing mode of organisation is presumed to be efficient if no superior feasible alternative can be described and implemented, does not solve the problem.

Given this lack of analytical preciseness of the concepts, inhibiting a stringent test and application of the model, the best way forward would be to test it with cases where plenty of 'objective' information – preferably quantitative – is available on the different variables. And this is where the problem with applying it to the German and British trade fair promotion cases lies:

As presented at the outset of the thesis, the data situation in the field of government export support services is poor. Despite finally concentrating on only one export support service in only two countries, using all available data sources, the available evidence for the postulated cause–effect links between organisation and effectiveness and efficiency has been indicative rather than comprehensive.

However, I believe that in spite of these weaknesses, the contribution made has been substantial. The transparent presentation of all analytical steps, combined with the available evidence, can both broaden and focus scholarly discussion on the causality between organisation and outputs, provoke a closer look at the evidence, and contribute to the dynamics of the research development in this field. The presented case studies certainly add to the public knowledge on trade fair support organisation in the two countries. The difficulties in accessing data on the research topic may well have been the major reason that it has found so little attention, and the present work might help to encourage future efforts.

Epilogue

As of April 1st, 2004 the British trade fair support organisation has undergone another wave of changes. On the one hand, this has been bad news for the author of the thesis. Many pieces of information about the British trade fair services delivery organisation, which were painstakingly collected, are now out of date. But on the other hand, the timing has been lucky. The changes that were introduced, based on a major TPUK client review and 'much external and internal consultation', provide further evidence for organisation having the postulated impacts on effectiveness and efficiency.

BTI, renamed 'UK Trade & Investment' in October 2003, introduced the following changes to the organisation (UK Trade & Investment:2004a,b; 2003):

Selection: Since 2003, sponsors have had to gain accreditation from TPUK to qualify for being part of the SESA programme. These 'Accredited Trade Organisations' have now been allocated to one or more 'Sector Panels' on the basis of the supported events they had in their programmes for 2001–02, 2002–3 and 2003–04. Each sponsor has received an indicative budget, adding up to a joint budget for the respective Sector Panels. The panels consist of representatives from all 'Accredited Trade Organisations' with an indicative budget in the sector. Each sponsor proposes their prioritised list of fairs to the panel, and overseas posts and market sections also have the opportunity to identify key exhibitions for inclusion in the programme. On the basis of these lists and the indicative budget, the Sector Panel jointly decides about the fairs that are to become part of the programme. The list is then submitted for clearance to UK Trade & Investment.

Effectively, this is a re-organisation according to the German 'quota' model, while taking into account, via Sector Panels, that sector representation in Britain is not as clearly defined as in Germany. The problem, that the British organisation implied a market determination by the state, with very low responsiveness to new market prospects, was responded to. The increased flexibility for trade associations to react to market trends is supported by the fact that events in target markets now longer receive additional funding.

However, it can be predicted that there will still be problems with the representation of sub-sectors. Also, the number of companies that are expected to participate is still a criterion for selection, and therefore the tendency to select fairs that can attract a broad group of companies will pertain. But – presumably in recognition of the problem that highly specialised SMEs find it difficult to receive support for relevant trade fair visits under the organisation of the current programme – a pilot scheme was introduced in May 2003. The 'Solo Show Support Scheme', extended to 2004–5, allows an individual firm to receive a grant for a participation in an exhibition that is not in the main programme. Also, addressing the problem that the demands of experienced exporters would influence sponsors' trade fair selection disproportionately, the sponsors have to predict how many new exporters are expected to participate. Their actual participation is now being controlled.

Recruitment: One of the three major problems that were identified in conjunction with the recruitment organisation, was that large firms and experienced exporters were far more likely to be recruited. Now UK Trade & Investment introduced the measure that only SMEs are eligible for a grant (fewer than 250 employees, an annual turnover of less than £25m, and less than 25% of their voting right owned by an enterprise with more employees or a higher turnover). Large companies can join a group at their own cost. Application forms now allow categorising participating businesses as SMEs, new to export, new to market and the figures are linked to a new performance measurement system of sponsors.

The two other identified problems – many companies' unawareness of the programme, and the invitation of companies who might not be export-ready, have also been diagnosed (TPUK 2002). By reducing the number of eligible participants and controlling the type of participant, sponsors' recruitment effort presumably will have to increase. The 'preparedness' of participants for an exhibition and market is now to be judged by UK Trade & Investment staff overseas, and included in the performance measurement report of sponsors.

Exhibition Support: The accreditation requirement for sponsors aims to reduce the diagnosed wide variability in sponsors' knowledge-related performance. It is also planned that they will benefit from benchmarking exercises, feedback reports, and 'best practise' exchange of experiences. The performance measurement of sponsors that has been introduced increases the incentives of sponsors to provide value-added services to participants. It is based on mandatory participants' feedback, feedback from UK Trade & Investment staff overseas on their perceived quality of the sponsor's services, and an assessment of sponsors' compliance with TPUK's terms and conditions (UK Trade & Investment 2004: Dear Sponsor Letter 2/2004). A further change in the programme aims to eliminate the competition of sponsors at the same event. Now the Sector Panels have to decide on lead sponsors, and other sponsors must either collaborate or withdraw.

These changes have also proven an additional point: The organisation of British trade fair support services is functionally adaptable, certainly compared with Germany. Only five years after the major reviews of the export support services, and the introduction of British Trade International, another major restructuring has taken place under the same government. In Germany, the only problem area that has been somewhat addressed is the programmes' limited impact on SMEs. In 2003 a measure was introduced with the result that companies will receive subsidies on their exhibition costs (granted through a reduction of the square metre exhibition space price) only up to a maximum of 100 square metres. For 2004 the maximum space has been further reduced to 50 square metres (Deutscher Bundestag 2003, BMWI 2003).

Annex

List of fairs looked up in the AUMA trade fair database to establish their size and the product range they cover

Medica
Arab Health
Hida
China Coal & Mining
International Water & Gas
International Aid & Trade
Seramitek
Atlanta International Gift Fair
International Contemporary Furniture Fair
World Education Market International
World Shoe Fair
Micam
Riva-Garda
International Furniture Fair
Basel World Watch
The Gourmet Products Show
International Space Symposium
Pitti Imagine Uomo 1 + 2
American International Toy Show
Securex
Plan Expo
Agrafood Tec
IPC Expo
Gardenex
New York International Gift Fair
Comdex Egypt
IT.com India
Infosystem Poland
L.A.Defentech

Interviews

Reference to interviewees has been coded to keep their identity confidential. Interview partners in Germany received the codes D-A, D-B, etc., while interview partners in the UK are referred to as UK-A, UK-B, etc.

In Germany 25 interviews were carried out. Out of these 14 were specifically about the trade fair support organisation, while the remainder concerned also the wider government export support organisation, including the organisation of other government promotion programmes. The interview partners were from the BMWi (2), BfAI (2), AUMA (2), public and private DFGs (4), trade associations (4), a 'regional association' (*Laenderverein*) (1) IHKs (4), Länder ministries and export agencies in Baden Württemberg and North-Rhine Westphalia (6). Informal interviews with firm representatives were conducted at MIDEST (Marché International de la Sous-Traitance Industrielle), an international supplier fair, Paris, Nov. 2000.

In the UK 22 interviews were held. They included representatives from different sections of TPUK (7), its predecessor JEPD (3), the Foreign Office (1), government sector support units (2), trade associations (4), Chambers of Commerce (3), an Area Advisory Group (1), and the Institute of Export (1).

To gather more detailed information about the British trade associations' role as sponsors in the governments' trade fair support programme ten associations that have regularly sponsored events over the past four years were contacted. The choice was made with the intention to cover a range of different industries but, for comparative purposes, also associations that compete with each other. Another factor influencing the choice was to cover associations that sponsored only one or two events versus those that sponsored more, and to cover associations with a fairly homogeneous group of members vs. organisations with very heterogeneous subgroups. These criteria led to picking W (185 members, six staff, sponsor for one event in 2001–02) and X (222 members, 24 staff, one event in 2001–02). They partly cover the same market and have a fairly homogeneous membership. The next couple picked represent an old industry that is exposed to strong international competition. Both associations did not respond. Another group were three large associations, with many trade fair participations, that stand in competition with each other. They represent firms of the 'new economy' as well as traditional manufacturers. Only one, association Z (192 members, 34 staff, 14 events) responded. Association Y, of another industry has 230 members, nine staff, and sponsors around seven events.

Bibliography

ABRAHAM, F. and G. DEWIT (2000). "Export Promotion via Official Export Insurance." Open Economies Review 11(1): 5-26.

AGASSI, J. (1960). "Methodological Individualism." The British Journal of Sociology 11(3): 244-270.

AGASSI, J. (1975). "Institutional Individualism." The British Journal of Sociology 26(2): 144-155.

AKERLOF, G. A. (1970). "The Market for 'Lemons': Quality Uncertainty and the Market Mechanism." Quarterly Journal of Economics 85: 488-500.

ALCHIAN, A. A. (1965). "Some Economics of Property Rights." Il Politico 30(4): 816-829.

ALCHIAN, A. A. and H. DEMSETZ (1972). "Production, Information Costs and Economic Organization." American Economic Review 62(5): 777-795.

ALCHIAN, A. A. and H. DEMSETZ (1973). "The Property Rights Paradigm." Journal of Economic History 33(1): 16-27.

ALCHIAN, A. A. and S. L. WOODWARD (1988). "The Firm is Dead, Long Live the Firm: A Review of Oliver E. Williamson's New Economic Institutions of Capitalism." Journal of Economic Literature 26(1): 65-79.

ALLEN, D. W. (1991). "What are Transaction Costs?" Research in Law and Economics 14: 1-18.

ALSTON, L. J., EGGERTSSON, T., D. NORTH (1996). Empirical Studies in Institutional Change. Cambridge, Cambridge University Press.

ARROW, K. J. (1985). The Economics of Agency. Principals and Agents: The Structure of Business. J. W. Pratt and R. J. Zeckhauser. Boston, Harvard Business School Press: 37-54.

ASTLEY, G. W. and A. H. VAN DE VEN (1983). "Central Perspectives and Debates in Organization Theory." Administrative Science Quarterly 28(2): 245-273.

ATKINSON, J. and N. MEAGER (1986). Changing Working Patterns. How Companies Achieve Flexibility to Meet New Needs. London, Institute of Manpower Studies in association with the Department of Employment: National Economic Development Office.

AUCOIN, P. (1990). "Administrative Reform in Public Management: Paradigms, Principles, Paradoxes and Pendulums." Governance 3(2): 115-137.

AUDITOR GENERAL OF CANADA (1999). Report of the Auditor General of Canada. Follow-Up on the Recommendations in Previous Reports: Canada's Export Promotion Activities -1996, Chapter 25. http://www.oag-bvg.gc.ca/domino/reports.nsf/html/9932ce.html . 2002.

AUMA (1983). AUMA: 75 Jahre im Dienst der Messewirtschaft. Köln, AUMA.

AUMA (1992). Die Messewirtschaft 1991. Köln, AUMA.

AUMA (1994). Die Messewirtschaft 1995. Köln, AUMA.

AUMA (1995). Satzung. Köln, AUMA.

AUMA (1997). Die Messewirtschaft 1996/97. Köln, AUMA.

AUMA (1997a). Der Messeplatz Deutschland im globalen Wettbewerb. 1.AUMA Messeforum, Bonn-Bad Godesberg, AUMA.
AUMA (1998). Die Messewirtschaft 1997/98. Köln, AUMA.
AUMA (1998a). Successful Participation in Trade Fairs Made in Germany. Cologne, AUMA.
AUMA (1998b). Erfolg auf Auslandsmessen. Ein Ratgeber fuer Auslandsmessebeteiligungen. Köln, AUMA.
AUMA (1998c). Auswertung der Ausstellerbefragung 1997. Köln, AUMA.
AUMA (1998d). AUMA Austellerbefragung 97. Ergebnisse einer schriftlichen Nachbefragung der Aussteller, die an Messen und Ausstellungen des Auslandsmesse-programms 1997 teilgenommen haben. Köln, AUMA.
AUMA (1998e). Kommunikation mit dem Weltmarkt. Die deutsche Messewirtschaft - Fakten und Perspektiven. Köln, AUMA.
AUMA (1998f). AUMA Handbuch International 1999. Köln, AUMA. Nr.22.
AUMA (1998g). Auslandsmesseprogramm 1999. Köln, AUMA.
AUMA (2001). Messewirtschaft Kennzahlen 2000, AUMA; http://www.auma.de/templates/display.asp?sprache=1&kapitel=020507&index=517&kapindex=510&parentidx=514 . 2001.
AUMA (2001a). Zusammenfassung der Beiträge auf dem Deutschen Messeforum 2001: Globalisierung und Kundennutzen, AUMA; http://www.auma.de/templates/display.asp?sprache=1&kapitel=020402&index=590&kapindex=510&parentidx=513#5 . 2001.
AUSTRADE (1994). Helping to Meet the Export Challenge : An Evaluation of the Export Market Development Grants Scheme and the International Trade Enhancement Scheme. Canberra, Australian Trade Commission.
AUSTRADE (2000). Austrade. The Australian Government's Export and Investment Facilitation Agency. Corporate Profile. Canberra, Australian Trade Commission.
AXINN, C. N., SAVITT, R., SINKULA, J.M., S.V.THACH (1995). "Export Intention, Beliefs, and Behaviors in Smaller Industrial Firms." Journal of Business Research 32(1): 49-56.
BANK OF ENGLAND (1998). Smaller Exporters. A Special Report. London, Bank of England.
BANNOCK, G. and A. PEACOCK (1989). Small Firms as Exporters. Governments and Small Business. G. Bannock and A. Peacock. London, Paul Chapman Publishing Ltd.: 24-59.
BANNOCK, G. and M. DALY (1994). Small Business Statistics. London, Paul Chapman Publishing Ltd.
BARNEKOV, T. K. and J.RAFFEL (1990). "Public Management of Privatisation." Public Productivity and Management Review, XIV(2):135-152.
BARNEY, J. B. and W. K. G. OUCHI, Eds. (1986). Organizational Economics. Toward a New Paradigm for Understanding and Studying Organizations. San Francisco, London, Jossey-Bass Publishers.
BARZEL, Y. (1997). Economic Analysis of Property Rights. Cambridge, Cambridge University Press.
BATES, R. H. (1995). Social Dilemmas and Rational Individuals. An Assessment of the New Institutionalism. The New Institutional Economics and Third World Development. J. Harriss, J. Hunter and C. M. Lewis. London, New York, Routledge: 27-48.
BCC (1997). BCC Policy Brief - International Trade, February 1997. London.
BCC (1997a). Exporting. Small Firms Survey No.22, British Chambers of Commerce.

BCC (1998). BCC Response. DTI Review of Export Promotion, BCC; http://www.britishchambers.org.uk/newsandpolicy/international/Response%20to%20DTI%20review%20on%20export%20promotion.htm . 2000.

BDI (1996). Beurteilung des Staatlichen Deutschen Außenwirtschaftsförderungssystems. Ergebnissse und Empfehlungen aus der Unternehmensbefragung. Köln, BDI.

BDI (1998). Benchmarking Außenwirtschaftsförderung. Köln, Bundesverband der Deutschen Industrie e.V.

BECKER, G. S. and K. M. MURPHY (1992). The Division of Labor, Coordination Costs, and Knowledge. Quarterly Journal of Economics 107(4): 1137-60.

BENNETT, R. J. (1996). Can Transaction Cost Economics Explain Voluntary Chambers of Commerce? Journal of Institutional and Theoretical Economics, 152(4): 654-680.

BENNETT, R. J. (1997a). Trade Associations: Britain and Germany Compared. Trade Associations in Britain and Germany: Responding to Internationalisation and the EU. R. J. Bennett. London, Anglo-German Foundation for the Study of Industrial Society: 12-22.

BENNETT, R. J. (1997b). SMEs, Business Associations and their Potential Contribution to Business Competitiveness. Working Paper. Cambridge.

BENNETT, R. J. (Ed.). (1997). Trade Associations in Britain and Germany: Responding to Internationalisation and the EU. London: Anglo-German Foundation for the Study of Industrial Society.

BERRY, A. J., BROADBENT J., D.OTLEY (1995). Structures of Control. Management Control. Theories, Issues and Practices. A. J. Berry, J. Broadbent and D. Otley. Houndmills, Basingstoke and London, Macmillan Press Ltd.: 27-40.

BESLEY, T. (1995). "Property Rights and Investment Incentives: Theory and Evidence from Ghana." Journal of Political Economy 103(5): 903-937.

BGA (1996). Positionspapier: Außenwirtschaftsförderung in der Bundesrepublik Deutschland. Bonn, 1.3.1996.

BMWi (1990). Exportfibel. Wegweiser für kleinere und mittlere Unternehmen. Cologne.

BMWi (1992). Auslandsmessepolitik für das Vereinte Deutschland. Bonn, Bundesministerium für Wirtschaft, Referat Öffentlichkeitsarbeit.

BMWi (1993). Auslandsmessepolitik fuer die Bundesrepublik Deutschland. Bonn, Bundesministerium für Wirtschaft, Referat Öffentlichkeitsarbeit.

BMWi (1995). Verbesserung der Transparenz und Konsistenz der Mittelstandsförderung. 1. Bericht der gemeinsamen Arbeitsgruppe des Bundes und der Länder unter Vorsitz des Beauftragten für den Mittelstand. Bonn, BMWi Dokumentation Nr. 379.

BMWi (1997). Unternehmensgrößenstatistik 1996/97 - Daten und Fakten -. Bonn, Erstellt vom Institut für Mittelstandsforschung Bonn.

BMWi (1998a). Auslandsmessepolitik für die Bundesrepublik Deutschland. Bonn, Bundesministerium für Wirtschaft, Referat Öffentlichkeitsarbeit.

BMWi (1998b). Unternehmensgrößenstatistik 1997/98 - Daten und Fakten -. Bonn, Erstellt vom Institut für Mittelstandsforschung.

BMWi (2000). Auslandsmessepolitik für die Bundesrepublik Deutschland. Bonn, Bundesministerium für Wirtschaft, Referat Öffentlichkeitsarbeit.

BMWI (2001). Wirtschaft in Zahlen, BMWI;
http://www.bmwi.de/Homepage/download/wirtschaftspolitik/WIZ05.pdf . 2001.

BMWI (2003). Auslandsmesseförderung noch starker auf Belange des Mittelstandes ausrichten.
http://www.bmwi.de/Navigation/Service/bestellservice,did=18428,render=renderPrint.html .

BOERNER, C. H. (1989). Aktiv als Veranstalter oder ideeller Traeger. Die Rolle der Verbände bei Messen und Ausstellungen. Blick durch die Wirtschaft 4/1989.

BOERNER, C. H. (1992). Der Ausstellungs- und Messe-Ausschuß der Deutschen Wirtschaft e.V. (AUMA) und seine Aufgaben. Handbuch Messemarketing. K. H. Strothmann and M. Busche. Wiesbaden, Gabler: 597-605.

BOESSMANN, E. (1980). Information. Handwörterbuch der Wirtschaftswissenschaften. W. Albers, K.E. Born, et.al. Vol. 3. Stuttgart et al.: Fischer et al.: 184-200.

BOESSMANN, E. (1982). "Volkswirtschaftliche Probleme der Transaktionskosten." Journal of Institutional and Theoretical Economics 138(4): 664-679.

BOLEAT, M. (1996). Trade Association Strategy and Management. London, Association of British Insurers.

BOLEAT, M. (1997). Trade Associations: Facing up to New Challenges. Trade Associations in Britain and Germany: Responding to Internationalisation and the EU. R. J. Bennett. London, Anglo-German Foundation for the Study of Industrial Society: 52-58

BOLEAT, M. (2000). Models of Trade Association Co-operation. Trade Association Forum. http://www.taforum.org/attach.pl/89/6/Models%20of%20trade%20association%20co-operation%20_Jan%202000_.pdf . 2002

BOLTON, P. and M. DEWATRIPONT (1994). "The Firm as a Communication Network." Quarterly Journal of Economics 109(4): 809-839.

BONUS, H. (1987). "Property Rights and Transaction Costs: Theory and Evidence of Privately-Owned and Government-Owned Enterprises. Comment." Journal of Institutional and Theoretical Economics 143 (1): 27-33.

BOOTH DI GIOVANNI, H. (2001). DTI Sector Sponsorship Evaluation 1998-99. London, Stationery Office.

BORCHERDING, T. E., POMMEREHNE, W. W., F. SCHNEIDER (1982). Comparing the Efficiency of Private and Public Production: The Evidence from five Countries. International Seminar in Public Economics, Bonn, Zeitschrift fuer Nationaloekonomie/ Journal of Economics 89(Supplement 2): 127-156.

BORENSTEIN, G. S. (1999). How to Pick the Right Trade Show for Your Company, The Borenstein Group; http://www.borenstein-online.com/volume13.htm . 2001.

BORRMANN, A., HOLTHUS, M., MENCK, K.W., B. SCHNATZ (1996). Investitionschancen und Erfahrungen kleiner und mittlerer deutscher Unternehmen im asiatisch-pazifischen Raum. Zusammenfassung der Ergebnisse eines Forschungsauftrages des BMWi. Bonn, BMWi.

BOTB (1993). 1992/93 Annual Report and Forward Plan. London, Department of Trade and Industry.

BOTB (1994). 1993/94 Annual Report and Forward Plan. London, Department of Trade and Industry.

BOTB (1998). 1997/98 Annual Report and Forward Plan. London, Department of Trade and Industry.

BOWEN, D.E. and G.R. JONES (1986). "Transaction Cost Analysis of Service Organisation-Customer Exchange." Academy of Management Review 11(2): 428-441.

BOWEN, S. (1997). Companies, Trade Associations and Information Advantage. Trade Associations in Britain and Germany: Responding to Internationalisation and the EU. R. J. Bennett. London, Anglo-German Foundation for the Study of Industrial Society: 35-39.

BRAEUNIG, K. (1997). Federations with a Future - a Future with Federations. In R. J. Bennett (Ed.), Trade Associations in Britain and Germany: Responding to Internationalisation and the EU. London: Anglo-German Foundation for the Study of Industrial Society: 40-45.

BRETON, A and R. WINTROBE (1975). "The Equilibrium Size of a Budget Maximizing Bureau: A Note on Niskanen's Theory of Bureaucracy." Journal of Political Economy 83(1): 195-207.

BRINCKMANN, H. (1994). Strategien fuer eine effektivere und effizientere Verwaltung. Produktivität öffentlicher Dienstleistungen. F. Naschold and M. Pröhl. Gütersloh, Verlag Bertelsmann Stiftung. 1. Dokumentation eines wissenschaftlichen Diskurses zum Produktivitätsbegriff: 167-242.

BRUDNEY, J. L. and D. R. MORGAN (1988). Local Government Productivity: Efficiency and Equity. Promoting Productivity in the Public Sector. R. M. Kelly. Houndsmills and London, Macmillan Press: 161-177.

BRUNNER, K. (1987). "The Perception of Man and the Conception of Society: Two Approaches to Understanding Society." Economic Inquiry XXV(3): 367-388.

BRYMAN, A. (1995). Research Methods and Organization Studies. London and New York, Routledge.

BTI (1999). National Strategy for International Trade Development and Promotion. London, DTI/Pub 4532/20k/10/99/NP.Urn 99/1178.

BTI (1999a). Markets and Sectors Matrix. London, DTI, URN 99/209.

BTI (2000). Building British Business Success Overseas: The First Year of British Trade International, BTI/Pub0004/25K/05/00, URN 00/778.

BURRELL, G. and G. MORGAN (1985 (1979)). Sociological Paradigms and Organisational Analysis. Aldershot, Gower.

BUSCHE, M. (1992). Staat und Wirtschaft als Traeger und Gestalter des Messewesens. Handbuch Messemarketing. K. H. Strothmann and M. Busche. Wiesbaden, Gabler: 69-80.

CABINET OFFICE (1998). Finding your way round Whitehall and beyond, British Council; http://www.britishcouncil.org/governance/manag/whitehal/ . 2001.

CAMINO, D. (1991). Export Promotion Policies in Spain and Other E.E.C. Countries: Systems and Performance. Export Development and Promotion: The Role of Public Organizations. F. H. R. Seringhaus and P. J. Rosson. Boston, Dordrecht, London, Kluwer Academic Publishers: 119-143.

CAMPBELL, S. (1998). Case Studies in Planning: Comparative Advantages and the Problem of Generalization. University of Michigan, Urban and Regional Research Collaborative: http://www.caup.umich.edu/acadpgm/urp/research/workingpapers/ URRC%2002-7.pdf 2002

CASSON, M. (1994). Economic Perspectives on Business Information. Information Acumen: The Understanding and Use of Knowledge in Modern Business. L. Bud-Friedman. London and New York: Routledge: 136-167.

CASSON, M. (1997). "Institutional Economics and Business History: A Way Forward?" Business History 39(4): 151-171.

CAVUSGIL, S. T. and P. L. YEOH (1994). "Public-Sector Promotion of United States Export Activity - A Review and Directions for the Future." Journal of Public Policy & Marketing 13(1): 76-84.

CAWSON, A. (1985). Corporatism and Local Politics. Political Economy of Corporatism. W. Grant (eds.). London, Macmillan Publishers: 126-147.

CBI (1996). Maximising Export Potential in SMEs. London, Confederation of British Industry.

CBI (1997). International Trade & Investment Issues: A Paper for Ministers. London, CBI.

CHANLAT, J.-F. (1994). "Francophone Organizational Analysis (1950-1990): An Overview." Organization Studies 15(1): 47-80.

CHEUNG, S. N. S. (1992). On the New Institutional Economics. Contract Economics. L. Werin and H. Wijkander. Cambridge Mass., Oxford, Basil Blackwell Ltd: 48-75.

CHI, T. (1994). "Trading in Strategic Resources: Necessary Conditions, Transaction Cost Problems, and Choice of Exchange Structure." Strategic Management Journal 15(4): 271-290.

COASE, R. H. (1937). "The Nature of the Firm." Economica 4(16): 386-405.

COASE, R. H. (1960). "The Problem of Social Costs." Journal of Law and Economics 3(1): 1-44.

COEURDEROY, R. and B. QUELIN (1997). "L'Économie des Couts de Transaction, un Bilan des Études Empiriques sur l'Intégration Verticale." Revue d'Économie Politique 107(2): 145-181.

CONNER, K. R. and C. K. PRAHALAD (1996). "A Resource-Based Theory of the Firm: Knowledge versus Opportunism." Organization Science 7(5): 477-501.

CONWAY, C. and W. NOTHDURFT (1996). The International State: Crafting a Statewide Trade Development System. Washington D.C.

COOPER, R. and G. BURRELL (1988). "Modernism, Postmodernism and Organizational Analysis. An Introduction." Organization Studies 9(1): 91-112.

CORDATO, R. E. (1994). Efficiency. The Elgar Companion to Austrian Economics. P. J. Boettke. Aldershot, Edward Elgar: 131-136.

CORNISH, S. L. (1997). Strategies for the Acquisition of Market Intelligence and Implications for the Transferability of Information Inputs. Annuals of the Association of American Geographers, 87(3), 451-470.

CYERT, R. M. and P. KUMAR (1996). "Economizing by Firms through Learning and Adaptation." Journal of Economic Behavior and Organization 29(2), 211-31.

CZINKOTA, M. R. (1996). "Why National Export Promotion." International Trade Forum(2): 10-16.

DAILY TELEGRAPH (1.6.1994). Diplomacy is now big business - I've become Britain's tradesman, Douglas Hurd tells Julie Kirkbride."

DAILY TELEGRAPH (18.1.1989). Export services hived off in drive for foreign trade.

DALTON, T. C. and L. DALTON (1988). The Politics of Measuring Public Sector Performance. Productivity and the Public Organization. Promoting Productivity in the Public Sector. Problems, Strategies and Prospects. R. M. Kelly. Houndsmills and London, Macmillan Press: 19-65.

DAVENPORT, T. H. (1997). Information Ecology. New York and Oxford: Oxford University Press.

DAWSON, S. and C. DARGIE (1999). New Public Management: Dead or Alive? The Third International Research Symposium on Public Management, March 1999.

DE ALESSI, L. (1980). "The Economics of Property Rights: A Review of the Evidence." Research in Law and Economics 2: 1-47.

DE ALESSI, L. (1983). "Property Rights, Transaction Costs and X-Efficiency: An Essay in Economic Theory." American Economic Review 73(1): 64-81.

DE ALESSI, L. (1990). "Form, Substance, and Welfare Comparisons in the Analysis of Institutions. " Journal of Institutional and Theoretical Economics, 146(1): 5-23.

DEKIMPE, M. G., FRANCOIS, P., LILIEN, G., C. VAN DEN BULTE (1997). "Generalizing about Trade Show Effectiveness: A Cross-National Comparison." Journal of Marketing 61(4): 55-65.

DEMSETZ, H. (1967). "Towards a Theory of Property Rights." American Economic Review 57(2): 347-359.

DEMSETZ, H. (1991). The Theory of the Firm Revisited. The Nature of the Firm. O. E. Williamson and S. Winter. New York, Oxford University Press: 159-178.

DEMSETZ, H. (1992). Comments: Specific and General Knowledge, and Organizational Structure. Contract Economics L. Werin and H. Wijkander. Oxford and Cambridge, MA: Blackwell: 275-281.

DENIS, D. J. and D.K. DENIS (1995). "Performance Changes Following Top Management Dismissals." Journal of Finance 50(4): 1029-1057.

DePASQUALE, D. (2000). Choosing a Trade Show - An Interview with Denise Moyer. http://www.microsoft.com/directaccess/channelbiz/valueadded/2000/1120/choosing.as p . 2001.

DEUTSCHER BUNDESTAG (1995a). Drucksache 13/2236, 01.09.1995. Antwort der Bundesregierung - Unterstützung deutscher Unternehmen auf den Weltmärkten und Sicherung von Arbeitsplätzen durch eine umfassende Außenwirtschaftskonzeption.

DEUTSCHER BUNDESTAG (1995b). 72. Sitzung. Tagesordnungspunkt 14 und Zusatzpunkt 8, Deutscher Bundestag, 24.November 1995: 6637-6653.

DEUTSCHER BUNDESTAG (1996). Drucksache 13/3888, 28.02.1996. Beschlußempfehlung und Bericht des Ausschusses für Wirtschaft (9. Ausschuß) zu dem Entschließungsantrag der Fraktionen der CDU/CSU und F.D.P. zur Beratung der Großen Anfrage 'Unterstützung deutscher Unternehmen auf den Weltmärkten und Sicherung von Arbeitsplätzen durch eine umfassende Außenwirtschaftskonzeption' und zum Antrag 'Neue Außenwirtschaftskonzeption zur Unterstützung deutscher Unternehmen auf den Weltmärkten'.

DEUTSCHER BUNDESTAG (1998). Drucksache 13/10300, 01.04.1998. Antwort der Bundesregierung - Reform des Auswärtigen Dienstes.

DEUTSCHER BUNDESTAG (2000a). Drucksache 14/3174, 11.04.2000. Antwort der Bundesregierung - Die Bedeutung Neuer Medien für das Auslandsgeschäft von kleinen und mittleren Unternehmen und die praktizierte staatliche Außenwirtschaftsförderung in Deutschland.

DEUTSCHER BUNDESTAG (2000b). Drucksache 14/3398, 17.05.2000. Antrag: Organisatorische Straffung und mehr Transparenz in der deutschen Außenwirtschaftsförderung.

DEUTSCHER BUNDESTAG (2000c). Drucksache 14/3870, 05.11.2000. Antwort der Bundesregierung - Chancen des Mittelstandes in der globalisierten Wirtschaft.

DEUTSCHER BUNDESTAG (2001). Drucksache 15/5581, 14.03.2001. Antwort der Bundesregierung - Zukunft der deutschen Messewirtschaft in der Globalisierung.

DEUTSCHER BUNDESTAG (2003). 15.Wahlperiode. 47.Sitzung. Tagesordnungspunkt 2. Befragung der Bundesregierung zum Thema Weltweit aktiv –Außenwirtschaftsoffensive der Bundesregierung für mehr Wachstum und Beschäftigung. 04.06.2003.

DIE WELT (17.2.1998). "DIHT startet Standort-Offensive."

DIETL, H. (1995). Institutionelle Koordination spezialisierungsbedingter wirtschaftlicher Abhängigkeit. Zeitschrift fur Betriebswirtschaft, 65(6), 569-585.

DIETRICH, M. (1991). "Firms, Markets and Transaction Cost Economics." Scottish Journal of Political Economy 38(1): 41-57.

DiLORENZO, T. J. (1988). "Property Rights, Information Costs, and the Economics of Rent Seeking." Journal of Institutional and Theoretical Economics 144(2): 318-332.

DONALDSON, L. (1990). "A Rational Basis for Criticisms of Organizational Economics: A Reply to Barney." Academy of Management Review 15(3): 394-401.

DONALDSON, L. (1994). The Liberal Revolution and Organization Theory. Towards a New Theory of Organizations. J. Hassard and M. Parker. London and New York, Routledge: 190-208.

DONALDSON, L. (1995). American Anti-Management Theories of Organization. A Critique of Paradigm Proliferation. Cambridge, Cambridge University Press.

DONALDSON, L. and J. B. BARNEY (1990). "The Ethereal Hand: Organizational Economics and Management Theory." Academy of Management Review 15(3): 369-381.
DOWDING, K. (1995). The Civil Service. London and New York, Routledge.
DOWDING, K. and D. KING (1995). Introduction. Preferences, Institutions and Applied Rational Choice. K. Dowding and D. King. Oxford, Clarendon.
DOWNS, A. (1967). Inside Bureaucracy. Boston, Mass., Little, Brown and Company.
DRUCKER, P. F. (1993). Post-capitalist Society. Oxford et al., Butterworth-Heinemann Ltd.
DTI (1991). Review of the Operation and Future Status of Fairs and Promotions Branch: Scrutiny Report. J. Rhodes and K. Rodrigues. Microfiche. Cambridge, Chadwyck-Healey Ltd: Pos: fiche no. 91.2560: 189.
DTI (1994). Evaluation of the Trade Fairs Support Scheme. London, HMSO.
DTI (1996). Competitiveness White Paper: Study on Outward Investment. Final Report by KPMG. Department of Trade and Industry. London, HMSO.
DTI (1997). The Way Forward for Overseas Trade Fairs. Press Release, 21.5.1997, P/97/340.
DTI (1998). Record Number of Companies to Receive Export Support. Press Release, 9.10.1998, P/98/773.
DTI (1998a). Support for Exhibitions and Seminars Abroad. An Overview, DTI: Export Services Directorate.
DTI (1998b). The Overseas Promotions Guide. A Guide to Events Supported by the DTI on Behalf of UK Exporters. London, DTI: Export Services Directorate.
DTI (1998c). Export Directions: Your Guide to UK Government Departments Export Services and Contacts. London, DTI/Pub 3421/10k/5/98/NP, URN 98/696.
DTI (1998d). Support for Exhibitions and Seminars Abroad - An Overview. London, DTI, Export Services Directorate.
DTI (1998e). Major Package to Help Firms to Export Announced. Press Release, 25.3.1998, P/98/229.
DTI (1999). Support for Exhibitions and Seminars Abroad - An Overview. London, DTI, Export Services Directorate.
DTI and FCO (1996). Overseas Trade Services: Exporting, A Guide to Export Services. London, DTI/Pub 1711/50k/1/96; URN 95/898.
DTI and FCO (1997). Towards an Export Initiative. A report by the Export Forum. London, DTI/Pub 3053/6k/11/97/NP, URN97/948.
DTI and FCO (1999). The Review of Export Promotion. A Report by the Secretary of the Cabinet, Sir Richard Wilson. London, DTI / Pub 4003/8k/3/99 NP; URN 99/686.
DTI and H. M. Treasury (1997). Trade and Industry 1997: The Government's Expenditure Plans 1997-98 to 1999-2000. Department of Trade and Industry; Export Credits Guarantee Department; Office of Fair Trading; Office of Telecommunications; Office of Gas Supply; Office of Electricity Regulation. London, Stationary Office; Cm 3605.
DTI and H. M. Treasury (2000). The Government's Expenditure Plans 2000-1 to 2001-2. Department of Trade and Industry; Export Credits Guarantee Department; Office of Fair Trading; Office of Telecommunications; Office of Gas and Electricity Markets. London, Stationary Office; Cm 4611.
DTI and H. M. Treasury (2001). The Government's Expenditure Plans 2001-2 to 2003-4 and Main Estimates 2001-2. Department of Trade and Industry; Export Credits Guarantee Department; Office of Fair Trading; Office of Telecommunications; Office of Gas and Electricity Markets; Postal Services Commission. London, Stationary Office; Cm 5112.
DTI, FCO, et al. (2001). British Trade International : The Government's Expenditure Plans 2001-02 to 2003-04 and main estimates 2001-02. London, Stationary Office, Cm 5123.

DUNLEAVY, P. (1991). Democracy, Bureaucracy and Public Choice: Economic Explanations in Political Science. New York, London et al.: Harvester Wheatsheaf.

DUNLEAVY, P. and C. HOOD (1994). "From Old Public Administration to New Public Management." Public Money & Management 14(3): 9-16.

DUNN, M. H. (1994). "Public Enterprises, Private Enterprises and Property Rights Theory. The Case of the Indian Steel Industry." Jahrbuch fuer Nationaloekonomie und Statistik 213(3): 305-320.

DUNSIRE, A. (1999). "Then and Now: Public Administration, 1953-1999." Political Studies 47(2): 360-378.

DUNSIRE, A. and C. HOOD (1989). Cutback Management in Public Bureaucracies: Popular Theories and Observed Outcomes in Whitehall. Cambridge, Cambridge University Press.

ECON-CONSULT and ISG (1994). Die Erschließung neuer Märkte der mittelständischen Wirtschaft durch Auslandsmessen. Untersuchung im Auftrag des Bundesministeriums für Wirtschaft. Abschlußbericht. Köln, ECON-CONSULT Wirtschafts- und Sozialwissenschaftliche Beratungsgesellschaft m.B.H.& Co.KG und ISG Sozialforsch-ung und Gesellschaftspolitik GmbH.

EGEBERG, M. (1994). "Research Note: Bridging the Gap between Theory and Practice: The Case of Administrative Policy." An International Journal of Policy and Administration 7(1): 83-98.

EGGERTSON, T. (1990). Economic Behavior and Institutions. Cambridge, New York,Victoria, Cambridge University Press.

EHRENFELD, H. (1997). Außenwirtschaftsfördernde Infrastruktur der Länder der Bundesrepublik Deutschland. Ergebnisse und Analyse einer empirischen Studie. Hildesheim, CEC Publication.

EISENHARDT, K. M. (1989). "Agency Theory: An Assessment and Review." Academy of Management Review 14(1): 57-74.

ENGELHARD, J. (1992). Exportförderung. Exportentscheidungsprozesse und Exporterfolg. Wiesbaden, Gabler.

ESER, S. (2000). "Mitgliederorientierung in Verbänden." Verbändereport 4(4).

ETZIONI, A. (1964). Modern Organizations. Englewood Cliffs, N.J., Prentice Hall.

EVERS, H. (1995). Entgeltpolitik fuer Führungskräfte. Handwörterbuch der Führung. A. Kieser. Stuttgart: Schaeffer-Poeschel: Sp.297-306.

EXPORT PUBLICATIONS UNIT (1996). Trade Fairs Support Scheme: Sponsors' Guide to Best Practice. Cambridge, Chadwyck-Healey Ltd.

FAYOL, H. (1997 (1916)). General Principles of Management. Organization Theory. Selected Readings. D. S. Pugh. London et al., Penguin: 253-274.

FAZ (1998). Messen müssen systematischer vorbereitet werden. Frankfurter Allgemeine Zeitung. Frankfurt: 34.

FCO and DTI (1996). Free Trade and Foreign Policy: A Global Vision. London, Stationery Office, Cm; 3437.

FERLIE, E. (2000). Public Management in the UK: Efficiency and Accountability. Paper presented at the Colloque International on 'Les Nouvelles Exigences de la Responsibilité Publique', Paris, February 2000.

FINANCIAL TIMES (13.5.1993). "DTI aims to sharpen export campaign."

FINANCIAL TIMES (14.10.1998). "FO Set to Lose Fight for Exclusive Role on Exports."

FINANCIAL TIMES (15.3.1991). "Exporters' Support Services will Merge."

FINANCIAL TIMES (17.2.1997). "Tories consider trade role for Foreign Office."

FINANCIAL TIMES (18.1.1989). "Shake-Up for Export Services. "

FINANCIAL TIMES (18.1.1997). "Exporters Angry at Trade Fair Aid Cuts."

FINANCIAL TIMES (22.4.1991). "The Queen's Awards For Export And Technology 1991."

FINANCIAL TIMES (25.5.1995). "Change to Put Mandarins at the Sharp End."

FINANCIAL TIMES (4.2.1997). "Exporters Back Drive on Aid For Trade Fairs."

FINANCIAL TIMES (4.7.1998). "Britain: Export Promotion Teams may Face Wind of Change: Government Help for Companies Seeking Business Abroad is Under Review."

FINANCIAL TIMES (5.11.1997). "Business Urges Review of Trade Promotion."

FINANCIAL TIMES (5.5.1994). "FT Exporter (2): The Shift Towards Intervention."

FINANCIAL TIMES (8.7.1997). "Trade Fair Scheme Changes."

FIRTH, M. (1991). "Corporate Takeovers, Stockholder Returns and Executive Rewards." Managerial and Decision Economics, 12(6), 421-428.

FLORIO, M. (1994). "Fair Trades by Trade Fairs. Information Providing Institutions under Monopolistic Competition." Small Business Economics 6(4): 267-281.

FOREIGN AFFAIRS COMMITTEE (1999). Foreign and Commonwealth Office Resources. House of Commons papers. 1998-99 ; 271. London, Stationary Office.

FOSS, N. J. (1993). "Theories of the Firm: Contractual and Competence Perspectives." Evolutionary Economics 3(2): 127-144.

FOSS, N. J. (1996a). "Knowledge-based Approaches to the Theory of the Firm: Some Critical Comments." Organization Science 7(5): 470-476.

FOSS, N. J. (1996b). "Harald B. Malmgren's Analysis of the Firm: Lessons for Modern Theorists?" Review of Political Economy 8(4): 349-66.

FRANT, H. (1991). The New Institutional Economics: Implications for Policy Analysis. Policy Analysis and Economics. Developments, Tensions, Prospects. D. L. Weimer. Boston, Dordrecht, London, Kluwer Academic Publishers: 111-125.

FREY, B. S. (1990). "Institutions Matter - The Comparative Analysis of Institutions." European Economic Review 34(2-3): 443-449.

FREY, B. S. (1997). Not Just for the Money. An Economic Theory of Personal Motivation. Cheltenham, UK and Brookfield, US: Edward Elgar Publishing.

FURUBOTN, E. (1990). "Different Approaches to the Economic Analysis of Institutions: Some Concluding Remarks." Journal of Institutional and Theoretical Economics 146(1): 226-232.

FURUBOTN, E. G. and R. RICHTER (1997). Institutions and Economic Theory. The Contribution of the New Institutional Economics. Ann Arbor, The University of Michigan Press.

FURUBOTN, E. G. and S. PEJOVICH (1972). "Property Rights and Economic Theory: A Survey of Recent Literature." Journal of Economic Literature 10(4): 1137-1162.

GALAL, A., JONES, L, TANDON, P, and O. VOGELSANG (1994). Welfare Consequences of Selling Public Enterprises: An Empirical Analysis. New York, Published for the World Bank by Oxford University Press.

GALUNIC, C. D. and S. RODAN (1997). Resource Recombinations in the Firm: Knowledge Structures and the Potential for Schumpeterian Innovation. INSEAD Working Paper: 96/75/OB, 5.August 1997.

GANLEY, J. A. and J. S. CUBBIN (1992). Public Sector Efficiency Measurement. North Holland et al., Elsevier Science Publishers B.V.

GEORGE, K. D., JOLL, C., and LYNK, E. L. (1992). Industrial Organisation: Competition, Growth, and Structural Change. (4th ed.). London. Routledge.

GERHART, B. and MILKOVICH, G. T. (1992). Employee Compensation: Research and Practice. Handbook of Industrial and Organisational Psychology. M. D. Dunnette and L. M. Hough. Palo Alto, CA., Consulting Psychologists Press, Inc.: 3:481-569.

GIBBONS, R. (1998). "Incentives in Organizations." Journal of Economic Perspectives 12(4): 115-132.

GLYNN, J., A. GRAY, et al. (1991). Discussion Paper on Effectiveness Audit prepared for the National Audit Office. Canterbury, Public Sector Management Unit, Canterbury Business School, University of Kent.

GODOY, R., O'NEILL, K., McSWEENEY, D., WILKIE, V., FLORES, D., BRAVO, P., KOSTISHACK, P., A. CUBAS (2000). "Human capital, wealth, property rights, and the adoption of new farm technologies: The Tawahka Indians of Honduras." Human Organization 59(2): 222-233.

GOODMAN, P. S. and J. M. PENNINGS (1977). Perspectives and Issues: An Introduction. New Perspectives on Organizational Effectiveness. P. S. Goodman, J. M. Pennings and Associates. San Francisco, Washington, London, Jossey-Bass Publishers: 1-12.

GOODSELL, S. (1996). The Role of Exhibitions in the European Marketing Mix. Paper given at Kawalek Software Marketing Perspectives, June 1996, San Francisco, http://www.international-marketing.co.uk/www/exhibit.ppr.html.

GOPALAKRISHNA, S., LILIEN, G. L., WILLIAMS, J. D. and I. K. SEQUERIA (1995). "Do Trade Shows Pay Off? " Journal of Marketing 59(3): 75-84.

GORDON, D. M. (1996). Fat and Mean: The Corporate Squeeze of Working Americans and the Myth of Managerial Downsizing. New York.,Free Press.

GRANICK, D. (1988). "Property Rights vs. Transaction Costs in Comparative Systems Analysis." Journal of Institutional and Theoretical Economics 144(5): 871-877.

GRANOVETTER, M. S. (1985). "Economic Action and Social Structure. The Problem of Embeddedness." American Journal of Sociology 91(3): 481-510.

GRANT, R. M. (1996). "Prospering in Dynamically-Competitive Environments: Organizational Capability as Knowledge Integration." Organization Science, 7(4), 375-387.

GRAVELLE, H. S. E. (1982). Incentives, Efficiency and Control in Public Firms. International Seminar in Public Economics, Bonn, Zeitschrift fuer Nationaloekonomie/ Journal of Economics 89(Supplement 2): 79-104.

GREENBURY, R. et al. (1995). Directors' Remuneration. London, The Study Group on Directors' Remuneration, CBI.

GROSSMAN, S. J. and O. D. HART (1983). "An Analysis of the Principal-Agent Problem." Econometrica 51(1): 7-45.

GROTH, C. (1992). Determinanten der Veranstaltungspolitik von Messegesellschaften. Handbuch Messemarketing. K. H. Strothmann and M. Busche. Wiesbaden, Gabler: 159-189.

GROTH, C. (1997). Die Deutschen Messegesellschaften - Dienstleister auf dem Weg in das 21. Jahrhundert. 1. AUMA Messe Forum 1997: Der Messeplatz Deutschland im globalen Wettbewerb. AUMA. Cologne, AUMA: 13-16.

HABUDA, J., HILPERT, H. G., and S. MARTSCH (1998a). Neue Ansätze und Instrumente der Außenwirtschaftsförderung in ausgewählten Industrieländern. München.

HABUDA, J., HILPERT, H. G., and S. MARTSCH (1998b). "Außenwirtschaftsförderung im internationalen Vergleich - Implikationen für Deutschland." ifo Schnelldienst 51(16): 13-28.

HALL, M. (1997). British Commercial and Service Association: The FLA. Trade Associations in Britain and Germany: Responding to Internationalisation and the EU. R. J. Bennett. London, Anglo-German Foundation for the Study of Industrial Society: 108-115.

HALLIBURTON, K. and S. R. HENNEBERRY (1995). "The Effectiveness of US Nonprice Promotion of Almonds in the Pacific Rim." Journal of Agricultural and Resource Economics 20(1): 108-121.

HANNAH, M. (2002). The National Trade Support Network - Is there a Case for a Formal Structure? International Trade Centre, Executive Forum. Discussion Brief for the Export Strategy Maker. http://www.intracen.org/execforum/ef2001fhannah.htm . 2002.

HANNAN, M. T. and J. FREEMAN (1977). Obstacles to Comparative Studies. New Perspectives on Organizational Effectiveness. P. S. Goodman and J. M. Pennings. San Francisco, Washington, London, Jossey-Bass Publishers: 106-131.

HANSARD (1997). Trade Fair Support Scheme. House of Commons, Mr. Nelson, 18.2.1997; Column 480.

HANSARD (2000). British Firms (Government Support). House of Commons, 24.5.2000; Column 500W, [123866].

HANSARD (2000a). Trade Partners UK. House of Commons, Mr. Caborn, 29.11.2000; Column 647W.

HARDIN, G. J. (1968). "The Tragedy of the Commons." Science 162:1243-1248.

HAUSWIRTH, I. (2000). "Business Associations within Public-Private Partnerships." International Journal of Public-Private Partnerships 2(3):367-386.

HAUSWIRTH, I. and D. BORGER (1997). Conceptualising Export Readiness. A Review of Research on Exporting Small and Medium Sized Companies. Paper for the International Trade Centre, Geneva.

HAYEK, F. A. (1945). "The Use of Knowledge in Society." American Economic Review 35(4): 519-530.

HEMMERSBACH, A. (1993). Wirkungen von Instrumenten der Technologie- und Exportförderungspolitik fuer kleine und mittlere Unternehmen. Eine empirische Analyse für Rheinland-Pfalz. Frankfurt am Main, Verlag Peter Lang GmbH.

HERBIG, P., PALUMBO, F., and B. O'HARA (1996a). "Differences in Trade Show Behavior between North American-Focused Firms and Worldwide-Oriented Firms." International Journal of Commerce & Management 6(1-2): 97-110.

HERBIG, P., PALUMBO, F., and B. O'HARA (1996b). "Differences in Trade Show Behavior between Manufacturers and Service-Oriented firms." Journal of Professional Services Marketing 14(2): 55-78.

HERZBERG, F. (1974 (1966)). Work and the Nature of Man. London: Crosby Lockwood Staples.

HESTERLY, W. S., LIEBESKIND, J., T. R. ZENGER (1990). "Organizational Economics: An Impending Revolution in Organization Theory?" Academy of Management Review 15(3): 402-420.

HEWITT-DUNDAS, N. (1997). Corporate Flexibility: A Comparative Analysis of Small Firms in Northern Ireland and Massachusetts. Aldershot and Brookfield, VT, Avebury, Ashgate Publishing Ltd.

HIRSCH, W. Z. (1995). "Contracting Out by Urban Governments: A Review." Urban Affairs Review 30(3): 458-472.

HIRSCHMAN, A. O. (1982). Shifting Involvements: Private Interests and Public Action. Princeton, N.Y., Princeton University Press.

HODGSON, G. M. (1988). Economics and Institutions: A Manifesto for a Modern Institutional Economics. Cambridge and Philadelphia, Polity and University of Pennsylvania Press.

HODGSON, G. M. (1989). "Institutional Economic Theory: The Old versus the New." Review of Political Economy 1(3): 249-269.

HODGSON, G. M. (1993). "Institutional Economics: Surveying the "Old" and the "New"." Metroeconomica 44(1): 1-28.

HODGSON, G. M. (1994). Methodological Individualism. The Elgar Companion to Institutional and Evolutionary Economics. L-Z. G. M. Hodgson, W. J. Samuels and M. R. Tool. Aldershot;Brookfield Vermont, Edward Elgar Publishing Company. 2: 63-67.

HOLMSTROM, B. and P. R. MILGROM (1991). "Multi-Task Principal Agent Analyses: Incentive Contracts, Asset Ownership, and Job Design." Journal of Law, Economics and Organization 7(Special Issue.): 24-52.

HOOD, C. (1991). "A Public Management for all Seasons?" Public Administration 69(1): 3-19.

HOOD, C. (1995). "Emerging Issues in Public Administration." Public Administration 73 (Spring): 165-183.

HOOD, C. (1996). Control Over Bureaucracy: Cultural Theory and Institutional Variety. Journal of Public Policy, 15(3), 207-30.

HOUSE OF COMMONS (1999). Foreign and Commonwealth Office Resources. Foreign Affairs Committee. London, Stationary Office, House of Commons papers. 1998-99; 271.

HOUSE OF COMMONS (2000). 5th report, (session 1999-00): Annual Reports of Foreign and Commonwealth Office and British Trade International 2000: Report, Together with the Proceedings of the Committee, Minutes of Evidence and Appendices. Defence Committee. London, Stationary Office; House of Commons papers. 1999-00; 507.

HOUSE OF REPRESENTATIVES (2001). International Trade Administration: The Commerce Department's Trade Policy Agenda. Hearing before the Committee on International Relations, House of Representatives. One Hundred Seventh Congress, First Session, June 21; Serial No.107-19; http://www.house.gov/international-relations. 2002

IMF (2001). Global Trade Liberalization and the Developing Countries. IMF Issues Brief. 01/08.

INDUSTRY WEEK (24.1.2000). Industry Week's Global Manufacturers' Resource Guide, Industry Week, http://www.industryweek.com/iwinprint/data/chart3.html. 2002

INSTITUTE OF EXPORT (1998). The Institute's Response to the Export Promotion Review. London.

INTERNATIONAL TRADE FINANCE (17.7.1998). "UK Government not Convinced About Independent Export Agency Proposal."

JAMES, O. (2001). "Business Models and the Transfer of Businesslike Central Government Agencies." Governance: An International Journal of Policy and Administration 14(2): 233-252.

JENSEN, M. C. (1983). "Organization Theory and Methodology." The Accounting Review 58(2): 319-338.

JENSEN, M. C. and W. H. MECKLING (1976). "Theory of the Firm: Managerial Behaviour, Agency Costs, and Ownership Structure." Journal of Financial Economics 3(2): 305-360.

JENSEN, M. C. and W.H. MECKLING (1992). "Specific and General Knowledge, and Organizational Structure." Contract Economics. L. Werin and H. Wijkander. Oxford and Cambridge, MA: Blackwell: 251-274.

JENSEN, M. C. and K. J. MURPHY (1990). "Performance Pay and Top-Management Incentives." Journal of Political Economy, 98(2): 225-64.

KANFER, R. (1992). Work Motivation: New Directions in Theory and Research. International Review of Industrial and Organizational Psychology, Vol. 7. C. L. Cooper and I. T. Robertson. London, John Wiley & Sons, Ltd.: 1-53.

KASPER, W. and M. STREIT (1998). Institutional Economics: Social Order and Public Policy. Cheltenham, UK; Northampton, MA, USA, Edward Elgar.

KAY, J. (1993). Foundations of Corporate Success. How Business Strategies add Value. New York: Oxford University Press.

KELLER, B. (1988). "Olsons 'Logik des kollektiven Handelns'. Entwicklung, Kritik - und eine Alternative." Politische Vierteljahresschrift 29(3), 388-406.

KELLY, R. M. (1988). Success, Productivity, and the Public Sector. Promoting Productivity in the Public Sector. R. M. Kelly. Houndsmills, Basingstoke and London, MacMillan Press in association with the Policy Studies Organisation: 1-16.

KHALIL, E. L. (1995a). "Organizations versus Institutions." Journal of Institutional and Theoretical Economics 151(3): 445-466.

KHALIL, E. L. (1995b). "Institutional Theory of the Firm? Extension and Limitation." Review of Political Economy 7(1): 43-51.

KIEFER, T. (1996). Partner für das Asiengeschaeft, local@global; http://www.localglobal.de/96/asiapart.htm. 1999.

KIESER, A. (1987). "Book Review: Lex Donaldson: In Defence of Organization Theory. A Reply to the Critics. 1985, Cambridge University Press, Cambridge." Organization Studies 8(4): 375-378.

KINNUCAN, H. W. and J. E. CHRISTIAN (1997). "A Method for Measuring Returns to Nonprice Export Promotion." Journal of Agricultural and Resource Economics 22(1): 120-132.

KIRSCH, G. (1993). Neue Politische Ökonomie. Duesseldorf, Werner.

KLAGES, H. and E. LOEFFLER (1996). Public Sector Modernization in Germany - Recent Trends and Emerging Strategies. Public Sector Management in Europe. N. Flynn and F. Strehl. New York, Prentice Hall: 132-145.

KNILL, C. (1999). "Explaining Cross-National Variance in Administrative Reform: Autonomous versus Instrumental Bureaucracies. " Journal of Public Policy 19 (2): 113-139.

KOERNER, H., Ed. (1989). Zur Analyse von Institutionen im Entwicklungsprozess und in der internationalen Zusammenarbeit. Schriften des Vereins für Socialpolitik. Neue Folge Band 186. Berlin, Duncker & Humblot.

KOHLER-KOCH, B. and C. QUITTKAT (1999). Intermediation of Interests in the European Union. Mannheim, Mannheimer Zentrum fuer Europaeische Sozialforschung; MZES Working Papers No.9, 1999.

KOTABE, M. and M. CZINKOTA (1992). "State Government Promotion of Manufacturing Exports: A Gap Analysis." Journal of International Business Studies 23(4): 637-658.

KRESSE, H. (1997). Internationale Rahmenbedingungen des Messeplatzes Deutschland. 1. AUMA Messe Forum 1997: Der Messeplatz Deutschland im globalen Wettbewerb. Köln, AUMA: 17-22.

LABOUR PARTY (1996). New Labour, New Life for Britain: New Opportunities for Business. London.

LAFFONT, J. J. and J. TIROLE (1990). Privatization and Incentives. Massachusetts Institute of Technology, Department of Economics, Working Paper 572.

LANE, C. (1997). Trade Associations and Inter-Firm Relations in Britain and Germany. Trade Associations in Britain and Germany: Responding to Internationalisation and the EU. R. J. Bennett. London, Anglo-German Foundation for the Study of Industrial Society: 23-32

LANE, E. and R. BACHMANN (1996). "The Social Constitution of Trust: Supplier Relations in Britain and Germany." Organization Studies 17(3): 365-395.

LANGLOIS, R. N. (1984). Internal Organization in a Dynamic Context: Some Theoretical Considerations. Communication and Information Economics. New Perspectives. M. Jussawalla and H. Ebenfield. Amsterdam, New York, Oxford, Elsevier Science Publishers B.V.: 23-49.

LANGLOIS, R. N. (1989). "What was wrong with the Old Institutional Economics (and what is still wrong with the New)?" Review of Political Economy 1(3): 270-298.

LAWLER, E. E. and G.D JENKINS (1992). Strategic Reward Systems., Handbook of Industrial and Organizational Psychology. M. D. Dunnette and L. M. Hough. Palo Alto, CA: Consulting Psychologists Press, Inc.:3: 1009-1055.

LAWRENCE, P. R. and J. W. LORSCH (1997 (1967)). High-Performing Organizations in Three Environments. Organization Theory. Selected Readings. D. S. Pugh. London et al., Penguin: 111-129.

LAZEAR, E. P. (1991). "Labor Economics and the Psychology of Organizations." Journal of Economic Perspectives 5(2): 89-110.

LAZEAR, E. P. and S. ROSEN (1981). "Rank-Order Tournaments as Optimum Labor Contracts." Journal of Political Economy 89(5): 841-64.

LEGLER, H., U. SCHASSE, et al. (1994). Analyse der Wirkungen der niedersächsischen Auslandsmesseförderung. Bericht zu einem Gutachten im Auftrag des Niedersächsischen Ministeriums fuer Wirtschaft, Technologie und Verkehr. Hannover, Niedersächsisches Institut fuer Wirtschaftsforschung e.V.

LEHMBRUCH, G. (1994). Dilemmata verbandlicher Einflusslogik im Prozess der deutschen Vereinigung. Staat und Verbaende. W. Streek.. Politische Vierteljahres-schrift 35, Sonderheft 25: Westdeutscher Verlag: 370-392.

LEONIDOU, L. C. (1995a). "Export Barriers: Non-Exporters' Perceptions. " International Marketing Review 12(1): 4-26.

LEONIDOU, L. C. (1995b). "Empirical Research on Export Barriers: Review, Assessment, and Synthesis. " Journal of International Marketing 3(1): 29-44.

LIBECAP, G. D. (1989). Contracting for Property Rights. Cambridge et al., Cambridge University Press.

LIEBESKIND, J. P., OLIVER, A. L., ZUCKER, L.G. and M. B. BREWER. (1996). "Social Networks, Learning, and Flexibility: Sourcing Scientific Knowledge in New Biotechnology Firms." Organization Science 7(4): 428-443.

LOEFFLER, E. (2000). "Germany." Governance & Public Sector Reform Sites: Administrative & Civil Service Reform: Designing and Implementing Reforms: Country Reforms Summaries. World Bank.
http://www1.worldbank.org/publicsector/civilservice/rsGermany.pdf

LOROT, P. (1998). "French Foreign Economic Policy." The International Spectator 23(1): http://www.ciaonet.org/olj/iai/iai_98lop01.html. 2002

LYNN, L. H. and T. J. McKEOWN (1988). Organizing Business. Trade Associations in America and Japan. Washington, D.C., AEI.

LYONS, B. R. (1996). "Empirical Relevance of Efficient Contract Theory: Inter-Firm Contracts." Oxford Review of Economic Policy 12(4): 27-49.

m+a (1970). Zwischen Organisation und Improvisation. Aufgaben und Probleme deutscher Durchführungsgesellschaften. m+a report: 24-25.

m+a (1986). Auslandsmessebeteiligungen. Schlüssel zu Exportmärkten für die deutsche Wirtschaft. m+a Gespräch mit Ministerialrat Winfried Wachendorfer. m+a: 31-32.

MacBEAN, A. (2000). Export Promotion in Transitional Economies. Trade and Transition. Trade Promotion in Transitional Economies. A. Macbean. London and Portland, OR, Frank Cass: 1-17.

MACHLUP, F. (1967). "Theories of the Firm: Marginalist, Behavioral, Managerial." The American Economic Review LVII(1): 1-33.

MACHLUP, F. (1978). Methodology of Economics and other Social Sciences. New York, San Francisco, London, Academic Press.

MACHLUP, F. (1980). Knowledge: Its Creation, Distribution, and Economic Significance. (Vol. Volume 1 - Knowledge and Knowledge Production). Princeton, NJ: Princeton University Press.

MACHLUP, F. (1983). Semantic Quirks in Studies of Information. The Study of Information. Interdisciplinary Messages. F. Machlup and U. Mansfield. New York et al., John Wiley & Sons: 641-671.

MACLEOD, W. B. (1995). Incentives in Organizations: An Overview of Some of the Evidence and Theory. Trends in Business Organization: Do Participation and Cooperation Increase Competitiveness? H. Siebert. Tuebingen, J.C.B.Mohr: 3-42.

MADHOK, A. (1996). "The Organization of Economic Activity: Transaction Costs, Firm Capabilities and the Nature of Governance." Organization Science 7(5): 577-590.

MAGUIRE, M. (1993). Pay Flexibility in the Public Sector - An Overview. Pay Flexibility in the Public Sector. O. P. M. Studies. Paris, OECD: 9-17.

MARITI, P. and R. H. SMILEY (1983). "Cooperative Agreements and the Organization of Industry." Journal of Industrial Economics 31(4): 437-51.

MARRIS, R. (1963). "A Model of the 'Managerial' Enterprise." The Quarterly Journal of Economics 77(2): 185-209.

MARRIS, R. (1992). Equity, Efficiency, and the Managerial Paradigm. Equity and Efficiency in Economic Development. Essays in Honour of Benjamin Higgins. D. J. Savoie and I. Brecher. McGill and Queen's University Press.

MARSCHAK, T. (1987). Organization Theory. The New Palgrave. A Dictionary of Economics. J. Eatwell, M. Milgate and P. Newman. London, New York, Tokio, The Macmillan Press Ltd. 3, K-P: 757-760.

MARSHALL, A. (1994 (1890)). Principles of Economics. London, Macmillan.

MARTIN, R. (1993). "The New Behaviorism: A Critique of Economics and Organisation." Human Relations 46(9): 1085-1101.

MAYHEW, A. (1989). "Contrasting Origins of the two Institutionalisms: The Social Science Context." Review of Political Economy 1(3): 319-333.

McAFEE, R. P. and J. McMILLAN (1987). "Competition for Agency Contracts." Rand Journal of Economics 18(2): 296-307.

McALEESE, D. and M. O'DONNELL (2000). Institutional Support for Exporting: Issues and Evidence. Trade and Transition. Trade Promotion in Transitional Economies. A. Macbean. London and Portland, OR, Frank Cass: 18-28.

McCLELLAND, D. C. (1976 (1953)). The Achievement Motive. New York, London, etc.: Irvington.

MECKLING, W. H. (1976). "Values and the Choice of the Model of the Individual in the Social Sciences." Schweizer Zeitschrift fur Volkswirtschaft und Statistik 112(4): 545-560.

MEFFERT, H. (1996). Ziele und Nutzen von Messebeteiligungen. Zusammenfassung einer empirisch gestützten Untersuchung auf der Grundlage einer Befragung deutscher Aussteller. Bergisch Gladbach, Heider.

MICHIGAN SMALL BUSINESS DEVELOPMENT CENTER (1998). Trade Secrets. The Export Answer Book - Ch.7 Trade Shows. http://www.tradenet.gov/Tutorial/Secrets/ch07.htm . 2001.

MIESENBOCK, K. J. (1988). "Small Businesses and Exporting: A Literature Review. " International Small Business Journal 6(1): 42-61.

MILGROM, P. R. (1988). "Employment Contracts, Influence Activities and Efficient Organizational Design." Journal of Political Economy 96(1): 42-60.

MILGROM, P. R. and J. ROBERTS (1992). Economics, Organization and Management. London et al., Prentice Hall.

MINKLER, A. P. (1993). "Knowledge and Internal Organization." Journal of Economic Behavior & Organization 21(1): 17-30.

MOE, T. M. (1984). "The New Economics of Organization." American Journal of Political Science 28(4): 739-777.

MORGAN, G. (1990). Paradigm diversity in organizational research. The Theory and Philosophy of Organizations. Critical Issues and New Perspectives. J. Hassard and D. Pym. London and New York, Routledge: 13-29.

MOTWANI, J., RICE, G., and M. ESSAM (1992). "Promoting Exports Through International Trade Shows: A Dual Perspective." Review of Business 13(4): 38-44.

MOXENES, E. (1998). "Not only the Tragedy of the Commons: Misperceptions of Bioeconomics." Management Science 44(9): 1234-1248.

MURPHY, K. J. (1996). "Reporting Choice and the 1992 Proxy Disclosure Rules." Journal of Accounting, Auditing and Finance 11(3): 497-515.

NALBANTIAN, H. R. (1987). Incentive Compensation in Perspective. Incentives, Cooperation, and Risk Sharing. Economic and Psychological Perspectives on Employment Contracts. H. R. Nalbantian. New Jersey, Rowman & Littlefield: 3-43.

NAO (c.{1994}). The Audit of Efficiency: A Structured Approach. London, National Audit Office.

NAO (1996). Overseas Trade Services: Assistance to Exporters. London, HMSO.

NASCHOLD, F. (1994). Produktivität öffentlicher Dienstleistungen. Produktivität öffentlicher Dienstleistungen. F. Naschold and M. Pröhl. Gütersloh, Verlag Bertelsmann Stiftung. Band 1 Dokumentation eines wissenschaftlichen Diskurses zum Produktivitätsbegriff: 363-413.

NASCHOLD, F. and M. PRÖHL, Eds. (1994). Produktivität öffentlicher Dienstleistungen. Gütersloh, Verlag Bertelsmann Stiftung.

NEALE, W. C. (1994). Institutions. The Elgar Companion to Institutional and Evolutionary Economics. A-K. G. M. Hodgson, W. J. Samuels and M. R. Tool. Aldershot, Brookfield, VT, Edward Elgar Publishing Limited: 402-406.

NEGELEIN, H. G. (1992). Das Messewesen in Deutschland. Handbuch Messemarketing. K. H. Strothmann and M. Busche. Wiesbaden, Gabler: 15-27.

NEWMAN, J. (1999). The New Public Management, Modernisation and Organisational Change: Disruptions, Disjunctures and Dilemmas. Paper presented to the ESRC Seminar 'Recent Developments in the New Public Management', Aston University, November 1999.

NISKANEN, W. A. (1971). Bureaucracy and Representative Government. Chicago, Aldine.

NONAKA, I. and H. TAKEUCHI (1995). The Knowledge-Creating Company. New York, Oxford University Press.

NOOTEBOOM, B. (1992). "Towards a Dynamic Theory of Transactions." Evolutionary Economics 2(4): 281-299.

NORTH, D. C. (1990). Institutions, Institutional Change and Economic Performance. Cambridge, New York, Victoria, Cambridge University Press.

NOTHDURFT, W. (1992). Going Global. How Europe Helps Small Firms Export. Washington DC, The Brookings Institution.

NUGENT, J., A. BERRY, et al. (1999). Implications for Theory, Policy and Future Research. Fulfilling the Export Potential of Small and Medium Firms. B. Levy, A. Berry and J. Nugent. Boston, Dordrecht, London, Kluwer Academic Publishers: 261-275.

OECD (1991). Public Management Developments. Paris, PUMA, OECD.

OECD (1997). Industrial Competitiveness in the Knowledge-Based Economy: A New Role of Governments. Paper presented at 'Industrial Competitiveness in the Knowledge-Based Economy: A New Role of Governments', Stockholm.

OECD (1997a). Globalisation and Small and Medium Enterprises. Paris, OECD.

OECD (1998). Past, Present and Future Policies for Industrial Development in Member Countries. Paris, OECD.

O'HARA, B., PALUMBO F., and P. HERBIG (1993). "Industrial Trade Shows Abroad." Industrial Marketing Management 22(3): 233-237.

OLSON, M. (1971). The Logic of Collective Action. Public Goods and the Theory of Groups. Cambridge, Mass. and London, Harvard University Press.

OLSON, M. (1982). The Rise and Decline of Nations. Economic Growth, Stagflation, and Social Rigidities. New Haven, London, Yale University Press.

ONDRACK, D. A. (1995). Entgeltsysteme als Motivationsinstrument. Handwörterbuch der Führung. A. Kieser. Stuttgart, Schaeffer-Poeschel: Sp.307-330.

ONIDA, F. (2002). The (Italian) Network's Fundamental Challenge: Addressing Conflicting Objectives, International Trade Centre, Executive Forum. Discussion Brief for the Export Strategy Maker.
http://www.intracen.org/execforum/ef2001/cponida.htm. 2002.

ORUM, A. M., FEAGIN, J. R., and G. SJOBERG. (1991). Introduction: The Nature of the Case Study. A Case for the Case Study. J. R Feagin, A. M. Orum, and G. Sjoberg. Chapel Hill, NC: University of North Carolina Press: 1-26.

OSTROM, E. (1986). "An Agenda for the Study of Institutions." Public Choice 48(1): 3-25.

OSTROM, E. (1990). Governing the Commons. The Evolution of Institutions for Collective Action. Cambridge, Cambridge University Press.

OTZEL, H. and S. MARTIN (1998). "Local Partnership for Economic Development: Business Links and the Restructuring of SME Support Networks in the United Kingdom." Economic Development Quarterly 12(3): 266-278.

OUCHI, W. G. (1991 (1980)). Markets, Bureaucracies and Clans. Markets, Hierarchies and Networks. The Coordination of Social Life. G. Thompson, J. Frances, R. Levacic, and J. Mitchel. London, New York, New Delhi, Sage Publications: 246-255.

PARKER, M. (1992). "Post-Modern Organizations or Postmodern Organization Theory?" Organization Studies 13(1): 1-17.

PAVLIK, E. L. and A. BELKAOUI (1991). Determinants of Executive Compensation: Corporate Ownership, Performance, Size, and Diversification. New York, Westport Conneticut, London, Quorum Books.

PAYNE, S. L. (1993). Exploring Multiple Epistemologies for the Study and Teaching of Management. Academy of Management Best Paper Proceedings 1993, 53rd Annual Meeting Atlanta, Georgia.

PEACOCK, A. (1983). Public Inefficiency: Informational and Institutional Constraints. Anatomy of Government Deficiencies. H. Hanusch. Proceedings of a Conference held at Diessen, Germany, July 22-25, 1980. Berlin et al., Springer-Verlag: 125-148.

PEJOVICH, S. (1995). Economic Analysis of Institutions and Systems. Dordrecht, Boston, London, Kluwer Academic Publishers.

PENROSE, E.T. (1959). The Theory of the Growth of the Firm. Oxford, Blackwell.

PERROW, C. (1986). Complex Organizations: a Critical Essay. New York, London, McGraw-Hill.

PETERS, B.G. (1988) Comparing Public Bureaucracies. Problems of Theory and Method. Tuscaloosa, University of Alabama Press.

PETERS, B.G. (2000). "Administrative Traditions." Governance & Public Sector Reform Sites: Administrative & Civil Service Reform: Architecture of the Public Sector. World Bank. http://www1.worldbank.org/publicsector/civilservice/traditions.htm .

PFAFF, M. (1994). Von Betriebs- und Volkswirtschaftlichen hin zu Sozialen und Gesamtgesellschaftlichen Produktivitätsbegriffen: das Beispiel des Deutschen Krankenhauses. Produktivität Öffentlicher Dienstleistungen. F. Naschold and M. Pröhl. Gütersloh, Verlag Bertelsmann Stiftung. 1: 13-50.

PFEFFER, J. (1993). "Barriers to the Advance of Organisational Science: Paradigm Development as a Dependent Variable." Academy of Management Review 18(4): 599-620.

PFEFFER, J. (1997). New Directions for Organization Theory. Problems and Prospects. New York, Oxford, Oxford University Press.
PICOT, A., DIETL, H., E. FRANCK (1997). Organisation: Eine Ökonomische Perspektive. Stuttgart, Schaeffer-Poeschel.
PINCH, S., MASON, C., and S. WITT (1991). "Flexible Employment Strategies in British Industry: Evidence from the UK 'Sunbelt'." Regional Studies 25(3): 207-218.
POLLERT, A. (1989). "The 'Flexible Firm': Fixation or Fact?" Work, Employment and Society 2(3): 281-316.
POLLITT, C. and G. BOUCKAERT (2000). Public Management Reform. A Comparative Analysis. Oxford, New York, Oxford University Press.
POLLITT, C. and H. SUMMA (1999). Performance Audit and Public Management Reform. Performance or Compliance? Performance Audit and Public Management in Five Countries. C. Pollitt, X. Girre, J. Lonsdale et al. Oxford, New York, Oxford University Press: 1-10.
POLLITT, C. and R. MUL (1999). Criteria. Performance or Compliance? Performance Audit and Public Management in Five Countries. C. Pollitt, X. Girre, J. Lonsdale et al. Oxford, New York, Oxford University Press: 79-104.
PRATT, J. W. and R. J. ZECKHAUSER (1985). Principals and Agents: An Overview. Principals and Agents: The Structure of Business. J. W. Pratt and R. J. Zeckhauser. Boston, Harvard Business School Press: 1-36.
PRENDERGAST, C. (1999). "The Provision of Incentives in Firms." Journal of Economic Literature 37(March): 7-63.
PRIEST, S. (1999). "Business Link Services to Small and Medium-Sized Enterprises." Environment and Planning C - Government and Policy 17(2): 177-193.
PRINTING WORLD (29.5.2000). "The Government Speaks."
PUGH, D. S. (1997 (1973)). Does Context Determine Form? Organization Theory. Selected Readings. D. S. Pugh. London et al., Penguin: 16-35.
PUGH, D. S., HICKSON, D.J., and C. R. HININGS (1964). Writers on Organizations. London et al., Hutchinson & Co.
RAINEY, H. G. (1983). "Public Agencies and Private Firms." Administration & Society 15(2): 207-242.
RAUCH, B. v. (1997). German Manufacturing Associations: the VDMA. Trade Associations in Britain and Germany: Responding to Internationalisation and the EU. R. J. Bennett. London, Anglo-German Foundation for the Study of Industrial Society: 99-101.
REED, M. I. (1992). The Sociology of Organizations. Themes, Perspectives and Prospects. Hemel Hempstead, Harvester Wheatsheaf.
REINHARD, H. W. (1997). Globalisierungstendenzen im internationalen Messewesen. European Business School, Schloss Reichartshausen am Rhein.
REUTER, N. (1994). "Institutionalismus, Neo-Institutionalismus, Neue Institutionelle Ökonomie und andere 'Institutionalismen': eine Differenzierung konträrer Konzepte." Zeitschrift fuer Wirtschafts- und Sozialwissenschaften 114(1): 5-23.
REUTHER, H. J. (1982). Der AUMA im Dialog mit den Verbänden. m+a: 27-28.
RICHARDS, T. J. and P. M. PATTERSON (1998). "Dynamic Complementarity in Export Promotion: The Market Access Program in Fruits and Vegetables." Journal of Agricultural and Resource Economics 23(2): 319-337.
RICHARDS, T. J., VanISPELEN, P., and A. KAGAN (1997). "A Two-Stage Analysis of the Effectiveness of Promotion Programs for US Apples." American Journal of Agricultural Economics 79(3): 825-837.
RICHARDSON, G. B. (1972). "The Organisation of Industry." The Economic Journal, 82(Sept.), 883-897.

RIKER, W. H. (1990). Poltitical Science and Rational Choice. Perspectives on Positive Political Economy. J. E. Alt and K. A. Shepsle. Cambridge et al: Cambridge University Press: 163-181.

ROBSON, P. J. A. and R. J. BENNETT (1999). "Central Government Support to SMEs Compared to Business Link, Business Connect and Business Shop and the Prospects for the Small Business Service." Regional Studies 33(8): 779-787.

ROEPKE, J. (1992). Cooperative Entrepreneurship. Marburg, Marburg Consult for Self-Help Promotion.

ROSEN, E. D. (1993). Improving Public Sector Productivity. Concepts and Practice. Newbury Park, London, New Delhi, SAGE Publications.

ROSS, S. A. (1973). "The Economic Theory of Agency: The Principal's Problem." The American Economic Review 63(2): 134-139.

ROSSON, P. J. and F. H. R. SERINGHAUS (1991a). Export Promotion and Public Organizations: Present and Future Research. Export Development and Promotion: The Role of Public Organizations. F. H. R. Seringhaus and P. J. Rosson. Boston, Dordrecht, London, Kluwer Academic Publishers: 3-18.

ROSSON, P. J. and F. H. R. SERINGHAUS (1991b). International Trade Fairs: Firms and Government Exhibits. Export Development and Promotion: The Role of Public Organizations. F. H. R. Seringhaus and P. J. Rosson. Boston, Dordrecht, London, Kluwer Academic Publishers: 163-188.

ROTH, A. E. (1996). Comments on Tversky's Rational Theory and Constructive Choice. The Rational Foundations of Economic Behavior. K. Arrow, E. Colombatto, M. Perlman and C. Schmidt. London, Macmillan: 198-202.

RUNIEWICZ, M. (1996). The Fourth Survey of International Services Provided to Exporters. London, Institute of Export & NCM Credit Insurance LTD.

RUNIEWICZ, M. (1997). The Fifth Survey of International Services Provided to Exporters. London, Institute of Export & NCM Credit Insurance LTD.

RUTHERFORD, M. (1989). "What is wrong with the New Institutional Economics (and what is still wrong with the Old)?" Review of Political Economy 1(3): 299-318.

RUTHERFORD, M. (1994). Institutions in Economics: the Old and the New Institutionalism. Cambridge, Cambridge University Press.

SAMUELSON, P. A. (1954). "The Pure Theory of Public Expenditure." Review of Economics and Statistics 36(4): 387-389.

SAPPINGTON, D. E. M. (1991). "Incentives in Principal-Agent Relationships." Journal of Economic Perspectives 5(2): 45-66.

SCHELLKES, W. (1987). "Auslandsmesseförderung unter der Lupe. 10 Jahre Ausstellerbefragungen." m+a Report: 50-54.

SCHLICHT, E. (1990). "Rationality, Bounded or not, and Institutional Analysis." Journal of Institutional and Theoretical Economics (JITE) 146: 703-719.

SCHLITT, T. (1997). Beteiligungskonzept der Elektroindustrie für Gemeinschaftsstände bei offiziellen Auslandsmessebeteiligungen. ZVEI Tätigkeitsbericht 1996/97: 63-65.

SCHMID, A. A. and D. SOROKO (1997). Interest Groups, Selective Incentives, Cleverness, History and Emotion: The Case of the American Soybean Association. Journal of Economic Behaviour and Organization 32(2): 267-286.

SCHOENIG, W. (1996). Alimentierung und Entlastungsleistungen von Wirtschaftsverbänden - Anmerkungen zum Erklärungswert der Theorie des Rent Seeking. Hamburger Jahrbuch für Wirtschafts- und Gesellschaftspolitik 41: 111-127.

SCHOTTER, A. (1981). The Economic Theory of Social Institutions. Cambridge, Cambridge University Press.

SCHREITER, C. (1994). Evolution und Wettbewerb von Organisationsstrukturen: ein Evolutionsökonomischer Beitrag zur Volkswirtschaftlichen Theorie der Unterneh-mung. Goettingen, Vandenhoeck & Ruprecht.

SCHREYOEGG, G. (1988). Die Theorie der Verfügungsrechte als allgemeine Organisationstheorie. Betriebswirtschaftslehre und Theorie der Verfügungsrechte. D. Budäus, E. Gerum and G. Zimmermann: 151-167.

SCHULTZ, S., VOLZ, J., and C. WEISE (1991). Die Außenwirtschaftsförderung der wichtigsten Konkurrenzländer Deutschlands. Frankreich, Grossbritannien, Japan und USA im Vergleich. Berlin, Duncker & Humblot.

SCOTT, W. R. (1981). "Developments in Organization Theory, 1960-1980." American Behavioral Scientist 24(3): 407-422.

SCOTT, W. R. (1987). Organizations. Rational, Natural, and Open Systems. Englewood Cliffs, N.J. et al., Prentice-Hall, Inc.

SELTEN, R. (1990). "Bounded Rationality." Journal of Institutional and Theoretical Economics 146: 649-658.

SERINGHAUS, F. H. R. and P. J. ROSSON (1990). Government Export Promotion. A Global Perspective. London and New York, Routledge.

SERINGHAUS, F. H. R. and P. J. ROSSON (1991). Export Promotion and Public Organizations: State-of-the-Art. Export Development and Promotion: The Role of Public Organizations. F. H. R. Seringhaus and P. J. Rosson. Boston, Dordrecht, London, Kluwer Academic Publishers: 3-18.

SERINGHAUS, F. H. R. and P. J. ROSSON (1998). "Management and Performance of International Trade Fair Exhibitors: Government Stands vs Independent Stands." International Marketing Review 15(5): 398-412.

SERVICEVERBUND AUSSENWIRTSCHAFT (2001). Finanzierungs- und Rechtsfragen. http://www.ixpos.de/finanzierung_und_rechtsfragen/finanzierung_und_rechtsfragen.html 2001.

SHARFMAN, M. P. and J.W. DEAN (1997). "Flexibility in Strategic Decision Making: Informational and Ideological Perspectives." Journal of Management Studies 34(2): 191-217.

SHARKEY, T. W., LIM, J. S., and K. I. KIM (1989). "Export Development and Perceived Export Barriers. An Empirical Analysis of Small Firms. " Management International Review 29(2): 33-41.

SHELANSKI, H. A. and P. G. KLEIN (1995). "Empirical Research in Transaction Cost Economics: A Review and Assessment." Journal of Law, Economics and Organisation 11(2): 335-361.

SHOHAM, A. (1999). "Performance in Trade Shows and Exhibitions: A Synthesis and Directions for Future Research." Journal of Global Marketing 12(3): 1999.

SIMON, H. A. (1959). "Theories of Decision-Making in Economics and Behavioural Sciences." American Economic Review 49: 253-83.

SIMON, H. A. (1964). "On the Concept of Organizational Goal." Administrative Science Quarterly (June): 1-22.

SIMON, H. A. (1991). "Organizations and Markets." Journal of Economic Perspectives 5(2): 25-44.

SIROWER, M. (1997). The Synergy Trap. New York: Free Press.

SMALL BUSINESS SERVICE (2001). Small and Medium Enterprises (SME) Statistics for the UK 2000, Small Business Service. http://www.sbs.gov.uk/press/news44.pdf 2001.

SMITH, A. (1993). An Inquiry into the Nature and Causes of the Wealth of Nations. A Selected Edition. Oxford, New York: Oxford University Press.

SOEDERMAN, S. (2002). Some Aspects of Sweden's Trade Support Network, International Trade Centre, Executive Forum. Discussion Brief for the Export Strategy Maker. http://www.intracen.org/execforum/ef2001/fpsweden.htm 2002.

SOMEREN, T. C. R. v. (1992). Emulation and Organizational Change. Entrepreneurship, Technological Innovation, and Economic Growth. Studies in the Schumpeterian Tradition. F. M. Scherer and M. Perlman. Ann Arbor, The University of Michigan Press: 201-216.

STAKE, R. E. (2000). Case Studies. Handbook of Qualitative Research. N. K. Denzin and Y. S. Lincoln. Thousand Oaks, London, New Delhi, Sage Publications Inc.: 435-454.

STATIONERY OFFICE (2000). The Whitehall Companion 2001. London, Stationery Office.

STATISTISCHES BUNDESAMT (2.11.2001). Deutschland im Jahr 2000 wieder weltweit zweitgrößter Exporteur. http://www.destatis.de/presse/deutsch/pm2001/p3950181.html

STIGLITZ, J. E. (1987). The Design of Labor Contracts: The Economics of Incentives and Risk Sharing. Incentives, Cooperation and Risk Sharing. Economic and Psychological Perspectives on Employment Contracts. H. R. Nalbantian. New Jersey, Rowman & Littlefield: 47-68.

STIGLITZ, J. E. (1989). Principal and Agent. The New Palgrave: Allocation, Information, and Markets. J. Eatwell, M. Milgate and P. Newman. New York, London, Macmillan Press Ltd: 241-253.

STIGLITZ, J. E. (1991). "Symposium on Organizations and Economics." Journal of Economic Perspectives 5(2): 15-24.

STINCHCOMBE, A. L. (1990). Information and Organizations. Berkeley, Los Angeles, Oxford, University of California Press.

SUEDDEUTSCHE ZEITUNG (22.2.1996). BDI fordert Exportoffensive in Japan.

SYDOW, J. (1992). Strategische Netzwerke: Evolution und Organisation. Wiesbaden, Gabler.

TANNER, J. (1997). The Power of Trade Shows II or Maximizing the Role of Exhibitions in the Total Marketing Mix. Executive Summary. Bethesda, MD., Centre for Exhibition Industry Research.

TAYLOR, F. W. (1997 (1912)). Scientific Management. Organization Theory. Selected Readings. D. S. Pugh. London et al., Penguin: 275-295.

TAYLOR, J. (1992). "Information Networking in Public Administration." International Review of Administrative Sciences 58(3): 375-389.

THE ECONOMIST (11.11.1989). "Export Promotion: Diplomats for Sale."

THE ECONOMIST (1.2.1997a). "Governments and Exports: Uncommercial Travellers."

THE ECONOMIST (1.2.1997b). "Governments and Exports: Thoroughly Modern Mercantilists."

THE ECONOMIST (1.2.1997c). "Governments and Exports: Don't be Salesmen."

THE ECONOMIST (17.6.2000). "Aid with Strings."

THE INDEPENDENT (11.11.1996). "Diplomats to join trade spotting business."

THE INDEPENDENT (15.1.1989). "Government to Revamp Support for Exporters."

THE INDEPENDENT (18.1.1989). "Cost of Export Advice to Climb."

THE TIMES (13.2.1997). "DTI's Sector Challenge Inclined Towards Competitive Advantage." Letters to the Editor.

THE TIMES (25.2.1997). "Sector Challenge Extends Scope of Government Help to Exporters." Letters to the Editor.

THE TIMES (4.3.1997). "British Firms Face Fee for Envoys' Role in Clinching Deals."

THOENE, M. (1997). Die Auslandmesseförderung des Bundes. Ordnungspolitische Aspekte und gesamtwirtschaftliche Wirkungen. Bergisch Gladbach, Heider.

TIETZEL, M. (1981). "Zur Ökonomie der Property Rights: Ein Überblick." Zeitschrift für Wirtschaftspolitik 30(3): 207-243.

TOMKINS, C. R. (1987). Achieving Economy, Efficiency and Effectiveness in the Public Sector. Edinburgh, Institute of Chartered Accountants of Scotland.

TPUK (2000). Building British Business Success Overseas. Your Guide to our Services. London, BTI/Pub0004/25K/05/00, URN:00/157.

TPUK (2000a). 2001-2002 SESA Programme. Final Version, 30.10.2000.

TPUK (2000b). Sector Partnership Report: Promotion and Development of Export Trade. London, DTI, URN 00/1110: 58.

TPUK (2001). Support for Exhibitions and Seminars Abroad - An Overview, TPUK; http://www.tradepartners.gov.uk/sesa/overview/overview/sesa.shtml . 2001.

TPUK (2001a). Support for Exhibitions and Seminars Abroad - Terms and Conditions, TPUK; http://www.tradepartners.gov.uk/sesa/terms/seminars/sesaterms.shtml . 2001.

TPUK (2001b). Sector Profile: Chemicals, TPUK; http://www.tradepartners.gov.uk/gateway/staging/data/sector_overview/chemicals/profile/index/overview.shtml . 2001.

TPUK (2002). Customer Needs Review. Final Report. 6.November 2002. PricewaterhouseCoopers.

TPUK and TAYLOR NELSON SOFRES HARRIS (2000). Quality Management Survey Satisfaction Report, SESA Trade Fairs, October 1999 - March 2000. London, TPUK.

TPUK and TAYLOR NELSON SOFRES HARRIS (2000a). Quality Management Survey Satisfaction Report, SESA Trade Fairs, July - September 1999. London, TPUK.

TPUK and TAYLOR NELSON SOFRES HARRIS (2001). Quality Management Survey Satisfaction Report, SESA Trade Fairs, April - September 2000. London, TPUK.

TRADE ASSOCIATION FORUM (2001). Online Directory, Trade Association Forum; http://www.martex.co.uk/taf/ . 2001.

TROCHIM, W. (1989). "Outcome Pattern Matching and Program Theory. " Evaluation and Program Planning 12(4): 355-366.

TULLOCK, G. (1987). Public Choice. The New Palgrave: A Dictionary of Economics. J. Eatwell, M. Milgate and P. Newman. London et al., Macmillan Press Ltd. 3: 1040-1044.

TYRE, M. J. and E.v. HIPPEL (1997). "The Situated Nature of Adaptive Learning in Organizations." Organizational Science 8(1): 71-83.

UESDIKEN, B. and Y. PASADENOS (1995). "Organizational Analysis in North America and Europe: A Comparison of Co-citation Networks." Organization Studies 16(3): 503-526.

UK TRADE & INVESTMENT (2003). Dear Sponsor Letters. http://www.tpuk-sponsor-accred.org.uk/sponsorsletters.htm

UK TRADE & INVESTMENT (2004). Dear Sponsor Letters. http://www.tpuk-sponsor-accred.org.uk/sponsorsletters.htm

UK TRADE & INVESTMENT (2004). International Business Schemes (SESA). http://www.trade.uktradeinvest.gov.uk/sesa/overview/overview/sesa.shtml

VDMA (1997). "Eiserner Sparzwang bei Bundesbeteiligungen 1998. " Maschinenbau Nachrichten 11-97: 64-67.

VICKERS, J. and G. YARROW (1987). Privatization: An Economic Analysis. Cambridge, Mass., MIT Press.

VOLBERDA, H. W. (1996). "Towards the Flexible Form: How to Remain Vital in Hypercompetitive Environments." Organization Science 7(4): 359-374.

WALKER, G. (1988). "Strategic Sourcing, Vertical Integration and Transaction Costs." Interfaces 18: 62-73.

WALZENBACH, G. P. E. (1998). Co-ordination in Context. Institutional Choices to Promote Exports. Aldershot; Brookfield USA, Ashgate.

WEBER, H. (1987). Unternehmerverbände zwischen Markt, Staat und Gewerkschaften: zur intermediären Organisation von Wirtschaftsinteressen. Frankfurt a.M., New York, Campus.

WEBER, M. (1997 (1924)). Legitimate Authority and Bureaucracy. Organization Theory. Selected Readings. D. S. Pugh. London et al., Penguin: 3-15.

WEIDIG, I. and W. RUPRECHT (1996). Kooperationschancen mittelständischer Unternehmen im Auslandsgeschäft. Untersuchung staatlicher Förderinstrumente im Hinblick auf die für mittelständische Unternehmen entscheidungsrelevanten Faktoren. Basel, Prognos - Europäisches Zentrum für Wirtschaftsforschung und Strategieberatung. Commissioned by Bundesministerium für Wirtschaft, Bonn.

WELCH, D. E., L. S. WELCH, et al. (1998). "The Importance of Networks in Export Promotion: Policy Issues." Journal of International Marketing 6(4): 66-82.

WIERSMA, U. J. (1992). "The Effects of Extrinsic Rewards in Intrinsic Motivation: A Meta-Analysis." Journal of Occupational and Organizational Psychology 65(Part 2): 104-114.

WILKINSON, T. J. and L. E. BROUTHERS (2000a). "An Evaluation of State Sponsored Promotion Programmes." Journal of Business Research 47(3): 229-236.

WILKINSON, T. J. and L. E. BROUTHERS (2000b). “Trade Shows, Trade Missions and State Governments: Increasing FDI and High-Tech Exports.” Journal of International Business Studies 31(4): 725-734.

WILLIAMSON, O. E. (1963). The Economics of Discretionary Behavior: Managerial Objectives in a Theory of the Firm. Englewood Cliffs, N.J.: Prentice Hall, Inc.

WILLIAMSON, O. E. (1975). Markets and Hierarchies: Analysis and Antitrust Implications. New York, Free Press.

WILLIAMSON, O. E. (1985). The Economic Institutions of Capitalism. New York, Free Press.

WILLIAMSON, O. E. (1989a). Internal Economic Organization. Perspectives on the Economics of Organization. Lund, Lund University Press: 9-48.

WILLIAMSON, O. E. (1989b). Transaction Cost Economics. Handbook of Industrial Organisation. R. Schmalensee and R. D. Willig. Amsterdam, London, New York, Tokyo, Elsevier Science Publishers. 1: 135-182.

WILLIAMSON, O. E. (1990a). "Political Institutions: The Neglected Side of the Story - Comment." Journal of Law, Economics, and Organization 6(Special Issue 1990): 263-266.

WILLIAMSON, O. E. (1990b). "A Comparison of Alternative Approaches to Economic Organization." Journal of Institutional and Theoretical Economics 146(1): 61-71.

WILLIAMSON, O. E. (1991). "Comparative Economic Organization - The Analysis of Discrete Structural Alternatives." Administrative Science Quarterly 36(2): 269-298.

WILLIAMSON, O. E. (1992). Comments: Specific and General Knowledge, and Organizational Structure. Contract Economics. L. Werin and H. Wijkander. Oxford and Cambridge, MA, Blackwell: 282-291.

WILLIAMSON, O. E. (1993). The Economic Analysis of Institutions and Organisations - In General and with Respect to Country Studies. Paris, OECD.

WILLIAMSON, O. E. (1998). "Transaction Cost Economics: How it Works; Where it is Headed." De Economist 146(1): 23-58.

WILSON, G. K. (1990). Business and Politics. Basingstoke and London, Macmillan.

WINSHIP, C. and S. ROSEN (1988). "Introduction: Sociological and Economic Approaches to the Analysis of Social Structure." American Journal of Sociology 94(Supplement): S1-S16.

WIRTSCHAFTSWOCHE (2.1.1997). "Wirkung völlig Schnuppe."

WOEHE, G. (1986). Einführung in die Allgemeine Betriebswirtschaftslehre. München, Verlag Franz Vahlen GmbH.

WTO (2000a). International Trade Statistics 2000. WTO. http://www.wto.org/english/res_e/statis_e/stat_toc_e.htm . 2000.

WTO (2000b). World Merchandise Exports by Region and Selected Economies, 1980, 1985, 1990 and 1995-99, WTO. http://www.wto.org/english/res_e/statis_e/statis_e.htm . 2000.

WTO (2000c). World Trade in Commercial Services by Region and Selected Economies, 1980, 1985, 1990 and 1995-99, WTO. http://www.wto.org/english/res_e/statis_e/statis_e.htm . 2000.

WTO (2002). World Merchandise Exports by Region and Selected Economies, 1980, 1985, 1990 and 1995-2000, WTO. http://www.wto.org/english/res_e/statis_e/statis_e.htm. 2000.

YIN, R. K. (1994). Case Study Research: Design and Methods. Thousand Oaks, London, New Delhi, Sage Publications.

YUHAS, D. (2000). How to Choose the Right Trade Show. Market Impact. http://www.market-impact.com/htmlfiles/articles/show.htm . 2001.

ZALD, M. N. (1987). "The New Institutional Economics." American Journal of Sociology 93(3): 701-708.

ZWONIECK, C. (1988). "Exportkreditversicherungen im internationalen Vergleich." Versicherungswirtschaft 43(1): 45-49.

Printing: Krips bv, Meppel
Binding: Stürtz, Würzburg